51A2

D0811759

World Handbook of Political and Social Indicators

WORLD HANDBOOK

OF POLITICAL AND SOCIAL INDICATORS

SECOND EDITION

by

Charles Lewis Taylor

and

Michael C. Hudson

With the collaboration of Katherine H. Dolan, Edwin G. Dolan,
John T. Dow, and John D. Sullivan

New Haven and London, Yale University Press, 1972

Copyright © 1972 by Yale University.
All rights reserved. This book may not be
reproduced, in whole or in part, in any form
(except by reviewers for the public press),
without written permission from the publishers.
Library of Congress catalog card number: 70-179479
International standard book number: 0-300-01555-0

Designed by John O. C. McCrillis
and set in IBM Press Roman type.
Printed in the United States of America by
The Murray Printing Co., Forge Village, Massachusetts.

Most of the tables and graphs of this book
were composed on an IBM 7094-7040 DCS computer
and listed by an IBM 1401. The graphs were
drawn by a CALCOMP plotter.

Published in Great Britain, Europe, and Africa by
Yale University Press, Ltd., London.
Distributed in Canada by McGill-Queen's University
Press, Montreal; in Latin America by Kaiman & Polon,
Inc., New York City; in Australasia and Southeast
Asia by John Wiley & Sons Australasia Pty. Ltd.,
Sydney; in India by UBS Publishers' Distributors Pvt.,
Ltd., Delhi; in Japan by John Weatherhill, Inc., Tokyo.

To Mary Frances and Vera

Contents

Foreword

When I agreed to write this introduction my first thought was that its title would be spelled "Forward." Actually, I think that spelling would be equally appropriate. The authors of this new edition have carried forward, in almost every way, the work of the 1964 edition. This new version is entirely their responsibility. They used all the resources of the Yale University World Data Analysis Program, including the intellectual resources of those of us who worked on the first edition. We offered many suggestions and urgings, but all final decisions on inclusion and exclusion rested with Charles Taylor and Michael Hudson. There are several major changes from the first edition.

Most obviously, the data are newer. All the attribute data in this volume apply approximately to 1965; the event data are carried through 1967. Furthermore, the coverage is more complete. The number of units examined has risen only slightly, from 133 to 136, but there are fewer absent observations per variable. Missing data for circa 1965 account for only 15 percent of the relevant data cells in the slightly more than 100 series in the book. The collection, therefore, is one of the most complete of its kind.

In addition, the number of variables is substantially larger than in the first edition. The 1964 book presented 75 variables; a few were shown merely to illustrate stages in the data-making process and 70 were made available to the scholarly community in machine-readable form. Most of these variables appear again in this volume with updated information. A few were omitted because (1) there was little new information available, in which case the reader can consult the first edition; (2) the variable proved not to be as relevant to the substantive and theoretical concerns of readers as we had expected, and so it was dropped in favor of one whose probable utility seemed greater; or (3) problems of reliability seemed especially great, particularly given the decision to try to use only variables with adequate data on 60 countries (adequate data on 30 countries was the goal for each variable used in the first edition).

To the variables carried over from the earlier book were added about as many new ones. Originally we had concerned ourselves very largely with the social and economic environment of politics. (Kenneth Boulding, noting the importance of his own discipline, observed that more than 40 percent of the initial "political and social" indicators either were derived from national income accounts or measured the distribution of factors of production—land and labor force.) Although such influences are still accorded much attention in the new edition, there has been a shift, with the addition of new variables, to a more detailed attention to political output and performance. Among the new data series reflecting this interest are measures of the age of national institutions, expenditure for public education, internal security forces, party fractionalization, press freedom, and electoral irregularity. Ten new event series tapping elements of political protest and executive change are also included with frequencies reported annually over a twenty-year period (1948-67). Attribute data on other variables, attribute data for other time periods (usually 1950, 1955, and 1960), and 57,268 daily reports of events are available on magnetic tape from the Inter-University Consortium for Political Research in Ann Arbor, Michigan.

Other major additions to the attribute data in this edition include information on food supply, ethnic and linguistic fractionalization, and scientific capacity. Another important difference is that this edition displays a more explicit concern with nations' external relations as compared with the domestic basis for comparative foreign policies. New variables in this category include external interventions in nations' politics, memberships in international organizations, diplomatic representation, foreign aid, export concentration by country and commodity, and economic distance from the superpowers.

Another major innovation in this volume is the use of computer programs to generate all the tables and graphs. The basic form of tabular presentation, with countries ranked by variable, is the same as before, but this time the tables were set entirely from the data tapes using programs devised by John Dow and Charles Taylor. This procedure both reduces costs and eliminates the errors that would otherwise unavoidably slip in during the usual process of compiling manuscript tables that are then typeset by conventional methods. Moreover, such summary statistics as the mean, median, and measures of skewness are generated and printed at the same time the table is produced. Computer-generated graphics, produced by other programs written especially for this volume, include pie charts, frequency distributions, and Lorenz curves where appropriate. Particularly striking is the presentation of a time-series plot for each country showing all the political events occurring over a twenty-year period. Like the data, these programs are available on tape from the Inter-University Consortium.

The authors of this volume, like those of the first edition, have provided extensive discussion of the reliability and validity of the data presented. Some sections of the discussion are substantially unchanged from the first edition, while others are quite new. An effort to include time-series was less successful than we had hoped. This book is limited to the 1948-67 period, although within that period some important changes can be identified. We leave for others the demanding task of compiling good cross-national data on the decades or century preceding World War II.[1]

1. See, for instance, Arthur Banks, *Cross-Polity Time-Series Data* (Cambridge, Mass.: M.I.T. Press, 1971); William Flanigan and Edwin Fogelman, "Patterns of Political Violence in Comparative Historical Perspective," *Comparative Politics,* 3 (1970); Flanigan and Fogelman, "Patterns of Political Development and Democratization," and "Patterns of Democratic Development: An Historical Comparative Analysis," both in John Gillespie and Betty Nesvold, eds., *Macro-Quantitative Analysis* (Beverly Hills, Calif.: Sage, 1971); Stein Kuhnle, "Time-Series Data for

Also, except for a fairly brief discussion of patterns in the political event data, no analysis is presented in this volume. The first edition devoted over 100 pages to analysis. Even so it did no more than identify some of the basic kinds of procedures to which the data might be subjected. Such an illustration may have been useful nearly a decade ago when quantitative cross-national study was in the early stages of its development; now it would be superfluous. Instead a separate volume is planned that will contain a few studies which employ the data, and we shall use some of the data in books and articles that relate to our particular interests. Many, indeed, have already appeared.[2] In this we follow the pattern set by the first edition. Such current or former associates of the World Data Analysis Program as Hayward Alker, Karl Deutsch, Michael Hudson, Richard Merritt, Bruce Russett, and Charles Taylor have used the data from the first edition in at least eight books and sixteen articles. Scholars at other universities also have already made substantial use of the data. Although the material appears only now in this "literary" form, the basic data set has been available in final form from the Inter-University Consortium since early 1970.

Bruce M. Russett

Eleven Smaller European Democracies" (Paper for the ISSC Workshop on Indicators of National Development, Lausanne, 1971); Simon Kuznets, *Modern Economic Growth: Rate, Structure, and Spread* (New Haven: Yale University Press, 1966); J. David Singer and Melvin Small, *The Wages of War: A Statistical Handbook, 1815-1960* (New York: Wiley, 1972) and subsequent publications; and Wolfgang Zapf and Peter Flora, "Some Problems of Time-Series Analysis in Research on Modernization," *Social Science Information,* 10 (1971): 53-102.

2. See Michael C. Hudson, "Conditions of Political Violence and Instability: A Preliminary Test of Three Hypotheses," *Sage Professional Papers in Comparative Politics,* no. 5 (1970); "Some Quantitative Indicators for Explaining and Evaluating National Political Performance" (Paper presented at the Annual Meeting of the American Political Science Association, 1967), "Toward a Comparative Analysis of Political Performance in the Arab States" (Paper presented at the Annual Meeting of the Middle East Studies Association, 1967); Bruce M. Russett, *What Price Vigilance? The Burdens of National Defense* (New Haven: Yale University Press, 1970) and "The Rich Fourth and the Poor Half: Some Speculations on International Politics in 2000 A.D." (Paper presented at the ISSC Conference on the Comparative Analysis of Industrialized Countries, Bellagio, 1971); John D. Sullivan, "Co-operating to Conflict: Sources of Informal Alignments," in Bruce Russett, ed., *Peace, War, and Numbers* (Beverly Hills, Calif.: Sage, 1972); and Charles L. Taylor, "Statistical Typology of Micro-States and Territories," *Social Science Information,* 8 (1969): 101-17, and "Communications Development and Political Stability," *Comparative Political Studies,* 1 (1969): 557-63.

Preface

This book was sponsored by the World Data Analysis Program in Yale University and was supported by funds from the National Science Foundation (GS 614), the Ford Foundation, and the Advanced Research Projects Agancy (N0014-67-A-0097-0007, monitored by the Office of Naval Research). Brooklyn College in the City University of New York was generous in granting a partial leave of absence for one of the authors and the International Data Archive of the University of Michigan provided summer support for the other. Our present institutions, Virginia Polytechnic Institute and State University and the School of Advanced International Studies of the Johns Hopkins University, have provided assistance in the completion of the project. But our greatest debt for institutional support is to Yale University, its Department of Political Science and its World Data Analysis Program.

Our teacher, Karl W. Deutsch, became interested in cross-national aggregate data collection a decade or so ago. His interest led to the first edition of the *World Handbook,* ably presided over by Bruce M. Russett. To the two of them and to their coauthors, Hayward R. Alker, Jr., and Harold D. Lasswell, we are indebted both for their published work and for their encouragement and suggestions in the preparation of this edition. Also generous in advice were Robert Hefner, Lester Warner, P. J. Loftus and others of the United Nations Statistical Office, Dankwart Rustow, Lincoln Day, Frederick Barghoorn, Robert Dahl, Joseph LaPalombara, Martin Needler, Ted Gurr, Samuel Huntington, Phillips Cutright, Robert Tilman, Hugh Stevens, Richard Ruggles, Lutz Erbring, Steven Brams, David Barrett, Ralph Lowenstein, Raymond Tanter, Derek de Solla Price, and many others far too numerous to mention by name. Douw Fonda and Arnold Sox of the Associated Press, Thomas O'Neill and Edward O'Neill of the Yale Computer Center, Robert Beattie and Susan Cowart of the Inter-University Consortium for Political Research, and Marian Ash of the Yale University Press have all in their sundry skillful ways been of considerable help to us.

A data collection of this magnitude obviously must be a cooperative effort; the title page attests to that. People other than those listed there, however, provided essential assistance in this joint effort. Coders for the event data series included Walter Barrows, Karyl Lee Kibler, Donna Lustgarten, Ann Morgan, Robin Nadel, John Parker, Bruce Rogers and Shirley Schiff. Other research assistants included John Bolton, Heidi Cochran, Samuel Fitch, William Freeman and Elizabeth Massey. Nathaniel Beck, Donald Blake, Richard Norling and David Seidman helped with the programming. Patricia Froehlich was a very able, energetic and pleasant secretary, keypuncher, data manager, and programmer. Without her, the collection would simply never have been completed. Many other people worked with us for shorter periods of time and to all of them we gratefully acknowledge their cooperation.

There was also a division of labor among the authors and contributors. Michael Hudson and Katherine Dolan developed seventeen of the event series that appear in chapter 3 and Katherine Dolan coded more than half the total number of countries and of years. John Sullivan developed the eighteenth event series, i.e. external interventions. Edwin Dolan wrote and described the computer program that merged the event data gathered from multiple sources into our final series. John Dow wrote the programs that created most of the tables, graphs, and other displays in the book. Michael Hudson also supervised the gathering of data on electoral irregularity, internal security forces, age of national institutions, diplomatic representation, press freedom, and air fares. The rest of the data collection was primarily the responsibility of Charles Taylor and to him fell the tasks of organizing all of the series, designing the tables and displays, and editing the manuscript. Most of chapter 3 and parts of chapters 1 and 2 were written by Hudson. The section on interventions in chapter 3 was written by Sullivan. Drafts for appendix 1 were written by Katherine and Edwin Dolan. Otherwise, the manuscript is the work of Charles Taylor and the responsibility for the final form of the product should rest on him.

C.L.T.
M.C.H.

Ellett Valley, Virginia
Washington, D.C.

1 Introduction

The first edition of the *World Handbook of Political and Social Indicators* stated as its purpose the "attempt to compare nations on a great variety of politically relevant indices . . . to present some of the data necessary for the further development of a science of comparative and international politics, and to illustrate some of the means of analyzing the data." The second edition continues in that tradition. As in the first, a number of political, economic, social, and cultural series—along with information on their quality—are presented in a manner designed to be most informative on their internal structure. We believe that the visual inspection of the data to gain insight into the nature of their distributions will lead to more effective research into the patterns among cross-national variables.

Our data collection should facilitate quantitative cross-national research in the future—just as did the first *World Handbook* in the past—by providing theory-relevant data in a convenient form. A great deal of effort was expended to make this dataset one of the largest and best documented in political science. The collection and processing of data are expensive, and whenever one collection can appropriately serve many purposes the economies argue for doing a thorough job with that collection both in the gathering, processing, and evaluation of the data and in the distribution of the results to other scholars. Parts of this dataset, therefore, are being made available to the scholarly community in this book, and the entire collection of approximately 70,000 machine readable records, along with the appropriate codebooks, can be obtained from the International Relations Archive of the Inter-University Consortium for Political Research. (See appendix 3 for further information.)

We do not test hypotheses in this volume. Rather our purpose is to make certain kinds of data readily available and interpretable to persons (including ourselves) with hypotheses to test.[1] No doubt the data will sometimes be used imprudently or ineffectively, but we feel that the benefits in providing them to scholars who are developing well-specified models far outweigh the disadvantages. Our choice to build a larger, better-documented data base rather than to produce three or four chapters of analysis for this particular book was one of allocation of our own resources and priorities; we are

---

1. The tendency to divide all political science into two parts—mindless empiricism and theoretically relevant work, the latter being whatever one is doing at the moment—is not very helpful to the development of the discipline. The interplay between data and thinking (perhaps the word "theory" should be banished for a while) is essential to our growing understanding of political phenomena; but, as Knorr and Rosenau put it, the demand for new theory and the demand for new data do not have to be met by the same person. They certainly need not be met in the same book, if this means a diminution of the quality of either. See Klaus Knorr and James N. Rosenau, *Contending Approaches to International Politics* (Princeton: Princeton University Press, 1969), p.17.

engaged elsewhere in comparative and international political research based upon the handbook data.

What are "theory-relevant data"? It now seems obvious to us, although it was not so clear when we began our work, that it is impossible to produce a dataset, much less a handbook, containing a "complete" or "comprehensive" collection of series[2] for comparative and international politics. Even if our resources had been ten times greater than they actually were, it would have been both futile and presumptuous to pretend to meet every need. The vast quantitative and qualitative developments in these fields precluded such an objective. Although the dataset of the second *World Handbook* is several times larger than that of the first, the first edition may have been relatively more "comprehensive" in its time. What, then, would be the rationale for the selection of series? After considerable discussion with our colleagues, we decided to pursue a few main themes in comparative and international politics and, within this narrower framework, to include only those series that seemed to us to be highly reliable.

Taking the nation-state as the unit of analysis and accepting the attendant analytic limitations, we have tried to present indicators for comparing nation-state *performance,* nation-state *environments,* and internation *transactions.* Our conceptual point of departure is the political system—sets of interrelated structures and processes that allocate value resources in society through the creation, exercise, and transfer of power. "The polity," in Harold D. Lasswell's words, "is the regime and the rule. . . . [It] is thus the political structure in the full sense, comprising both the authority and control structures."[3] We do not pretend that the political performance variables in this handbook in themselves allow for a comprehensive or detailed comparison of the public decision making and policy implementation of powerholders in 136 nation-states over a twenty-year period. Selected aspects of performance, however, are perhaps susceptible of measurement: certain kinds of structural data, for example, such as political party representation, size of internal security forces, or government budget allocations may provide some clues about the relative degree of democracy or coercive capacity, cross-nationally. The pattern of political violence or governmental change events over time may help confirm or reject hypotheses

2. We have used several words to describe data: series, measure, indicator, index, and variable. By *series* we mean simply a set of numbers together in a table. A *measure* is the quantitative statement of a phenomenon. An *indicator* is a gauge that points out more or less exactly a phenomenon. An *index* is a series of numbers derived from observations and used as an indicator or measure. A *variable* is a symbol in a mathematical function that can be replaced by any one of the elements of the specified set of numbers. Indexes is used as the plural of index; indices, as the plural of indicator. We have attempted to observe these distinctions but may seem frequently to have failed since one man's index becomes another man's variable.

3. Harold D. Lasswell and Abraham Kaplan, *Power and Society* (New Haven: Yale University Press, 1950), pp. 75, 214-15.

about the instability of regimes. While we do not wish to force our own metaphors or models on anybody, we might suggest that we have been concerned here with the *outputs* and the *outcomes* of political systems, and we believe that the political data series in this handbook, sensibly interpreted, may help political scientists in their triple functions of explaining, predicting, and evaluating political behavior.[4]

While we think that our indicators of political performance may be useful for simple descriptive purposes, we have also undertaken the larger task of providing indicators of the "political environment" that may facilitate the testing of hypotheses about political performance. Metaphorically, our political performance indicators might be thought of as germane to the "output" side of the political system schema of David Easton, while the environmental indicators are relevant to the "input" side.[5]

One of the central concerns of recent comparative politics has been the modernization process. Accordingly, we have tried to supply in convenient form certain data pertaining to social mobilization and economic development aspects of modernization at the nation-state level. Our indebtedness to Karl Deutsch for his formulations and contributions in this area is manifest.[6] We have also been intrigued by the modernization hypotheses put forth by Daniel Lerner, David Apter, Mancur Olson, and Seymour Martin Lipset, among others.[7]

While modernization bulks large among the preoccupations of comparative political theorists, it hardly encompasses what one might think of as the "ecology" of political systems. Students of political development in the Third World have long been particularly sensitive to another analytically distinct factor—"primordial sentiments," as the anthropologist Clifford Geertz has called them.[8] Much of the civil strife of the post-World War II period that is depicted in this volume has arisen out of racial, religious, ethnic, and linguistic conflict. But primordial conflict, just like the tensions of the modernization process, is not confined solely to the Third World;

4. J. Roland Pennock, "Political Development, Political Systems, and Political Goods," *World Politics,* 18 (1966): esp. 420-32.

5. David Easton, *A Systems Analysis of Political Life* (New York: Wiley, 1965), pp. 29-33.

6. Karl W. Deutsch, "Social Mobilization and Political Development," *American Political Science Review* 55 (1961): 493-514; and Karl W. Deutsch, "Toward an Inventory of Basic Trends and Patterns in Comparative and International Politics," *American Political Science Review* 54 (1960): 34-57.

7. Daniel Lerner, *The Passing of Traditional Society* (Glencoe, Ill.: Free Press, 1958), chap. 2; David Apter, *The Politics of Modernization* (Chicago: University of Chicago Press, 1965); Mancur Olson, "Rapid Growth as a Destabilizing Force," *Journal of Economic History,* 23 (1963): 529-58; Seymour Martin Lipset, *Political Man* (New York: Doubleday, 1959), chap. 2.

8. Clifford Geertz, "Primordial Sentiments and Civil Politics in the New States," *Old Societies and New States,* ed. Clifford Geertz (New York: Free Press, 1963), pp. 105-57.

violence in the United States, Canada, and Ireland—to name three prominent examples—has shown otherwise. It is, therefore, not surprising that students of comparative politics have become increasingly interested in the degree of fragmentation in national political cultures.[9] Thus it is appropriate that a handbook of environmental-political indicators should include some mea- surements of the distribution of certain prenational, supranational, and subnational communities. As Sidney Verba has observed, "To concentrate only on shared beliefs might lead one to overlook situations where significant political beliefs were held only by certain groups, and where the very fact that these attitudes were not shared by most members of the system was of crucial importance."[10]

Political culture, like modernization, development, and several other "grand concepts" in comparative politics, is so spongy a term that it can be approached in several ways, of which one of the most prominent has been survey research.[11] It is unrealistic to suppose that we could measure "political culture fragmentation" as sensitively with aggregate data as with attitude surveys; only a handful of indicators with worldwide applicability are available. Certain gross measurements, however, may provide indirect evidence of political culture fragmentation and so we have included series on ethnolinguistic and religious distribution.

The third main component in our concept of the political system environment is the external world. As there is great scholarly interest among both the "comparativists" and the "internationalists" about the interaction between internal and international behavior, we have sought to include certain indicators that help show a nation's transactions in the fields of international trade, aid, communications, and politics. Once again, we have refrained from proposing how users of this handbook frame their hypoth- eses; while our selection criteria may have rested on propositions linking the external environment causally to various kinds of domestic political performance, we are mindful of the concerns of those whose primary interest is in explaining international transactions by looking at internal conditions.

Our interest in the "political environment" as a source of explanations of political performance reflects the great emphasis on the "input" side of the political system evinced by comparative politics theorists of the period from the mid 1950s to the mid 1960s. It was inevitable and salutary that a certain

9. See, for example, Robert Melson and Howard Wolpe, "Modernization and the Politics of Communalism: A Theoretical Perspective," *American Political Science Review*, 64 (1970): 1112-30; and Richard Rose and Derek Urwin, "Social Cohesion: Political Parties and Strains in Regimes," *Comparative Political Studies*, 2 (1969): 7-67.

10. Sidney Verba, "Conclusion," *Political Culture and Political Development,* ed. Lucian Pye and Sidney Verba (Princeton: Princeton University Press, 1965), p. 525.

11. See, for example, Gabriel A. Almond and Sidney Verba, *The Civic Culture* (Princeton: Princeton University Press, 1963).

reaction to this emphasis should have gained momentum in the late 1960s. Critics of systems imagery wanted to know more about the transformations going on inside the "black box." There was a revival of interest in the previously maligned formal structures of government and politics and more than one prominent writer charged that the comparative political theorists had neglected politics itself as a causal factor.[12] We were particularly influenced by some of the propositions put forth in Samuel P. Huntington's *Political Order in Changing Societies.*[13] The concept of institutionalization seemed to be worth pursuing on theoretical grounds and feasible for cross-national macroanalysis, even though the problems of operationalizing Huntington's dimensions of institutionalization were, and are still, formidable. There will doubtless be divergences among readers interested in testing or refining some of Huntington's notions as to which (if any) of the political structure and performance indicators can be used to measure the various aspects of institutionalization.

The compilers of this handbook, like those of the first edition, thus have a number of specific theoretical concerns in mind and are not simply attempting to assemble the data that were easily available. Nor are we presenting them as a coherent and complete operationalized model for explaining political performance; to do so would violate what Martin Landau has called "due process of inquiry."[14] Doubtless, few of our colleagues will feel that we have been able to meet their ideal criteria of relevance and comprehensiveness. Nevertheless, it is our hope that this handbook will still be useful to established scholars and to students for reference, for training in quantitative analysis, and for at least partial help in clarifying some of the issues of current interest in comparative and international politics.

It will be gratifying if scholarly use of our dataset results in the statement of new hypotheses and the further development of theory. Such developments will create additional and different data needs and our book will have accomplished its purpose.

There have been other more mundane criteria for inclusion and omission of data, of course. Many phenomena of interest in the study of cross-national politics cannot easily be stated as precise and replicable quantities. Certain indicators that at first seemed both theoretically interesting and feasible were subsequently deleted because of serious doubts or disagreements concerning accuracy. Other important data were not included because

---

12. Dankwart A. Rustow, "Modernization and Comparative Politics: Prospects in Theory and Research," *Comparative Politics,* 1 (1968): 38-39.

13. Samuel P. Huntington, *Political Order in Changing Societies* (New Haven: Yale University Press, 1968), esp. chap. 1.

14. Martin Landau, "Due Process of Inquiry," *American Behavioral Scientist,* 9 (1965): p. 6.

they did not exist in comparable terms for a sufficient number of countries. Except for some series that were desirable theoretically, e.g. educational stocks and indexes of inequality, our practice was to include only a series for which adequate information existed on at least 60 countries. Thus survey and content analytic data, available for only a few countries, were excluded.

The authors of the first *World Handbook* stated their hope that future editions would be "expanded, improved, and, where necessary, corrected." The two major improvements, we feel, are the inclusion of a much larger number of explicitly political variables and the collection of certain data for multiple points in time. Two of the five data chapters are devoted to political structure, performance, and change, to power distribution, and to civil disorder; and a third is given to external relations, political and otherwise. Eighteen series measuring political events were collected day-by-day over the twenty-year period 1948-67. Other data were collected circa 1965, 1960, 1955, and 1950, although by no means did we succeed in collecting each series for all four dates. Data are 85 percent complete for 1965, but the percentage falls rapidly for the other three dates.

A large proportion of our work went into the creation of the eighteen government-change and civil-disorder data series coded from the *New York Times* and its *Index* and from secondary sources for each country. These series include several types of governmental change (regular and irregular, successful and unsuccessful) and political violence (such as riots, demonstrations, and armed attacks). They were gathered directly under the auspices of the Yale World Data Analysis Program. In chapter 3, we describe the definitions and coding procedures that we used in order that the reader may obtain some feel for the theoretical relevance of each series. Annual aggregations for ten of these series are printed in chapter 3; space limitations prevented their publication in more detail. The daily reports as well as the annual aggregations for all eighteen series, however, are available in machine readable form from the Consortium in Ann Arbor.

Other political variables are reported in chapter 2. Data in chapters 4-6 refer to size and resources of the country, its economic structure, its social patterns, and its relations with other countries. Most of these series are based on the work of other political scientists, economists, demographers, journalists, historians, and sociologists. In a few cases we report their work without changes but with comments, because we believe that these particular indexes are the best available measures of some phenomena. Sometimes these data have been previously made available in studies published by governments, international organizations, private agencies, or university presses. In other instances they were made available to us directly by their collectors. In the case of still more series, we have taken data from several sources, weighing varying estimates, to produce as complete and as accurate a series as we can. Frequently, this meant calculating percentages or rates of change or doing aggregations, transformations, or manipulations to make comparisons more meaningful. Occasionally, it was necessary to modify certain items of data substantially to make them more nearly comparable to other items in the series. For some series we had to compile our data from private studies and national statistical yearbooks since preexisting compilations were inadequate or nonexistent. Frequently, especially with the latter series, we used raw data from other sources to develop indexes that went far beyond the original purposes of the data gatherers. For all the series, we comment upon the quality of the data, explain what we have done with them, give their sources, and display them in a way that makes their internal structure as clear as possible.

The ability of others to replicate our collection is of great importance if these data are to contribute to the advancement of knowledge. Thus we have tried to state our definitions clearly and to include all information necessary for other scholars to see just what was collected and how it was modified. Ambiguity or the absence of full discussion in our sources sometimes made this impossible, however.

Effort is also made to discuss accuracy. Here we are interested both in *reliability,* i.e. whether or not the numbers are exaggerations or underestimates, and *comparability,* i.e. whether the definition of the series remains the same from country to country. We have tried to think of the permissible error that can be tolerated in relation to the inferences to be drawn. This permissible error is in part related to the range of the series. When the value of a variable in two countries differs by 20 percentage points, an error margin of 15 points will have crippling effects; when they differ by 40 or 50 percentage points an error margin of 15 points, while damaging, may nonetheless be tolerable.

In deciding whether or not to collect a given series we had to make a preliminary judgment about the data's accuracy. Furthermore, we have attempted to assess for many of the series fairly precise statements of error. This, of course, was a difficult and uncertain task given the paucity of existing information. Few previous data collections, other than the first edition of the *World Handbook,* have made more than the grossest assessments, frequently warning the reader to use the data only with caution and due regard for noncomparability. Obviously it is not easy to give any precise error margin for a single datum, much less for a whole series. If we knew that much about the error, we could simply adjust the series. In addition, there is always the problem that our opinions on quality, meant to give only a very general order of magnitude, may be taken too seriously by the reader. Nevertheless it seemed to us that refusal to make any statements on error when presenting series of this sort would be an avoidance of responsibility.

Some of the specific problems affecting data accuracy are discussed with each series. In general, we believe that there is a clear tendency for the quality and availability of data to rise with the level of economic development in a country. This is simply a matter of resources. The collection and evaluation of adequate data is an expensive process requiring personnel; in many countries neither the human nor the financial raw material is available. This is particularly true in small countries and with respect to data normally collected by sample survey methods. With a population of a million or more inhabitants the size of the sample needed for reliable data collection is not responsive to the size of the total population. The results of a sample survey of, say, 5,000 individuals, are virtually as reliable for a country of 200 million as for a country of 1 million. The costs of the survey are not very different in the large country, but the burden on the small country may be relatively great, especially if it is not wealthy. Thus sample surveys, which can form an important supplement to decennial censuses, are often not undertaken in smaller states.

Another problem stems from the lack of international agreement on the definition of certain items. The United Nations has performed a major service in attempting to establish standard definitions for census-taking, accounting, and other data-gathering and data analysis procedures. Yet the task is far from complete and often one cannot be sure that standard definitions were used in published data.

A final major difficulty is the deliberate or semideliberate distortion of data by national governments. Sometimes a government does not want to admit that certain data are unavailable; such an admission may seem to reflect on its own competence or the state of the nation's development. In these cases "data" may be created without much empirical referent. One branch of a government may even undertake such fabrication without the knowledge of another. A regional office faced with a demand for data beyond its resources to collect may find quite ingenious ways of reporting something. And, on a national scale, the appearance of economic strength or rapid development or a literate and healthy population may be an important asset in international politics. Where the true data indicate otherwise, they may be modified, and it may be extraordinarily difficult for an independent examiner to determine the presence or degree of modification. Some governments, like some businessmen, keep two sets of books.

Despite these difficulties, we feel that use of the data is valid if care is given to caveats stated in the text.

Units of Collection

The assumption, implicit thus far, is that countries are important units for analysis; the comparison of national aggregates with each other or the comparison of a country's score on some value at one point in time with its scores at other points in time is meaningful for some analytical purposes. There is, of course, a rather strong tradition for the use of the country as a unit of analysis in qualitative as well as quantitative scholarship in politics.

Bibliographies of some of the quantitative research of interest to political scientists are found in the introduction to the first edition of the *World Handbook,* and in Bruce M. Russett's review of uses of that edition's data.[15]

W. S. Robinson demonstrated long ago that statistical analysis performed on aggregate units overstates the true relationship among individuals.[16] Thus the use of the country as the unit of analysis is quite unjustified for some purposes. For example, one cannot relate GNP and literacy data for several countries and come to the conclusion that rich people tend to be better educated than poor people; the variability that exists among the individuals is partially lost when averaging them into country figures and this reduction increases correlation coefficients. In making such an inference, one runs afoul of the ecological fallacy. Interest, however, is not always centered on the individual. Erwin Scheuch reminds us that the territorial units are a part of a reality and their use as units of analysis may be appropriate if they are considered a contextual property in accounting for the variation in other variables. He described the individualistic fallacy as the negation of the utility of an explanation "that treats the collectivity as a collectivity . . . and the phrasing of explanations for properties of the collectivity entirely in terms of the individual units, whose aggregated values should be the 'true' value for the collectivity."[17] Simon Kuznets, in studying economic growth, justifies the use of countries as units of analysis on the grounds that these sovereign entities, with their communities of feeling, have the interest and power to make many long-term decisions that promote or impede economic growth and that a complex and widespread process is best studied by considering units that affect its course rather than units such as race or letters of the alphabet that do not.[18] In comparative politics, the appropriateness of the nation-state as a unit is even clearer. The analyses of conditions of irregular government change, civil strife, and resource allocation are best done with reference to national governmental and territorial units.

15. Bruce M. Russett, "The *World Handbook* as a Tool in Current Research," in *Aggregate Data Analysis: Political and Social Indicators in Cross-National Research,* ed. C. L. Taylor (The Hague: Mouton, 1968), pp. 243-59.

16. W. S. Robinson, "Ecological Correlations and the Behavior of Individuals," *American Sociological Review,* 15 (1950): 351-57.

17. Erwin K. Scheuch, "Cross-National Comparisons Using Aggregate Data: Some Substantive and Methodological Problems," in *Comparing Nations: The Use of Quantitative Data in Cross-National Research,* ed. Richard L. Merritt and Stein Rokkan (New Haven: Yale University Press, 1966), pp. 131-67, esp. 150-51, 158. Hayward Alker, using the covariance theorem, developed a cache of fallacies. For a mathematical summary of the problem, see his "A Typology of Ecological Fallacies," in *Quantitative Ecological Analysis in the Social Sciences,* ed. Mattei Dogan and Stein Rokkan (Cambridge, Mass.: M.I.T. Press, 1969), pp. 69-86.

18. Simon Kuznets, *Modern Economic Growth: Rate, Structure, and Spread* (New Haven: Yale University Press, 1966), pp. 16-19.

Our decision to collect national aggregate data called for a comprehensive list of countries. Creating such a list is not quite so straightforward as might first appear. Does one include dependent territories as well as independent states? Must a state be independent for the full 20 years of the study? Are some places too small for inclusion, and, if so, what is the proper threshold? Indeed, is that threshold to be set in terms of population, gross national product, or land area? In a cluster analysis, Charles Taylor found that in terms of any one of these variables or of all of them in combination there is no very obvious cut-off point between mini-states and "real" states.[19] We chose to include all states and territories that had 1 million people or more in 1965. Five of these—Angola, Hong Kong, Mozambique, Papua/New Guinea, and Puerto Rico—were still dependent territories in 1971 and approximately a third of all the others became independent only between 1948 and 1967. One table in chapter 2 lists dates of independence and the user may filter the sample to suit himself. In addition to these larger territories, all other states that were members of the United Nations in June 1968 were included. Data were collected, therefore, on such places as Iceland and Luxembourg, whose sizes alone do not indicate their importance in world affairs. Excluded were tiny places like Andorra and Liechtenstein and inactive places like Bhutan and Sikkim (for which relatively few data are available anyway).

The states and territories of the world are listed in appendix 2. Indicated there are the countries included in this handbook.

Presentation of the Data

Tables are usually either reference sources, complex and detailed repositories of information, or summary capsules, concise and simple explications of a limited number of findings. The purpose of this handbook dictates an intermediate kind of table. In such a table, a great deal of data must be presented but the presentation should reveal as much about the structure of the series as possible. This has inevitably led to compromises. The publication of the whole dataset was not feasible; only a small proportion of it is in this book. Except for the event data, therefore, emphasis is given to the period circa 1965 and data for other dates and variables are available on magnetic tape from the Consortium in Ann Arbor. This reduction of data for the printed tables allows more comparisons among series and a larger number of charts and graphs than would otherwise be possible.

The first edition of the *World Handbook* had 75 tables with one series per table. This second edition has 56 tables with a total of 107 series. Of course, many items that were not a part of the first edition are included here. A few

19. Charles L. Taylor, "Statistical Typology of Micro-States and Territories," *Social Science Information,* 8 (1969): 101-17.

items in the first edition are not reprinted here. In some cases we were not able to improve on data published earlier and readers are asked to return to the earlier edition for these series.

The inclusion of multiple series in a single table allows the reader readily to see relationships among selected variables. Some series are brought together because they are related by theory. Others are placed together because they measure similar phenomena. In these tables the rank ordering of one variable is very much like that of the others. Some tables, however, are a hodgepodge of rank orderings; their series have been brought together because, although they have substantive or descriptive similarity, they are statistically unrelated. Although tables are usually ordered from high to low on the rightmost series, occasionally there are reasons to change this procedure. The important series is sometimes elsewhere in the table. In a few cases, ranking is done on the sum of more than one series or by some other means. These exceptions are explained in notes to the appropriate tables. Rank numbers appear to the left of the country names; median ranks are assigned to tied scores and countries are listed alphabetically within the tie.

The date around which a table is built is generally given as a footnote to the table. If the date for a particular country is different from this base date, the year will be noted somewhere to the right of the datum in question. Symbols to indicate notes, sources, and biases are also frequently found there and operate essentially as directors to footnotes. If a note refers to all the countries it appears as a footnote without a directing symbol in the body of the table. Bias, as we have judged it, has the following indicants:

$$-2, \text{ extreme underbias}$$
$$-1, \text{ underbias}$$
$$1, \text{ overbias}$$
$$2, \text{ extreme overbias}$$

A blank indicates *no known* bias. Notes to the table attempt to explain what these indicants mean in terms of particular series. Usually, any one series has a general source supplemented by others. A blank in the source column indicates the datum is from the general source, which is given at the bottom of the table; numbers in that column refer to numbers and sources also at the end of the table. Other special notes and symbols are explained within the contexts of specific tables.

Each table (with the exception of the few embedded in the text) includes all 136 countries one way or another. If a country's datum is available for any one series in the table, it appears in the appropriate place and the country's values on the other series are left blank. If data are unavailable for all of the series, the country is listed in a footnote to the table. Sometimes series are thought irrelevant to the country. For example, party fractional-ization is meaningless for a country without parties or elections and defense expenditures in dependent territories are not quite the same as those in independent states. Such countries are listed in a separate footnote to the table. These explicit statements of missing and inapplicable as well as available data should make the tables easier to use.

Six summary statistics are printed at the top of each table for each series included in the table. These are the mean, standard deviation, median, range, skewness, and number of countries. The number of countries refers to the count for which data are available and listed and *does not* include those for which the series is deemed irrelevant. The other five measures are calculated only on the values of the countries included. The mean is defined as

$$\overline{x} = \sum_{i=1}^{n} x_i/n.$$

The standard deviation is obtained by

$$s = \sqrt{\sum_{i=1}^{n} (X_i - \overline{X})^2 / n - 1}.$$

The median is the midpoint in the distribution above and below which one-half of the cases lie and the range is the distance between the smallest and the largest case. Skewness is arrived at by

$$Sk = \sum_{i=1}^{n} (X_i - \overline{X})^3.$$

These measures are generally given to the same number of decimal places as are the original data except that skewness, as a standardized measure, is always given with two significant places after the decimal.

Accompanying each table are selected pie graphs, frequency distributions, and (occasionally) Lorenz curves. The division of the world pie into pieces accounted for by national units is an appropriate method for picturing some distributions, such as defense dollars, population, or gross national product. The frequency distributions printed in this book all have as vertical axes values of a selected series and as horizontal axes country rankings. The highest ranking country's value is marked to the left; the lowest ranking country's value is to the right. The connecting line traces the distribution of values for the countries between. The median country is marked with a short vertical line. The Lorenz curves, built upon cumulative percentages of population and of values of the selected series, demonstrate the deviation from equality of distribution in the series. (See p. 212 for further information.)

A few of the values are estimations obtained from general knowledge. For example, it seemed relatively safe to insert zeros for foreign aid to countries when sources on American and Soviet aid did not mention the country. Similarly, literacy for some countries could be assumed to be very high since a figure for some previous year had been near 100 percent and nothing was known of a rapid decrease in the pace of the country's educational effort.

Some thought was given to the possibilities of estimating missing data by statistical routines. One procedure would have been to form a giant matrix, to make estimates for the missing cells by inserting means, intelligent guesses, or whatever else possible, and with the aid of factor analysis or multiple regression to find coefficients that would allow new estimates for the missing cells. Finding new coefficients and revising the cells would have continued until the estimates began to stabilize. The most obvious difficulty with any scheme of this sort is that future manipulations of the data including the estimates will be tainted by the previous building in a part of any relationship to be found. In short, it would be a case of statistical incest. Others using our data may in many cases wish to estimate missing values. By choosing variables that maximize correlations with the variable being estimated and minimize correlations with the proposed dependent variable, the optimal properties of regression will be maintained.[20] In any event, however, the estimations should most appropriately be made in terms of the particular theoretical relationship being tested and on the basis of variables not otherwise included in the particular analysis.

The authors of the first edition described their work as "beginnings." They hoped one of the major results of that work would be an emphasis on the gaps in available data and on the problems of comparability in those that did exist. We would modestly claim the work in this volume as "continuations." Some of the gaps have been filled. Explicitly political indicators that measure governmental stability, civil order, distribution of power, and allocation of political resources have been created. Indexes have been built from new data to provide new series on sectoral income distribution, ethnic fractionalization, export concentration, and the like. We have been able to build a much larger and more complete dataset. The cursory reader will perhaps be impressed by the large amount of data reported here and on magnetic tape. The person who looks somewhat more closely will be skeptical. The scholar who digs into our sources and into work in the fields touched upon here will find numerous problems of data gathering that plague the collector of comparable data. So the work of aggregate data collection has hardly begun. The many gaps that still exist, to say nothing of the problem of error, provide sufficient evidence of that. It is our hope that the discipline will encourage the intelligent, theory-informed accumulation of data that is essential to sound empirical analysis.

20. See J. Johnston, *Econometric Methods* (New York: McGraw-Hill, 1963), chap. 6.

Polities differ in their degrees of institutionalization, civil order, and government stability, in the allocation of their resources, in the extent of the freedom allowed their populations, and in the level of participation by those populations. This chapter reports data on age, budget and manpower allocations, and political freedom. Chapter 3 gives data on government stability, civil order, and political participation.

Political institutions as objects of study in political science were casualties of the behavioral revolution of the 1950s. This fact may explain to some extent why political scientists in the 1970s have available to them only the most rudimentary measurements of governments, which, despite behavioralism, remain at the focus of the discipline. Two currents, however, one methodological and one theoretical, have developed during the 1960s, and they both point up the need for better institutional indicators. The methodological emphasis on systematic cross-national comparison, as opposed to the looser parallel descriptions that have long dominated comparative politics, requires that the units of comparison be strictly defined. Quantitative terminology should provide the most precise description for large-scale comparative analysis; thus aggregate, interval-scaled indicators have assumed considerable importance. As we shall see, however, ideal quantitative indicators are not yet within our grasp. The theoretical emphasis on political institutions as important mediating variables between a changing socioeconomic environment and various kinds of political performance also suggests a return to the systematic observation of party, legislative, executive, constitutional, and administrative structures.

Given these reasons for studying institutional development, it is curious if not dismaying that so little work has been done to measure the size, age, and complexity of national political structures. In attempting to provide some indicators along these lines, however, we have come to appreciate the difficulties inherent even in the most rudimentary efforts. The following tables present data on the age of modern national political entities and the size of government sectors measured in monetary terms against the economy as a whole. Two measurement problems strike us as particularly difficult. One is that of arbitrary judgment. Historians who have labored for years trying to decide when a particular country became the political entity it is today will find the designation of particular years arbitrary if not capricious. The second problem is uncertainty as to whether or not the variable definition, no matter how well specified, is adequately met by the data. As yet, political scientists have not devoted the painstaking effort needed to gather precise data about structures ambiguously located on the boundaries of government. Neither of these problems can be met to the satisfaction of all the likely users of these data. It is possible, however, to reduce them somewhat by estimating, to the best of our imperfect knowledge, the quality of the data and by specifying the known idiosyncracies in particular figures. Users of the data may thereby find themselves in a better position than they would be otherwise to pursue "prudent" or "conservative" types of analysis. Our over-all intuitive judgment is that the indicators of institutional development are crude but still useful measures of the basic dimensions of national governments. We would be more uneasy about resting any analytic conclusions on the difference between the scores for two adjacent countries than we would about drawing conclusions from differences between countries at different deciles on the rank-order listing.

Longevity, it has been suggested, begets legitimacy; habituation to procedures produces consent. Political scientists from Hume to Huntington have hypothesized that the age of the political system may have important bearing on a nation's performance, particularly in terms of stability and order. One possible indicator of the continuity of contemporary political systems is the number of years the major national ruling institutions have maintained roughly their present form.

For more than half the countries in the world the beginning of present national political identity can be dated from the achievement of independence from an occupying or colonial power. A number of states, however, particularly the developed nations of Western Europe, are traceable as coherent political entities for many hundreds of years; for them, the date of independence is irrelevant as a criterion. Furthermore, political scientists interested in systemic continuity will properly question whether the political system of, let us say, China is continuous back to 221 *B.C.*, even though historians with the depth of vision of a Toynbee may accept such an idea.

We must, therefore, establish additional limiting criteria to locate these "older" states. One is the criterion of modernity. Before "modern" times the nation-state unit itself, if it can be said to exist at all, is only remotely comparable to the sovereign state of the late twentieth century. Modern nation-state institutions perform, however imperfectly, in modern or modernizing societies whose functional political requisites are qualitatively different from those of preindustrial and feudal environments. We are therefore excluding the possibility of modern political system continuity before the seventeenth century.

Three indicators of institutional age are presented in table 2.1: period of the consolidation of modernizing leadership, date of current constitution, and date of national independence. C. E. Black classified countries according to dates of the consolidation of modernizing leaderships. Modernization, says Black, is "the process by which historically evolved institutions are adapted to the rapidly changing functions that reflect the unprecedented increase in man's knowledge, permitting control over his environment, that accompanied the scientific revolution."[1] The consolidation of modernizing

1. C. E. Black, *The Dynamics of Modernization: A Study in Comparative History* (New York: Harper & Row, 1966), pp. 6-7, 73-74.

leadership is seen as the first stage of modernization; it is followed by the economic and social transformation and then by the integration of society. Black's classification is of interest to students of the longevity of political structures. The consolidation is marked by three characteristics: (1) the assertion of the determination to modernize; (2) an effective and decisive break with the institutions of an agrarian way of life; and (3) the creation of a national state with an effective government and a reasonably stable consensus on political means and ends by the inhabitants.

Dankwart Rustow has assembled basic data on dates of independence for countries. His series lists in a group 22 countries independent before 1775. Countries that became independent between 1776 and 1966 are listed with the year of independence. No formal criteria for independence or additional notations are presented. The question of national identity—what it is, how it arises, and its relation to the modernizing process—is treated at length in his book *A World of Nations,* especially on pages 20-31. Rustow recognizes the difficulties inherent in using a particular date to establish the longevity of a given nation when he comments, "If a nation is conceived of as a group of people bound together by common loyalty, it follows that nationhood, like loyalty itself, is a matter of degree. A given people at a given time may be more or less of a nation; and none fully approximates the ideal type."[2]

The third series included in table 2.1 is the year in which the present constitution or extraconstitutional operative rules as of 1970 came into effect. This series is intended to indicate a structural dimension distinct from both elites and the nation-state structure itself; it is perhaps a more sensitive measure of structural performance than the other two. On the other hand, it is not intended to measure types of power transfer that occur routinely ("within the norms of the system") or that rupture the normal governmental change procedures only temporarily without necessarily altering the formal power relationships of the system. These more sensitive fluctuations are charted over a 20-year period in chapter 3.

The establishment of a new constitution or governing rules may indicate one or more of the following changes in executive power relationships: (1) a change in the method of selection of the chief executive; (2) the emergence (or disappearance) of elites, groups, classes, or other sectors of the population into positions of power and influence; (3) a change in the powers and decision-making procedures of the national government; and (4) a change in the prevailing ideology. All these changes occur when a communist or other fundamentally revolutionary constitution is established, and for these countries we see the most significant deviations from the dates for modernizing elites and independence. The series distinguishes quite effectively, in addition, the instability in formal power relationships in those nonrevolutionary states that show impressive elite and nation-state dura-

2. Dankwart Rustow, *A World of Nations: Problems of Political Modernization* (Washington: Brookings Institution, 1967), pp. 24-25.

bility, such as France and several Latin American states. It must be noted, however, that the series does not indicate the full scope, intensity, or legality of constitutional establishment. It would be premature, to say the least, to infer that Jordan (1951) is slightly more institutionalized than Denmark (1953). It might also be premature, however, to conclude on the basis of such comparisons that the series has no value as an indicator. The purpose of the series, after all, is to facilitate research into the role of formal structures in national political performance.

For most countries a constitution is a written document, specifying the permanent structures, scope of authority, basis of legitimacy, and rule-making procedures of the government; the United States Constitution may be taken as a model. Also included are "unwritten constitutions," common agreements about these basic matters. We have designated the years of emergence of such agreements in accordance with conventional historical assessments; e.g. the United Kingdom is dated 1832. Some countries' constitutions consist of a series of ordinary but "basic" laws. In such cases we have selected the date of the first of them; e.g. Israel is dated 1948. Not every country was operating under a constitution in the Western sense in 1970, but it is assumed that every regime was operating according to some general, though not necessarily legitimate, rules.

Amendments and revisions to an existing constitution have been excluded, on grounds of comparability and because of a theoretical interest in the durability and flexibility of the formal core conception. For this reason and others, the establishment of the constitution preceded the date of independence in some countries (Laos and Lebanon, for example).

Draft constitutions, if judged to be in force, are also accepted. Changes of form of government are also judged as constitutional establishments; e.g. the Maldive Islands became a republic in 1968. Territorial losses or additions do not signify constitutional changes in the present use of the term, if a case can be made that constitutional forms were subsequently maintained; e.g. Malaysia is considered a continuation of Malaya. Partitions or federations that do appear to alter the previous forms are counted as new constitutions; e.g. East and West Germany are dated 1949.

The less stable countries present some coding difficulties. A few countries have reverted to an original constitution after a period with a different constitution or without any constitution; in these cases (Argentina, for example) the coding rule has been to accept the date of the original constitution. Military coups are not evidence of constitutional change unless there is explicit suspension of the previous constitution beyond some temporary abridgement. A further complexity arises in the case of countries that have undergone more than one change of regime after a constitution was originally suspended; in such countries the rule has been to designate the most recent coup as the date of current constitution-regime rule. Pakistan, for example, ended its brief constitutional period in 1958, but the

Mirza-Ayoub rule was terminated in 1969 by the establishment of a new regime and so 1969 is the date assigned to Pakistan. The same procedure requires assigning to Syria the date 1966, the year in which a new regime succeeded, through a coup, a regime that had itself come to power through a coup. In both cases the change of regime is judged to have altered the formal structures of the system, even though in the latter case the new regime ostensibly belongs to the same party as the old one. General Suharto's displacement of President Sukarno in Indonesia in 1966 could be regarded as the establishment of a new constitution, even though there is no explicit evidence of constitutional innovation. Alternatively, President Sukarno's extension of his powers in 1959 and 1960 constituted very fundamental changes in the power relationships; yet he claimed to be acting on the basis of the 1945 constitution. As further investigation reveals no evidence that the 1945 constitution is *not* formally in effect in the Suharto era, the coding rules indicate that 1945 must be the designated date.

Budgetary and Manpower Allocations

Tables 2.2 and 2.3 give data on education and defense expenditure. In each is reported the aggregate expenditure, the per capita expenditure, and expenditure as a percentage of gross national product. The first two figures for each country are given in United States dollars.

The educational data refer to public expenditure on both current and capital accounts for preschool, primary, secondary, and higher education. Whenever possible expenditure of all levels of government are included, but in a few cases data refer only to expenditures by the ministry of education or by the central government. Private expenditures assigned to private education are excluded except in the cases of Japan and India.

Military expenditures are defined as current and capital expenditures to meet the needs of the armed forces and to cover all expenditures of national defense agencies other than those expenditures used for civilian projects. They also include the distinguishable military component of such activities as atomic energy, space, research and development, and paramilitary forces. Where possible, military assistance to foreign countries, retirement pensions of career personnel, and military equipment stockpiling are included, but civil defense, civilian space exploration, and industrial stockpiling are excluded.[3]

Data in each of these tables are subject, first of all, to errors in the denominators. Difficulties in measuring gross national product and total population are discussed in chapter 5. In addition, the numerators of the ratios are subject to substantial error due to inadequacies in the published data. Since military expenditures and numbers of personnel are sometimes

---

3. United States Arms Control and Disarmament Agency, Economics Bureau, *World Military Expenditures and Related Data, Calendar Year 1966 and Summary Trends, 1962-1967.* Research Report 68-52 (Washington, D.C.: U.S. Government Printing Office, 1968), p. 22.

highly sensitive items of political information, deliberate distortion is sometimes a factor. Given the nature of their political systems, data for Western democracies are likely to be most reliable. Figures for defense expenditure as a percentage of gross national product for the Soviet Union, on the other hand, ranged from 4.6 percent to 14 percent. The datum of 9 percent is something of a compromise although we feel it is a reasonable one. China's figure, reported as 7.9 percent by one source and 10 percent by another, is anybody's guess. The very high percentage for Laos may also be more guess than anything else.

Several scholars have worked with cross-national defense expenditures and have attempted to draw together comparable figures for a large number of countries. Their estimates are by no means independent of one another since the publications cite one another frequently.[4] Our primary source was the work of the United States Arms Control and Disarmament Agency (ACDA). That agency in turn relied heavily upon the work of the Institute for Strategic Studies in London. Not surprisingly, estimates by the two organizations are very close for most countries. This is especially true when currency exchange rates are not a serious problem. We feel that the Arms Control and Disarmament Agency has given more attention than the Institute for Strategic Studies to the problem of converting data in national currencies into comparable figures in United States dollars and we have tended to report ACDA data when the two sets diverged. ACDA data were also available for a larger number of countries. Incidently, data reported in table 2.3 are not always those in the tables of the sources but are sometimes adjusted on the basis of information in the sources' texts.

The military effort for a given country may be high for many reasons. It may indicate tension with neighboring states; the data in table 2.3 are essential in testing theories about arms races. Inspection of the table will show a clear tendency for high ratios to be associated with alliance with either of the two major world power blocs. High levels of military expenditure are often made possible by substantial foreign assistance; this is clearly true for most of the smaller countries at the top of the expenditure table. But a high rate of military expenditure or participation need not be directed externally. In many states it indicates substantial internal tension or repression.

The consequences may be as diverse as the causes. Large armies serve as a major source of social mobility in some countries where advancement through the ranks has long been one of the easiest means of moving up in the larger society. The army may also be a source of social mobilization; it may bring into the modern and politically relevant sectors many people who would otherwise have remained in the traditionally oriented sectors. Military conscription may provide an opportunity for many young men to become

4. See Emile Benoit, "Economics of Arms Control and Disarmament; the Monetary and Real Costs of National Defense," *American Economic Review,* 58 (1968): 398-416.

literate and skilled in modern technology. In some underdeveloped countries the primary source of such people is the army. On the other hand, military careers, which provide the experience of certain aspects of modern life, may produce in some men great dissatisfaction with civilian political control. The bargaining process, coupled with the apparent and often real inefficiency of democratic government, may be incomprehensible to one who has experienced the seemingly rational order of a military hierarchy. Young officers exposed to modern technology in the army may become impatient with civilian inefficiencies and step directly into politics. A large army created to suppress domestic opposition may turn against its creators. Large armies thus may indicate both actual domestic instability (opposition to be suppressed) and a potential instability on the part of the suppressors.

Military manpower is given in table 2.4. In this table data on armed forces refer to military personnel actually on duty, including paramilitary forces where significant. Reserve forces are excluded except in Switzerland, where the national militia includes all able-bodied males, and Israel, where reserves account for a high percentage of the readily mobilized fighting force.

Table 2.5 reports data on internal security forces. These include police forces at all levels of government and such paramilitary internal security forces as gendarmeries, active militias, and active national guards. Data are generally drawn from publications of the Institute for Strategic Studies, but several governmental statistical reports as well as data compiled by Ted Gurr were also consulted and used in the collection.[5] Gurr's data were drawn from a variety of sources including the Institute for Strategic Studies, the *Statesman's Year-Book,* J. Cramer's *The World's Police* (London: Cassell, 1964), the *New York Times,* the United States Army, and the official publications of embassies of several countries. Gurr suggests that error, due largely to definition and identification, is of two kinds: underreporting owing to lack of information about "hidden" internal security force units, and overreporting resulting from the use of figures authorized rather than actual strength. While we agree that both kinds of error exist, we are not certain that they cancel each other out, resulting in a random pattern. We are instead inclined to think that underreporting is the more serious error of the two. Figures and estimates from reputable sources of certain countries, such as China, vary enormously. Similarly, in countries that are experiencing or waging insurgency warfare, such as North and South Vietnam, the range of internal security force units possibly warranting inclusion also varies greatly. In both these cases we have excluded the estimates at both the high and low extremes. Moreover, we have graded each datum as follows: A, reliable; B, good; and C, questionable. We have also indicated the direction and likely degree of bias.

5. Ted Gurr, *New Error-Compensated Measures for Comparing Nations* (Princeton: Center for International Studies Monograph, 1966). Later modifications were supplied by Professor Gurr in December 1967.

Freedom and Political Participation

Some measures of political participation and governmental restrictions are given in tables 2.6, 2.7, 2.8, and 2.9 although others coded on a daily basis from newspapers and similar sources are reported in chapter 3.

According to Douglas Rae and Michael Taylor, cleavage in a society can be categorized into three types; ascriptive, attitudinal, and behavioral.[6] By ascriptive is meant such "trait" cleavages as race or caste; our ethnolinguistic fractionalization measure of chapter 4 attempts to get at that kind of cleavage. By attitudinal is meant such "opinion" cleavages as ideology or preference; unfortunately, the instruments for providing comparable data of this sort have not been used in a very large number of our countries. By behavioral is meant such "act" cleavages as those elicited through voting and organizational membership; we have attempted to measure that cleavage in our indexes of party fractionalization.

Data were gathered for an election between 1963 and 1968 for each country and indexes of fractionalization were calculated based upon the party cleavages both in legislative seats and in original votes cast. Fractionalization was found as follows:

$$F = 1 - \sum_{i=1}^{N} \left(\frac{n_i}{N}\right)\left(\frac{n_i - 1}{N - 1}\right)$$

where n_i = the total number of votes (or seats) received
by the ith party
N = the total number of votes cast (or seats).

Fractionalization indicates the likelihood that two randomly selected members of the legislature will belong to different parties. Data refer to elections for the lower (or only) house of the legislature and exclude appointed members. Votes and seats are assumed to be divided into mutually exclusive categories attached to distinct parties. For some countries, this assumption—necessary for the index—is unreal; they may be without elections, legislatures, and/or parties. These countries are listed in a note at the bottom of table 2.6.

The press freedom index, reported in table 2.7, was created by the University of Missouri School of Journalism, and is designed to measure the freedom of a country's broadcasting and press systems to criticize their own local and national governments. Two native and two nonnative judges for each of 115 countries were asked to rate their countries on fixed scales for 23 items. For example, they were asked to mark "legal controls, not including libel and obscenity laws" as none, weak, moderate, strong, or severe and to rate "favoritism in the release of government news" as none, little, some, much, or complete. If there were disagreement between the

6. Douglas W. Rae and Michael Taylor, *The Analysis of Political Cleavages* (New Haven: Yale University Press, 1970), p. 1.

native and nonnative judges of more than 6 percent, judgments of the nonnatives only were used. Judges were carefully selected and their results were further selected; 24 percent of all questionnaires were voided because of irregularities or because respondents were not in consensus with judges for the same country.[7] The index, which consists of averages of the judges' scores, has a range from −4.00 for least freedom to +4.00 for greatest freedom.

Voter turnout data, given in table 2.8, can be helpful in ascertaining institutionalized mass participation in a political system. Such data can indicate, partially at least, the degree to which the electorate engages in active and formal political behavior. Within the limitations suggested below these data may provide a clue as to the scope of the political system and its effectiveness. As such, they may indicate indirectly the extent of a political system's structural development.

Voters were defined as individuals casting valid ballots in national legislative elections. In countries with bicameral legislatures the votes selected were those cast in elections to the lower house. In a few cases voting turnout for presidential elections was recorded; these cases are indicated in the notes to the table. Voters are given as a percentage both of the electorate and of the total population age twenty and over. The electorate was defined as those individuals legally able to vote in given elections. The number of eligible voters is determined by the political system's own formal criteria of participation, and these criteria vary from country to country. Universal adult male and female suffrage is certainly predominant in postwar electoral systems, but at the time these data were collected there were notable exceptions, such as Switzerland, which prohibited female suffrage. The minimum voting age also varied from place to place, and in 1970 at least 36 countries were reported to allow voting at age eighteen.[8] Governments also may diminish the size of the electorate for security reasons, as in the 1967 senatorial election in South Vietnam.[9] Voter turnout as a percentage of the electorate thus provides a measure of participation, but in the system's own terms. It is also desirable for cross-national analysis that turnout be compared in terms of a uniform demographic denominator in order that political systems can be evaluated in terms of their full possibilities for participation. Population age profiles reported in the United Nations *Demographic Yearbooks* provided the percentage of total population age twenty or over and these percentages were used to discover the absolute number of persons in that category from population estimates for the year

7. See Ralph L. Lowenstein, "World Press Freedom, 1966," University of Missouri, Freedom of Information Center Publication No. 181 (1967) and Ralph L. Lowenstein, "Measuring World Press Freedom as a Political Indicator," (Ph.D. diss., University of Missouri, 1967).

8. *New York Times,* 23 June 1970, citing data provided by the Library of Congress.

9. *Facts on File,* 1967.

of the election. In some countries with high participation and a voting age limit of eighteen the percentage of age twenty-plus voters actually exceeded 100 percent but in such cases the percentage was rounded back to 100 percent.

It would not be prudent to rely upon voter turnout alone as a measure of institutionalized participation. The just-mentioned technical problems with the categories and others involving data reliability reduce the analytic power of such an indicator, and the matter of context may be important. Elections obviously vary in significance from country to country. In some systems people may go to the polls and yet be deeply cynical about the electoral process; in others they may be required or coerced into voting; in others they may be rewarded with bribes. As the first edition of this handbook showed, the linear correlation between voter turnout and per capita GNP is not very strong, suggesting that voter turnout and wealth (one of the familiar indicators of development) do not go hand in hand.[10] One can see merely by inspecting table 2.8 that the rank order of countries on this variable does not coincide with several conventional notions about advanced, developed, differentiated, or civic polities. We feel nevertheless that the functional and normative significance of voter turnout is a matter that deserves further investigation.

Recognizing the problems of reliability and context inherent in voter turnout data, we attempted to devise a supplementary indicator that would permit cross-national comparisons of the regularity of national elections. By so doing, we hoped to facilitate the interpretation of voting statistics as well as to provide a somewhat more sensitive—albeit crude—measurement of structured participation.

We classified selected elections in three groups, according to whether they were reported to be (1) competitive and free, with no manifest coercion of voters; (2) marked by significant deviation from the competitive and free norm; or (3) marked by extreme deviation from that norm, i.e. allowing no effective voter choice. Classification was made on the basis of summary information about the election in question gathered from the sources reported in the notes to table 2.8. While a more elaborate typology of electoral regularity might have been desirable, the paucity of information would not support more than this threefold classification.

An election was classified as competitive or free if it were judged to conform to four criteria proposed by W. J. M. Mackenzie:

> An independent judiciary to interpret electoral law; . . . an honest, competent, non-partisan administration to run elections; . . . a developed system of political parties, well enough organized to put their policies, traditions and teams of candidates before the electors as alternatives between which to choose; . . . a general acceptance throughout the

---

10. Bruce M. Russett et al. *World Handbook of Political and Social Indicators* (New Haven: Yale University Press, 1964), pp. 305-06.

political community of certain rather vague rules of the game, which limit the struggle for power because of some unspoken sentiment that if the rules are not observed more or less faithfully the game itself will disappear amid the wreckage of the whole system.[11]

Mackenzie has proposed these as the conditions *ideally* necessary for the holding of free elections. These conditions served as general guidelines only; in many cases classified as competitive and free we lacked detailed information as to whether and to what extent each condition was met. It was not difficult, however, to recognize reported gross deviations from these norms.

The different types of deviation were distinguished. The countries classified under category 2, "significant deviation," were reported to exhibit one or more of the following characteristics: elections accompanied by extreme violence; fraud; intimidation of voters; a boycott by one or more major political groups; the outlawing of any major parties; single-party systems; manipulation of the electoral system so as to guarantee results beforehand, e.g. the practice in Colombia of dividing all seats between the two main parties; other kinds of ad hoc electoral "deals," such as those made in Guatemala in 1958 following an electoral impasse; and tampering with the electoral law and voting procedures to affect the outcome, e.g. through the last-minute relocation of polling stations.

An even more serious class of deviations from Mackenzie's ideal free election is that in which the fundamental electoral structure prohibits a competitive and free choice, whether because there are irregularities in electoral procedures (as in category 2) or because the election itself is annulled and its results immediately overturned. These might be called "rigged." In the rigged election there is no real choice for the voter, either among candidates or in the selection of candidates. Elections are considered rigged when racial discrimination disenfranchises most of the voters. Normal single-party elections were placed in category 2 because they deviated from the Mackenzie ideal; but single-party elections in which the candidates are selected by the ruling group and not on local initiative are considered even more deviant and are placed in the rigged category.

It was found easier to distinguish between free elections and the other two types than it was between the substantially deviant and the rigged types. For example, reported interference by interested foreign parties or occupation by foreign troops was judged to indicate at least an irregular election, but occasionally the interference appeared to be so pervasive that it required classification in the extreme category. Elections of certain Communist governments in Eastern European states such as Poland were scored as rigged because the parliament was judged as nonfunctioning in Mackenzie's terms. On the other hand, elections in the single-party state of Tanzania and in

11. W. J. M. Mackenzie, *Free Elections* (London: George Allen and Unwin, 1958), p. 14.

Yugoslavia were classified in the intermediate category. Indeed, one-party systems presented the most difficult judgmental problem, because it was not always possible to determine precisely how candidates were selected. Another problem was assessing to what extent the opposition was "token," as is the case, for example, in certain Latin American systems.

We realize that many users of the handbook will find this classification unsatisfactory for their purposes. It is arguable whether the Mackenzie criteria are relevant to non-Western systems and whether the reported information and coding judgments are uncritically biased against the communist and other single-party systems. Rather than asserting ethical judgments, however, our main intention has been to indicate groups of countries in which elections would seem to perform fundamentally different normative and empirical functions.

Table 2.1
Age of National Institutions

Countries as ranked below

Mean	years since independence	72
Standard Deviation	years since independence	72
Median	years since independence	38
Range	years since independence	193
Skewness	years since independence	.67
Number of Countries		131

Rank	Country	Consolidation of Modernizing Leadership	Year of Current Constitution	Year of Independence
11	Afghanistan	1923–	1965	1775
11	Austria	1848–1918	1945	1775
11	China	1905–1949	1949	1775
11	Denmark	1807–1866	1953	1775
11	East Germany	1803–1871	1949	1775
11	Ethiopia	1924–	1955	1775
11	France	1789–1848	1958	1775
11	Iran	1906–1925	1906	1775
11	Italy	1805–1871	1948	1775
11	Japan	1868–1945	1947	1775
11	Nepal		1962	1775
11	Netherlands	1795–1848	1814	1775
11	Portugal	1822–1910	1933	1775
11	Soviet Union	1861–1917	1936	1775
11	Spain	1812–1909	1938	1775
11	Sweden	1809–1905	1809	1775
11	Switzerland	1798–1848	1874	1775
11	Thailand	1932–	1968	1775
11	Turkey	1908–1923	1961	1775
11	United Kingdom	1649–1832	1832	1775
11	West Germany	1803–1871	1949	1775
22	United States	1776–1865	1787	1776
23	Paraguay	1841–	1967	1811
24	Guatemala	1881–	1966	1813
25	Argentina	1853–1946	1853	1816
26	Chile	1861–1925	1925	1818
27	Colombia	1863–	1963	1819
28	Mexico	1867–1910	1917	1820
29	Peru	1879–	1821	1821
30	Brazil	1850–1930	1967	1822

Table 2.1 Age of National Institutions—*Continued*

Rank	Country	Consolidation of Modernizing Leadership	Year of Current Constitution	Year of Independence
31	Bolivia	1880-1952	1947	1825
32	Uruguay	1828-1911	1966	1828
34	Ecuador	1875-	1967	1830
34	Greece	1863-1918	1968	1830
34	Venezuela	1870-1958	1958	1830
36	Belgium	1795-1848	1831	1831
38.5	Costa Rica	1889-1948	1871	1838
38.5	El Salvador	1939-	1962	1838
38.5	Honduras	1919-	1965	1838
38.5	Nicaragua	1909-	1963	1838
41	Haiti	1879-	1964	1840
42	Dominican Republic	1881-	1966	1844
43	Liberia	1847-	1847	1847
44	Canada	1791-1867	1867	1867
45.5	Rumania	1878-1918	1965	1878
45.5	Yugoslavia	1878-1918	1963	1878
47	Luxembourg	1795-1867	1868	1890
48.5	Australia	1801-1901	1900	1901
48.5	Cuba	1898-1959	1959	1901
50	Panama	1903-	1946	1903
51	Norway	1809-1905	1814	1905
52	New Zealand	1826-1907	1852	1907
53	Bulgaria	1878-1918	1947	1908
54	South Africa	1910-1962	1961	1910
55	Albania	1912-1925	1946	1912
58.5	Czechoslovakia	1848-1918	1948	1918
58.5	Finland	1863-1919	1919	1918
58.5	Hungary	1848-1918	1949	1918
58.5	Iceland	1874-1918	1944	1918
58.5	Poland	1863-1918	1952	1918
58.5	Yemen	1963-	1965	1918
62.5	Ireland	1870-1922	1937	1921
62.5	Mongolia	1921-1950	1960	1921
64	United Arab Republic	1922-1952	1964	1922
65	Saudi Arabia	1964-	1962	1925
66	Iraq	1921-1948	1964	1932
67.5	Lebanon	1920-1941	1926	1943
67.5	Syria	1920-1941	1966	1943
69.5	North Korea	1910-1946	1948	1945
69.5	South Korea	1910-1946	1962	1945
71.5	Jordan	1923-1946	1951	1946
71.5	Philippines	1899-1946	1935	1946
74	Ceylon	1920-1948	1947	1947
74	India	1919-1947	1950	1947
74	Pakistan	1919-1947	1969	1947
76.5	Burma	1923-1948	1962	1948
76.5	Israel	1920-1948	1948	1948
78.5	Indonesia	1922-1949	1945	1949
78.5	Taiwan	1895-1945	1950	1949
80	Libya	1952-	1963	1951
82.5	Cambodia	1949-	1955	1954
82.5	Laos	1949-	1947	1954
82.5	North Viet Nam	1949-	1960	1954

Table 2.1 Age of National Institutions—*Continued*

Rank	Country	Consolidation of Modernizing Leadership	Year of Current Constitution	Year of Independence
82.5	South Viet Nam	1949–	1966	1954
86	Morocco	1934–1956	1962	1956
86	Sudan	1924–1956	1956	1956
86	Tunisia	1922–1955	1959	1956
88.5	Ghana	1957–	1966	1957
88.5	Malaysia	1963–	1957	1957
90	Guinea	1958–	1958	1958
99.5	Cameroon	1960–	1961	1960
99.5	Central African Republic	1960–	1960	1960
99.5	Chad	1960–	1960	1960
99.5	Congo – Brazzaville	1960–	1960	1960
99.5	Congo – Kinshasa	1960–	1967	1960
99.5	Cyprus	1878–1946	1960	1960
99.5	Dahomey	1960–	1960	1960
99.5	Gabon	1960–	1960	1960
99.5	Ivory Coast	1960–	1960	1960
99.5	Malagasy Republic	1960–	1959	1960
99.5	Mali	1960–	1960	1960
99.5	Mauritania	1960–	1960	1960
99.5	Niger	1960–	1960	1960
99.5	Nigeria	1960–	1966	1960
99.5	Senegal	1960–	1960	1960
99.5	Somalia	1960–	1960	1960
99.5	Togo	1960–	1960	1960
99.5	Upper. Volta	1960–	1967	1960
110	Kuwait		1961	1961
110	Sierra Leone	1961–	1961	1961
110	Tanzania	1961–	1965	1961
114.5	Algeria	1847–1962	1962	1962
114.5	Burundi	1962–	1966	1962
114.5	Jamaica	1924–1962	1962	1962
114.5	Rwanda	1962–	1961	1962
114.5	Trinidad and Tobago	1959–	1962	1962
114.5	Uganda	1962–	1967	1962
118	Kenya	1963–	1963	1963
120	Malawi	1964–	1966	1964
120	Malta	1921–1961	1964	1964
120	Zambia	1965–	1964	1964
123.5	Maldive Islands	1965–	1968	1965
123.5	Rhodesia	1965–	1965	1965
123.5	Singapore	1965–	1965	1965
123.5	The Gambia	1965–	1963	1965
127.5	Barbados		1961	1966
127.5	Botswana		1965	1966
127.5	Guyana	1928–1966	1965	1966
127.5	Lesotho		1966	1966
130	Southern Yemen		1967	1967
131	Mauritius		1968	1968

Table 2.1 Age of National Institutions—*Continued*

Notes: Dependent territories of 1 million or more population in 1970 were Angola, Hong Kong, Mozambique, Papua/New Guinea, and Puerto Rico. They were omitted from this table, of course.

Summary statistics at the beginning of the table refer to the numbers of years since independence (to 1970), not to the dates of occurrence. The arbitrary choice of 1775 for the older countries, although reasonable as a convention, does affect the summary statistics and should affect one's interpretation of them.

Dates assigned to the consolidation of modernizing leadership are those of Cyril E. Black, published in *The Dynamics of Modernization: A Study in Comparative History* (New York: Harper & Row, 1966), pp. 90-94.

The year of current constitution was coded by Michael Hudson from *The Statesman's Year-Book, Statistical and Historical Annual of the States of the World for the Year, 1969-1970,* ed. S. H. Steinberg and John Paxton (London: Macmillan, 1969) and selected earlier editions; Moshe Y. Sachs, ed., *The Worldmark Encyclopedia of Nations* (New York: Harper & Row, 1967); and Dankwart Rustow, *A World of Nations: Problems of Political Modernization* (Washington, D.C.: Brookings, 1967), p. 290.

The year of independence is that given by Rustow, table 6, pp. 292-93, supplemented by Bruce M. Russett, J. David Singer, and Melvin Small, "National Political Units in the Twentieth Century: A Standardized List," *American Political Science Review* 62 (1968): 932-51.

Table 2.2
Education Expenditure

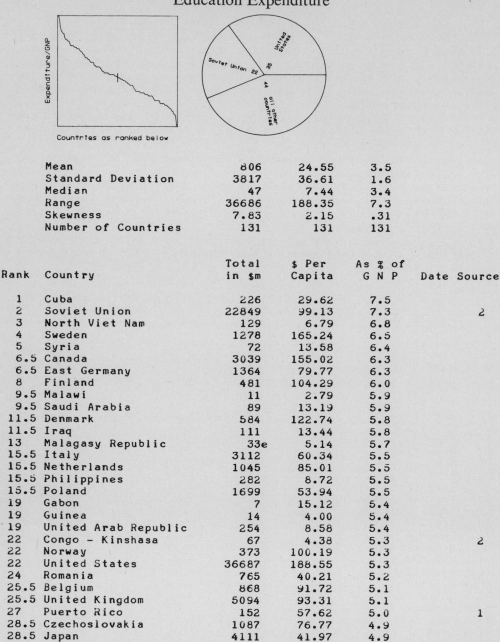

Countries as ranked below

Mean	806	24.55	3.5
Standard Deviation	3817	36.61	1.6
Median	47	7.44	3.4
Range	36686	188.35	7.3
Skewness	7.83	2.15	.31
Number of Countries	131	131	131

Rank	Country	Total in $m	$ Per Capita	As % of G N P	Date Source
1	Cuba	226	29.62	7.5	
2	Soviet Union	22849	99.13	7.3	2
3	North Viet Nam	129	6.79	6.8	
4	Sweden	1278	165.24	6.5	
5	Syria	72	13.58	6.4	
6.5	Canada	3039	155.02	6.3	
6.5	East Germany	1364	79.77	6.3	
8	Finland	481	104.29	6.0	
9.5	Malawi	11	2.79	5.9	
9.5	Saudi Arabia	89	13.19	5.9	
11.5	Denmark	584	122.74	5.8	
11.5	Iraq	111	13.44	5.8	
13	Malagasy Republic	33e	5.14	5.7	
15.5	Italy	3112	60.34	5.5	
15.5	Netherlands	1045	85.01	5.5	
15.5	Philippines	282	8.72	5.5	
15.5	Poland	1699	53.94	5.5	
19	Gabon	7	15.12	5.4	
19	Guinea	14	4.00	5.4	
19	United Arab Republic	254	8.58	5.4	
22	Congo – Kinshasa	67	4.38	5.3	2
22	Norway	373	100.19	5.3	
22	United States	36687	188.55	5.3	
24	Romania	765	40.21	5.2	
25.5	Belgium	868	91.72	5.1	
25.5	United Kingdom	5094	93.31	5.1	
27	Puerto Rico	152	57.62	5.0	1
28.5	Czechoslovakia	1087	76.77	4.9	
28.5	Japan	4111	41.97	4.9	
31	Hungary	524	51.64	4.7	
31	Mali	14	3.06	4.7	

Table 2.2 Education Expenditure—*Continued*

Rank	Country	Total in $m	$ Per Capita	As % of G N P	Date	Source
31	Yugoslavia	414	21.22	4.7		
33.5	Israel	169	65.94	4.6		
33.5	Singapore	43	22.83	4.6		1
35	Algeria	118	9.94	4.5		
37.5	Luxembourg	29	87.61	4.4		
37.5	Malta	7	21.63	4.4	1962	1
37.5	Uganda	29	3.84	4.4		
37.5	Venezuela	340	38.98	4.4		
40.5	Ceylon	68	6.05	4.2		
40.5	Ghana	93	12.02	4.2		
44	Central African Republic	5	3.70	4.1		
44	Kenya	35	3.74	4.1		
44	Lesotho	2	2.44	4.1		1
44	Malaysia	118	12.55	4.1		
44	Tunisia	39	8.84	4.1		
47	Guyana	8	12.75	4.0		1
48	Mauritania	5	4.76	3.9		
49.5	Bolivia	23	6.22	3.8		
49.5	Morocco	99	7.43	3.8		
53	Bulgaria	255	31.10	3.7		
53	Cambodia	31	5.07	3.7		
53	China	2800e	4.00	3.7		
53	France	3439	70.30	3.7		
53	Panama	23	17.69	3.7		
58.5	Austria	338	46.59	3.6		
58.5	Ivory Coast	35	9.13	3.6		
58.5	North Korea	90	7.44	3.6		
58.5	Switzerland	494	83.10	3.6		
58.5	Tanzania	27	2.57	3.6		
58.5	The Gambia	1	3.44	3.6	1962	1
63	Australia	788	69.37	3.5		
63	Costa Rica	21	14.65	3.5		
63	Sudan	47	3.47	3.5		
66	Argentina	590	26.40	3.4		
66	New Zealand	177	67.05	3.4		
66	West Germany	3832	64.90	3.4		
69	Barbados	3	11.50	3.3	1962	1
69	Ireland	92	32.02	3.3		
69	South Viet Nam	80	4.96	3.3		
72	Iceland	15	78.13	3.2		
72	Lebanon	36	14.04	3.2		
72	Senegal	22	6.30	3.2		
74.5	Ecuador	34	6.69	3.1		
74.5	Mauritius	6	8.59	3.1		1
76.5	Kuwait	47	100.64	3.0		
76.5	South Korea	89	3.14	3.0		
79.5	Burundi	4	1.37	2.9	1964	1
79.5	Hong Kong	46	12.09	2.9		
79.5	Iran	170	7.26	2.9		
79.5	Laos	5	2.50	2.9		
82	Taiwan	78	6.28	2.8		
83	Chile	130	15.17	2.7		
84	Jordan	13	6.58	2.6		
87	Cameroon	17	3.25	2.5		

Table 2.2 Education Expenditure—*Continued*

Rank	Country	Total in $m	$ Per Capita	As % of G N P	Date	Source
87	El Salvador	20	6.83	2.5		
87	Libya	22	13.61	2.5		
87	Trinidad and Tobago	16	16.26	2.5	1964	1
87	Turkey	221	7.11	2.5		
92	Colombia	120	6.64	2.4		
92	Cyprus	10	16.84	2.4		
92	Dahomey	4	1.69	2.4		
92	Jamaica	21	11.74	2.4		
92	South Africa	258	14.44	2.4		
96.5	Dominican Republic	22	6.08	2.3		
96.5	Liberia	5	4.67	2.3		
96.5	Peru	100	8.58	2.3		
96.5	Sierra Leone	8	3.49	2.3		
101	Burma	39	1.58	2.2		
101	Congo - Brazzaville	3	3.57	2.2		
101	Honduras	11	4.82	2.2		
101	Southern Yemen	3	2.89	2.2	1961	1
101	Thailand	86	2.81	2.2		
104	Chad	5	1.51	2.1		
105	India	1002	2.06	2.0		
108.5	Mexico	365	8.55	1.9		
108.5	Portugal	71	7.89	1.9		2
108.5	Rwanda	3	1.06	1.9	1963	1
108.5	Togo	3	1.83	1.9		
108.5	Upper Volta	5	1.03	1.9		
108.5	Zambia	15	4.04	1.9		
114	Brazil	381e	4.63	1.7		
114	Greece	100	11.69	1.7		
114	Mozambique	9	1.24	1.7	1964	1
114	Nigeria	84	1.46	1.7		
114	Rhodesia	17	3.99	1.7		
118	Nicaragua	9	5.44	1.6		
118	Niger	4	1.20	1.6		
118	Paraguay	7	3.45	1.6		
120.5	Guatemala	21	4.73	1.5		
120.5	Pakistan	165	1.60	1.5		
122.5	Angola	7	1.36	1.4		
122.5	Spain	244	7.72	1.4		
124	Somalia	2	.80	1.3		
125.5	Haiti	4	.91	1.2		
125.5	Uruguay	18	6.63	1.2		
127.5	Afghanistan	12	.80	1.0		
127.5	Ethiopia	10	.44	1.0		
129	Indonesia	92	.87	.9		
130	Nepal	2	.20	.3		
131	Yemen	1	.20	.2		

Notes: Data are missing for Albania, Botswana, Maldive Islands, Mongolia, and Papua/New Guinea.

An "e" indicates data reported as estimated in the source.

Date, unless otherwise noted, is 1965.

Source, unless otherwise noted, is United States, Arms Control and Disarmament Agency,

Table 2.2 Education Expenditure—*Continued*

Economics Bureau, *World-Wide Military Expenditures and Related Data, Calendar Year 1965,* Research Report 67-6 (Washington, D.C.: U.S. Government Printing Office, 1967.

  1. UNESCO, *UNESCO Statistical Yearbook, 1966* (Paris, 1967).

  2. UNESCO, *UNESCO Statistical Yearbook, 1967* (Paris, 1968). Only educational expenditure as a percentage of GNP was taken from this source; other data for these countries were taken from the main source.

Table 2.3
Defense Expenditure

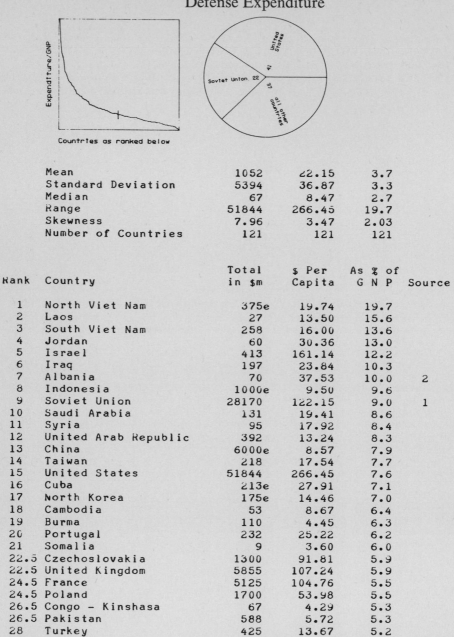

Mean	1052	22.15	3.7
Standard Deviation	5394	36.87	3.3
Median	67	8.47	2.7
Range	51844	266.45	19.7
Skewness	7.96	3.47	2.03
Number of Countries	121	121	121

Rank	Country	Total in $m	$ Per Capita	As % of G N P	Source
1	North Viet Nam	375e	19.74	19.7	
2	Laos	27	13.50	15.6	
3	South Viet Nam	258	16.00	13.6	
4	Jordan	60	30.36	13.0	
5	Israel	413	161.14	12.2	
6	Iraq	197	23.84	10.3	
7	Albania	70	37.53	10.0	2
8	Indonesia	1000e	9.50	9.6	
9	Soviet Union	28170	122.15	9.0	1
10	Saudi Arabia	131	19.41	8.6	
11	Syria	95	17.92	8.4	
12	United Arab Republic	392	13.24	8.3	
13	China	6000e	8.57	7.9	
14	Taiwan	218	17.54	7.7	
15	United States	51844	266.45	7.6	
16	Cuba	213e	27.91	7.1	
17	North Korea	175e	14.46	7.0	
18	Cambodia	53	8.67	6.4	
19	Burma	110	4.45	6.3	
20	Portugal	232	25.22	6.2	
21	Somalia	9	3.60	6.0	
22.5	Czechoslovakia	1300	91.81	5.9	
22.5	United Kingdom	5855	107.24	5.9	
24.5	France	5125	104.76	5.5	
24.5	Poland	1700	53.98	5.5	
26.5	Congo - Kinshasa	67	4.29	5.3	
26.5	Pakistan	588	5.72	5.3	
28	Turkey	425	13.67	5.2	
29.5	Iran	296	12.63	5.0	
29.5	Mongolia	25e	22.64	5.0	
31	Yugoslavia	396	20.30	4.5	

Table 2.3 Defense Expenditure—*Continued*

Rank	Country	Total in $m	$ Per Capita	As % of G N P	Source
32.5	Sweden	843	109.00	4.4	
32.5	West Germany	4979	84.33	4.4	
34	Guinea	11	3.14	4.3	
35.5	India	2077	4.27	4.2	
35.5	Malaysia	117	12.44	4.2	
37.5	Morocco	103	7.73	4.0	
37.5	Netherlands	750	61.02	4.0	
39	South Korea	113	3.98	3.9	
41	Algeria	127	10.69	3.8	1
41	East Germany	1000	58.48	3.8	
41	Norway	266	71.45	3.8	
43	Australia	838	73.77	3.7	
45	Congo - Brazzaville	5e	5.95	3.6	
45	Dominican Republic	35	9.67	3.6	
45	Greece	210	24.56	3.6	
48	Italy	1939	37.60	3.4	
48	Mali	10	2.19	3.4	
48	Romania	500	26.28	3.4	
50.5	Canada	1535	78.30	3.2	
50.5	Libya	28	17.32	3.2	
52.5	Belgium	501	52.94	3.0	
52.5	South Africa	320	17.91	3.0	
56	Brazil	641	7.80	2.9	
56	Bulgaria	200	24.39	2.9	
56	Denmark	286	60.11	2.9	
56	Paraguay	13	6.40	2.9	
56	Peru	123	10.56	2.9	
59	Haiti	9	2.05	2.8	
61	Hungary	300	29.56	2.7	
61	Lebanon	30	11.70	2.7	
61	Spain	587	18.57	2.7	
63.5	Ethiopia	30	1.33	2.6	
63.5	Switzerland	356	59.88	2.6	
65	Central African Republic	3e	2.22	2.5	
67.5	Chile	102	11.91	2.4	
67.5	Dahomey	4	1.69	2.4	
67.5	Niger	6	1.80	2.4	
67.5	Sudan	33	2.44	2.4	
70.5	Gabon	3e	6.48	2.3	
70.5	Venezuela	174	19.95	2.3	
75	Bolivia	13	3.52	2.2	
75	Cameroon	15	2.87	2.2	
75	Cyprus	9	15.15	2.2	
75	New Zealand	113	42.80	2.2	
75	Senegal	15	4.30	2.2	
75	Thailand	84	2.75	2.2	
75	Yemen	11	2.20	2.2	
79	Ecuador	24	4.72	2.1	
80.5	Colombia	102	5.65	2.0	
80.5	Kuwait	31	66.38	2.0	
82.5	Malagasy Republic	11	1.71	1.9	
82.5	Togo	3	1.83	1.9	
84	Afghanistan	23	1.53	1.8	
85.5	Argentina	272	12.17	1.7	

Table 2.3 Defense Expenditure—*Continued*

Rank	Country	Total in $m	$ Per Capita	As % of G N P	Source
85.5	Finland	139	30.14	1.7	
68	Ghana	36	4.65	1.6	
88	Luxembourg	10	30.21	1.6	
88	Mauritania	2e	1.90	1.6	
91	Philippines	76	2.35	1.5	
91	Tunisia	14	3.17	1.5	
91	Uruguay	23	8.47	1.5	
95	Honduras	7	3.06	1.4	
95	Liberia	3	2.80	1.4	
95	Nicaragua	8	4.83	1.4	
95	Nigeria	66	1.15	1.4	
95	Uganda	9	1.19	1.4	
99.5	Austria	118	16.26	1.3	
99.5	Chad	3	.91	1.3	
99.5	El Salvador	10	3.42	1.3	
99.5	Ivory Coast	13	3.39	1.3	
102.5	Ireland	33	11.49	1.2	
102.5	Upper Volta	3	.62	1.2	
104	Zambia	9	2.43	1.1	
105.5	Guatemala	14	3.15	1.0	
105.5	Rhodesia	10	2.35	1.0	
108	Japan	781	7.97	.9	
108	Kenya	8	.85	.9	
108	Sierra Leone	3	1.31	.9	
111	Ceylon	13	1.16	.8	
111	Mexico	153	3.58	.8	
111	Tanzania	6	.57	.8	
114	Burundi	1	.31	.7	1
114	Nepal	5	.50	.7	
114	Rwanda	1	.32	.7	1
116.5	Jamaica	5	2.80	.6	
116.5	Malawi	1	.25	.6	
118	Trinidad and Tobago	3	3.08	.4	1
119	Costa Rica	2	1.40	.3	
120	Panama	1	.77	.2	
121	Iceland	0	.00	.0	

Notes: Datum is missing for Malta.

This series is inapplicable for Angola, Barbados, Botswana, Guyana, Hong Kong, Lesotho, Maldive Islands, Mauritius, Mozambique, Papua/New Guinea, Puerto Rico, Singapore, Southern Yemen, and The Gambia. They were dependent territories in 1965.

An "e" indicates data reported as estimated in the source.

Date is 1965.

Source, unless otherwise noted, is United States, Arms Control and Disarmament Agency, Economics Bureau, *World-Wide Military Expenditures and Related Data, Calendar Year 1965,* Research Report 67-6 (Washington, D.C.: U.S. Government Printing Office, 1967).

1. For Burundi and Rwanda, David Wood, *The Armed Forces of African States,* Adelphi Papers, no. 27 (London: Institute for Strategic Studies, 1966); for Trinidad and Tobago, David Wood, *Armed Forces in Central and South America,* Adelphi Papers, no. 34 (London: Institute for Strategic Studies, 1967); for the USSR and Algeria, *The Military Balance, 1968-1969* (London: Institute for Strategic Studies, 1968).

Table 2.3 Defense Expenditure—*Continued*

2. United States, Arms Control and Disarmament Agency, Economics Bureau, *World Military Expenditures and Related Data, Calendar Year 1966 and Summary Trends, 1962-1967*, Research Report 68-52 (Washington, D.C.: U.S. Government Printing Office, 1968). Only defense expenditure as a percentage of GNP was taken from this source; other data for Albania were obtained from the main source.

Table 2.4
Military Manpower

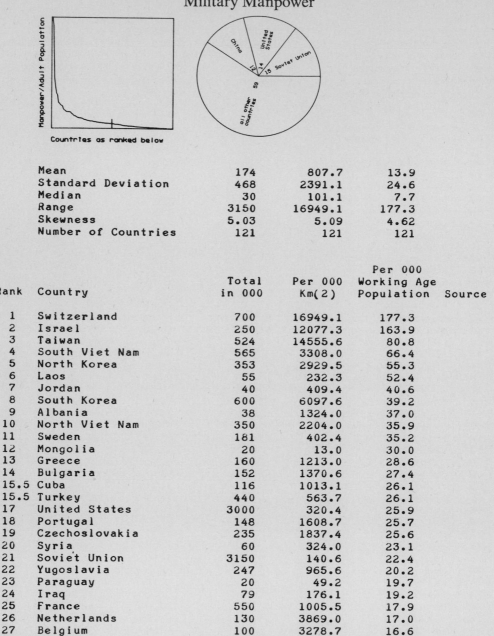

Mean	174	807.7	13.9
Standard Deviation	468	2391.1	24.6
Median	30	101.1	7.7
Range	3150	16949.1	177.3
Skewness	5.03	5.09	4.62
Number of Countries	121	121	121

Rank	Country	Total in 000	Per 000 Km(2)	Per 000 Working Age Population	Source
1	Switzerland	700	16949.1	177.3	
2	Israel	250	12077.3	163.9	
3	Taiwan	524	14555.6	80.8	
4	South Viet Nam	565	3308.0	66.4	
5	North Korea	353	2929.5	55.3	
6	Laos	55	232.3	52.4	
7	Jordan	40	409.4	40.6	
8	South Korea	600	6097.6	39.2	
9	Albania	38	1324.0	37.0	
10	North Viet Nam	350	2204.0	35.9	
11	Sweden	181	402.4	35.2	
12	Mongolia	20	13.0	30.0	
13	Greece	160	1213.0	28.6	
14	Bulgaria	152	1370.6	27.4	
15.5	Cuba	116	1013.1	26.1	
15.5	Turkey	440	563.7	26.1	
17	United States	3000	320.4	25.9	
18	Portugal	148	1608.7	25.7	
19	Czechoslovakia	235	1837.4	25.6	
20	Syria	60	324.0	23.1	
21	Soviet Union	3150	140.6	22.4	
22	Yugoslavia	247	965.6	20.2	
23	Paraguay	20	49.2	19.7	
24	Iraq	79	176.1	19.2	
25	France	550	1005.5	17.9	
26	Netherlands	130	3869.0	17.0	
27	Belgium	100	3278.7	16.6	
28.5	Denmark	50	1162.8	16.2	
28.5	Hungary	109	1172.0	16.2	
30	Romania	198	833.7	15.8	

Table 2.4 Military Manpower—*Continued*

Rank	Country	Total in 000	Per 000 Km(2)	Per 000 Working Age Population	Source
31	Iran	180	109.2	15.4	
32	Poland	277	886.4	14.2	
33.5	Luxembourg	3	1153.8	13.6	
33.5	Norway	32	98.7	13.6	
35	Finland	38	112.8	12.7	
36	Spain	250	495.3	12.4	
37	United Kingdom	424	1737.7	12.1	
38.5	Afghanistan	90	139.0	11.6	
38.5	West Germany	450	1810.9	11.6	
40	Italy	390	1294.8	11.5	
41	United Arab Republic	180	180.0	11.3	
42.5	Dominican Republic	19	390.1	10.6	
42.5	East Germany	112	1034.2	10.6	
44	Canada	120	12.0	10.3	
45	Uruguay	17	91.0	9.8	
46	Libya	8	4.5	9.7	
47	Chile	45	59.4	9.4	
48	Argentina	132	47.5	9.3	
49	Cambodia	30	165.8	9.2	
50	Tunisia	21	127.9	8.8	
51	Nicaragua	7	50.1	8.7	
52	Australia	60	7.8	8.5	
53	New Zealand	13	48.4	8.3	
54	Lebanon	12	1153.8	8.2	
55	Peru	50	38.9	8.1	
56	Thailand	132	256.8	8.0	
58	Burma	110	162.2	7.9	
58	Ireland	13	184.9	7.9	
58	Saudi Arabia	30	13.3	7.9	
60	Algeria	48	20.1	7.8	
61	Bolivia	15	13.6	7.7	
62	Ecuador	19	67.0	7.2	
63	Venezuela	30	32.9	6.7	
65	China	2500	261.5	6.6	
65	Colombia	60	52.7	6.6	
65	Morocco	45	101.1	6.6	
67	Liberia	4	35.9	6.3	
68	Indonesia	350	234.6	6.0	
69	Malaysia	29	87.2	5.8	
70	Austria	25	298.3	5.4	
71	Pakistan	260	253.0	4.9	
72	Honduras	5	44.6	4.6	
73	Brazil	200	23.5	4.5	
74.5	Panama	3	39.6	4.3	
74.5	Somalia	6	9.4	4.3	
76.5	Congo — Kinshasa	35	14.9	4.0	
76.5	Guatemala	9	82.6	4.0	
78	El Salvador	6	280.4	3.9	
79.5	India	1000	314.1	3.7	
79.5	Japan	250	676.2	3.7	
81	Gabon	1	3.7	3.6	
82	Nepal	20	142.0	3.5	
83	Mexico	68	34.5	3.2	

Table 2.4 Military Manpower—*Continued*

Rank	Country	Total in 000	Per 000 Km(2)	Per 000 Working Age Population	Source
84.5	Cyprus	1	107.5	2.9	
84.5	Guinea	5	20.3	2.9	
86	Ethiopia	35	28.6	2.8	
87	South Africa	27	22.1	2.7	
88	Sudan	18	7.2	2.6	
89	Ghana	10	41.9	2.5	
90.5	Philippines	37	123.3	2.3	
90.5	Rhodesia	5	12.8	2.3	
93	Congo – Brazzaville	1	2.9	2.1	
93	Jamaica	2	181.8	2.1	
93	Senegal	4	20.4	2.1	
96	Haiti	5	179.9	1.9	
96	Ivory Coast	4	12.4	1.9	
96	Trinidad and Tobago	1	196.1	1.9	1
99.5	Ceylon	9	137.2	1.5	
99.5	Mauritania	1	1.0	1.5	
99.5	Sierra Leone	2	27.9	1.5	
99.5	Zambia	3	4.0	1.5	
103	Central African Republic	1	1.6	1.3	
103	Mali	3	2.5	1.3	
103	Togo	1	17.7	1.3	
105	Rwanda	2	76.0	1.2	1
106	Cameroon	3	6.3	1.0	
107	Malagasy Republic	3	5.1	.9	
108	Dahomey	1	8.9	.8	
109	Yemen	2	10.3	.7	
111	Burundi	1	36.0	.6	1
111	Kenya	3	5.1	.6	
111	Niger	1	.8	.6	
113.5	Malawi	1	8.4	.5	
113.5	Uganda	2	8.5	.5	
115	Upper Volta	1	3.6	.4	
116	Nigeria	9	9.7	.3	
117	Tanzania	1	1.1	.2	
119.5	Chad	0	.0	.0	
119.5	Costa Rica	0	.0	.0	
119.5	Iceland	0	.0	.0	
119.5	Kuwait	0	.0	.0	

Notes: Datum is missing for Malta.

This series is inapplicable for Angola, Barbados, Botswana, Guyana, Hong Kong, Lesotho, Maldive Islands, Mauritius, Mozambique, Papua/New Guinea, Puerto Rico, Singapore, Southern Yemen, and The Gambia. They were dependent territories in 1965.

The Swiss national militia includes all able-bodied males. Israeli reserves are included because they represent a high proportion of the readily mobilized fighting force. Otherwise, these data refer to military personnel actually on duty, including paramilitary forces where significant.

Date is 1965.

Source, unless otherwise noted, is United Nations, Arms Control and Disarmament Agency, Economics Bureau, *World-Wide Military Expenditures and Related Data, Calendar Year 1965,*

Table 2.4 Military Manpower—*Continued*

Research Report 67-6 (Washington, D.C.: U.S. Government Printing Office, 1967), which in turn compiled data from *The Reference Handbook of the Armed Forces of the World, 1966* (Washington, D.C.: Robert C. Sellers) and from *The Military Balance, 1965-1966* (London: Institute for Strategic Studies, 1965), and David Wood, *Armed Forces in Central and South America* Adelphi Papers, no. 34 (London: Institute for Strategic Studies, 1967).

  1. For Burundi and Rwanda, David Wood, *The Armed Forces of African States*, Adelphi Papers, no. 27 (London: Institute for Strategic Studies, 1966); for Trinidad and Tobago, David Wood, *Armed Forces in Central and South America*, Adelphi Papers, no. 34 (London: Institute for Strategic Studies, 1967).

Table 2.5
Internal Security Forces

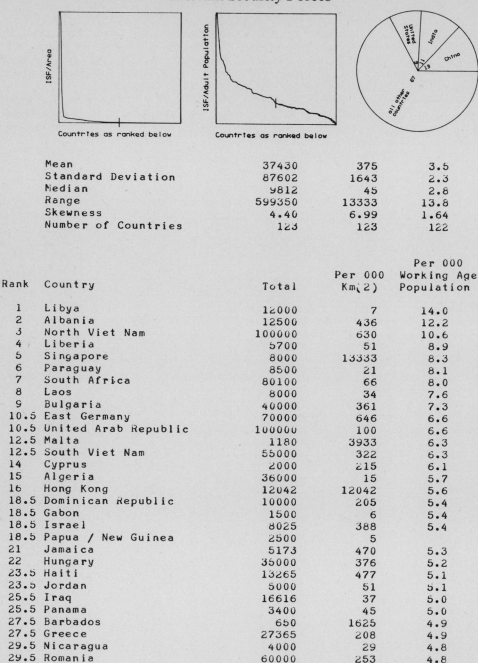

Countries as ranked below   Countries as ranked below

Mean	37430	375	3.5
Standard Deviation	87602	1643	2.3
Median	9812	45	2.8
Range	599350	13333	13.8
Skewness	4.40	6.99	1.64
Number of Countries	123	123	122

Rank	Country	Total	Per 000 Km(2)	Per 000 Working Age Population
1	Libya	12000	7	14.0
2	Albania	12500	436	12.2
3	North Viet Nam	100000	630	10.6
4	Liberia	5700	51	8.9
5	Singapore	8000	13333	8.3
6	Paraguay	8500	21	8.1
7	South Africa	80100	66	8.0
8	Laos	8000	34	7.6
9	Bulgaria	40000	361	7.3
10.5	East Germany	70000	646	6.6
10.5	United Arab Republic	100000	100	6.6
12.5	Malta	1180	3933	6.3
12.5	South Viet Nam	55000	322	6.3
14	Cyprus	2000	215	6.1
15	Algeria	36000	15	5.7
16	Hong Kong	12042	12042	5.6
18.5	Dominican Republic	10000	205	5.4
18.5	Gabon	1500	6	5.4
18.5	Israel	8025	388	5.4
18.5	Papua / New Guinea	2500	5	
21	Jamaica	5173	470	5.3
22	Hungary	35000	376	5.2
23.5	Haiti	13265	477	5.1
23.5	Jordan	5000	51	5.1
25.5	Iraq	16616	37	5.0
25.5	Panama	3400	45	5.0
27.5	Barbados	650	1625	4.9
27.5	Greece	27365	208	4.9
29.5	Nicaragua	4000	29	4.8
29.5	Romania	60000	253	4.8

Notes	Bias	Date	Source
b		1966	
c	-1	1965	
c		1964	5
b		1966	
		1963	3
b		1966	
b		1965	
c	-1	1965	
b		1966	3
b	-1	1965	
c		1963	3
b		1965	1
b	-1	1966	
c		1965	
c		1966	
b		1965	2
b		1966	
b		1966	
b		1964	2
		1965	
b		1965	1
b	-1	1965	
b	+1	1966	
b		1965	
b		1965	2
b		1966	
b		1966	
		1965	3
b		1966	
b	-1	1965	

Table 2.5 Internal Security Forces—*Continued*

Rank	Country	Total	Per 000 Km(2)	Per 000 Working Age Population
31	France	140000	256	4.7
33	Chile	22500	30	4.6
33	Italy	150000	498	4.6
33	Malaysia	23000	69	4.6
35.5	Guyana	1500	7	4.5
35.5	Trinidad and Tobago	2377	466	4.5
37	Cambodia	12000	66	4.1
39.5	Congo – Brazzaville	1900	6	4.0
39.5	Ghana	16500	69	4.0
39.5	Ireland	6568	93	4.0
39.5	Tunisia	9600	59	4.0
42.5	North Korea	25000	208	3.9
42.5	The Gambia	658	58	3.9
44.5	Czechoslovakia	35000	274	3.8
44.5	Syria	9800	53	3.8
46.5	Colombia	35000	31	3.7
46.5	Zambia	6134	8	3.7
49	West Germany	130000	523	3.6
49	Yemen	10000	51	3.6
49	Yugoslavia	43000	168	3.6
53.5	Cameroon	10700	23	3.5
53.5	Mauritius	1314	692	3.5
53.5	Morocco	24000	54	3.5
53.5	Somalia	5000	8	3.5
53.5	Spain	70000	139	3.5
53.5	United States	401000	43	3.5
57.5	Puerto Rico	4765	535	3.3
57.5	Thailand	53732	105	3.3
59	Taiwan	20000	556	3.1
60	Malagasy Republic	9000	15	2.9
61.5	Peru	18000	14	2.8
61.5	Rhodesia	6400	16	2.8
63.5	Afghanistan	21000	32	2.7
63.5	United Kingdom	94520	387	2.7
66.5	Brazil	120000	14	2.6
66.5	Kenya	11705	20	2.6
66.5	Pakistan	135000	131	2.6
66.5	Soviet Union	350000	16	2.6
70	Australia	17587	2	2.5
70	Bolivia	5000	5	2.5
70	Portugal	13900	151	2.5
72.5	Botswana	708	1	2.4
72.5	Congo – Kinshasa	21000	9	2.4
76.5	Ethiopia	29200	24	2.3
76.5	Japan	156848	424	2.3
76.5	Netherlands	17500	521	2.3
76.5	Poland	45000	144	2.3
76.5	Senegal	4500	23	2.3
76.5	South Korea	34058	346	2.3
82	Honduras	2500	22	2.2
82	Indonesia	130000	87	2.2
82	Iran	26000	16	2.2
82	Lebanon	3250	313	2.2

Notes	Bias	Date	Source
b		1963	3
b		1966	
b		1961	3
b		1965	
b		1966	
b		1965	1
c		1965	3
b		1966	
b		1966	
a		1964	2
b		1966	
b	-1	1965	
b		1965	4
b	-1	1965	
b		1965	
b		1966	
b		1965	
c		1963	3
c	+1	1967	4
b		1963	3
b		1966	
b		1964	4
b		1966	
b		1966	
b		1963	3
b		1964	3
b		1964	1
b		1965	2
		1963	3
b		1966	
b		1966	
b	-1	1966	
c		1965	1
a		1964	2
b	-1	1966	
b		1964	2
b		1965	
c	-1	1963	3
a		1965	2
b·		1966	
c		1966	3
b		1964	4
b		1966	
b		1966	
a		1965	2
b		1966	1
b	-1	1965	
b		1966	
c		1964	2
b		1966	
b		1965	
b	-1	1965	
b		1965	

Table 2.5 Internal Security Forces—*Continued*

Rank	Country	Total	Per 000 Km(2)	Per 000 Working Age Population
82	Venezuela	10000	11	2.2
87	Belgium	12645	415	2.1
87	Denmark	6400	149	2.1
87	Ecuador	5800	21	2.1
87	India	504016	158	2.1
87	Switzerland	8200	199	2.1
90.5	Norway	4500	14	2.0
90.5	Sweden	10000	22	2.0
92.5	Central African Republic	1530	3	1.9
92.5	Lesotho	832	28	1.9
94	Dahomey	2200	20	1.8
95.5	Angola	5000	4	1.7
95.5	New Zealand	2698	10	1.7
99	Ceylon	9812	150	1.6
99	China	600000	63	1.6
99	Costa Rica	1200	24	1.6
99	El Salvador	2500	117	1.6
99	Togo	1300	23	1.6
103.5	Cuba	6000	52	1.5
103.5	Malawi	3000	25	1.5
103.5	Sierra Leone	2050	29	1.5
103.5	Sudan	10000	4	1.5
106	Chad	2500	2	1.4
108	Guatemala	3000	28	1.3
108	Mozambique	5310	7	1.3
108	Uganda	5500	23	1.3
111	Argentina	17000	6	1.2
111	Burundi	1850	67	1.2
111	Mauritania	800	1	1.2
113.5	Guinea	1900	8	1.1
113.5	Ivory Coast	2300	7	1.1
115.5	Burma	13000	19	1.0
115.5	Niger	1700	1	1.0
117	Philippines	15500	52	.9
119	Mali	1600	1	.7
119	Nigeria	24000	26	.7
119	Upper Volta	1800	7	.7
121	Canada	7102	1	.6
122	Rwanda	750	29	.4
123	Tanzania	1350	1	.2

Notes: Data are missing for Austria, Finland, Iceland, Kuwait, Luxembourg, Maldive Islands, Mexico, Mongolia, Nepal, Saudi Arabia, Southern Yemen, Turkey, and Uruguay.

These data were selected from a variety of possibilities by Michael Hudson who graded them A (reliable), B (good), or C (questionable). He assigned them "+1" when he felt an overestimate was likely and "−1" when an underbias was likely.

Source, unless otherwise noted, is *The Military Balance, 1965-1966* (London: Institute for Strategic Studies, 1965); *The Military Balance, 1966-1967* (London: Institute for Strategic Studies, 1966); David Wood, *The Armed Forces of African States*, Adelphi Papers, no. 27 (London: Institute for Strategic Studies, 1966); David Wood, *The Military Strength of Israel's Arab Neighbors* (London: Institute for Strategic Studies, 1965); or David Wood, *Armed*

Notes	Bias	Date	Source
b		1966	
b		1964	2
b		1961	3
b		1966	
b		1965	1
b		1963	3
b		1961	3
b		1961	3
b		1966	
c		1965	1
b		1966	
		1963	3
b		1965	1
b		1964	1
c	-1	1962	3
c		1966	
b		1966	
b		1966	
c		1965	
b		1966	
b		1966	
c		1964	
c		1966	
b		1966	
b		1965	2
b		1966	
b		1966	
b		1966	
b		1966	
b		1966	
b		1966	
c		1961	1
b		1966	
b		1966	
b		1966	
b		1966	
b		1966	
b		1965	1
b		1966	
b		1966	

Forces in Central and South America, Adelphi Papers, no. 34 (London: Institute for Strategic Studies, 1967).

1. *The Statesman's Year-Book, Statistical and Historical Annual of the States of the World for the Year, 1966-1967*, ed. S. H. Steinberg (London: Macmillan, 1966).

2. Annual governmental fiscal and statistical reports.

3. Ted Gurr, *New Error-Compensated Measures for Comparing Nations*, Research Monograph, no. 25 (Princeton: Center of International Studies, 1966), pp. 111-26.

4. Nonannual governmental and statistical reports.

5. *The Statesman's Year-Book, Statistical and Historical Annual of the States of the World for the Year, 1964-1965*, ed. S. H. Steinberg (London: Macmillan, 1964).

Table 2.6
Party Fractionalization

Countries as ranked below

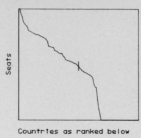

Countries as ranked below

Mean	.502	.379
Standard Deviation	.276	.305
Median	.610	.438
Range	.838	.945
Skewness	-.88	-.09
Number of Countries	64	101

Rank	Country	F Votes	Source	F Seats	Source	Date
1	Lebanon			.945	2	1964
2	Hong Kong			.900		1967
3	Indonesia			.877	1	1967
4	Netherlands	.838		.830		1967
5	Switzerland	.822		.815		1967
6	Finland	.808		.803		1966
7	Israel	.789		.794		1965
8	Venezuela	.791		.760		1963
9	Colombia			.753		1966
10	Denmark	.763		.752		1966
11	Ecuador			.741		1966
12	Peru			.738		1967
13	Italy	.758		.734		1963
15	Belgium	.748		.725		1965
15	Ceylon	.743		.725		1965
15	Iceland	.735	3	.725		1967
17	Norway	.743		.720		1965
18	Panama	.666		.713		1964
19	Sudan			.709	3	1965
20	Chile	.769		.704		1965
21	Luxembourg			.697		1964
22	Sweden	.708		.693		1964
23	India	.806		.682		1967
24	France	.755		.668		1967
25	Australia	.593	3	.625		1966
26	Ireland	.632		.624		1965
27	Turkey	.631		.620		1965
28	Guyana	.610		.617		1964
29	Canada	.699		.616		1965
30	Malaysia	.598		.589		1964
31	Japan	.671		.586		1967

Table 2.6 Party Fractionalization—*Continued*

Rank	Country	F Votes	Source	F Seats	Source	Date
32	West Germany	.610		.582		1965
33	Guatemala	.725		.572		1966
34	El Salvador	.628		.566		1967
35.5	Barbados	.638		.565		1966
35.5	Uruguay	.590		.565		1966
37	Costa Rica	.500		.541		1966
38	Austria	.581		.535		1966
39	New Zealand	.614		.512		1966
40	United Kingdom	.588		.507		1966
41.5	Honduras	.495		.503		1965
41.5	Malta	.589		.503		1966
43	Paraguay	.482		.496		1967
44	Lesotho	.642	3	.494		1966
45	United States			.491	1	1966
46	Mauritius			.481		1967
47	Jamaica	.503		.479		1967
48	Philippines			.475		1965
49	Nicaragua	.399		.463		1967
50	Trinidad and Tobago	.602		.457		1966
51	Brazil	.620		.438		1966
52	Dominican Republic	.545		.430		1966
53	Singapore	.630		.416		1963
54	Uganda			.414	1	1962
55	Zambia			.402	1	1964
56	The Gambia	.463	4	.401	1	1966
57	South Africa	.518	3	.397	1	1966
58	South Korea	.633		.387		1967
59	Rhodesia	.684	5	.385	3	1965
60	Pakistan			.377		1965
61	Puerto Rico			.370	6	1965
62	Bolivia	.593		.358		1966
63	Mexico	.280		.303		1967
64	Somalia			.280	1	1964
65	Iran			.276		1967
66	Botswana			.181		1966
67	Kenya			.101	1	1967
68	Malagasy Republic			.055		1965
85	Albania	.000		.000		1966
85	Bulgaria	.003		.000		1966
85	Cambodia			.000		1966
85	Cameroon	.300	2	.000		1964
85	Chad	.031	2	.000		1963
85	China			.000		1964
85	Congo – Brazzaville	.189	2	.000		1963
85	Czechoslovakia	.001		.000		1964
85	East Germany	.001		.000		1967
85	Gabon	.624	2	.000		1964
85	Guinea			.000		1968
85	Haiti			.000		1961
85	Hungary	.006		.000		1967
85	Ivory Coast	.020	3	.000		1965
85	Liberia			.000		1964
85	Malawi			.000		1966
85	Mali	.002	2	.000		1964

Table 2.6 Party Fractionalization—*Continued*

Rank	Country	F Votes	Source	F Seats	Source	Date
85	Mauritania			.000		1965
85	Mongolia			.000		1966
85	Niger	.020	3	.000		1965
85	North Korea			.000		1967
85	North Viet Nam			.000		1964
85	Poland	.026		.000		1965
85	Portugal			.000		1965
85	Rumania	.005		.000		1965
85	Rwanda			.000	1	1965
85	Senegal	.099	2	.000		1963
85	Soviet Union	.005		.000		1966
85	Spain			.000	1	1967
85	Tanzania			.000	1	1965
85	Tunisia			.000		1964
85	United Arab Republic			.000		1964
85	Yugoslavia			.000	1	1967

Notes: This series is inapplicable for Afghanistan, Algeria, Angola, Argentina, Burma, Burundi, Central African Republic, Congo-Kinshasa, Cuba, Cyprus, Dahomey, Ethiopia, Ghana, Greece, Iraq, Jordan, Kuwait, Laos, Libya, Maldive Islands, Morocco, Mozambique, Nepal, Nigeria, Papua/New Guinea, Saudi Arabia, Sierra Leone, Southern Yemen, South Viet Nam, Syria, Taiwan, Thailand, Togo, Upper Volta, and Yemen. In several cases, e.g. Angola, Burma, Cuba, Nepal, Saudi Arabia, and Syria, there was no legislature. In others, e.g. Afghanistan, Ethiopia, and Laos, elections were not on the basis of party. In still others, e.g. Algeria, Greece, Nigeria, and Togo, duly elected legislatures were suspended. The last election in Cyprus was in 1960 and the last in Taiwan was in 1947. Data for the table were for elections held between 1962 and 1968.

Source, unless otherwise noted, is United States, Department of State, Bureau of Intelligence and Research, *World Strength of the Communist Party Organizations,* Twentieth Annual Report (Washington, D.C.: U.S. Government Printing Office, 1968).

1. Walter H. Mallory, ed., *Political Handbook and Atlas of the World, 1968* (New York: Council on Foreign Relations, 1968).

2. *Review of Elections* (London: Institute of Electoral Research, 1964).

3. *Keesing's Contemporary Archives* (London: Keesing's, 1968).

4. *Africa Diary* (New Delhi: By M. Chhabra for Africa Publications, 1968).

5. *Africa Research Bulletin* (London: Africa Research, 1968).

6. Operations and Policy Research, Inc., Institute for the Comparative Study of Political Systems, *Puerto Rico: Election Factbook* (Washington, 1968).

Table 2.7
Press Freedom

The highest possible score for press freedom is +4.00 and the lowest possible score for the lack of it is —4.00.

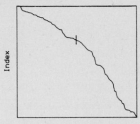

Countries as ranked below

Mean	.42
Standard Deviation	2.01
Median	1.00
Range	6.56
Skewness	-.55
Number of Countries	91

Rank	Country	Index	Notes
1.5	Norway	3.06	
1.5	Switzerland	3.06	
3	Netherlands	3.02	
4	Sweden	2.83	
5	Canada	2.78	
6	Peru	2.76	
7.5	Finland	2.72	
7.5	United States	2.72	
9	Costa Rica	2.68	1
10	Philippines	2.66	
11	Denmark	2.65	
12	Uruguay	2.61	
13	Venezuela	2.54	
14.5	Australia	2.53	
14.5	Belgium	2.53	
16	Japan	2.44	
17	West Germany	2.43	
18	Bolivia	2.39	
19.5	Ireland	2.37	
19.5	United Kingdom	2.37	
21	El Salvador	2.26	
22	New Zealand	2.24	
23	Colombia	2.21	
24	Jamaica	2.16	2
25	Ecuador	2.12	2
26	Austria	2.10	
27	Italy	1.98	
28	Cyprus	1.96	
29	France	1.92	
30	Singapore	1.81	
31	Israel	1.75	
32	Panama	1.69	

Table 2.7 Press Freedom—*Continued*

Rank	Country	Index	Notes
33.5	Malaysia	1.66	
33.5	Turkey	1.66	2
35	Mexico	1.46	
36	Greece	1.37	
37	Brazil	1.25	
38	Kenya	1.20	2
39	Chile	1.19	
40	Lebanon	1.18	2
41.5	Dominican Republic	1.16	2
41.5	Rhodesia	1.16	
43	Ceylon	1.14	
44	South Africa	1.07	
45	Zambia	1.05	
46	Morocco	1.00	2
47	India	.98	
48	Argentina	.92	2
49	Tanzania	.87	
50	Uganda	.77	
51	Thailand	.70	2
52	Taiwan	.61	
53	Malawi	.52	1
54	Nigeria	.45	2
55	South Korea	.42	2
56	Burma	.38	
57	Ghana	.34	
58	Yugoslavia	.08	2
59	Pakistan	-.01	
60	Indonesia	-.39	
61	South Viet Nam	-.44	2
62	Congo - Kinshasa	-.45	1
63	Laos	-.46	2
64	Jordan	-.51	2
65	Nepal	-.59	
66	Tunisia	-.66	
67	Spain	-.99	2
68	Iran	-1.02	2
69	Cambodia	-1.14	1
70	Afghanistan	-1.29	1
71	Iraq	-1.35	1
72	Portugal	-1.42	2
73	Hungary	-1.57	2
74	Senegal	-1.98	1
75	Syria	-1.99	
76	United Arab Republic	-2.31	2
77	Cameroon	-2.41	2
78	Czechoslovakia	-2.50	2
79	Poland	-2.53	1
80	Bulgaria	-2.70	1
81	Chad	-2.71	2
82	Cuba	-3.01	1
83	Soviet Union	-3.07	1
84	Upper Volta	-3.08	1
85	Ethiopia	-3.09	2
86	China	-3.15	1
87.5	East Germany	-3.19	1

Table 2.7 Press Freedom—*Continued*

Rank	Country	Index	Notes
87.5	Romania	-3.19	1
89	Algeria	-3.25	2
90	North Korea	-3.38	1
91	Albania	-3.50	1

Notes: Data are missing for Angola, Barbados, Botswana, Burundi, Central African Republic, Congo-Brazzaville, Dahomey, Gabon, Guatemala, Guinea, Guyana, Haiti, Honduras, Hong Kong, Iceland, Ivory Coast, Kuwait, Lesotho, Liberia, Libya, Luxembourg, Malagasy Republic, Maldive Islands, Mali, Malta, Mauritania, Mauritius, Mongolia, Mozambique, Nicaragua, Niger, North Viet Nam, Papua/New Guinea, Paraguay, Puerto Rico, Rwanda, Saudi Arabia, Sierra Leone, Somalia, Southern Yemen, Sudan, The Gambia, Togo, Trinidad and Tobago, and Yemen.

In the *notes* column, a 1 indicates that no native scores were used in calculating the index. A 2 indicates that there was a disagreement of more than 6 percent between native and nonnative scores. For countries for which there were such large differences, only nonnative scores were used to build the index.

The data were provided by Ralph L. Lowenstein, Freedom of Information Center, The School of Journalism, The University of Missouri.

Table 2.8
Voter Turnout

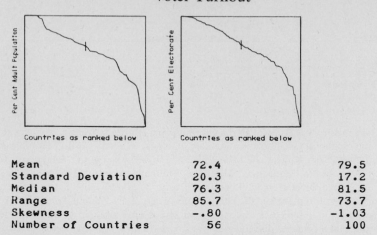

Mean	72.4	79.5
Standard Deviation	20.3	17.2
Median	76.3	81.5
Range	85.7	73.7
Skewness	-.80	-1.03
Number of Countries	56	100

Rank	Country	Voters as % of Population 20+	Date	Voters as % of Electorate	Date
1.5	Albania	100.0	1966	100.0	1962
1.5	North Korea			100.0	1962
3	Soviet Union	97.7	1966	99.9	1966
4	Romania	99.6	1965	99.8	1965
5	Bulgaria	100.0	1966	99.7	1962
6	Ivory Coast			99.6	1965
7	Guinea			99.5	1963
8.5	Czechoslovakia	100.0	1964	99.4	1964
8.5	Gabon	97.3	1964	99.4	1967
10	East Germany	92.1	1967	99.2	1963
11	Netherlands	87.9	1967	98.9	1959
12	United Arab Republic			98.5	1964
13	Niger			98.2	1965
14	Upper Volta			97.4	1965
15	Hungary	100.0	1967	97.2	1963
16	Tunisia			96.7	1964
17	Poland	100.0	1965	96.6	1965
18	Guyana	85.2	1964	96.3	1964
19	Australia			95.7	1963
20	Malawi			95.6	1961
21	Chad			95.4	1963
22.5	Dahomey			94.3	1964
22.5	Zambia			94.3	1964
24	Singapore	71.8	1963	94.2	1963
25	Senegal	66.6	1963	94.0	1966
26	Austria	88.9	1966	93.8	1966
27	Malta	80.9	1966	93.4	1966
28	Italy	89.2	1963	92.9	1963
29	Mauritania			92.8	1965
30	Mauritius			91.8	1959
31	Belgium	79.4	1965	91.6	1965

Table 2.8 Voter Turnout—*Continued*

Rank	Country	Voters as % of Population 20+	Date	Voters as % of Electorate	Date
32	Togo			91.1	1963
33	Yugoslavia			90.9	1963
34	New Zealand	77.1	1966	90.5	1963
35	Luxembourg			90.0	1959
36	Paraguay	49.2	1967	89.9	1963
37	Mali			88.9	1964
38	Ethiopia			88.4	1961
39	Peru			87.6	1963
40	West Germany	77.6	1965	86.8	1965
41	Iceland	85.8	1967	86.6	1963
42	Denmark	86.8	1966	85.5	1964
43	Norway	81.9	1965	85.4	1965
44	Algeria			85.0	1964
45	Venezuela	78.8	1963	84.9	1963
46	Central African Republic			84.2	1964
47	Sweden	78.1	1964	83.9	1964
48	Cameroon	83.3	1964		
49.5	Finland	82.1	1966	83.0	1966
49.5	Puerto Rico			83.0	1964
51	Ceylon	75.0	1965	81.5	1965
52	Greece			81.0	1961
53	Argentina			80.9	1963
54	France	66.5	1967	80.0	1967
55	Brazil	44.2	1966	79.6	1962
56.5	Israel	84.1	1965	79.1	1965
56.5	Nicaragua	87.1	1967	79.1	1963
58	Costa Rica	69.8	1966	79.0	1966
59	Tanzania			78.1	1965
60	Chile	54.1	1965	77.8	1965
61	United Kingdom	72.4	1966	77.1	1964
62	Botswana			76.5	1965
63	Malaysia	48.0	1964	76.4	1964
64	Philippines			76.1	1961
65	Ecuador			75.9	1960
66	Ireland	72.1	1965	75.1	1965
68	Malagasy Republic			75.0	1960
68	Portugal			75.0	1961
68	The Gambia	70.2	1966	75.0	1962
70	Uruguay	70.5	1966	74.3	1966
71	Canada	67.7	1965	74.0	1965
72.5	Morocco			73.0	1963
72.5	South Africa	14.3	1966	73.0	1966
74	Jamaica	46.6	1967	72.9	1962
75	Papua / New Guinea			72.3	1964
76	Turkey	61.2	1965	71.3	1965
77	Japan	72.3	1967	71.1	1963
78	Bolivia			70.0	1964
79	Dominican Republic	82.8	1966	69.9	1962
80	South Korea	76.3	1967	69.8	1963
81	Kenya			69.3	1963
82	Honduras	67.3	1965		
83.5	Iran			66.7	1963
83.5	Kuwait			66.7	1963
85	Jordan			66.6	1963

Table 2.8 Voter Turnout—*Continued*

Rank	Country	Voters as % of Population 20+	Date	Voters as % of Electorate	Date
86	Switzerland	23.3	1967	66.1	1963
87	Uganda			66.0	1963
88	Trinidad and Tobago	64.7	1966		
89	Lesotho	68.6	1965	62.3	1965
90	Cyprus			61.6	1960
91	Barbados			60.0	1961
92	United States	56.8	1964	58.7	1964
93	Mexico	49.8	1967	54.1	1964
94	Panama	53.9	1964		
95	Lebanon			53.4	1964
96	India	55.8	1967	53.1	1962
97	Syria			53.0	1961
98	Guatemala	25.9	1966	47.8	1966
99	Ghana			47.7	1956
100	Cuba			40.0	1958
101	Colombia			36.9	1964
102	El Salvador	34.3	1967	33.4	1966
103	Nigeria			28.0	1964
104	Nepal			26.3	1959

Notes: Data are missing for Afghanistan, Angola, Burma, Burundi, Cambodia, China, Congo-Brazzaville, Congo-Kinshasa, Haiti, Hong Kong, Indonesia, Iraq, Laos, Liberia, Libya, Maldive Islands, Mongolia, Mozambique, North Viet Nam, Pakistan, Rhodesia, Rwanda, Saudi Arabia, Sierra Leone, Somalia, Southern Yemen, South Viet Nam, Spain, Sudan, Taiwan, Thailand, and Yemen.

Sources include *Review of Elections* (London: Institute of Electoral Research), Department of State, Bureau of Intelligence and Research, *World Strength of the Communist Party Organizations* (Washington, D.C.: U.S. Government Printing Office, selected annual editions, 1965-1968), Walter H. Mallory, ed., *Political Handbook and Atlas of the World, 1968* (New York: Council on Foreign Relations, 1968), *Keesing's Contemporary Archives, Europa Yearbook, Africa Diary, Africa Research Bulletin, Africa Report, Asian Recorder, Parliamentary Affairs, Interparliamentary Bulletin,* selected *Election Factbooks* on several Latin American countries (Washington, D.C.: Institute for the Comparative Study of Political Systems), *The Statesman's Year-Book*, official statistical publications, and selected academic studies.

Qualifications. As the data presented usually are drawn from official sources, one's assessment of their accuracy will depend on his confidence in the government's capabilities and integrity. In many cases, however, unofficial estimates have been reported; such figures are usually qualified as "approximately," "around," "a little more (less) than," or are obviously rounded. Data for the following countries were reported to be underestimates: Iceland, Luxembourg, South Africa, and Yugoslavia. Data for the Netherlands were reportedly overestimated. Data for the following countries were reported to be "approximate" or "not rigorously exact" but no direction of error was suggested: Barbados, Costa Rica, Dominican Republic, Gabon, Iran, Jordan, Mali, Mexico, Morocco, Portugal, Puerto Rico, and Syria. Guinea's figure is "an official estimate."

Data for Costa Rica, Guatemala, and United Arab Republic refer to presidential elections. For India, Kenya, and Tanzania, figures are for contested constituencies only. For Zambia, calculations are from the main roll, not the very much smaller reserve roll.

Table 2.9
Electoral Irregularity

A. Countries for which elections were scored as competitive and reasonably free:

Australia (1963)	Guyana (1964)	Pakistan (1965)
Austria (1966)	Iceland (1963)	Panama (1964)
Barbados (1966)	India (1967)	Papua (1964)
Belgium (1965)	Ireland (1965)	Peru (1963)
Botswana (1965)	Israel (1965)	Philippines (1965)
Canada (1965)	Italy (1963)	Puerto Rico (1964)
Ceylon (1965)	Jamaica (1962)	Sweden (1964)
Chile (1965)	Japan (1963)	Switzerland (1963)
Costa Rica (1966)	Lebanon (1964)	Thailand (1957)
Denmark (1964)	Luxembourg (1964)	Trinidad and Tobago (1966)
Ecuador (1966)	Malaysia (1964)	Turkey (1965)
El Salvador (1966)	Malta (1966)	Uganda (1963)
Finland (1966)	Mexico (1964)	United Kingdom (1964)
France (1967)	Nepal (1959)	United States (1964)
Gambia (1966)	Netherlands (1963)	Uruguay (1966)
West Germany (1965)	New Zealand (1963)	
Greece (1964)	Norway (1965)	

B. Countries for which elections were scored as displaying significant deviation from the competitive and free norm:

Afghanistan (1965)	Guatemala (1964)	Singapore (1963)
Argentina (1963)	Iran (1963)	Sudan (1965)
Bolivia (1964)	Jordan (1963)	South Vietnam (1966)
Brazil (1966)	Kenya (1963)	Syria (1961)
Burma (1960)	South Korea (1963)	Tanzania (1965)
Burundi (1965)	Kuwait (1963)	Tunisia (1964)
Cambodia (1962)	Laos (1965)	Venezuela (1963)
Colombia (1966)	Lesotho (1965)	Yugoslavia (1966)
Congo-Kinshasa (1965)	Libya (1965)	Zambia (1964)
Cyprus (1960)	Morocco (1963)	
Dahomey (1959)	Nigeria (1964)	
Dominican Republic (1966)	Rwanda (1965)	
Ethiopia (1965)	Senegal (1966)	

C. Countries for which elections were scored as displaying extreme deviation from the competitive and free norm:

Albania (1962)	Indonesia (1960)	Rhodesia (1965)
Algeria (1964)	Iraq (1958)	Rumania (1965)
Bulgaria (1962)	Ivory Coast (1965)	Sierra Leone (1965)
China (1962)	Liberia (1963)	South Africa (1966)
Czechoslovakia (1964)	Nicaragua (1967)	Togo (1963)
East Germany (1963)	Niger (1965)	United Arab Republic (1964)
Ghana (1965)	North Korea (1962)	Soviet Union (1962)
Guinea (1963)	Paraguay (1963)	North Vietnam (1964)
Haiti (1961)	Poland (1965)	
Hungary (1963)	Portugal (1965)	

Table 2.9 Electoral Irregularity—*Continued*

D.   Countries for which there was insufficient information available for judgments:

Cameroon	Honduras (1965)	Mauritania
Central African Republic (1964)	Malagasy Republic	Mauritius
Chad (1963)	Malawi (1964)	Mongolia
Congo-Brazzaville (1963)	Maldive Islands	Mozambique
Gabon	Mali (1964)	Somalia
	Upper Volta	

E.   Countries that were scored as inapplicable on this variable, because they had no known recent elections:

Angola	Saudi Arabia	Taiwan
Cuba	Southern Yemen	Yemen
Hong Kong	Spain	

3 Political Protest and Executive Change

Order and stability are central themes in classical political theory; violent upheaval is the basic operational doctrine of the more than fifty liberation movements found mainly throughout the Third World of Asia, Africa, and Latin America. But protest and change have come to the "developed" world too. Americans experienced a wave of civil protest in their cities and on their campuses during the 1960s over the issues of racial equality and the war in Indochina. Political scientists came to the realization that politics has a violent dimension even in the most "civic" polities. The compilers of the violence and instability event data in this collection sought to carry out their coding with a degree of clinical detachment, concentrating on the quantitative aspects of strife and change. But such events also have important qualitative aspects that defy systematic comparison. We experienced, albeit vicariously and peripherally, the quality of a violent event when, in the spring of 1970, the expectation of violence at a rally on behalf of the Black Panthers in New Haven caused us to remove our data to the safer suburbs. The episode held a certain irony. But it was also sobering and perhaps useful to imagine how this rally or the Kent State tragedy might appear in our violence profiles and analyses. The mind balks at comprehending the hope and suffering that are represented in these data.

We must leave to others the task of showing the human dimensions of violence. Our aim instead is to portray quantities of violence and change for purposes of comparative analysis. To do so requires one to accept the proposition that violence events are indeed comparable and that one can sensibly add them together. Some political scientists, believing a knowledge of the context of an event to be paramount, will reject that proposition outright. Most others, ourselves included, will accept it only for limited purposes. To one user, for example, it may be admissible to compare two countries in terms of aggregate violence and draw certain inferences about the relative capabilities or stability of those systems; to another, however, an event called a riot in the Philippines may be a completely "different" phenomenon from a riot in the Netherlands. The latter user still may find it desirable to compare riots within the Philippines over time and thus may still find this handbook useful, although some may still argue that time alone invalidates such comparisons. The same issue of interpretation, of course, applies to political deaths, voter turnout, and many other "political" indicators. Our own view is that aggregations of armed attack events have much the same analytic utility in political analysis as aggregate gross national products in economic analysis.

The first edition of the *World Handbook* made a path-breaking contribution toward the systematic comparative analysis of instability by presenting aggregate indicators of executive stability and political deaths per

1,000 population. These indicators could begin to serve as rough measures of one of the central dependent variables in modernization theory—system "stability." Our concern in this edition is to provide a richer array of "instability" data than was included in the first edition. One means of doing this is to assemble date-specific event data over a considerable time period, thus permitting the plotting of protest patterns longitudinally. Before undertaking the data collection we consulted numerous colleagues and nearly all of them recommended collecting time series data. We at first planned to supply only annual aggregations, but the scope of the project was soon vastly broadened to include the recording of single date-specific events separately. Work in progress by others on typologies of violence guided us in developing a variety of indicators.[1] While a composite index of instability, possibly using weighted scores for different types of events, has proved and still might prove useful, we felt it was most appropriate for our purposes to distinguish different kinds of protest and to present the data in their most basic form, thus leaving a wider variety of research options for the users of the handbook. After a period of experimentation it was decided to collect 18 event series, of which 10 are presented in summary tables by variable, annually aggregated, with countries rank-ordered on the basis of a 20-year aggregation. In addition, we present plots depicting the distribution of all 10 events over time for each country, because we believe that there is a useful purpose to be served in allowing visual inspection of the fuller range of a political system's violence and instability performance.

It may be appropriate to dwell briefly upon "events" as analytic units. In common parlance an event is an occurrence or noteworthy happening. We have assembled reports of "noteworthy happenings" in the domain of political violence and governmental change, because we have felt that events of this sort may be suitable units of measurement for discovering quantitative relationships in this domain. Specifically, we have been guided by Lasswell's call for developmental analysis of the power process in which he argues that "the subject of political science [may be expressed] in terms of a certain class of *events* (including subjective events), rather than timeless institutions or political patterns. We deal with power as a process in time . . . . The developmental standpoint is concerned, not with systems in equilibrium, but with patterns of succession of events. . . . "[2]

1. E.g. Harry Eckstein, ed., *Internal War* (New York: Free Press, 1964); Rudolph J. Rummel, "Dimensions of Conflict Behavior Within and Between Nations," *General Systems: Yearbook of the Society of General Systems,* 8 (1963): 1-50; Raymond Tanter, "Dimensions of Conflict Behavior, 1958-1960," *Journal of Conflict Resolution,* 10 (1966): 41-64; Ivo K. and Rosalind L. Feierabend, "Aggressive Behaviors Within Politics, 1948-1962: A Cross-National Study," *Journal of Conflict Resolution,* 10 (1966): 249-71. We are deeply indebted to Katherine H. Dolan for her crucial role in formulating, refining, and operationalizing the event indicators. We were also influenced at an early stage by Rummel's definitions of antigovernment demonstrations, riots, and deaths from political violence (Rummel, "Dimensions of Conflict Behavior," p. 5).

2. Harold D. Lasswell and Abraham Kaplan, *Power and Society: A Framework for Political Inquiry* (New Haven: Yale University Press, 1950), pp. xiv-xv.

It would be misleading to claim that the event reports coded here are precise units; our data sources—journalists and editors—think of events in conventional rather than metaphysical terms. But we do not feel that our borrowing of others' conventional usage is undesirable; it may be preferable to the opacity and false precision of more elaborate conceptualizations. A violence or change event in our dataset is an occurrence judged important enough by a professional journalist or editor to merit reporting in a daily newspaper, a daily wire-service file, or a specialized publication dealing with politics in a particular area. From the historian's perspective the French Revolution may be considered an event taking place over several years; from the journalist's perspective an event is an occurrence that took place within perhaps a 24-hour period and that would be "noteworthy" for at least another 24-hour period—or for tomorrow's paper. The cabinet shuffle may have been contemplated for months but it takes place within a given time period measurable in hours rather than weeks or months. The coup d'état may be the product of years of discontent but the removal of the ruler can be rather precisely pinpointed; and, as the new leadership struggles to consolidate its power—successfully or unsuccessfully—it will do so through a rapid series of moves that will also be recorded as part of the power process, even though from the usual perspective these events may appear as a single change. Similarly, demonstrations and riots can be observed as discrete social processes that begin and end within a period of hours, and an armed attack may take only a matter of minutes. Events like riots, whose form is sometimes hard to discern and which may seem to last for days, continue to be news and are usually reported in effect as new events; so they are thus appropriately weighted for quantitative analysis. In a rough sense, therefore, the events reported here are comparable in terms of duration and longevity.[3]

Even if event-units are comparable, the question remains as to how adequately they are reported and coded. Because this is an exceedingly complex question, we have felt it desirable to present our discussion in an appendix. Suffice it to say here that we make no claim to have coded all the events that happened and that the following indicators would be more accurately thought of as "event reports" than as simple "events." We do feel, however, that they can be reliably used for those kinds of analysis that take into account the areas of strength and weakness—by indicator, by region, by perceived importance to Americans, etc.—in the data. If this dataset and its

3. Our procedure differs from that of violence archivists who sometimes reported cumulative incidents of strife as single events. See, for example, Ted Gurr, "A Causal Model of Civil Strife," *American Political Science Review,* 62 (1968): 1104-24, esp. 1108, n. 16. Gurr reports, for example, that all European-OAS terrorism in Algeria was treated as a single event (presumably he assigned to such an event very high pervasiveness, duration, and intensity). Rudolph Rummel also created certain event categories of greater duration than ours (for example, his "presence or absence of guerrilla warfare," "number of major government crises," and "number of purge" indicators): see Rummel, "Dimensions of Conflict Behavior," p. 5. On this point see also Charles Tilly and James Rule, *Measuring Political Upheaval,* Center of International Studies Research Monograph no. 19 (Princeton: Princeton University, 1965), pp. 61-62.

categories arouse sufficient interest among political scientists, it should be possible for intensive partial studies, using a wider array of local sources, to reveal the strengths and weaknesses in this dataset. Such revelations would be interesting, particularly since this dataset is drawn from roughly the same information flow that forms and influences educated American perceptions of politics in the world's nation-states.

Our primary intention has been to compile indicators that would be helpful in the study of participation and power transfer in national political systems. Initially, our conception of protest and participation events was quite simple, but during four months of preliminary coding it became clear that each process was multifaceted. It became clear almost immediately that power transfers could not be adequately categorized under one or two rubrics and that protest events take several forms. The result was an array of indicators. Not only does the array permit of more complex analyses of the various dimensions of protest and power transfer, it also allows one to perceive a given country's "profile" of performance on them.

Indicators of Political Protest

Comparative research on political violence suggests that it is not necessarily a homogeneous, unitary concept. It follows that data on various types of civil disorder may be more helpful at this stage than a premature composite "violence index." Furthermore, current work in the field suggests the importance of the following characteristics of civil disorder: magnitude, amplitude, direction, sequence, and combination of disorder events. We have made an attempt to serve these needs with our violence event data.

Inasmuch as the political protest and executive change data comprise 57,268 event reports for 136 countries from two sources over the 1948-67 period, there are certain problems in presenting these data on a daily basis in a handbook. We have been obliged therefore to present only a part of the violence dataset and to summarize it in a manner that we hope is convenient for users. Thus, six series, selected to represent distinct types of violence and coercion, and four others, chosen to depict types of executive change, are presented here in annual aggregations and in totals for the entire 20-year period. These violence and government change events have also been computer-plotted by country. We know that this mode of presentation is inadequate for many scholars, but we suspect that they will find the complete data tapes far more manipulable than even a gargantuan handbook.

The behavior we have tried to measure in these series is often called "violence," "strife," or "disorder," but we have some hesitation about these terms as labels for events as diverse as protest demonstrations, riots, armed attacks, and acts of coercion by a government itself. As Henry Bienen notes, "violence" connotes the exercise of illegitimate or unnecessary force.[4]

4. Henry Bienen, *Violence and Social Change: A Review of Current Literature* (Chicago: University of Chicago Press, 1968), p. 4.

Clearly we are in no position to assert that the events of these types that we have recorded are in any way "deviant" from moral or empirical norms. Protest demonstrations, for example, are frequently legal within a given political system and generally nonviolent in terms of bloodshed or damage to property.

In a broad sense, these event variables are indicators of different kinds of participation within the political system. Furthermore, they represent participatory behavior of an anomic rather than a formally structured type. Handbook users interested in comparing these two types of participation may find it possible to do so by comparing the violence event indicators with the indicators of structural participation in the preceding chapter. Analysts interested in assessing political system capabilities and responses to stress may find these comparisons helpful.

These event series are more specifically concerned with protest of various kinds. Our intent has been to provide a typology of protest behavior on a figurative spectrum of intensity, ranging from the relatively normal and legitimate demonstration, which is essentially nonviolent, to the comparatively subversive or revolutionary violence of the armed attack, which in one of its most typical forms involves the bombing of government facilities. Our data should make it possible to formulate and test hypotheses relating to the sequential relationships between different kinds of protest. Students interested in the anatomy of crisis behavior may find these "graded" indicators of protest helpful.

From still another perspective these indicators are possible measurements of relations between the rulers and the ruled. The demonstration, riot, and armed attack events coded for this handbook are acts of protest mainly targeted against a regime or its policies. We have also attempted to code governmental sanctions (short of a government's armed counterattacks in full-fledged civil war) against opposition through acts of coercion or threatened coercion, sometimes involving violence. Thus, within limits, it should be possible for analysts to explore the relationships in time, type, and quantity between acts of protest against a regime and acts by a regime against an opposition.

Having suggested some ways in which we think these protest series might be useful in comparative analysis, we wish to reiterate a caveat that applies to virtually every other indicator in this handbook: The "meaning" or relevance of these indicators, in our view, cannot be unilaterally dictated by the coders but is rather a question that needs to be studied by analysts with particular hypotheses and research designs. For example, it would be premature if not erroneous for us to propose that these indicators measure system stability. Some may find it satisfactory simply to assert an arbitrary definition equating stability and number of riots, perhaps discounting for a country's population size and density. Others may find it plausible to use riots as an indicator for some hypothetical predictor of instability (operationally defined, perhaps, as revolution). Still others might argue that political systems on the verge of major transformation may not manifest any such "symptom" of malfunctioning: A regime's coercive forces may be so effective that open disorder and even measurable acts of coercion by those forces simply may not occur, and yet the system's equilibrium may be like that of an egg balanced on its top, vulnerable to the merest accident of fate.[5] Issues of this kind are as important as the problem of data reliability, which is discussed below.

The six civil strife indicators that follow are reports of peaceful protest by the ruled (protest demonstrations), anomic action by the ruled (riots), organized violent action by the ruled (armed attacks and political deaths), coercive action by the rulers (governmental sanctions), and violent action originating outside the country against the rulers (interventions). We found three problems in coding protest event data of which users should be aware. One was that riots and demonstrations sometimes occur over issues (quarrels between individuals or public confrontations that get out of hand, for example) that have no relevance to politics. While events like these were occasionally reported and excluded from coding, the coders were urged to take a very broad view of the political arena. Thus, for example, a major feud between local families in Lebanon was coded, inasmuch as these families are an integral part of the Lebanese political system. Similar disputes, to which a government itself might not be a direct party, were also included. Furthermore, it is our impression that the judgments of "newsworthiness" that greatly determined the content of our event sources selected out clear nonpolitical protest.

The second problem in coding the data concerned the comprehensiveness of our event sources in reporting violence. Indeed, we were less alarmed about including nonpolitical protest events than with missing relevant internal conflict events—particularly in the rural parts of underdeveloped countries. Communal rioting in India or racial-tribal-religious violence in southern Sudan are examples of the kind of conflict that our sources are likely to have underreported. We shared with many of our colleagues uncertainties about the possibility of compiling data that would be sufficiently accurate to permit both cross-national and longitudinal within-country comparisons. Previous analysts of violence data had shown that the *New York Times Index* was the most comprehensive single data source, but we shared the considerable uncertainty of these analysts (not to mention their critics) as to the ability of the *Times* to cover world instability evenly, consistently, and objectively.[6]

---

5. Chalmers Johnson, *Revolutionary Change* (Boston: Little, Brown, 1966), chap. 5, esp. pp. 89-92.

6. Ted Gurr, with Charles Ruttenberg, *The Conditions of Civil Violence: First Tests of a Causal Model* (Princeton: Princeton University, Center of International Studies, 1967), pp. 36-37. See the discussion of our and others' source comparisons in appendix 1. Although it did not change

The comparisons of primary and secondary sources reported in appendix 1 suggest that the merging of secondary sources did contribute to a more even coverage, both by country and by variable. In particular, it may have alleviated the strain on news reporting capacities during a period of simultaneous world violence crises. However, we still cannot be sure about evenness of coverage over time. It remains a matter for investigation whether the intensiveness of reporting does not in fact vary with the degree of crisis perceived by the media. Such a phenomenon would produce underreporting in relatively quiet periods and, possibly, exaggerated reporting in crisis periods. Relatively nonviolent protest such as demonstrations may be underreported by the *Times* in a country not perceived as being strategically important to the United States, as long as the protest is not considered an immediate and serious problem to the government.

The third problem concerning the coding of the data involved ambiguous or incomplete reporting by our sources, especially during periods of sustained violence. In such periods the boundaries of events, in time and space, could not be ascertained precisely, yet there was usually enough general information available to permit rough estimates as to the quantity or intensity of protest events. The magnitude of an event in terms of numbers of participants was estimated whenever possible (see appendix 1). The number of events taking place on a given date and in a given report was also estimated from clues in the report. Judging from the context of events, we feel that these estimates probably underreport rather than exaggerate the quantity of protest events. If "several demonstrations" were reported, for example, five events were assigned to the date. In light of contextual considerations such as the size of the locality of disorder, a report such as "widespread rioting" would be assigned a value of ten. If rioting were reported to have continued for three days and no other information were available, the coder would make the minimal assumption that there was one riot a day and enter three events on the date of this report. If "demonstrations were reported in three cities," again the minimal assumption would be made that there was only one demonstration in each city, and a value of three would be reported for that date. Coders were instructed to be careful to detect separate reports of the same event, which occasionally were filed during violent crisis periods when "wrap up" stories appeared, and to avoid reporting the same event more than once. A procedure for merging reports from the two different sources, with minimum duplication, by

---

its policy of trying to serve as the newspaper of record, the *Times* as an organization underwent changes toward the end of the period for which we coded data, according to accounts by a former writer and the retired managing editor. These controversies and bureaucratic struggles may have made the *Times* a better paper at the end of the 1960s than it was at the beginning. However, they did not necessarily make it a better record of worldwide protest events (see Gay Talese, *The Kingdom and the Power* [New York: World, 1969], passim; and Turner Catledge, *My Life with the Times* [New York: Harper & Row, 1971], esp. chap. 18, pp. 209-15 and chap. 25).

computer, is described in appendix 1, along with further information on coding procedures.

A *protest demonstration* is a nonviolent gathering of people organized for the announced purpose of protesting against a regime, government, or one or more of its leaders; or against its ideology, policy, intended policy, or lack of policy; or against its previous action or intended action. The protest issues involved are perceived as significant at the national level, but within that framework demonstrations directed at all branches and levels of government are included. This category of events includes demonstrations for or against a foreign government, its leaders, or its visiting representatives when such a demonstration is reported to indicate opposition to the demonstrators' own government.

The category excludes election meetings, rallies, and boycotts, because such meetings are associated with a particular formal process that is unevenly distributed over the countries and time period covered and because the variable is intended to encompass peaceful protest outside the formal structures of government. There is inevitably a degree of ambiguity over the criteria of "nonviolence" in such demonstrations. Biased reporters may occasionally underplay or exaggerate the extent of turmoil associated with a particular gathering, just as they can misreport the size of a demonstration; but we detect no particular direction of bias. The incompleteness of our sources makes it impossible for us to assert that some damage and even occasional serious injury does not accompany some of these demonstrations. However, if destruction of property or bloodshed is observed as more than marginal to a demonstration, then the event is judged to have been transformed into a riot and is coded as such. It is not coded as a demonstration, even if it began as one. If there is some indication that a demonstration terminated peacefully, with the crowd dispersing, but that after a period of time a new crowd began rioting in the same place and presumably over the same issue, then two events—a demonstration and a riot—would be recorded. For example, had we been coding the gathering on the New Haven Green on 1 May 1970, protesting the trial of the Black Panthers, the activities during the day would have been coded as a demonstration, but the violence that erupted that night after the demonstration ended would have been coded as a riot. The actions of the police to end the turmoil would have been coded as a governmental sanction.

We expressed above our reservations about possible underreporting of protest demonstrations. In addition, we note that the category of demonstrations, even assuming it is well reported, may not represent adequately the total volume of nonviolent protest behavior. Acts of protest carried out by individuals or very small groups are not included, nor are "negative demonstrations," such as organized boycotts of governmental services. We have concentrated on extraordinary nonviolent protest, but we have not been able to measure the volume of "ordinary" protest reflected in activities such as the electoral process, communications to editors and politicians, or campaigns in the mass media. Elsewhere, however, we have provided data relating to governmental change, voting, and press freedom, from which inferences about "normal" protest and a system's capacity to tolerate it might be made.

A *riot* is a violent demonstration or disturbance involving a large number of people. "Violent" implies the use of physical force, which is usually evinced by the destruction of property, the wounding or killing of people by the authorities, the use of riot control equipment such as clubs, gas, guns, or water cannons, and by the rioters' use of various weapons.

Riots, in comparison with demonstrations and armed attacks, are characterized by spontaneity and by tumultuous group behavior. We are not asserting that riot events are unplanned, but rather that the riot organizers constitute a small, often invisible, portion of the rioters. Events were classified as riots if it appeared from the report that most of those involved were violently agitated in their behavior, that they formed an excited or confused crowd or mob, that they were engaged in unpredictable acts of disorder, and that the objects of their violence would not seem to be closely related to the objects of their political discontent in the analysis of a dispassionate observer. Our data sources rarely reported the number of people involved in a riot; even when they did we have no way of assessing the accuracy of the estimates. Therefore, it was impossible to assert that a riot involved, let us say, at least 100 people. In common parlance it is possible to speak of a riot involving as few as three people. We doubt very much that any of the reported riots involved that small a number, and we suspect that for a riot to be reported at all its participants could have been numbered in the hundreds and thousands rather than in tens.

Coders were instructed to distinguish between riots and armed attacks on grounds of apparent spontaneity of most of the participants. Violent raids against property and persons were occasionally reported; coders were instructed to exclude such events from the riots variable and to code them as armed attacks if they were directed by opposition to the government or as governmental sanctions if they were directed by the government against its opposition. Coders were instructed to count as riots events that began as demonstrations but became riots, and such events were not counted as demonstrations. Riots taking place within parliaments or other ruling bodies were also included.

An *armed attack* is an act of violent political conflict carried out by (or on behalf of) an organized group with the object of weakening or destroying the power exercised by another organized group. It is characterized by bloodshed, physical struggle, or the destruction of property. A wide variety of weapons may be utilized, including guns, explosives, bricks, spears, gasoline bombs, chemicals, and knives. The category is intended to encompass all organized political violence in a political system, and it is intended to exclude all nonviolent protest and incidents of turmoil (riots), as well as organized violence such as crime that is not observed to be directly relevant to cleavages, conflicts, and issues in the state's political process.

Excluded from the category of armed attacks, in addition to acts of nonpolitical violence, are acts of political violence organized and carried out by foreign groups within the country. (These acts are presented as a separate indicator, interventions, which we discuss later.) Exception is made, however, for colonies in which the forces of the metropole engage indigenous forces. Confrontations of the armed forces of two or more countries in a situation of international war are also excluded, as are the security measures undertaken by governments in conditions short of civil war (raids and arrests, for example). Assassinations, which were relatively few in number, are also excluded, but they have been coded separately and are available on the *World Handbook* data tape.

The target of an armed attack typically is a regime, government, or political leader, or its (his) ideology, policy, or actions; it may also be a religious, ethnic, racial, linguistic, or special interest minority. In general insurgency situations a government may itself resort to organized violence; in such cases the target may be an insurgent or rebel movement or pretender-government. Armed attacks are organized by political groups that wish to displace an established regime or gain for themselves substantial power or autonomy. Typically, such groups include liberation movements, revolutionary ideological parties, and unintegrated minority communities, and, in cases of major insurgency, the military and security forces of the state. When an insurgency situation reaches such proportions that the government can no longer control it by normal punitive measures (such as those coded below as governmental sanctions), the government's actions as well as those of the insurgents fall within the definition of armed attacks.

Examples of armed attacks include attacks on government buildings and personnel, public utilities, roads and transport facilities, dwelling places, factories, and markets. Occasionally whole villages are the target of armed attacks. Armed attacks are often reported as acts of sabotage, terrorism, or liberation.

Unlike the other indicators in this section, *deaths from political violence* is not an event variable but a body count. The deaths reported here occurred mainly in conjunction with armed attacks, but also in conjunction with riots and (to a much lesser extent) demonstrations. Our coders predicted and some preliminary correlations corroborated that deaths were more strongly related to armed attacks than to the other protest variables. Deaths were coded partly because they were a kind of absolute and unambiguous measure of political conflict, and partly because they provide a quasi-independent check or supplement to the other violence data.

The category includes persons of the country who die participating in foreign interventions in the country, but not foreigners. It excludes persons wounded in political violence. It does not include assassination victims; these are indicated in connection with the assassination variable on the data tape. Nor does it include victims of political execution (a category that is also scored separately on the data tape), deaths in enemy prisons, deaths in formal warfare, or deaths in border incidents with other countries. Victims of ordinary criminal homicide were, of course, also excluded.

In coding deaths, coders were instructed to be especially careful to detect duplicate reports. The publication of both daily reports and periodic summaries of deaths during periods of prolonged and widespread civil strife sometimes made this task difficult, particularly given the incomplete or ambiguous nature of the reports. Occasionally, sources would cite only a certain number of "casualties" or "victims," but only reports specifying "deaths" were included.

A *governmental sanction* is an action taken by the authorities to neutralize, suppress, or eliminate a perceived threat to the security of the government, the regime, or the state itself. Although the category encompasses a diversity of governmental activities, all of them share the characteristic of constituting specific responses to a perceived security problem at the national level, even though, in conformity with the particular constitution of the state, the sanctions are sometimes carried out by subnational governmental units. An attempt has been made to exclude sanctions against criminal behavior that has no observed relevance to the political security of the state; thus there are no reports of crackdowns against organized crime or drives by the police to reduce crime in the streets.

Governmental sanctions may be directed against either perceived internal or external threats or interference. The category includes three types of action. (1) Censorship. This type includes actions by the authorities to limit, curb, or intimidate the mass media, including newspapers, magazines, books, radio, and television. Typical examples of such action are the closing of a newspaper or journal, or the censoring of articles in the domestic press or dispatches sent out of the country. (2) Restrictions on political participation. This type includes general restrictive measures by the authorities, such as the act of declaring martial law, mobilizing troops for domestic security, or instituting a curfew. It also includes actions specifically directed against an individual, a party or other political organization. Such specific actions include the removal of a governmental official reportedly because of his political beliefs or activities, the banning of a political party or acts of harassment against it (denying it a permit to hold a public meeting, for example), the arrest of opposition politicians on grounds of state security, the exiling or deportation of persons for engaging in political actions or for expressing opposition regarded as detrimental to the national interest, and the arrest or detention of persons reportedly involved in political protest actions, including demonstrations, riots, political strikes, armed attacks, and assassination attempts. (3) Espionage. This type includes actions by the authorities in which one or more persons (nationals or foreigners) are arrested or detained on charges of spying, sabotage, or prohibited interference in the domestic politics of the state constituting a perceived threat to internal security.

One special problem with the governmental sanctions indicator is the boundary of such events in time. One usually thinks of the severity of a government's control over political participation as a condition or a state, rather than as a succession of events. A government that promulgates a censorship law, for example, is setting a constant limitation on political activity that may be unchallenged and therefore all the more effective. Thus the sanctions indicator may not be an appropriate measure of the intensity of a regime's restrictiveness. What it attempts to indicate is merely the frequency and concentration of sanction events. The expectation is that the relation between these twitches of governmental activity and the pattern of protest will prove interesting for comparative analysis. It is relatively easy to determine when a sanction event begins but not when it ends. Its beginning is marked by a discrete action, a departure from the normal behavior or inaction of the authorities. For example, a report that "the government began a massive wave of arrests of subversive elements, which is expected to last several weeks" would constitute a single sanction event, even though it denotes the beginning of a coherent process of behavior that may deviate considerably from the short time-frame, simplicity, and coherence of the typical riot or armed attack event.

A second problem is the heterogeneity of the indicator; the variety of governmental behavior it encompasses is wide indeed. We believe that all the actions described share conceptual unity, but we realize that some users still may find the indicator too inclusive for their purposes without weighting the various events included in terms of some criteria of significance. We were unable to devise a rational weighting procedure in light of the problems of information, context, and criteria; nevertheless, the frequency with which events of these types occur may alone be a useful indicator of system performance, regardless of the scope or severity of particular events. More serious than either of these problems, perhaps, is the old question of consistent reporting. In addition to the standard difficulties of information flow from remote places and the "attention span" of our sources, there is the likelihood of systematic underreporting from particularly repressive countries.

Indicators of External Interventions

It has been suggested by numerous observers that one of the important developments of the post-World War II international system is the extent to which the domestic affairs of nations have become of prime importance to other nations. This has led to an increased concern with various domestic political processes and developments and to an increased "penetration" of domestic political systems by countries and other actors outside those systems. One, but only one, means of intervention is the use of military troops engaging in armed attacks within the borders of another country. One of the event series collected in this dataset was foreign armed interventions.

To be considered a military intervention, the act must consist of the movement of troops or materials across national boundaries for the purpose of armed attacks. Not all such armed attacks, however, are counted as military interventions. For our purposes here, a military intervention must have two characteristics.[7] First, it must represent a break in an existing pattern of behavior between two or more nations. That is, the military intervention must be a departure from the pattern of relations previously existing between the nations involved. At some point, the military intervention may cease to represent a break in a pattern and become, in one sense, an accepted pattern of behavior. The military interaction between the protagonists becomes quite regularized and patterned and becomes the accepted mode of interaction between the countries. It can be argued, for instance, that the United States involvement in Vietnam ceased long ago to be an act of intervention and has evolved into a highly patterned and complex relationship between at least four prime actors. Similarly, although the shelling of Quemoy and Matsu by the Chinese Communists in the 1950s and 1960s at first represented quite a break in an accepted pattern of behavior and was very much a crisis situation, it eventually became a very regular, almost predictable, event. The United States intervention in the Dominican Republic is an example of a pattern-breaking event that did *not* evolve into some patterned relationship.

The second characteristic of an act of intervention is that it must be directed towards the authority structure of the target nation. This

7. This discussion, which is based on the work of James Rosenau, is developed as much greater length in John D. Sullivan, "International Consequences of Domestic Violence: Cross-National Assessment" (Paper delivered at the American Political Science Association Annual Meeting, New York, 1969).

The data described in this section were collected by one coder. In order to assess the reliability of the coding, a random sample of 100 events was selected for recoding by a second coder. It was not possible to find 6 of the events in the original sources because of the difficulties in those sources, and the sample was reduced to 94 events. The overall index of agreement for the two coders across all 20 variables was 94 percent. The areas of disagreement between two coders seemed to be limited to two variables. First, the coders disagreed on the direction of support of the intervener in the Congo. The original coder scored the United Nations intervention as supporting the government while the second coded it as nonsupportive. The data are presently coded as the original coder scored them.

The other area of disagreement had to do with the alignment of the intervener. The coders disagreed in some cases as to whether an intervener leaned to the West, to the East, or was nonaligned. Again, the data are as the original coder scored them. Given that these two variables require rather complex judgments, such disagreement is not too surprising; but these two variables should be used with caution. The disagreement between the two coders on the remaining variables was quite low.

stipulation excludes any action intended as a device designed to effect a change in some aspects of the target country's policy. For instance, disputes between countries with ill-defined borders over the exact extent of those borders are considered attempts to alter the policy of one of the nations involved and are not considered acts of intervention. Efforts to influence or control who will be the incumbents of a particular political system or what the form of that political system will be are considered to be acts of intervention. The Sino-Indian border dispute, for example, appears to have been primarily a dispute over the borders of the two countries and neither actor appeared interested in producing significant changes in the other's political system. On the other hand, the United States intervention in the Dominican Republic did constitute an attempt to influence patterns of power in that country. Thus, the former would not be considered an act of intervention, while the latter would.

According to this definition, then, approximately 1,000 intervention events during the period 1948-67 were identified for this series. In the process of collecting these data, it became apparent that each event had associated with it additional information that would be of interest both for analytical and for descriptive purposes. This information included such things as the amount and type of force employed when this information was available, the target of the act of intervention (that is, either a rebel group or the existing government), the alignment of the intervener (that is, with the Western bloc, the Eastern bloc, or the nonaligned bloc), and the extent to which it was possible to identify third-party statements either in support of the intervention or in opposition to it. While we will discuss some of this information below, it will not be possible to deal with all of it and the reader is referred to the code book available through the Inter-University Consortium for Political Research for a more complete description of these variables and the coding rules used in their collection.

There are two ways in which these data can be used. The first is to describe patterns and acts of intervention and the second is to perform analyses designed to identify the causes and consequences of acts of intervention. An investigator might wish to explore patterns of intervention and other types of political violence within a given country or small number of countries at one point in time or over some specified time period. The country charts at the end of this chapter can be used to explore patterns of violence within a specific country or across a group of countries. Within a country, the investigator can examine variations in patterns of intervention and visually inspect the extent to which there appears to be some similar variation in other forms of political violence or in forms of nonviolent political change. Thus, the investigator can use these tables to explore hunches about patterns of intervention and possible relationships between intervention and other types of event variables. In addition, the investigator can compare countries in terms of patterns of intervention and the frequency of occurrence of other types of violent and nonviolent events.[8]

The student of comparative and international politics is not always interested, however, in the events in just one or a very few countries. Frequently, he wishes to examine and explore patterns of events across a large number of countries, perhaps all national political units at some specified time point. It is possible with these data to perform various aggregations and to explore interventions across those aggregations. Scholars may wish to look at patterns of intervention and domestic political violence in different regions of the world and to compare regions with each other, or they may wish to identify types of nations, say underdeveloped versus developed or large versus small, and compare intervention within and between those groupings.

In this book we examine only a few patterns across all the countries. One question of interest is whether there appears to be any variation over time in the number of events that have occurred in the international system or whether the pattern appears roughly random. It is important to stress here that we are discussing a *systemic* characteristic and not a characteristic of any nation or group of nations. We will discuss below how such systemic description might play a role in research. As the data in figure 3.a indicate, there has been considerable variation in acts of intervention during the period 1948-67. The number of events that occurred in the early part of the period is quite small but it has increased considerably over time. It appears, however, that while there is a constant upward trend in most of the data, the frequency of these events may now be lessening somewhat. There are a number of possible explanations for the upward trend. An obvious one, of course, is that there are now more national political units in the world than in the late 1940s and 1950s. Thus there are more opportunities for nations to become involved in the affairs of other nations and to resort to armed intervention to achieve political goals. In addition, these national political units have become increasingly more interdependent politically, economically, and socially. Such linkages may lead, in certain circumstances, to acts of intervention. Thus, increasing interdependencies among nations can also result in increasing acts of intervention. A final candidate

8. Such country descriptions are not limited in utility to academics. They could be of great use to a foreign policy decision-maker as he responds to events in and between other countries. To give but one simple example, upon receipt of a message that a certain type of event has occurred in a country of interest to the United States, say an armed intervention, it would be of great use to a desk officer to know if this event differs greatly from an ongoing pattern. He can, of course, search his own memory and whatever organizational memory might be available about recent events in that country. Having access to a retrieval system that can print very quickly the type of profile given in this book would permit him to locate the new event in the context of the range and variation of both interventions and other political events in that country. In addition, he might be interested in comparing patterns in the country under question with other countries, say in the same region. Again, having access to these types of data and an appropriate retrieval system would permit him to make such comparisons. While such information would be only one component in his decision as to how to respond, it would provide him with fairly precise information and information that extended back in time.

explanation might lie in the increased diffusion of military and technological capability. Perhaps in the early part of this period many nations did not have the capability to carry out acts of armed intervention even if motivated to do so. As more nations achieved higher levels of development and as the major powers spread military and technological capability through foreign aid programs, more nations were able to resort to armed intervention as a technique of foreign policy. Whatever the explanation, it is clear that the frequency of intervention increased over this 20-year period. Although we will not elaborate the point here, the reader can see that these hypotheses could be explored with the data contained in the *World Handbook.*

In looking at acts of intervention, it is of interest to determine the types of actors involved and whether or not any patterns are apparent. Five types engage in acts of armed attacks within the borders of other countries: (1) a country crossing a border; (2) a rebel group residing in another country; (3)

Figure 3.a. Intervention Events (1948-1967)

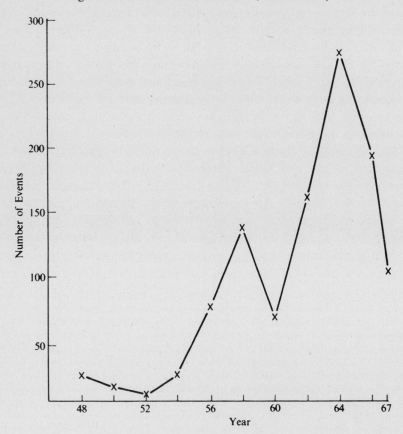

an international organization; (4) a nation whose troops were temporarily present in the target country although not previously engaged in armed attacks; and (5) mercenaries hired by the "attacking" country. (To the extent that rebels residing in another country received support and comfort from that country, as frequently was the case, their acts were counted as a type of intervention.)

Figure 3.b. Intervention Data: Type of Intervener

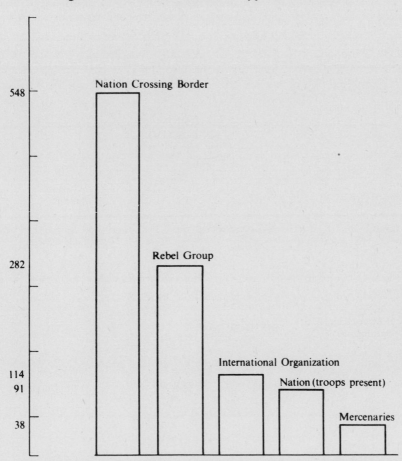

As the data in figure 3.b indicate, there has been considerable variation in the type of unit engaging in acts of intervention. By far the most frequent type of intervener is a nation crossing a border. The next most frequent is a rebel group, while the remaining three types of interveners comprise a relatively small percent of the total. Thus, it appears that national groups most frequently resort to intervention and that other actors intervene much less often. Again, one can explain this in terms of the capabilities of the

actors involved. National groups are most likely to have the capabilities
necessary for these types of acts; rebel groups are much less likely to have
them. International organizations rarely have such capabilities unless they

Figure 3.c. Intervener Supporting Government or Rebels

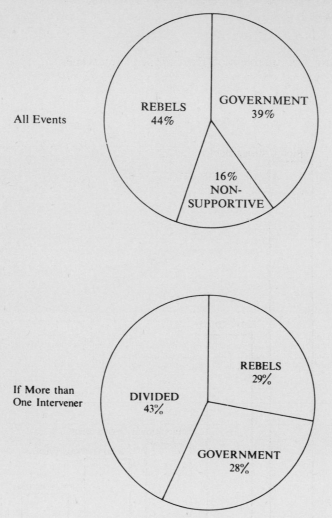

Note: Because percentages in the pie labeled *All Events* have been rounded to
the nearest whole number, they do not add up to 100 percent.

are granted by a significant number of their members and the small
frequency of international organizational interveners is thus not surprising.
    Given that an actor decides to engage in armed attack events to achieve
some policy objective, the next question relates to the exact target of his
activity in the country where it occurs. As figure 3.c indicates, when there is
only one intervener, the target of the activity is divided roughly in half

between rebels and the existing government with a small percentage of activity coded as nonsupportive. When there is more than one intervener, however, 48 percent of the time the interveners were divided in their support. When they acted in concert roughly half of the activity was directed at the rebels and half in support of the government. Thus, for the time period as a whole and for all national political actors, actors engaging in acts of intervention did not clearly act in support of either rebel groups or incumbent governments.

Figure 3.d. Nature of Action (1,073 Events) and Number of Interveners Per Event

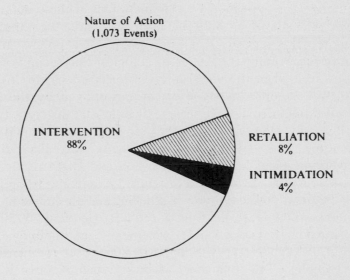

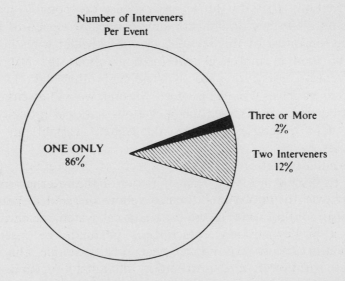

We indicated above the definition used to guide the collection of the intervention series. It was discovered that a small percentage of the 1,073 events did not conform exactly to that definition. Figure 3.d indicates the pattern of both interventions and other types of events and also provides a breakdown on the number of interveners in each event. Of the events collected 88 percent were clear acts of intervention as described above. Roughly 8 percent of the events collected consisted of events of retaliation for one or more acts of intervention. Clearly, to the extent that the pattern of retaliation persisted, the relationship was no longer one of an actor intervening in the affairs of another but one of warfare. Note that group acts of intervention appear to be extremely rare in these data. Fully 86 percent of the events involved only one intervener while the remainder involved two or more. This suggests that intervention, as a policy, may be difficult to achieve successfully for groups of actors or that second or third parties only get involved when the initial intervention has escalated to full-scale warfare.

A final factor is the type of force employed by the intervener. In the collection of these data, it became obvious that different types of force were employed by interveners and that separate codes should be developed for each type. The central assumption here was that different types of intervention might have different causes and might result in different kinds of consequences. As the data in figure 3.e indicate, troop intervention is the most frequent device employed. Shelling and air incursion are the next most frequent, while naval incursion is the least frequent. Within the category of air incursion, it was possible to separate out bombing, intimidation, and support and supply types of activities. The most frequently employed type was bombing. The separation of these types of force will permit a more complete investigation of the causes and the consequences of intervention.

We have just discussed some descriptive aspects of the data on armed intervention. They by no means exhaust the possible ways of looking at these data but they do indicate some important aspects of this phenomenon. In the remainder of this section, we will consider ways in which these data can be used in analytical investigations about the effects and causes of intervention. First, the use of these and other data in the handbook as *systemic* variables will be discussed. Second, we will discuss the way in which the frequency of intervention in various national groups can be employed both as a dependent and an independent variable in various types of analyses.

In our description of various aspects of intervention, we noted that we were exploring, in effect, characteristics of the international system. That is to say, each of the factors discussed above referred to patterns based on all national political units in the international system. Such data have a utility that goes beyond pure description. Students of international politics frequently discuss the impact that such systemic characteristics as the balance of power, the distribution of capability, and the diffusion of

Figure 3.e. Type of Force Employed by Intervener

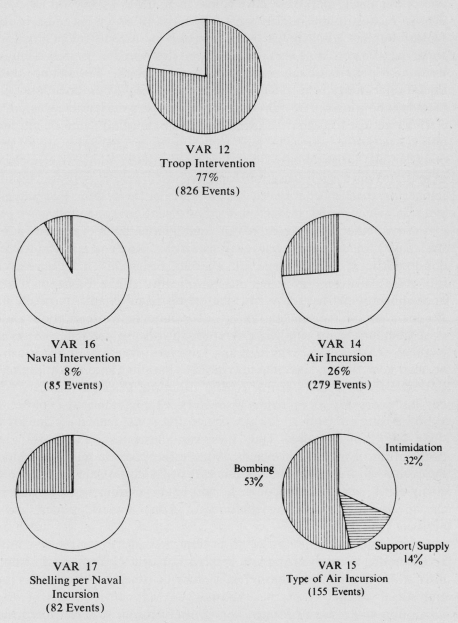

VAR 12
Troop Intervention
77%
(826 Events)

VAR 16
Naval Intervention
8%
(85 Events)

VAR 14
Air Incursion
26%
(279 Events)

VAR 17
Shelling per Naval
Incursion
(82 Events)

Bombing
53%

Intimidation
32%

Support/Supply
14%

VAR 15
Type of Air Incursion
(155 Events)

Note: Because in a number of events more than one type of force was employed by interveners, percentages in Var. 12, Var. 14, and Var. 16 add up to more than 100 percent, and the number of events adds up to more than the total of 1,073. Percentages in Var. 15 have been rounded to the nearest whole number and so do not add up to 100 percent.

technology have upon the behaviors of members of the international system. The focus here is not upon the characteristics of the members of the system and the impact that these have upon their behavior but rather upon the characteristics of the international system itself and how these contextual factors impinge upon the actions of members of the system. For instance, there has been a long-standing debate as to whether or not a bipolar or multipolar international system is more stable. Translating this into operational terms, the question here might be: Does one observe more international violence in a bipolar system than in a multipolar system?

If we return to figure 3.a, which describes the frequency of intervention events over the 20-year period, we note as indicated that there is considerable variation over these years. We might want to investigate the extent to which such variations on the systemic level appeared to have an impact on certain behaviors of the members of the system. For instance, for years in which there is a high rate of interventions, one might also wish to observe whether or not patterns of trade among pairs of nations also vary. One might want to push the analysis a step further and introduce level of development as a control and ask whether, in periods of high intervention, the trade between developed nations is not affected but that between undeveloped nations is. Again, the comparison is *not* between nations experiencing intervention and those not experiencing intervention. Rather, it is a comparison of the *behaviors* of nations in *different international systems,* that is, those with high and low rates of intervention. It can easily be seen how the student of international relations can employ the series on intervention as well as many of the other variables in this handbook to develop measures of systemic characteristics and then to explore various hypotheses about both national characteristics and national behavior within these different systems. Thus, systemic measures on the amount and distribution of national power, both military and economic, the amount of intervention in the system, the amount of domestic change, both peaceful and violent, can be developed and can play an extremely important role in the investigation of various theories of national development and international behavior.

In the analysis of the intervention series, two general problems are to be considered: (1) intervention as a response to other events, such as domestic disruption, and (2) intervention as a cause of other events, such as political and social change. It can be hypothesized that not all types of domestic disruption will result in foreign armed intervention. A further hypothesis is that certain characteristics of the nation experiencing the disruption may play a mitigating role in the tendency of intervention to occur. In exploring such hypotheses, a tendency was found for the more organized forms of domestic violence (e.g. armed attack events and unsuccessful irregular power transfers) to be significantly related to the occurrence of intervention in a country.[9] Furthermore, when certain characteristics of the nation experiencing the disruption were introduced as controls, small nations that had highly concentrated exports *and* that experienced high rates of organized domestic disruption tended also to experience foreign intervention.[10] Thus, in this particular analysis, foreign armed intervention was taken as a dependent variable and hypothesized causes of such intervention were explored. It should be stressed that the models employed in this study were rather simple and that much more complex models must be used in the future. The extensive information provided for each act of intervention will permit such an examination.

The phenomenon of intervention can also be viewed as a cause of events and developments within the nation experiencing the intervention. For instance, intervention by a foreign country on behalf of a rebel group may intensify the efforts of the incumbent government to put down the insurrection. Similarly, armed intervention may have an impact on the behavior of other parties in the international system. They may be impelled to come to the aid of either the intervener or the incumbent government either by means of verbal or military support. Alternatively, to the extent that they are dependent on the target country for trade or military support, they may be impelled to cease those relationships and to seek such aid elsewhere. Finally, both domestic violence and foreign armed intervention may have spillover effects in that they encourage or stimulate, for whatever reasons, other states to engage in similar activities. Thus, acts of foreign armed intervention can serve to stimulate developments and changes in domestic events and processes as well as to affect the relations between nations.

Indicators of Executive Change

Power is central to politics, and the process through which power is transferred, shared, or maintained is of basic concern to the comparative analysis of political systems. While the concept of power has been treated extensively, there has been relatively little systematic quantitative comparison of the power processes of nation-states. It is our hope that the executive change event data presented in this handbook and in the data tape will facilitate more work of this kind.

In trying to classify changes in the power structure cross-nationally, we have discovered that the variety and sequence of such changes is complex. Our event definitions are the result of a great deal of trial and error, and they reflect numerous compromises that were made in order to satisfy the

9. Sullivan, "International Consequences." It should be noted that the present intervention series represents a refinement and extension of the data employed in the 1969 study and that analyses are presently being conducted to explore these and other hypotheses.

10. The theoretical explication for these findings is in Sullivan, "International Consequences."

minimum requirements of clarity, theoretical relevance, and worldwide applicability. Area specialists looking at their country profiles will frequently find that the conventional interpretation of executive changes is challenged in many cases by our abstractions. To the charge that we have wrenched events out of a broader context and sacrificed nuance and interpretation, we can only plead guilty, for that was precisely our intention. By breaking down the power process into a series of events whose duration is typically a matter of minutes or hours, *what had been thought of, for example, as single crises may become a constellation of irregular, regular, major, and minor power change events.* These constellations indicate, we feel, more adequately than conventional means the variety and extent of system behavior at critical points in time. One major limitation in our typology of change events is that it deals only with formal executive power structures, such as cabinets, presidential offices, military juntas, and ruling party councils, and ignores "real" or informal powerholders. Another objection is that our typology fails to inform as to the intensity or significance of certain change events. An event in country X that fits perfectly our definition of minor executive adjustment, for example, may have a long-term importance and may signify a greater shift in power than a coup d'état in country Y. Like the journalist's sources upon which we draw, we can perceive and record only the immediate and manifest attributes of the event. It is for analysts of the pattern of events and their correlates to make more profound interpretations.

Our theoretical concern with measuring the frequency and extent of change and our preliminary coding efforts led to the construction of an array of governmental change events that would accommodate every particular instance of change that we came across. We developed three dimensions of executive change: regular-irregular, major-minor, and successful-unsuccessful. We also discovered events in the power process that did not involve, strictly speaking, a transfer of power at all: The power of incumbent authorities was frequently renewed. From our perspective it appeared that if one wished to analyze the power process comprehensively, one would have to examine regular (normal) transfers of executive power, irregular transfers, minor power adjustments within the executive body (such as cabinet reshuffles), and renewals of executive power. These data are presented in this book. Some analysts may wish to utilize the other types of change that we discovered, such as unsuccessful irregular changes ("abortive coups"), unsuccessful regular changes (e.g. in parliamentary systems, votes of no confidence that fail), and national elections; these are available on the handbook data tape.

A *regular executive transfer* is a change in the office of national executive from one leader or ruling group to another that is accomplished through conventional legal or customary procedures and that is not accompanied by actual or directly threatened physical violence. The office of national executive refers both to individual leaders such as presidents and prime ministers and also to collegial executive bodies such as cabinets composed of one or more parties or groupings. In the latter case a change is scored if a constituent element of the coalition is excluded from power, or if a new element is included, or if a new element replaces an old one. The term "regular" in this and subsequent executive change series definitions means that the change is not reported to be accompanied by actual or directly threatened violence or physical coercion and that it conforms to the prevailing conventional procedures of the political system; in contrast, "irregular" change events are characterized by actual or threatened violence and by abnormal procedures.

Chief executives include monarchs, presidents, prime ministers, and party chiefs in states where single parties exercise decisive power, paralleling or supervising the affairs of government. Also included are all other analogous offices and titles that may not enjoy general usage (e.g. the "head of state" in Baathist Syria or "the sole leader of the country" in Iraq under Abdel-Karim Qasim). For a transfer to be scored, it was necessary that the chief executive office change hands, but the new recipient of power could have held the office previously. Cases in which an executive's tenure was extended through elections or other means were coded as renewal events.

In some political systems there are two chief executive offices or officers. We decided not to make qualitative judgments about the relative significance of, say, prime ministers over presidents or kings, and we coded changes in both offices. We were unwilling to write off "ceremonial" or "symbolic" offices as unimportant. A number of countries were under some form of colonial administration during the period under investigation and in these countries changes in the colonial executive, such as the governor-general, were coded as power transfers. Most of these countries became independent during the coding period, and it was decided that the formal change to sovereign status must be recorded as a power transfer even if there happened not to be a simultaneous change of executive officers. Similarly, changes in a country's constitution that clearly increased or decreased a chief executive's powers were also counted. This variable is not presented as an indicator of basic structural or regime changes. Whether the transfers recorded here have long-run significance in terms of policy we cannot say. What we have tried to present is simply a record of the major changes that occurred in the highest national executive offices in the expectation that it will constitute a somewhat more sensitive barometer of system performance than is now available.

Certain additional coding rules should be mentioned. Some constitutions, notably those in Latin American countries, require the temporary resignation of a president when he is travelling abroad. Such resignations were not counted unless the president failed to resume office when he returned. Cabinet reshuffles occurring simultaneously with a change of prime minister were not counted as adjustments; only the regular power transfer was recorded. A change of premier and a simultaneous change in the composition of coalition cabinet as the result of the same election were counted as a single change. Another coding question concerned the duration of a change event; sometimes the consummation of a power transfer, without any discernible intermediate change, exceeded the 24-hour time boundary typical of most of our political events. Coders therefore were instructed to score the date of each power transfer event as the date on which it was reported completed. For example, if a cabinet were restructured to include a new party, the event would be scored on the day that the new cabinet assumed power, not when the old one resigned. In the case of a newly elected president or prime minister, the executive transfer was scored as occurring when he took office and not on the day the election results were announced.

A *renewal of executive tenure* is an act that reestablishes or reconfirms the term of office of the national executive incumbent leader or ruling group through the country's regular institutionalized channels for this procedure. Formal power is neither lost nor transferred, but renewed in those who currently hold it.

Examples of executive renewals include the reelection of a president, the reelection to parliament of the party or parties that support an incumbent president or premier, the reappointment of an incumbent premier who has resigned, a vote of confidence in a premier or his cabinet, and the defeat of a vote of censure.

No one will be surprised to note that executive renewals are concentrated in parliamentary systems, but we do not feel that the concept of renewal is relevant only to such systems. It is surely a significant fact that certain kinds of systems have built-in renewal procedures and that others do not.

We are reluctant to make any categorical assertions as to whether states displaying relatively large numbers of renewal events are more stable than those not displaying them. Renewals, after all, are only one type of government change event, and there is something to be said for looking at other types as well before making assertions about a country's stability. A system characterized by frequent renewals, especially if major change events are also present, might be evaluated as precarious while one with frequent renewals and little other change might appear solid. It would be premature to propose that a negative relationship between aggregate renewals and aggregate violence—should one be discovered—shows the importance of such institutionalized change procedures in preventing or minimizing civil strife. However, it might not be amiss to suggest that renewals seem to signify the capacity of a system to challenge leadership tenure, at least formally. Thus they may offer some basis for comparing the responsibility and responsiveness of executives to other elements in the system.

The counterpart of a power renewal is an event in which an incumbent leadership is *not* reconfirmed; such events are the regular executive transfers discussed above. Our coders discovered, however, that during a period of executive transfers and adjustments there occasionally occur events that are "intermediate" between renewals and regular changes. We have given such events the rather awkward label of unsuccessful regular changes. These consist of abortive attempts to choose a successor to an executive who has already lost or given up actual power, even though he may still hold office in a caretaker capacity. An example is the appointment of a premier who fails to form a coalition government. We did not feel that this series was sufficiently interesting theoretically to warrant inclusion in the handbook (it is available on the data tape), but we call the attention of handbook users to it, since it does seem to constitute a recurrent "stage" in the power transfer process of certain countries, notably the less stable parliamentary systems.

An *executive adjustment* event is a modification in the membership of a national executive body that does not signify a transfer of formal power from one leader or ruling group to another. National executive bodies include cabinets, councils of ministers, presidential offices, military juntas, and ruling party councils in states in which authoritative power is wielded by a single party. Modification in the membership of such a body, short of a major executive transfer, typically include "reshuffles" or "shakeups" in which one or a small number of men are removed from or added to the membership. Frequently an adjustment involves the substitution of a new man for an old one. Executive adjustments always involve the movement of men into or out of the executive; they do not include acts such as the redistribution of ministerial portfolios within an executive body.

It is possible that executive adjustments might serve as an adequate indicator of the institutional adaptability of executive structures. Analysis might also show that in some systems a rapid series of adjustments precedes a violent crisis. Political scientists interested in the response of systems to violent crises may wish to utilize adjustment events as a relatively minor response that can be compared with renewals, major regular transfers, and irregular transfers of power.

Executive adjustments are considered "minor" in the power process because only one or a few positions change hands; the control exercised by the leader or ruling group is not reported to have been transferred or lost either wholly or partially to another group, faction, or coalition. In most cases, according to our coders, the ruling group makes such adjustments to consolidate or strengthen its security or popularity. They are also considered "regular" in that they are not reported to be accompanied by actual or threatened coercion or by unconventional procedures. We recognize, however, that we have no very adequate means for judging the significance of any particular adjustment event; nor can we easily ascertain what "conventional procedures" in the politics of some executive bodies really mean; so we use the terms *minor* and *regular* advisedly.

According to our coding rules, power adjustments could be scored at any

time during the tenure of a government. They could also be scored
simultaneously with renewals; frequently, when a premier is reconfirmed in
office he makes modifications in his cabinet, and such modifications were
counted as adjustments as long as they did not involve changes in the
governing coalition of such importance that they constituted major
executive changes. Adjustments occurring simultaneously with major regular
executive transfers or irregular power transfers (described below) were not
scored, however, because they were considered an integral part of the
executive transfer; a reported major transfer in effect obliterated the context
in which a mere adjustment could occur. The removal of a member from an
executive body and his simultaneous arrest was not coded as an adjustment
but rather as a governmental sanction.

Significant shakeups, of course, can occur in many executive structures
besides the highest ruling body; in some countries, for example, large-scale
purges of the military and civilian bureaucracy would seem to represent a
kind of power adjustment. But considerations of comparability of categories
and of available information led us to confine our arena to the pinnacle of
the national decision-making structure. Thus, changes in a country's general
staff have not been coded unless the general staff actually rules the country;
nor have we coded changes in deputy premiers. Adjustments in party central
committee membership in Communist countries has been excluded, but
changes in praesidium members and heads of ministries have been included.

An *irregular power transfer* event is a change in the office of national
executive from one leader or ruling group to another that is accomplished
outside the conventional legal or customary procedures for transferring
power in effect at the time of the event. Such events are accompanied either
by actual physical violence or by the clear threat of violence. These events
thus encompass bloodless depositions of rulers as well as the more
spectacular sanguinary variety. In conformity with our general practice, we
make no qualitative assessment of the subsequent significance of an irregular
power transfer as a criterion for coding. Such an event may precipitate a
fundamental change in the political system or the system may continue
substantially unchanged except for the irregularity of the power transfer
itself. Users of this series would be ill-advised to think of it as an indicator of
political or social revolution.

Irregular power transfers are close conceptually to what are conven-
tionally thought of as coups d'état. Our irregular transfers are probably more
numerous than conventional coups, however, because our coding rules
required that the many steps and maneuvers associated with a crisis be
recorded as distinct events. *There are a number of occasions in which events
that historians might consider a single coup are represented here by two or
more irregular change events.* The only criterion for a "successful" irregular
power transfer was that a report existed stating that the new leadership had
actually replaced the old, arrogating to itself the titles and functions of chief

executive; no minimum tenure limit could be imposed, we felt, without being unwisely arbitrary. Thus the indicator is relatively more sensitive to maneuverings and "countercoups" than an inspection of the definition alone might lead one to suppose. It follows that analysts interested only in coups in the conventional sense may want to edit out some of the events in this series. To repeat, however, our guideline with respect to measuring the "instability" of irregular power transfers, as with the other governmental change variables, is that the quantitative pattern and frequency of the events themselves may yield useful results. We do not seek to force upon the reader our imperfect judgment of the significance of particular events in their particular contexts. If an irregular transfer sometimes begot further irregular transfers during political crises, even more frequently an irregular transfer was closely followed by several other kinds of governmental change as a new regime sought to consolidate and legitimize its position. Coup leaders sometimes installed somebody either inside or outside their immediate group as president or premier. As a rule, such events were coded as regular executive transfers because in the new power context such delegations or transfers of authority conformed to new procedural norms and were not accompanied by threatened or actual coercion.

Irregular power transfers are initiated by groups, cliques, cabals, parties, and factions either inside or outside a government and its agencies. Sometimes they are carried out by rebellious elements within population minority groups; sometimes by foreign conspirators.

These "successful" irregular transfers are differentiated in our coding from another indicator—unsuccessful irregular power transfers. The latter variable (not included in this handbook but available on the data tape) is defined as a reported actual attempt to overthrow an incumbent executive that does not succeed. Reports of plotting alone were insufficient to designate such an "abortive coup": the plot must actually have been put into execution.

Table 3.1
Protest Demonstrations

A protest demonstration is a nonviolent gathering of people organized to protest the policies, ideology, or actions of a regime, a government, or political leaders.

	1948	1949	1950	1951	1952	1953	1954	1955
Total	125	87	138	119	180	163	116	159
Median								
United States	1	1	3	1		1	8	1
France	11	3	3	1	8	5	2	22
India	3	3		2	8	10	1	13
South Viet Nam			1				1	2
West Germany	12	1	24	17	22	9	13	6
Japan	11	2	5	4	17	7	5	10
South Africa	1	1	2	5	15	1	1	13
South Korea	1							1
Algeria			1		1			
United Kingdom		2	5	4	2		1	1
Italy	11	20	21	10	9	3		1
Pakistan	5				1	19	2	6
Argentina		1	2	3	2		2	22
Iran	2		1	18	8	31	3	
Spain	6	5					2	1
Jordan					4		10	13
Rhodesia								
Cyprus	3		2	1		5	2	18
Belgium	5	2	12		3	1		1
Cuba			1	1	4	10	2	3
Dominican Republic								
Poland								
Sudan	1		1	1			2	
Syria		5	2	2			5	1
Colombia		1				2		1
Turkey								
East Germany	11	1	4	4		8	5	
Indonesia					1	1	1	
Southern Yemen								
Czechoslovakia	13			5		6	2	

1956	1957	1958	1959	1960	1961	1962	1963	1964	1965	1966	1967	Total
245	178	144	185	472	508	324	450	356	605	443	375	54h 17
8	4	21	12	95	165	72	202	134	211	124	115	12h
32	3	8	19	35	39	1	12	9	3		7	223
9	17	4	14	6	5		2	1	39	27	37	201
			1				54	22	29	77	12	199
		1	1	1				1	57	9	19	193
1	4		3	71	9	11	3	2	2	4	2	173
2	8	10	16	26	16	11	6	7	1	2	1	145
		3	3	38	6		5	29	37	1	12	136
14	1	4	5	15	35	31		10	15	1	1	134
	1	7	21	14	15	13	6	3	13	8	16	132
1		4			2		1	5	4	3	14	109
1		2				26	4	24		16	2	108
2	8	4	3	7	3	10	2	8	10	10		99
				1	12	2	9					87
6	1	1		1		17			9	7	30	86
4	21						20			8		80
			2	8	13	16	4	10	16	10		79
6	9	11	2	1	1	2		5	1			69
	1	1	7	22	2	1	4		1	1	3	67
12	9	1	2	5	5	7						62
			1	2	24	1	13	1	13	6		61
27	11	1			1			1		13		54
1				5	5			15	23			54
1		5	1		7	1	17	1	5		1	54
	17			5		5	1	7	1	8	5	53
1		1	7	23	1	2	6			2	6	49
9	1	1			1			1				46
	1	3				1		1	3	18	15	45
7				1	7	7	3		7	7	5	44
7	6	1				2	1					43

89

Table 3.1 Protest Demonstrations—*Continued*

	1948	1949	1950	1951	1952	1953	1954	1955
Greece			5			1		
Lebanon	1	3	3	3	5	1	1	1
Panama		6		3	1	1		
Venezuela			1		5			
Israel		1		1	3	3		
Guatemala			2	3	3	9	1	1
Guyana							8	
Morocco			5	2	8	1	1	12
Tunisia			5		22		2	2
United Arab Republic	3			8	10		7	
Mexico	1				2			
Bolivia				1	2	5		
Chile							2	5
Denmark		2	7	1		5		
Ecuador	1				1	5		
Brazil				1	2	2	1	
Canada					1			
Iraq	2			2	1			
Peru								
Soviet Union								
Hungary	1							
Philippines	1			1				
Austria			9	5	4		2	
Ceylon					1			
Malaysia								
Puerto Rico	6							
Haiti								
Australia	1	2	2	1		1		
Congo - Kinshasa								
Norway		5		1				
Rumania		2						
Congo - Brazzaville								
Libya				1	1	5		5
Nepal				1	1			5
Finland	7	9						
Kenya	1							
Nigeria						6		
Portugal								
Singapore				1			7	2
Zambia						1		
Hong Kong	1			1				
Malawi								
Maldive Islands								
Somalia		5					1	
Burma		1				1		

1956	1957	1958	1959	1960	1961	1962	1963	1964	1965	1966	1967	Total
							4		23	2	7	42
2	8	10		1	1						2	42
8		2	2					10	5	2	1	41
	1	4		8	17	3			1			40
3	1	2			10	1	6		4	2	2	39
7			5		3	2				1		37
		1			1	6	20					36
		5					1			1		36
					1			1	1	1		35
									5			33
2	1	3	2	9	6	1	2		1		2	32
1			1	3	7		2	8	1			31
	6	3		1	2				7	5		31
		1		4	3	7				1		31
			2	2	6			2	6	4		29
		3	2	5	6	1			1	4		28
2		1		1		6	1	7	6	1	1	27
		1	6	2		5	2			5		26
5	5	2	1		1	11					1	26
15	1				5		1		1	1	1	25
19	3	1										24
					1			5	7	7	2	24
	1								1			22
		1			20							22
	2							5	1	7	7	22
		1	2	7	1			2	1	1	1	22
1	13		2		5							21
									2	11		20
			1	15		1	2	1				20
					2					11	1	20
15	1							1				19
			1				16			1		18
								5	1			18
	2				2	5					2	18
		1										17
		1	3	7	3	1	1					17
			1				1	2	1	5	1	17
		1			1	11		1	3			17
5					1						1	17
		1		8	7							17
											14	16
			8	7								15
			5			10						15
				2	6							14
					1				10			13

Table 3.1 Protest Demonstrations—*Continued*

	1948	1949	1950	1951	1952	1953	1954	1955
Ireland		1						
Uruguay			1					
New Zealand								
Paraguay								
Afghanistan		1						
Dahomey								
Netherlands			2			2		
Uganda							1	
Bulgaria								
China	2	1				1		
Gabon								
Ghana			1	1			1	
Kuwait								
Mali								
Malta								
Upper Volta								
Honduras							1	
Tanzania								
Nicaragua								
Senegal								
Thailand							1	
Yugoslavia								
Cambodia					2			
Iceland								
Lesotho								
Trinidad and Tobago								
Albania								
Chad								
El Salvador								
Ethiopia								
Liberia								
Papua / New Guinea								
Sweden								
Togo								
Yemen								

Notes: This event was not reported at any time during the twenty years for Angola, Barbados, Botswana, Burundi, Cameroon, Central African Republic, Costa Rica, Guinea, Ivory Coast, Jamaica, Laos, Luxembourg, Malagasy Republic, Mauritania, Mauritius, Mongolia, Mozambique, Niger, North Korea, North Viet Nam, Rwanda, Saudi Arabia, Sierra Leone, Switzerland, Taiwan, nor The Gambia.

An "h" indicates hundreds.

1956	1957	1958	1959	1960	1961	1962	1963	1964	1965	1966	1967	Total
									1	1	10	13
			1		6	2				1	2	13
										1	11	12
		5	6		1							12
			10									11
							5		6			11
									2	1	1	8
1	2		1	1	1	1						8
	6							1				7
			1							2		7
								7				7
				1	3							7
5			1									6
						5					1	6
									6			6
										5		5
2					1							4
					1	1				2		4
							1	2				3
					1		1			1		3
	1					1						3
			3									3
												2
					1		1					2
					1					1		2
	1			1								2
1												1
			1									1
						1						1
					1							1
								1				1
						1						1
											1	1
										1		1
					1							1

Table 3.2
Riots

A riot is a violent demonstration or disturbance involving a large number of people and characterized by material damage or bloodshed.

	1948	1949	1950	1951	1952	1953	1954	1955
Total	326	274	294	353	416	348	251	315
Median								
United States		7	9	13	2	2	1	
India	20	9	59	3	13	19	7	10
Italy	60	33	38	11	14	33	11	4
Morocco	10			7	65	20	26	78
South Africa	3	15	11	1	21	6	2	1
China	5	30	5	10	5		5	
Laos							45	
Algeria				1	3			20
Nigeria		17			1	12	1	
Iran	1	6	1	35	21	55	6	
Venezuela	5	1	1			5		
Philippines	5	4		79	33	7		28
Congo - Kinshasa								
Japan	12	14	16	4	27	1	2	2
South Korea	15	1	1		3			
Pakistan			2		8	16	9	
Mexico				7	16	1	12	1
France	16	1	19	6	6	5	1	24
Colombia	26	30	2	5	2	5	11	
Cyprus							1	32
Dominican Republic								
Malawi								
Rhodesia								
Uganda								
Bolivia		5	4	11	1			
Argentina			1	3	1	5	3	13
Panama	1	11		11	1	1		
West Germany		2	12	12	14	9	13	4
Iraq	11				11	5	1	
South Viet Nam		1	1				1	6

1956	1957	1958	1959	1960	1961	1962	1963	1964	1965	1966	1967	Total
519	294	389	536	659	522	447	435	471	390	569	621	84h 34
10	11	7	8	36	47	21	65	75	45	119	205	683
80	8	6	16	18	51	7		7	59	109	57	558
11	2	6	15	25	10	20	3	3	2	8	1	310
38	1	6	1			5			10	5		272
25	13	2	29	70	12	5	7			2	1	226
	12	1	3			1				21	97	195
				146								191
13	6	11	8	25	56	37	1		6			187
		5	5	8	2	2	1	31	38	52	2	177
	5			2	15	6	21					174
15	1	51	6	39	13	11	9	7	5	1		170
	2		1		2					2	2	165
			83	29	18	8	13	5	1	2	3	162
10	1	2	3	30	9	10	2			2	12	159
8	1	1		56	6		5	24	24	2	3	150
5	1	4			5	28	4	37	15	9	2	145
2	9	19	12	13	24	7		2	2	1	3	131
22	2	13	1	7		1					3	127
5	15	1	3					6		11	3	125
21	19	19	14					6	5	4		121
				1	44	25	5	6	11	29		121
			99	9				10	1			119
				36	11	27	9	14	5	11	1	114
1		1	2	11		28	53	2		6		104
6	6	1	8	9	22	3	1	17	6			100
6	7	7	3		6	8		1	13	22		99
7		17	10		2			24	5	8		98
1		1	1	2	4	12	1	1		1	8	98
25		22	12	5	5							97
							7	40	15	19	6	96

Table 3.2 Riots—*Continued*

	1948	1949	1950	1951	1952	1953	1954	1955
Brazil				6	7	7	13	
Kenya		1	1		2	7	1	
Malaysia	6							1
Indonesia	1		1	21	1		1	
Syria	20	1	3	1	9		1	4
United Kingdom		2	8	5	1			
Tunisia					55			1
Lebanon		5		12			10	
Zambia						1		
Ecuador					3	6		1
East Germany	2	1	1	7	1	37	6	
Poland	1					5	1	
United Arab Republic	18		2	29	10		6	
Jordan			1		4	1	1	15
Spain	1			11			7	
Chile		16			12			
Southern Yemen				1	5			
Ceylon	1					5		
Israel	5	1	1	11	2			1
Belgium		2	13	1	1			10
Hong Kong			1		2			
Sudan	11			1			5	1
Guyana						5		
Congo – Brazzaville								
Cuba			7	1	6	7	1	1
Burma				1				
Singapore		5	8		1		1	13
Czechoslovakia	5	7	6	2		16		
Greece							18	1
Haiti			5					
Soviet Union				6		1		
Ghana	13		10			5		
Peru	5							5
Turkey								10
Guatemala			2	5	3	4	5	
Austria		2	6	1	8		1	
Malta		5					1	1
Portugal				1				
Angola								
Hungary	1		1			1		
Somalia	5	7	6		1			
Libya	5	13		1	1			
Canada	1		2		2			
Nicaragua			1					
Cameroon								16

1956	1957	1958	1959	1960	1961	1962	1963	1964	1965	1966	1967	Total
2		13	11	1	2	6	1	4		22		95
	22	1	2	1	2	14	34	1	3	1		93
	17						1	36	2	6	20	89
	1		1	1		1	20	1	11	16	5	82
5	5				1	7	16	9				82
	1	15	4	8	4	21	3	2	2	2	4	82
11					1						11	79
5		30	7	1			1	1	1		3	76
			3	6	11	17	29	5		2		74
6		1	12	1	17	6			6	14		73
5			1	7					1			69
26	16	5	2	7	2	1	1			2		69
	1				1			1				68
14	15	5					1			9	1	67
5	1	5				1			5	8	21	65
	16	7		2	1	1			7		2	64
1		5				1	7		3	6	35	64
10	6	27			2	1			2	6		60
6	1	3	12		8		5		1	1	1	59
1				7	15	3	3		1	1		58
8										2	44	57
1					2		5	20	11			57
					5	6	27	11		1		55
		1	26			6	10	10				53
5	1	2	9	6	4	1						51
		3			5	5		2			34	50
13		5					2			1		49
2	1					6	2		1			48
	1			1		2		1	18	3	2	47
1	34			1	1		2					44
5		3	4		6	11	1	4	2		1	44
1	2	1	5		1					5		43
5		7	5		3	7		1	2		1	41
	7	1	3	7	4	1	1		1	3	3	41
	3			4	1	11				1		39
			15	1		1			1			36
	1	10	1	1	6	5		5				36
		19				13	1	1	1			36
			1	1	26	5						33
25	2	1										31
			5	1			6					31
			5					5				30
1		1	1	3			3	7	3	5		29
		5	12	1		1	6				1	27
	5		5									26

Table 3.2 Riots—*Continued*

	1948	1949	1950	1951	1952	1953	1954	1955
Dahomey								
Rumania	1							
Senegal								
Jamaica	1		5	1	5		1	
Paraguay	10							
Yugoslavia						17		
Uruguay	1				2			
Chad								
Ethiopia			11					
Nepal			1				6	
Gabon								
Guinea								
Tanzania								
Trinidad and Tobago								6
Afghanistan								2
Lesotho								
Finland	2	5						
Maldive Islands						1		
Papua / New Guinea						5		
Taiwan		5						
Bulgaria		1		5		1		
Sweden			5					
Costa Rica	6		1					1
Thailand		5		1				1
Botswana			1	1	5			
Ireland	5				1			
Denmark			1			5		
Puerto Rico		1						
Sierra Leone								
Togo								
Yemen	1							
Cambodia						4		
Honduras							1	
Mali								
Mauritius								
Mozambique							5	
Mauritania								
Netherlands	1							
North Korea	4							
Switzerland	1							
Australia		1						1
El Salvador	1							
Kuwait			1					
Mongolia		1						
Albania	1							

1956	1957	1958	1959	1960	1961	1962	1963	1964	1965	1966	1967	Total
			10	6				5	5			26
25												26
		1	11		1	1	12					26
	1	1				5					1	21
5		1	2				1					19
										2		19
			1		2			10	1			17
							5		11			16
						5						16
	5								1		1	14
						5		8				13
1		5	1		5					1		13
		1			11			1				13
7												13
			5						5			12
				5						6	1	12
						4						11
			5					5				11
					6							11
	5			1								11
	1						1	1				10
									5			10
												8
1												8
												7
									1			7
												6
									2		3	6
										6		6
		1					5					6
										5		6
								1				5
3	1											5
			5									5
										5		5
												5
										2	2	4
1										2		4
												4
			1		1			1				4
										1		3
				1								2
1												2
										1		2
												1

Table 3.2 Riots—*Continued*

	1948	1949	1950	1951	1952	1953	1954	1955
Liberia								
North Viet Nam							1	

Notes: This event was not reported at any time during the twenty years for Barbados, Burundi, Central African Republic, Iceland, Ivory Coast, Luxembourg, Malagasy Republic, New Zealand, Niger, Norway, Rwanda, Saudi Arabia, The Gambia, nor Upper Volta.

An "h" indicates hundreds.

1956	1957	1958	1959	1960	1961	1962	1963	1964	1965	1966	1967	Total
					1							1
												1

Table 3.3
Armed Attacks

An armed attack is an act of violent political conflict carried out by an organized group with the object of weakening or destroying the power exercised by another organized group.

	1948	1949	1950	1951	1952	1953	1954	1955
Total Median	17h	21h	19h	18h	18h	19h	23h	10t
Malaysia	389	673	690	570	670	663	97	17h
Indonesia	58	63	42	15	18	53	17	70h
South Viet Nam	14	37	151	116	299	167	23	113
Algeria			1				61	247
China	494	569	308	31	48	46	75	90
India	28	27	31		15	9	6	12
Cuba	14	9	4	6	5	25	15	18
Philippines	13	55	145	304	177	322	17	8
Burma	106	160	198	413	64	59	16	23
Morocco	1				6	11	832	141
Cyprus							1	202
Congo - Kinshasa						1		
United States	2	11	20	19	15	12	6	10
North Viet Nam							656	6
Laos						1	65	66
Greece	230	294	5	3		1		2
Colombia	27	49	11	80	33	19	16	23
France	17	2	25		3	2	2	5
Venezuela			3	6	9	4	1	
Taiwan			3	9	4	1	30	50
Lebanon		7	1	1	2	5		
Southern Yemen		1	2			2		3
Kenya			1		42	137	100	32
Nigeria								
Argentina	1	1	1	20	6	13	3	81
Angola								
South Africa	2	5	7	1	19	20	6	
Iraq	1			4				
Tunisia	1				118	17	68	17
United Arab Republic	12	11	6	92	62	81	15	

1956	1957	1958	1959	1960	1961	1962	1963	1964	1965	1966	1967	Total
26h	19h	31h	20h	17h	20h	22h	12h	22h	18h	18h	34h	49t
											1	47
610	612	607	601	351			3	5	4	6	1	83h
59	29	189	68	34	6	4		36	74	75	15	79h
4	4	13	7	43	127	234	191	686	598	917	556	43h
10h	492	534	445	167	642	622	17	51	2		1	43h
36	11	159	24	16		5	15	2	12	17	408	24h
36	22	31	18	64	27	4	8	18	159	78	11h	17h
47	225	412	62	204	146	35	30	20	9	7	1	13h
3	21	3	21	6	4	4	5	3	5	6	135	13h
17	11	9	4	9	11	8	7	37	12	1	4	12h
59	4	15	25	1		2	1	7			6	11h
266	64	172	8	5	10	10	21	154	23	21	26	983
			17	182	199	77	70	186	114	19	39	904
40	121	97	61	57	22	31	47	71	71	23	43	779
4												666
13		5	92	41	98	29	71	54	28	28	19	610
2	5				5		1	1	6		12	567
18	29	23	22	3	33	15	70	28	29	12	12	552
5	4	34	18	15	110	296	3	7	1		1	550
1	2	35	10	34	24	64	174	68	36	21	17	509
42	46	167	45	20	9	12	2	2	4			446
7	18	355	17	7	11	3		2		6	3	445
5	9	9	6		3	7	7	35	52	101	202	444
2		1	1	19	8	22	3	58	10	2	1	439
				8	7			115	7	46	210	393
24	47	6	41	27	15	48	5	31	8	10		388
				6	178	60	58	39	8	7	7	363
2	6	5	18	180	16	28	9	13		3	2	342
1		6	50	13	21	62	108	1	44	12	5	328
36	11	8	1		11				1			289
	4											283

Table 3.3 Armed Attacks—*Continued*

	1948	1949	1950	1951	1952	1953	1954	1955
Dominican Republic		1						
Italy	35	19	18	16	6	3		7
Bolivia	1	36	10	3	15	22		1
Guatemala		2	2		5	10	27	3
Yemen	4	5						
Hong Kong	1	2	10	1		1		1
Nepal			37	6	10	7	5	
Guyana							5	
Zambia								
Peru	14	1	2	1				
Haiti								
South Korea	73	16	16		2			1
Rhodesia								
Iran			7	1	50	17	6	
Syria		2	10	2	1	1	18	2
Brazil	3		13	8	1	4	5	1
Canada			3	1		13		
Cameroon								5
Sudan								9
Hungary				1				
East Germany	11		9	5	7	28	10	
West Germany	7		27	10	8	3	11	5
Israel	10	5		2	1	3	7	12
Mozambique								
Costa Rica	47	3		9	1		3	18
Mexico			1	3	10	3	9	1
Uganda					1	3	1	1
Ecuador	1		1	2	10	1	2	1
Spain	2	10	1	7				
Thailand	1	1		20	1			
Ethiopia	1	6	23	2		1		
Poland	1	1		2	2	15		
Pakistan	1				2	3	3	
Paraguay	9						2	8
Panama	7	1		3	1			
Malawi								
Honduras							2	1
Cambodia					2	12	23	2
United Kingdom			3	13	1			2
Nicaragua	2	1					2	
Soviet Union		2	2	1		1		
Ireland	1			2		1	1	1
Chile	1	2	7	1	2		1	4
Puerto Rico			16		2		2	
Japan		10	3	3	10		1	

1956	1957	1958	1959	1960	1961	1962	1963	1964	1965	1966	1967	Total
			15	6	16	17	20	3	126	33	20	257
1	5	4	7	5	57	17	23	7	2	6	11	249
12	1	13	6	19	5		3	29	25		25	226
2	1	1	13	14	1	30	14	6	15	39	31	216
			3	1		79	9	21	15	31	37	205
										183		199
	5			3	23	87		1				184
	1					6	43	84	16			155
		1	4	12	32	4	5	82	5	2	2	149
5	6	9	2		2	11	13	25	49	7		147
11	14	13	27	1	11		40	18		2	4	141
		2			11			3	9		5	138
				16	3	24	12	18	25	27	9	134
21	5	2			6		8		1	1		125
11	3		5	3	11	15	6	22	1	7	1	121
10	1	2	7	3	4	14	5	11	4	19	2	117
1		7	1			65	9	5	4	1	3	113
	2	60	14	19	12					7		112
	1				2			24	67	7		110
89	14		1							1		106
			10		3	14	3				1	101
		3	1		1	4	5	1	1		9	96
1	2		1		1		8		2	26	10	91
					5	1		33	32	20		91
		1		2								84
	5	3	5	1	9	8	10		3	2	9	82
		1	10	12	1	10	5	3	12	19		79
7		1	14	2	9	9	3	4	4	2	5	78
				6	1	18	10	12	1	6	2	76
	1				8	1		1	11	4	27	76
	1			11		1				1	27	74
27	6	6		5	1					3	2	71
	1	2	1			1	6	21	25		1	67
		11	30					6				66
		19	5	3	2	1		13	1			56
			13	8	3		1	17	10		3	55
6	1	1	31	1		2	5		3			53
										3	7	49
		3	4	1	2			1	2	8	5	45
		1	11	8	2						16	43
17			7		1	2	1				9	43
4	12	1	3	1	8				2	4	1	42
	2	1			2	5		1	3	1	8	41
				2	8	2					8	40
2		1		2	1						2	35

Table 3.3 Armed Attacks—*Continued*

	1948	1949	1950	1951	1952	1953	1954	1955
Belgium			19	2				
Ghana	1		1		1			
Jamaica	2	1	6	1	1	1		
Singapore	6		9	4	6		3	1
Ceylon						6		
Tanzania						5	5	
Austria	5	2	1	5	4	1	1	
Jordan							1	3
Libya	5				1			
Papua / New Guinea					1	1	5	
Somalia			5					
Congo - Brazzaville								
Portugal	1							
Rwanda								
Rumania		7				5		
Turkey								
Saudi Arabia						5		
Yugoslavia	1	1		1	2	2	1	
Netherlands								
Albania				2	2	2	1	
Australia				1				
Togo				5				
Afghanistan						1		
Dahomey								
Kuwait								
Niger								
Switzerland	1							1
Burundi								
Czechoslovakia		2			2			
Gabon								
Sierra Leone								1
Denmark				1		3		
El Salvador					1			
Maldive Islands								
Mauritius								
Upper Volta								
Uruguay								
Lesotho								
Bulgaria						1		
Finland	1		1					
Malta							1	
North Korea	1	1						
Norway					1			1
Trinidad and Tobago	1						1	
Botswana						1		

1956	1957	1958	1959	1960	1961	1962	1963	1964	1965	1966	1967	Total
				1	6		5			1		34
1		1			4	14			1	5	5	34
			2	3	1		2			10	1	31
1												30
	5	16										27
								15	1			26
					5		1					25
3	4	4		2						6		23
1			1	1				1	7		6	23
3	2	1	1			7		1				22
			1		1	10	5					22
			3				1		5	8		17
					3	3		1	2		5	15
							5	8		2		15
											1	13
		2	3			3				4	1	13
										1	6	12
										1	2	11
1										3	6	10
1												8
				6						1		8
		1					1			1		8
			1	5								7
			1				5	1				7
6	1											7
							1	6				7
	2	1						1			1	7
									6			6
										1	1	6
								6				6
				5								6
1												5
		1			1	1					1	5
			4					1				5
									5			5
										5		5
	1				1	1		1			1	5
	1					2					1	4
							1				1	3
				1								3
		1						1				3
										1		3
											1	3
							1					3
											1	2

Table 3.3 Armed Attacks—*Continued*

	1948	1949	1950	1951	1952	1953	1954	1955
Chad								
Mali								
New Zealand		1						
Iceland		1						
Luxembourg	1							
Mauritania								
Senegal								
Sweden					1			

Notes: This event was not reported at any time during the twenty years for Barbados, Central African Republic, Guinea, Ivory Coast, Liberia, Malagasy Republic, Mongolia, nor The Gambia. A "t" indicates thousands and an "h" indicates hundreds.

1956	1957	1958	1959	1960	1961	1962	1963	1964	1965	1966	1967	Total
	1										1	2
							1	1				2
										1		2
												1
												1
						1						1
						1						1
												1

Table 3.4
Deaths from Domestic Violence

This series records the number of persons reportedly killed in events of domestic political conflict. The data refer to numbers of bodies and not events in which deaths occur.

	1948	1949	1950	1951	1952	1953	1954	1955
Total Median	21t	12t	22t	99h	23t	13t	38t	28t
Indonesia	128	118	13h	22h	15h	493	419	45h
South Viet Nam	169	18	52h	24h	69h	25h	165	961
Algeria					2		49	27h
Hungary								
Angola								
North Viet Nam							27t	
Rwanda								
China	40h	236	86h	804	50h	1	39	
Cameroon								50h
Congo – Kinshasa								
Kenya	11		24		136	65h	49h	18h
Malaysia	175	501	19h	163	15h	12h	11h	997
Philippines	58	346	22h	33h	31h	535	94	67
Malagasy Republic	10t							
Nigeria		22				55	6	
Greece	37h	56h		13				
Colombia	15h	23h	54	129	833	39	51	714
Argentina		2	1	4	1	18	6	66h
Iraq	78	5		4	11	1	2	
Taiwan			19			14	23h	23h
India	84	29	554	6	28	109	23	280
Dominican Republic			8					
Burma	257	14h	472	199	301	536	140	217
Bolivia	1	163	3	13	30h	40		3
Cuba	10	1	2	2	5	74	1	9
Uganda								3
Yemen								
Tunisia			100		133	29	468	64
Laos							354	
Pakistan	4		1		47	24	424	

1956	1957	1958	1959	1960	1961	1962	1963	1964	1965	1966	1967	Total
42t	37t	25t	37t	14t	42t	16t	15t	50t	92t	611t	44t	1m 131
50h	41h	80	14t	48h	222	14			50t	525t	188	615t
20h	9	375	676	686	33h	66h	57h	54h	32t	69t	33t	177t
86h	97h	18t	12t	40h	779	32h	13	150	8		10	59t
20t	20t		2									40t
				30	31t	30h	25	31	105	243	71	34t
20										50	951	28t
					500			21t		50h		27t
4	1	399	42h			2	183			40	14h	25t
	26	51	73	328	187	20	1	10t				16t
			595	12h	23h	11h	36h	40h	953	3	240	14t
55	105		22	18	102	64	54	115	50	13	66	14t
962	932	920	919	921	459		29	55	2	29	33	13t
2	33	1	86	8	29	8	6	18	44	8	167	10t
												10t
		28		37	106			11h	153	42h	37h	94h
							1		1		3	93h
15h	154	212	171	38	242	185	92	740	66	40	32	91h
41	1			21	1	47	25	14	2	2		68h
8		85	23h	20	7		14h	300	10	20h		63h
42	4	96	2	27			470					53h
502	343	14h	23	58	152	76	18	39	112	394	931	51h
100			145	92	28	13	73	1	40h	36	7	45h
87	61		16	24	33	47	49	237	57	9	67	42h
4	4	7	105	271	25	9	14	322	119		61	42h
172	638	25h	16	92	203	45	311	35	11	6	1	42h
3	3		3	20	17	218	72		12	29h		33h
				4		26	607		201	274	22h	33h
253	44	79	1		20h				2			31h
			28	153	107	170	29	13h	412	36	430	30h
3		14			50	2	842	906	531	13	8	29h

Table 3.4 Deaths from Domestic Violence—*Continued*

	1948	1949	1950	1951	1952	1953	1954	1955
South Korea	609	13h	153		13			
Morocco	52			6	269	71	103	10h
Sudan	12						32	7
Syria	1	12	54		28		8	3
Venezuela			2	10	78	4	2	
Mozambique								
Zambia								
South Africa	25	181	58	16	59	23	12	1
Iran	70	9	12	45	130	322	1	
Peru		2	291	1				
Cyprus								13
Albania								
Southern Yemen			9			6	6	5
Poland		8		9				
United Arab Republic	61	9	26	223	108	15	13	
Ethiopia		1	32	45		200		
Nicaragua							13	
Mexico	2		14	9	47	1	46	44
Guatemala		40	26	4	6	16	144	12
Soviet Union								
Lebanon			2	25	4	1	1	
Somalia	53	4	234		3		1	
Rhodesia								
Ceylon						12		
Guyana								
United States	2	5	3	9	3			2
Hong Kong	30	2						1
Thailand		55		80	1	4		
Congo - Brazzaville								
Haiti		1						
Papua / New Guinea					2			
Paraguay	2						26	
Singapore	1		26	15	101		2	4
Honduras	2							1
Afghanistan								
Brazil	23	1	13	13	8	10	11	
East Germany	2	11	5	18	2	79	3	
Cambodia					8	2	100	21
Ecuador				2	4	1		
France	1		1		1	7		
Italy	13	17	14	19	2	6		5
Burundi								
Chad								
Malawi								
Panama	4			31				3

1956	1957	1958	1959	1960	1961	1962	1963	1964	1965	1966	1967	Total
1		3		502			9	1	15	9	1	26h
389	120	67	6	3		130	3	10	25		2	23h
	2				19		2	584	14h	100		22h
28	1				203	12	200	878	1	400		18h
25	5	705	5	27	35	620	62	36	26	10	21	17h
					13			410	11h	98		16h
			4	1	22	16	9	13h		1		13h
15	92	4	117	283	14	31	22	14		2	44	10h
127	34	1			8	1	190		3	11		964
1	2	5	5		8	9	8	345	195	10		882
170	26	153	2	4	2	4	168	187	5	3	67	804
778											4	782
3	4	5			16	3	7	131	37	68	255	555
536												553
	23											478
				12	2	5	100				78	475
2	35	1	235	12	8						151	457
3		11	13	19	112	20		24	20		61	446
5	6			3	2	18	27	9	15	22	53	408
100			2			287	9				1	399
	66	205	6	4	4	41		1	1	13	1	375
			27	1		33	9					365
			40	26	4	7		12	1	68	203	361
10	2	313			1					1		339
						9	10	308	2			329
7		12	11	7	3	10	13	14	105	15	99	320
115										1	94	243
						1			36	35	23	235
		3	220			2	9					234
1	60	18	7		4		62	9	61		4	227
58		2	45		2	102						211
			157	17			3		1			206
30												179
42	5		72	15	1	11	2		1			152
			143									143
3	1	5		2	5	17	8		1	22		143
						4	5	4	2	5		140
1												135
6			59	7	36		3		4	2	4	128
	1	15			3	81	1	1				112
3	3			11	3	9				4		109
									100	6		106
	31						19				56	106
			85					10	6	4	1	106
		10	4					44	1	2		99

113

Table 3.4 Deaths from Domestic Violence—*Continued*

	1948	1949	1950	1951	1952	1953	1954	1955
Ghana	25				3	10		1
Turkey								
Tanzania						5		
North Korea		5					70	
Nepal				2	1			
Costa Rica	12	6					1	56
Czechoslovakia	6		1	60	2			
Jordan				1			9	14
Chile		1	1		2			
Spain	39	1		4				
Israel	22				1			
Gabon								
Lesotho								
Puerto Rico			33		5			
Dahomey								
Japan		5		1	4		16	
Yugoslavia	1					21		
Portugal								
Niger								
Libya	7							
Sierra Leone								17
Senegal								
Kuwait								
Jamaica		1			1			
Denmark				14				
El Salvador								1
Belgium		4						
West Germany	1		1	2	2			
United Kingdom			6					
Canada								
Guinea								
Mali								
Austria	2				1	1	1	
Botswana						5		
Finland		1						
Mauritania								
Togo								
Central African Republic								
Maldive Islands							1	
Mauritius								
Trinidad and Tobago								1
Bulgaria								
Ireland								
Ivory Coast								
Uruguay								

Notes: This event was not reported at any time during the twenty years for Australia, Barbados, Iceland, Liberia, Luxembourg, Malta, Mongolia, Netherlands, New Zealand, Norway, Rumania, Saudi Arabia, Sweden, Switzerland, The Gambia, nor Upper Volta.

An "m" indicates millions, a "t" indicates thousands, and an "h" indicates hundreds.

1956	1957	1958	1959	1960	1961	1962	1963	1964	1965	1966	1967	Total
12		1				20		1	1	20	4	98
	3		14	7	25		5				44	98
			1	1	64			20				91
										7		82
				7	14	53						77
				1								76
4											1	74
11	3			11			12			11		72
	40			3		5				5	5	62
				7	1	1				1	1	55
1	1		4		5					14	1	49
						7		39				46
	31				6					8	1	46
				1							2	41
			2	2				12	20			36
				2								28
										5	1	28
		2				22	1	1				26
						1	20	1	1			23
								5			10	22
											4	21
		2	2				13					17
8	8											16
				3		1	7			1	1	15
												14
				6	5							12
				2	4							10
											4	10
		1	1		1							9
		1	1				3	2	1			8
		1	7									8
			3			2		3				8
							1					6
												5
				3								4
						3						3
		1				1	1					3
										2		2
			1									2
									2			2
					1							2
										1		1
1												1
								1				1
					1							1

Table 3.5
Governmental Sanctions

A governmental sanction is an action taken by the authorities to neutralize, suppress, or eliminate a perceived threat to the security of the government, the regime, or the state itself.

	1948	1949	1950	1951	1952	1953	1954	1955
Total	12h	13h	13h	11h	15h	12h	10h	10h
Median	1	1	2	2	1	2	2	1
Hungary	52	41	32	31	13	34	3	28
East Germany	130	64	103	56	92	141	45	28
Argentina	16	23	97	83	37	50	47	266
Cuba	7	10	10	9	39	43	31	17
United States	12	10	19	15	10	8	26	5
South Africa	11	10	17	5	104	28	20	60
Czechoslovakia	132	224	144	48	43	22	25	14
West Germany	58	21	89	76	142	60	32	23
China	25	45	26	89	42	15	24	44
Indonesia	11		16	9	3	4	13	14
Poland	41	83	45	29	16	28	18	19
Soviet Union	4	17	12	30	32	49	23	11
India	46	34	23	25	19	13	9	15
South Viet Nam	2	5	16	4	2	2	6	14
Iran	13	78	11	36	26	128	37	6
France	20	22	28	13	38	10	8	10
Algeria	2		2		4	2	39	34
Venezuela	17	4	30	14	18	13	3	5
United Arab Republic	27	13	16	48	59	43	41	2
Syria	13	11	4	5	9		13	8
Spain	26	10	18	13	16	13	14	6
Yugoslavia	52	42	50	47	53	12	9	10
South Korea	15	17	11	4	25	7	10	6
Lebanon	9	75	7	7	20	12	5	7
Greece	40	47	9	13	21	12	8	11
Brazil	11	10	19	14	28	13	12	17
Iraq	6	2	3	9	31	13	17	4
Rhodesia						1		
Congo – Kinshasa						1		
Italy	15	31	43	38	44	27	22	8

1956	1957	1958	1959	1960	1961	1962	1963	1964	1965	1966	1967	Total
11h	28h	15h	13h	15h	15h	13h	12h	11h	13h	16h	16h	28t
2	1	2	3	3	4	2	3	3	3	4	4	96
77	17h	123	13	6	8	16	5	8	10	11	8	23h
24	26	19	28	48	71	96	28	25	32	34	13	11h
64	47	39	47	30	11	52	19	27	12	40	18	10h
34	98	78	157	210	104	33	5	16	22	26	8	957
30	25	37	17	86	123	47	115	69	114	58	120	946
20	17	32	39	113	81	51	53	56	51	51	24	843
30	47	25	14	11	10	8	9	7	4	5	12	834
21	28	28	38	52	25	28	7	8	15	26	24	801
5	32	28	7	8	3	1	3	1	4	145	204	751
24	118	92	72	55	21	13	13	24	115	88	46	751
46	38	39	21	25	32	11	12	12	7	31	21	574
23	20	5	43	33	36	57	37	23	19	45	42	561
33	11	11	14	24	19	33	8	9	23	76	73	518
9	6	4	2	7	8	28	67	44	103	136	50	515
8	6	4	3	5	21	15	81	2	6	6	3	495
14	2	28	6	39	49	87	33	14	13	3	2	439
40	35	19	14	48	46	65	18	29	19	12	8	436
5	12	30	11	97	33	38	46	21	13	12	8	430
22	19	11	8	7	16	12	4	1	12	40	18	419
6	15	209	6	4	10	18	27	11	9	23	14	415
18	8	20	20	19	17	55	4	16	19	34	65	411
11	15	15	12	9	12	8	2	3	4	12	11	389
40	1	17	13	27	49	27	18	30	46	7	14	384
9	21	68	10	10	15	38	9	2	3	20	5	352
1	2			6	1	7	10	3	19	11	126	347
11	5	7	6	1	21	11	13	52	27	35	10	323
15	9	23	40	24	24	14	36	6	11	20	12	319
	1		32	26	20	32	16	55	44	59	32	318
			24	63	71	21	38	19	25	29	19	310
5	5	9	5	7	9	7	3	4	6	7	12	307

Table 3.5 Governmental Sanctions—*Continued*

	1948	1949	1950	1951	1952	1953	1954	1955
Kenya					49	55	33	8
Haiti		10		1			4	
Pakistan	4	1	1	11	8	26	34	18
Turkey	6	3	1	9	3	9	12	14
Japan	34	46	51	24	31	10	11	5
Morocco	5	4		11	25	12	26	48
Cyprus	1		4	6			6	28
Dominican Republic	1	2	6	2		1		2
Guatemala	2	5	13	6	8	14	64	20
Jordan		1	2	4	9	2	7	1
Colombia	7	10	15	7	17	14	14	12
Bolivia	5	17	15	15	11	20	4	4
Rumania	37	33	34	7	18	11	10	1
Nigeria		1				4	1	
United Kingdom	12	10	6	13	7	1	6	3
Malaysia	27	2	10	4	6	2	3	6
Tunisia			4	1	54	9	27	6
Portugal	5	12	8	4	6	2		1
Bulgaria	16	48	16	19	8	6	3	1
Ghana	3		4			2		
Austria	38	18	14	5	22	21	7	6
Thailand	8	5	4	6	10	12	6	1
Burma	16	5	10	5	5	4	2	10
Chile	16	15	4	6	5	5	13	19
Peru	11	23	9	7		3	4	2
Singapore	30	2	3	5	2	1	7	14
Philippines	4	6	16	24	33	7	8	4
Israel	5	3	28	9	8	13	2	2
Panama	13	10	9	20	5	4	1	17
Ceylon					2	16	6	6
Guyana						20	32	2
Mexico	1	4	1	3	19	6	13	2
Sudan	3		1	5		1	7	5
Ecuador	3	2	3	1	9	16	4	3
Uganda					1	3	24	4
Malawi								
Albania	18	9	11	17	9	13	3	
Hong Kong	5	2	8	4	12	1	1	
Southern Yemen			1					
North Viet Nam							1	
Tanzania	5				1	1	3	
Nepal			2	1	6	3	1	1
Zambia					1	4		
Switzerland	2	4	3	4	1	5	6	14
Canada	7	4	9	12	2	1	1	2

1956	1957	1958	1959	1960	1961	1962	1963	1964	1965	1966	1967	Total
6		6	13	17	11	17	28	23	11	19	3	299
9	43	28	33	26	17	12	62	19	8	4	15	291
4	4	36	23	13	5	20	12	24	7	13	13	277
23	21	20	27	56	23	12	16	11		7	2	275
2	7	4	1	19	8		2	5	1		3	264
8	8	21	17	16	6	7	9	4	9	17	11	264
126	35	29	3	5		1		6		4	6	260
1	2	1	17	33	54	22	32	17	30	19	11	253
22	12	4	3	9	9	10	14	2	6	15	1	239
10	66	26	20	23	3	3	10	2	2	18	12	221
24	21	8	21		6	3	13	3	6	7	4	212
8	6	6	8	1	9	6	4	17	24	2	20	202
15	4	7	7	4	1				1	1	3	194
		5		5	13	10	11	18	34	45	46	193
	8	7	6	12	11	22	10	4	10	13	22	183
6	8	4	7	3			8	28	13	12	33	182
8	9	14	12	1	16	1	3	4	3	2	6	180
	3	14	10	4	15	26	8	12	20	10	13	173
21	8	10		2	3	1	5	2	2	1		172
2	13	15	14	9	21	20	3	20	4	20	14	164
1	5	2	5	2	4	2		1	2	3	2	160
17	7	40	2	1	3	3	2	3	6	10	7	153
4	2	5	8	2	5	9	9	13	18	6	13	151
10	11	2	2	4	5	6		3	5	2	17	150
21	3	6	7	2	8	15	6	7	9	1	3	147
19	17	1	12	1	4	1	13		1	5	4	142
2	5	2	8	1	2	7		1	3	4	1	138
6	8	6	1	6	7	3	6	1	5	10	8	137
6	1	8	13	2	5	2		8	9	1	3	137
1		23	16	2	23	11	1	4	2	17	1	131
	1				4	7	27	22	1	5	1	122
3	2	10	17	6	10	6	2	1	4	5	4	119
1		6	11		8	2		31	30	6	1	118
7	3	6	6	2	14	4	6	7	11	8	1	116
1		1	7	5	2	7	12	7	4	28	7	113
			78	7	2	1		10	5	1	4	108
6		2			10	2		2		1	4	107
4		8			1		3			4	45	98
2		8	1		4	11	10	4	31	12	10	94
3	1	3	2	3			2	3		55	17	90
		1			3	9	8	34	8	8	9	90
2	3			12	24	18	4	4	4		3	88
			10	7	20		8	11	9	9	7	86
1	1	5	6	6	4	1	3	4	1	5	2	78
2		1		3	3	4	6	5	8	2	2	74

Table 3.5 Governmental Sanctions—*Continued*

	1948	1949	1950	1951	1952	1953	1954	1955
Taiwan		2	12	7	12	2	1	2
Paraguay	11	2	2	3	1		2	4
Honduras	3			1	1	1	7	5
Nicaragua	7	1	1	1			4	1
Costa Rica	21	3	3	6	1	3	1	9
Sweden		2	3	2	16	2	1	7
Yemen	1	1	1		1			1
Laos								
Belgium	1		12	3	2			2
Congo - Brazzaville								
Puerto Rico	5		11	3	1		7	
Libya	2	1	1	1	2		4	
Jamaica	4	2	3	2	3	3	8	
Uruguay	1	2		2	1		6	
El Salvador		4	2	2	4	2		1
Angola								
Australia	3	7	12	2		4	2	2
Finland	3	9	4			2	6	
Netherlands	2		3	3	7	5		
Togo					6			
Senegal								
Sierra Leone								
Mozambique							2	
Denmark			3	2		8		1
Ethiopia		2	1	5			1	
Cambodia					1			
Ireland	1				1	1		
Somalia		4				1	1	
Saudi Arabia			5		1			2
Norway		1		3		1	8	1
Guinea								
Liberia				2	1	1	1	2
Burundi								
Dahomey								
Kuwait								
Malta								1
Ivory Coast								
Cameroon								1
Mauritania								
Afghanistan		1	2		1			2
Papua / New Guinea								
Gabon								
Niger								
Botswana			4		3			
Chad								

1956	1957	1958	1959	1960	1961	1962	1963	1964	1965	1966	1967	Total
4	3	5		5	2	9	2	2	1	1	2	74
3	1	6	12	3	14	1	2	2	1		1	71
21	1	1	5	3	2		8	1	1			61
7	8	1	8	6	1	1	1	2	1		8	59
1	2	1		4	1				1	1		58
4	5	2		2	1	1	3	1	3			55
		1	2	1	1	3	3	3	8	12	12	51
1	1	2	17	13	1	2	1	5	2	3	1	49
1	1		2	7	3	6	9	2	1	3	3	47
			9		1	2	9	2	19	2		44
				5	6	1		4			1	44
14	1		5		2			4	1	1	4	43
		1	1	7						6	2	42
1	1	1	1	1	7	2		1	8	4	3	42
4	1	2	2	7	6	3			1			41
				5	27		2	4	1	1		40
							1			4	2	39
1	3		3	2		2	1	2			1	39
1	1	1		3	1				1	7	4	39
		2	1	1	6	1	5			7	5	34
			1		5	5	7	4	2	2	7	33
					3	3		1		1	25	33
			3		6	4	2	4	4	5	1	31
	8	1	2	1				2	1			29
				4	3	5		1			7	29
	1		2	5		1	7		2	1	8	28
1	10		1	2	2	1	1		2	3	1	27
			2	2	3		10	2		1	1	27
3	5	1			1			1	2	2	3	26
			2	2				1	1	1	4	25
			1		4	2	1	2	1	8	5	24
2	1	1			6		4	1	1	1		24
						3	2	1	12	4	1	23
					2	1	5	2	7	1	4	22
6		1	2		1				1	6	4	21
2		5	8	2				2	1			21
			1			2	13	1	1		1	19
1		2	7			5					2	18
		5		2		1	3	1	1	1	2	16
		1	6	1								14
	8	1		1	1	1			2			14
						1		12				13
				1			3	7	2			13
							1	1		2		11
			1		2		5	1	1	1	1	11

Table 3.5 Governmental Sanctions—*Continued*

	1948	1949	1950	1951	1952	1953	1954	1955
Lesotho								
North Korea	2				1	1	1	
Central African Republic								
Mali								
Mongolia								
Trinidad and Tobago			1	1		1	1	
New Zealand				1				
Upper Volta								
Iceland			1					
Malagasy Republic								
Mauritius		1						
Rwanda								
Luxembourg			1					
Maldive Islands						1		
The Gambia								

Notes: This event was not reported at any time during the twenty years for Barbados. An "h" indicates hundreds and a "t" indicates thousands.

1956	1957	1958	1959	1960	1961	1962	1963	1964	1965	1966	1967	Total
					4		2			1	4	11
		1								3	2	11
				1		1				5	1	8
			3	1		1		1	1			7
									5		2	7
1					1							6
						2				1		4
							2			1	1	4
						2						3
		1						1			1	3
									2			3
							1	1			1	3
												1
												1
										1		1

Table 3.6
External Interventions

An external intervention is an attempt by an actor, whether another nation-state or a rebel group operating from outside the country, to engage in military activity within the target country with the intent of influencing the authority structure of that country. The data are listed by target, not intervening, country.

	1948	1949	1950	1951	1952	1953	1954	1955
Total	25	6	8	2	1	2	14	23
Median								
Congo – Kinshasa								
Yemen								
Laos								3
Tunisia								
Kenya								
Dominican Republic								
Cuba								
Southern Yemen								
Hungary								
Lebanon								
Cyprus								
China	6	1	5					1
Costa Rica	8	1						14
Rhodesia								
Ethiopia								
Morocco								
Angola								
Mozambique								
Taiwan		1						
Burma							2	3
Guatemala							11	
Haiti								
Portugal								
Somalia								
Spain								
Greece	10		2					
Papua / New Guinea								
Thailand	1							
Algeria								
Nigeria								

124

1956	1957	1958	1959	1960	1961	1962	1963	1964	1965	1966	1967	Total
52	43	94	24	43	95	60	81	192	126	73	109	11h
				21	47	16	8	33	13	4	14	156
						18	16	6	6	14	19	79
			5	5	9	2	1	23	2	8	12	70
11	22	6	2	4	19	1			4			69
					9			31	20		2	62
			1					2	42	10		55
		3	1	1	7	7	13	4	2	4	2	44
	1	10						17	4	6	2	40
28					2					1		31
		27										27
								21			4	25
		9						1	1			24
1												24
										1	21	22
						2	13	3		2		20
3	8	7										18
					7	1	1			4	3	16
								9	6	1		16
		14										15
3	1		1	1	3							14
			1	2								14
		1	2				11					14
							8		6			14
							2	10	2			14
	7	7										14
												12
						11						11
							1			4	4	10
1	3	2			1	1	1					9
											8	8

Table 3.6 External Interventions—*Continued*

	1948	1949	1950	1951	1952	1953	1954	1955
Senegal								
Bolivia								
Nicaragua				1				1
Uganda					1	1		
Gabon								
Malaysia			2				1	
Rwanda								
Saudi Arabia								
Tanzania								
Panama								
Poland						1		
Hong Kong								
Iraq								
Jordan								
Venezuela								
Zambia								
Burundi								
Congo – Brazzaville								
Indonesia								
Maldive Islands								
Albania								
Cambodia								
Central African Republic								
Guinea								
Honduras								
Malawi								
Nepal				2				
Paraguay								
Botswana								
Cameroon								
Chad								
Czechoslovakia								
Dahomey								
El Salvador								1
Mali								
Mexico			1					
North Korea								

Notes: This event was not reported at any time during the twenty years for Afghanistan, Argentina, Australia, Austria, Barbados, Belgium, Brazil, Bulgaria, Canada, Ceylon, Chile, Colombia, Denmark, East Germany, Ecuador, Finland, France, Ghana, Guyana, Iceland, India, Iran, Ireland, Israel, Italy, Ivory Coast, Jamaica, Japan, Kuwait, Lesotho, Liberia, Libya, Luxembourg, Malagasy Republic, Malta, Mauritania, Mauritius, Mongolia, Netherlands, New

1956	1957	1958	1959	1960	1961	1962	1963	1964	1965	1966	1967	Total
							4		4			8
											7	7
			2	2	1							7
									4	1		7
						6						6
		1					1			1		6
							2			4		6
		1	2			1				2		6
							5			1		6
			1				4					5
4												5
										4		4
							4					4
		3								1		4
				2						1	1	4
								4				4
							3					3
										3		3
		3										3
			2			1						3
			1	1								2
1	1											2
								1		1		2
								2				2
			2									2
										2		2
												2
				2								2
										1		1
				1								1
										1		1
						1						1
			1									1
												1
									1			1
												1
											1	1

Zealand, Niger, North Viet Nam, Norway, Pakistan, Peru, Philippines, Puerto Rico, Rumania, Sierra Leone, Singapore, South Africa, South Korea, South Viet Nam, Soviet Union, Sudan, Sweden, Switzerland, Syria, The Gambia, Togo, Trinidad and Tobago, Turkey, United Arab Republic, United Kingdom, United States, Upper Volta, Uruguay, West Germany, nor Yugoslavia.

An "h" indicates hundreds.

Table 3.7
Regular Executive Transfers

A regular executive transfer is a change in the office of national executive from one leader or ruling group to another that is accomplished through conventional legal or customary procedures and unaccompanied by actual or directly threatened physical violence.

	1948	1949	1950	1951	1952	1953	1954	1955
Total	64	52	67	56	61	56	56	62
Median								
Syria	1	3	3	5	1		4	3
Greece		4	6	3	2			1
Cambodia		1	3		1	2		3
Jordan			3	3	2	1	1	3
Iraq	3	2	2		2	3	2	
South Viet Nam	1	1	2		1	1	2	3
Lebanon				2	6	2	1	1
South Korea	2		2		3		2	1
Finland	1		1	3		1	2	
United Arab Republic	1	2	1		7	1	3	
France	3	1	2	2	2	3	1	1
Morocco				2		1	1	5
Indonesia	3	2	2	1	1	1		1
Israel	1	2		1	1	3	1	3
Switzerland	1	1	1	1	1	1	1	1
Iran	3	1	2	3	2			1
Hungary	2		1		1	2	1	1
Laos							2	
Uruguay				2	1			1
Italy	1			1		1	1	2
Libya		2	2	2			2	
Malaysia	3				1		1	1
West Germany		3		1				2
Yemen	1							1
Congo – Kinshasa								
Japan	2		1	2	1		1	1
Nepal				2	1	2		1
Colombia	2	1	1	1		2	1	
Southern Yemen				1				
Tunisia			2		1		1	3	3

1956	1957	1958	1959	1960	1961	1962	1963	1964	1965	1966	1967	Total
66	73	70	50	72	67	70	64	76	67	68	60	1388
1	2	1	1		5	3	4	3	2	2		44
1		2			2		3	3	3	1	4	35
8	3	3		3	2	1				1	2	33
4	2	1	1	1		1	2	1	1		3	30
	2	2					2		2	3	2	27
							1	6	6	1	2	27
2		4		2	1			2	1	2		26
1				5	3	4	1	1				25
3	3	2	1		2	1	2	1		1		24
			1		2	1		1	1	1	1	23
1	2	1				1					1	21
3		2		1	2		1		1		2	21
1	3	2	2					1		1	1	20
		1	1	1	1	1	2	1		1	1	20
1	1	1	1	1	1	1	1	1	1	1	1	20
	1		1		1	1		1	1			18
4		1			1	1			1		1	17
1	1	1	3	6		1		2				17
1	1	1	1		1	1	1	1	1	2	2	17
1	1	1	2			2	2	1				16
	1			1			1	1	1		2	15
	1		2	2			2		1	1		15
		2			1	3	1	1		1		15
					2	2		1	2	3	3	15
				3	3	1	1	1	1	2	2	14
1	1			1	1	1		1				14
1	2	1	1	1			1		1			14
		2				1			1	1		13
1			1	1			2	1	2		4	13
2	1											13

Table 3.7 Regular Executive Transfers—*Continued*

	1948	1949	1950	1951	1952	1953	1954	1955
Algeria	1			1				1
Belgium		1	3	1	1		1	
Brazil				1				1
Haiti		1	2		1			
Kenya					1			
Pakistan	1			1		1	1	2
Ecuador	1		1		1			
Guatemala			1	1			2	
Malta		1	2			1	1	
Panama	1	1		1	1			2
Peru	1		1				1	
Argentina				1				1
Austria			1	1		1		1
Bolivia		1			1			
Burma	2	1			1			
Ceylon	1				1	1		
Jamaica			1	1				1
Rhodesia						2		
Rumania	2				2		1	1
Singapore					1			2
Soviet Union						3		1
Turkey		1	1					
Venezuela	1		2			1		
Dominican Republic					1			
El Salvador	1	1	1					
Ireland	1	1		1			1	
Malawi						1		
Sudan							2	
Uganda								
Zambia						1		
Burundi								
China	3	3						
Costa Rica	2				2	1		
Denmark		1				1		1
East Germany		1	1				2	1
Guyana						1		
Kuwait			1					
Luxembourg	1					1		
Senegal								
Somalia		1	1	1		1		
South Africa	1						1	
Tanzania								
Barbados								
Bulgaria		1	2					
Iceland		1	1		1	1		

1956	1957	1958	1959	1960	1961	1962	1963	1964	1965	1966	1967	Total
2		1		1		3		1	1			12
		2			1				1	1		12
1					3	3		1	1		1	12
1	5	1						1				12
		1	1		1	2	3	1		2		12
2	2	2										12
1					1	1			2	2		11
	5	1								1		11
		1	2		1	1		1				11
1	1				1				1		1	11
1		1	1		1		1		1		2	11
		1				2	2			2	1	10
	1				1			2	1	1		10
1	1		1					1		2	2	10
1	2	2		1								10
1			2	2				1	1			10
	1	2				2					2	10
1	1	1				1		2	1	1		10
		1			1				1		1	10
1	1		1	1			2		1			10
	1	1		1				2	1			10
		2	1	1	2	1	2		2	1		10
					2		2	1	2	1		9
1					1	2		1			1	9
	1		2		1					1		9
1	1				1		1	2		2		9
3									2	1	1	9
1	1				1	3	1	1		1		9
1	1		2			1		3				9
						1	1	4	2			8
			1								1	8
		1				1				1		8
	1			2		1		1				8
				2				1				9
	1		1		1		3		1			8
				1	1	1	2	2				8
		2	1				1		1	1		8
		1	2		2	2			1			8
1			1		1		1					8
		1		1				2	2			8
	1	1		2	2		2					8
		4		2					1			7
1	1			1		1						7
1		1			1							7

Table 3.7 Regular Executive Transfers—*Continued*

	1948	1949	1950	1951	1952	1953	1954	1955
India			1					
Netherlands	1							
Poland	1				1		1	
Thailand	2		1					
Afghanistan		1				1		
Chile					1	1		
Cyprus	1	1						1
Ghana		1			1		1	
Honduras		1						
Nicaragua			1					
Norway				1				1
Philippines	1					1		
Taiwan		1	2				1	
United Kingdom				1	1			1
Botswana			1			1		
Chad								
Czechoslovakia	1			1		1		
Dahomey								
Lesotho								
Mongolia		1			1	1	1	
Togo								
Albania	2					1	1	
Cameroon								
Maldive Islands					1	1	1	
New Zealand		1						
Nigeria								1
Paraguay	1	1					2	
Rwanda								
Saudi Arabia						1	1	
Sierra Leone								
Sweden			1	1				
Trinidad and Tobago								1
Angola								1
Australia		1						
Canada	1							
Central African Republic								
Cuba	1							
Ethiopia					1			
Gabon								
Ivory Coast								
Mali								
Mexico					1			
Mozambique								
Niger								
Portugal				2				

1956	1957	1958	1959	1960	1961	1962	1963	1964	1965	1966	1967	Total
					1		2		1	2	1	7
		1	1			1		1		1	1	7
2			1				1					7
	2		1				1					7
			1				1		1		2	6
		1			1		1				1	6
	1		1	1				1				6
	1				1			1				6
1	3								1			6
1	1						1			1	1	6
	1						2		1			6
	1				1	1			1			6
		1					1					6
	1						1	1				6
									1	2		5
			3	1		1						5
	1						1					5
			1	1				1	2			5
				1		1			2	1		5
							1					5
1			1				1				1	5
												4
	1		1		1	1						4
									1			4
	2		1									4
	1		1							1		4
												4
				3	1							4
			1					1				4
				1				1			2	4
	1	1										4
1		1					1					4
				1	1							3
										1	1	3
	1						1					3
		1	1	1								3
			2									3
										2		3
				2							1	3
			1	1			1					3
			1	2								3
		1						1				3
			1		1	1						3
		1		2								3
		1										3

133

Table 3.7 Regular Executive Transfers—*Continued*

	1948	1949	1950	1951	1952	1953	1954	1955
The Gambia								
United States					1			
Congo – Brazzaville								
Mauritania								
North Viet Nam							1	1
Papua / New Guinea						1		
Puerto Rico			1					
Upper Volta								
Guinea								
Malagasy Republic								
North Korea	1							
Yugoslavia								

Notes: This event was not reported at any time during the twenty years for Hong Kong, Liberia, Mauritius, nor Spain.

An "h" indicates hundreds.

1956	1957	1958	1959	1960	1961	1962	1963	1964	1965	1966	1967	Total
						2			1			3
				1			1					3
							1			1		2
				1	1							2
												2
						1						2
								1				2
				1		1						2
		1										1
				1								1
												1
										1		1

Table 3.8
Renewals of Executive Tenure

A renewal of executive tenure is an act that re-establishes or reconfirms the tenure of the incumbent national executive leader or group through the country's conventional procedures.

	1948	1949	1950	1951	1952	1953	1954	1955
Total Median	49	48	80	131	74	49	61	51
United Kingdom		3	23	59	12	3	4	5
France	19	9	19	25	20	4	10	8
Italy	5	4	3	7	1	7	6	3
Israel	1	4	3	3	3	2	1	3
Canada		2	1	3		3	2	6
Belgium	4	1	7	2	4	1	3	1
Greece	3	4	3	3	4		1	
Iran	4	1	4	9	4	2	2	2
Lebanon	1	1		1	1		2	
India			1		2		1	
Jordan		1	1	1	2	1	3	
Turkey	1		1				1	2
Japan		1	1		2	2	1	2
Syria	2	2	2	2		1	2	2
South Africa			1	1	5	2		1
Ceylon					1	2		2
Finland		2	4			2	1	
Australia	1			1	1	1	1	1
Ireland		1			1	1		
Cambodia				1			2	1
South Korea					2		2	
Soviet Union			1			1	1	
Sweden	1				1			
Iraq						1	1	1
Liberia					2			
Netherlands	1	1		1	1			1
Austria					1			
Indonesia				2	1		1	1
Malawi								
Rhodesia	1							

1956	1957	1958	1959	1960	1961	1962	1963	1964	1965	1966	1967	Total
91	75	59	58	58	54	68	67	64	68	58	41	13h 3
7	8	3	7	7	9	6	5	5	18	2	3	189
31	13	4	4	4	2	7		1		2	4	186
4	6	4	4	4	1	5	4	3	2	8	8	89
10	5	4	4	3	1	8	4	6	1	1	1	68
3	3	4		1		9	12	6	3	3	1	62
		5	2	5	5			1	1	2		44
2	1	2	1	1		2	2	2	2	2		35
1	2	1			1		2					35
3	1	4		3	3	1	1	2	1	3		28
	4					1	1	1	4	3	4	22
1	2		1		2	1	2	1	1		1	21
	4				2	1		3	4		1	20
		1		1			2	2	1	1	2	19
	1					1	1		2	1		19
1		3			1					1		16
	2	1	3	1	1					2		15
	1			1	1	1	1					14
		2			2		2			1		13
	1				1		2		2	2		11
		1			1	1	1	2				10
2		1		1			1				1	10
1		1				1	1			3		10
1	1	1	1	2				2				10
1	2						2	1				9
1				2		1		2			1	9
2		1			1			1				9
1			3	1		1	1					8
		1		1						1		8
		1	3			1	1	2				8
		1	3				1		2			8

Table 3.8 Renewals of Executive Tenure—*Continued*

	1948	1949	1950	1951	1952	1953	1954	1955
Singapore								1
Yugoslavia	1		1			1	1	
China	1						1	
East Germany						1	1	
Norway		1				1		
Pakistan								
Paraguay		1	1			1		
South Viet Nam								
United Arab Republic						2	2	
West Germany				1		1	1	1
Congo - Kinshasa								
Czechoslovakia	2							
Hungary		1		2				
Thailand		1		2				
Zambia								
Brazil							1	
Ghana							1	
Malta		1	1				1	1
Mauritania								
Nepal								
Nigeria								
Peru								
Philippines		1						1
Poland								
Portugal		1				1		
Puerto Rico					1			
Rumania						1		1
Senegal								
Somalia								
Sudan								1
Albania								
Algeria								1
Burma					1			
Laos								
New Zealand					1		1	
North Viet Nam								
Taiwan							1	
Bulgaria			1					
Cameroon								
Denmark			1			1		
Kenya								
Luxembourg					2		1	
Malagasy Republic								
Mongolia								
Sierra Leone								

1956	1957	1958	1959	1960	1961	1962	1963	1964	1965	1966	1967	Total
4			2		1							8
		1					1	1			1	8
1		1	1						1	1		7
	1	1					1				2	7
	1		1		1		1				1	7
1	1	1		1		2			1			7
		2					1				1	7
1			1		1		1			1	2	7
1								1	1			7
	1				1				1			7
			1			3	1		1			6
							1	2		1		6
		1	1			1						6
	3											6
			4				1		1			6
					1	2	1					5
2					1				1			5
										1		5
			1		1				2	1		5
			1	1				1			2	5
1			1	1			1	1				5
			1	3	1							5
	1							1			1	5
	1				1		1	2				5
		1			1				1			5
1	1		1	1								5
	1		1						1			5
			2			1	2					5
		1				1		3				5
1		2							1			5
1		1				1				1		4
						1	2					4
	1	1	1									4
					1		1	1		1		4
							1			1		4
	1		1	1			1					4
	1		1							1		4
		1								1		3
			2						1			3
										1		3
					1			1		1		3
												3
			1						2			3
			1		1		1					3
						2					1	3

Table 3.8 Renewals of Executive Tenure—*Continued*

	1948	1949	1950	1951	1952	1953	1954	1955
Togo								
United States	1							
Afghanistan								
Argentina					1			
Bolivia								
Chile								1
Congo – Brazzaville								
Cuba								1
Cyprus								
Dahomey								
Ecuador							1	
Gabon								
Guyana								
Haiti								
Iceland		1						
Jamaica		1						
Kuwait								
Libya						1		
Malaysia								
Mauritius						1		
Nicaragua				1				
North Korea								
Switzerland								
Trinidad and Tobago								
Tunisia								
Venezuela						1		
Barbados								
Botswana		1						
Central African Republic								
Chad								
Colombia								
Costa Rica		1						
Guinea								
Hong Kong					1			
Ivory Coast								
Lesotho								
Morocco								
Tanzania								
The Gambia								
Uganda								
Upper Volta								
Uruguay								

Notes: This event was not reported at any time during the twenty years for Angola, Burundi, Dominican Republic, El Salvador, Ethiopia, Guatemala, Honduras, Maldive Islands, Mali, Mexico, Mozambique, Niger, Panama, Papua/New Guinea, Rwanda, Saudi Arabia, Southern Yemen, Spain, nor Yemen.

An "h" indicates hundreds.

1956	1957	1958	1959	1960	1961	1962	1963	1964	1965	1966	1967	Total
					1		1			1		3
1								1				3
							1		1			2
								1				2
								1		1		2
1												2
			1				1					2
			1									2
									1	1		2
				1					1			2
						1						2
					1						1	2
					1	1						2
					1			1				2
				1								2
			1									2
								1		1		2
1												2
								2				2
										1		2
	1											2
1	1											2
			1				1					2
										2		2
			1					1				2
	1											2
										1		1
												1
								1				1
						1						1
	1											1
												1
					1							1
												1
									1			1
									1			1
1												1
									1			1
										1		1
										1		1
				1								1
						1						1

Table 3.9
Executive Adjustments

An executive adjustment is an event modifying the membership of a national executive body that does not signify a transfer of formal power from one leader or ruling group to another.

	1948	1949	1950	1951	1952	1953	1954	1955
Total	121	151	157	149	137	173	134	173
Median								
Soviet Union	13	9	9	5	4	18	10	16
Argentina		5	4	5	2	1	2	10
South Korea	1	4	5	5	3	6	1	5
Cuba	2	3	7	6	5	5	3	3
Poland	2	9	5	3	2		6	4
Rumania	2	4	4	5	9	7	6	2
United Kingdom	5		3	8	5	4	4	1
India	1		3		2	1	2	5
East Germany	4	1	4	1	6	16	3	4
Hungary	4	6	6	5	4	8	2	1
Turkey	1	1	4	2	1	1	1	7
Brazil	1	1		1	1	5	6	8
Chile	2		4	3	4	5	5	12
Colombia	3	7	8	8	2	2	3	
Iraq	3	2	1	2	1	1	5	4
Jordan		3	3	4	2	1	2	1
Syria	3	3	3	2	2	3	1	1
Bolivia	2	6	6	2	2	3	3	
Pakistan			1			1	5	4
United Arab Republic		6	2	2	9	4	4	3
Indonesia	1	1		4	2	5	2	1
Japan	3	1	3	1	4	3	4	4
Ecuador	2	2	4	1	2	8	1	5
Czechoslovakia	6	1	5	4	6	4	2	3
Iran	1	1	6	8	3	5		5
France	1	5	3	1		2	5	3
Lebanon	1	2				1	1	3
Peru	4	4	2	1	2	1	2	3
Bulgaria		10	5	4	2		1	
South Viet Nam			1	2	1	1	3	2

1956	1957	1958	1959	1960	1961	1962	1963	1964	1965	1966	1967	Total
163	128	172	140	125	143	167	183	180	175	163	107	30h
						1	1	1	1	1		13
9	10	12	3	4	3	9	7	3	10	3	6	163
9	7	6	11	2	6	20	7	2	2	6	1	108
1	6	1	2	10	8	1	8	3	1	2	2	75
		2	8	4	4	3	2	3	6	1	3	70
20	5	2	3	3	1	1	1	1	1	1		70
8	5	4	2		1	2			3	2		66
4	2	3	3	2	2	4	3	1	3	4	5	66
6	1	3	2		1	6	11	8		6	4	62
1	1	3		3	2	1	4		3	2	1	60
5	3	2	1	2	2	3	3		1	2		60
4	1	7		7	10	2	3	1	2	3	1	59
1	2	5	4	2	1	1	7	6	2	3		57
7	4	1	1	1	1	2	1	1		1	2	57
3	2		5	3	1		2	2	6			57
	1	3	3	4	2		6	9	5	2		54
2	4	6	3	1	4	1	4	1	6	2	2	52
2	2	4	3	6	3	3	5		1	3	1	51
4	7	1	6	1		2	1	1	2	1		50
4	3	10	1	3		6	3	1	1	5	1	49
2	1	2	1	1	2	1		3	1		3	47
3	1	1	1	2		3	2	5	6	4	2	46
1	1	2	2	2		2	2	2	3	4	1	45
2		1		1	5	4	1	1	3	1		44
2	1	2	1		1	1	2		1		1	43
		1	1		1	1	3	1	1	3	2	43
5		2	3	3	4	4					1	42
4	4	9	3		6			3	3	2		42
	1	4	2	3		3	2	3	3	1	1	42
1	4	1	3		2	4			1	1	3	39
2				1	2		2	6	7	6	3	39

Table 3.9 Executive Adjustments—*Continued*

	1948	1949	1950	1951	1952	1953	1954	1955
West Germany	1	2	1	1		1		5
Canada	2	1	2		1	2	1	
Ghana						1		
China	3	2	1		1	1	2	2
Greece	2		4	2	3		4	
Guatemala	2	1	4	2	3	1	4	4
Haiti	1	1	2					
Saudi Arabia						1	2	2
United States	3	3		2	1	1		1
Burma	4	3	2	1	1	3		2
Israel		1	3	1	3			2
Philippines	2	5	1	2	2	4	1	
Nepal				4	2	1		1
Venezuela	1	1			1	1		
Yugoslavia	4	2	2	5	2	1	1	1
Ceylon						1	1	
Panama	1	4	2	5	2		1	4
Finland	3	2	1		5	1		1
Italy	1	3		3	1	1	1	1
Libya		1		1		2	2	
Morocco				1	1	2		1
Rhodesia						1		
Southern Yemen								
Dominican Republic						1		
Albania	3	1	2	2	2	1		
Costa Rica	1	4	1	3	2		1	1
Belgium	2		2		3			1
Thailand	1		2	1	1	1		3
Algeria								
Australia			1	4			1	1
Kenya						1		1
El Salvador	2	2				1		
Guyana								
Nigeria								
Sudan							1	
Taiwan			2	1	1		3	1
Congo – Kinshasa								
Denmark	1		2			1		1
North Korea				2	1	4	1	1
Tunisia				1			1	1
Uruguay	1	1	1		1		1	1
Austria		1			3	3		
Mexico	3				1		1	2
Netherlands	1	1	2	3	1			
Nicaragua	2	1	1		1	1		1

1956	1957	1958	1959	1960	1961	1962	1963	1964	1965	1966	1967	Total
1	4	1	1	3	3	3	2	3	3	3		38
	1	1	1	1	1	3	6	2	7	1	3	36
1	2	3	2		7	4	5	3	5	2	1	36
1	1	3	2	2			3		2	7	2	35
2		1	1				2	3	1	6	4	35
2	4	3	1	1		1	1					34
2	10	7	4	2	1	1	3					34
1		7	3	2	3	5	1	2	1	1		31
1	2	3	2			2	1	5		1	3	31
	1	4	1	2	1		1	3	1			30
2		2	2	3	1		2	2	2	2	2	30
		1	1	3	2	2	1	1				28
	1	1	1	1	3	2		3	2	4	2	27
		12		2	3		3	1	1		1	27
1		1				1	1	1	2	1		26
3		1	6	2		4	3	2		1		24
	1	3	1									24
3	1	1			1		3				1	23
2	1		1	3		2			2	1		23
2		2		2	1	4		3	1	1	1	23
4		1			2	2	2	1	1	3	1	22
		1	1			2		13	1	1		20
			2	2	1		4	3	1	2	5	20
				3	4	3	2		2	4		19
1	1			1	1					3		18
2	1							1	1			18
1	1		2	3	1	1						17
1	5	1	1									17
		1				3	3	4	2	3		16
3				1	1	1	1	2				16
			2	1		3	3	2	1	1	1	16
		1	2	1	3			1	1		1	15
		3				1	1	5		2	2	14
1					1	1	1	3	3	2	2	14
		1				1	1	1	6	3		14
		2		1				1	1		1	14
			1		2		1	1	3	4	1	13
2	1	1						1		1	2	13
			2			1				1		13
	1	2			2	1		1	1	2		13
1	2					1		1			2	13
			1	1	1		1	1				12
1					1			2	1			12
		1	2							1		12
2					2	1						12

Table 3.9 Executive Adjustments—*Continued*

	1948	1949	1950	1951	1952	1953	1954	1955
Portugal			1				1	1
South Africa	1		1					1
Spain	1	2		2	1			
Malawi						1		
Yemen								
Honduras		1					2	1
Kuwait								
Malaysia			1					1
Mauritania								
Paraguay		3		1	1	1	1	1
Switzerland			1			2	1	
Liberia							1	
Sierra Leone						1		
Sweden	2	4						1
Afghanistan								1
Ivory Coast								
Puerto Rico				1	1			2
Laos						1		
Tanzania								
Uganda								
Zambia						2		
Dahomey								
Gabon								
Norway	2			1				
Burundi								
Cambodia						1		1
Guinea								
Mali								
Upper Volta								
Cameroon								
Chad								
Congo - Brazzaville								
Ethiopia		1						
Ireland			1	2				
Mongolia								
North Viet Nam							2	
Singapore								1
Togo								
Central African Repuolic								
Cyprus								
Jamaica						2		
New Zealand							1	
Senegal								
Somalia								
Lesotho								

1956	1957	1958	1959	1960	1961	1962	1963	1964	1965	1966	1967	Total
		1			3	2	1		1		1	12
2		1		1	2			1		2		12
1	1					1			1		2	12
			1		1		1	6		1		11
							2	3	1	1	4	11
1	2		2						1			10
					2		2	2	2	1	1	10
1			1	1		1		1	2	1	1	10
					1	1	2		4	1	1	10
1			1									10
			1		2	1					2	10
	1			1	1		2	2	1			9
						2	2	2	1		1	9
			1			1						9
1	2								1	3		8
							2	2	1	3		8
	1	1		2								8
			2					2	1		1	7
						1	1	1	1		3	7
					1		1	2	1	1	1	7
								1	1	2	1	7
			1			1	2				1	6
							3	1	2			6
				1			1	1				6
							1		2		2	5
							1		1		1	5
							2	2			1	5
					1	1		2		1		5
					1	1	2				1	5
					1		1		1	1		4
					1	1	1	1				4
						1		1	1	1		4
					1					2		4
	1											4
			1	1		1			1			4
							1		1			4
			2	1								4
							1			3		4
						2				1		3
1			1			1						3
											1	3
							1				1	3
		1						1	1			3
			1		1					1		3
								2				2

Table 3.9 Executive Adjustments—*Continued*

	1948	1949	1950	1951	1952	1953	1954	1955
Niger								
The Gambia								
Botswana								
Hong Kong								
Malagasy Republic								
Papua / New Guinea								
Rwanda								

Notes: This event was not reported at any time during the twenty years for Angola, Barbados, Iceland, Luxembourg, Maldive Islands, Malta, Mauritius, Mozambique, nor Trinidad and Tobago. An "h" indicates hundreds.

1956	1957	1958	1959	1960	1961	1962	1963	1964	1965	1966	1967	Total
						1	1					2
									1	1		2
									1			1
										1		1
									1			1
						1						1
									1			1

Table 3.10
Irregular Executive Transfers

An irregular executive transfer is a change in the office of national executive from one leader or ruling group to another that is accomplished outside the conventional legal or customary procedures for transferring formal power in effect at the time of the event and accompanied by actual or directly threatened violence.

	1948	1949	1950	1951	1952	1953	1954	1955
Total	9	9	2	5	6	5	8	9
Median								
South Viet Nam								3
Syria		3		2			1	
Yemen	2							2
Paraguay	2	3					1	
Argentina								2
China		1						
Haiti			1					
Algeria								
Dahomey								
Dominican Republic								
Guatemala							2	
Iraq								
Peru	1	1						
United Arab Republic					2		2	
Bolivia				1	1			
Brazil							1	1
Ecuador								
El Salvador	1							
Honduras							1	
South Korea								
Sudan								
Thailand				1				
Venezuela	1				1			
Burma								
Burundi								
Colombia							1	
Congo – Kinshasa								
Cuba					1			
Gabon								
Indonesia	1							

1956	1957	1958	1959	1960	1961	1962	1963	1964	1965	1966	1967	Total
2	5	8	1	6	7	9	13	12	11	11	9	147
							1	3	3			10
					1	1	1			1		10
						2			2		1	9
												6
						2				1		5
										4		5
1	2							1				5
		1			2				1			4
							1		2		1	4
						2	1		1			4
	1						1					4
		1					3					4
						1	1					4
												4
								1				3
								1				3
					1		1			1		3
				1	1							3
1							1					3
				1	2							3
		1						2				3
	1	1										3
		1										3
		1				1						2
										2		2
	1											2
				1					1			2
			1									2
								2				2
										1		2

Table 3.10 Irregular Executive Transfers—*Continued*

	1948	1949	1950	1951	1952	1953	1954	1955
Laos								
Morocco							1	1
Nepal			1					
Panama			1		1			
Togo								
Cambodia							1	
Central African Republic								
Congo - Brazzaville								
Cyprus								
Czechoslovakia	1							
France								
Ghana								
Greece								
Iran							1	
Maldive Islands							1	
Nigeria								
Pakistan								
Rhodesia								
Sierra Leone								
Tunisia					1			
Turkey								
Uganda								
Upper Volta								

Notes: This event was not reported at any time during the twenty years for Afghanistan, Albania, Angola, Australia, Austria, Barbados, Belgium, Botswana, Bulgaria, Cameroon, Canada, Ceylon, Chad, Chile, Costa Rica, Denmark, East Germany, Ethiopia, Finland, Guinea, Guyana, Hong Kong, Hungary, Iceland, India, Ireland, Israel, Italy, Ivory Coast, Jamaica, Japan, Jordan, Kenya, Kuwait, Lebanon, Lesotho, Liberia, Libya, Luxembourg, Malagasy Republic, Malawi, Malaysia, Mali, Malta, Mauritania, Mauritius, Mexico, Mongolia, Mozambique, Netherlands, New Zealand, Nicaragua, Niger, North Korea, North Viet Nam, Norway, Papua/New Guinea, Philippines, Poland, Portugal, Puerto Rico, Rumania, Rwanda, Saudi Arabia, Senegal, Singapore, Somalia, South Africa, Southern Yemen, Soviet Union, Spain, Sweden, Switzerland, Taiwan, Tanzania, The Gambia, Trinidad and Tobago, United Kingdom, United States, Uruguay, West Germany, Yugoslavia, nor Zambia.

1956	1957	1958	1959	1960	1961	1962	1963	1964	1965	1966	1967	Total
				1				1				2
												2
				1								2
												2
							1				1	2
												1
										1		1
							1					1
								1				1
												1
		1										1
										1		1
											1	1
												1
												1
										1		1
		1										1
									1			1
											1	1
												1
				1								1
										1		1
										1		1

Country Plots

The tables of annual aggregates obscure some variation over time. In them a year is treated as a homogeneous period. The tables are also unwieldy for comparisons among series. The country displays are designed to remedy both these problems, but the price paid is less specificity in the data. For some purposes, the tables will be more instructive; for others, the displays will be more useful. Hopefully, both will provide a little something for everybody.

The representation of events in the displays is of two kinds. Government changes occur with less frequency than do events of civil disorder and popular participation. Therefore, power renewals, minor regular power adjustments, major regular power transfers, and major irregular power transfers are denoted by symbols whereas antigovernment demonstrations, riots, armed attacks, deaths from domestic political violence, governmetal security sanctions, and foreign interventions are depicted in bar graphs. All ten series are placed along twenty-year time continua from a left of 1 January 1948 to a right of 31 December 1967. The midpoints of symbols are in the appropriate places along the timespan. The width of the pen with which the lines were drawn happens to be twelve days according to our scale before photographic reduction so that each vertical bar represents the number of designated events that happened in its particular twelve days. The resulting contrasts between dense and sparse segments enhance comparisons among and within countries.

A scale of heights was determined separately for each series because the ranges among series differ greatly. There are ten possible heights in each case and the longest is limited only by infinity. The divisions (by number of events) for the six series are:

demonstrations: 1, 2, 3, 4, 5, 6, 9, 13, 49, ∞
riots: 1, 2, 4, 5, 7, 9, 11, 17, 33, ∞
attacks: 1, 2, 3, 4, 6, 9, 15, 32, 55, ∞
deaths: 2, 12, 25, 39, 55, 77, 102, 149, 419, ∞
sanctions: 1, 2, 3, 4, 5, 6, 8, 10, 21, ∞
interventions: 1, 2, 3, 4, 5, 6, 7, 9, 11, ∞

Series names are included for a country only if that country was reported to have had an occurrence of the event at some time during the twenty years.

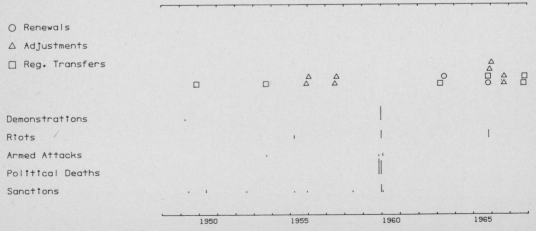

Albania

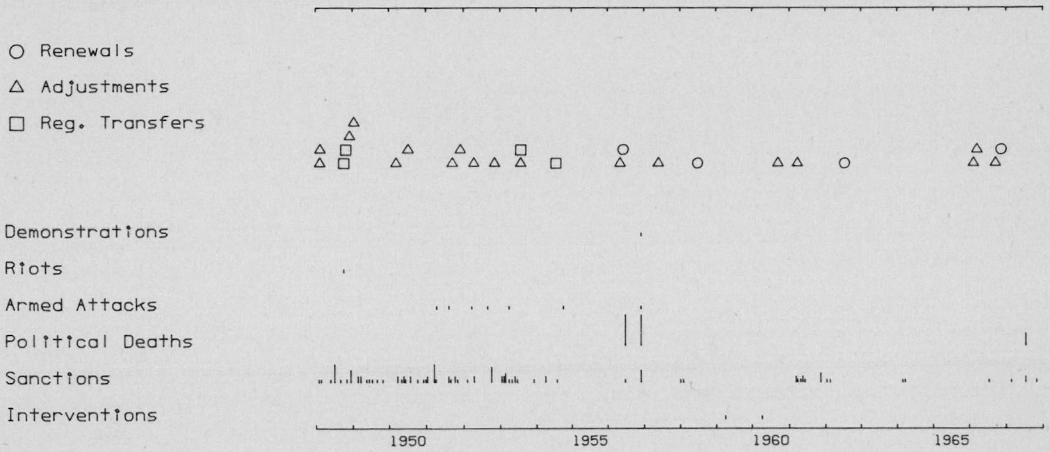

O Renewals
△ Adjustments
□ Reg. Transfers

Demonstrations
Riots
Armed Attacks
Political Deaths
Sanctions
Interventions

1950　　　　1955　　　　1960　　　　1965

Algeria

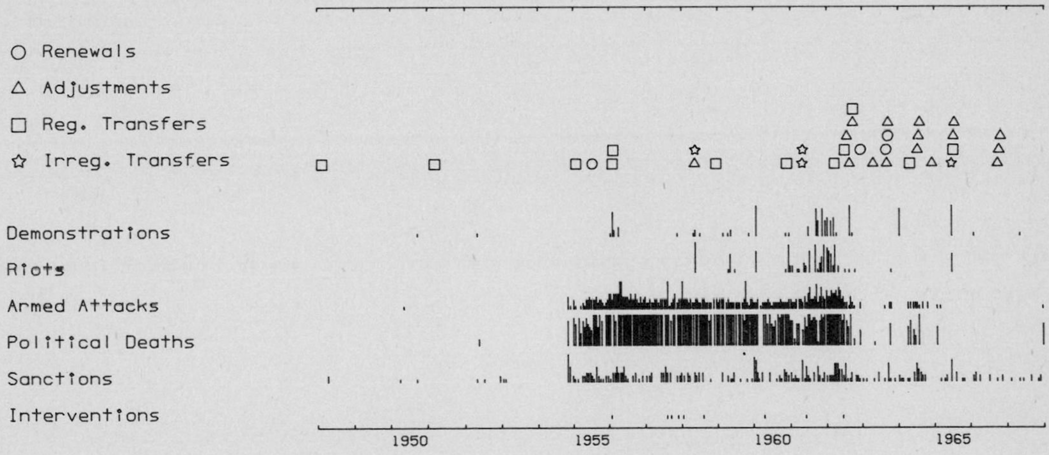

O Renewals
△ Adjustments
□ Reg. Transfers
☆ Irreg. Transfers

Demonstrations
Riots
Armed Attacks
Political Deaths
Sanctions
Interventions

1950　　　　1955　　　　1960　　　　1965

Angola

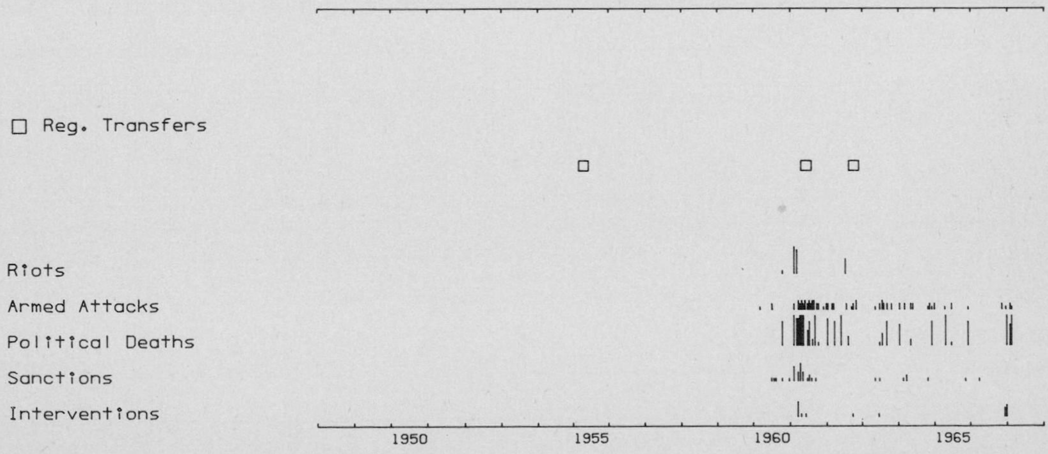

□ Reg. Transfers

Riots
Armed Attacks
Political Deaths
Sanctions
Interventions

1950　　　　1955　　　　1960　　　　1965

155

Argentina

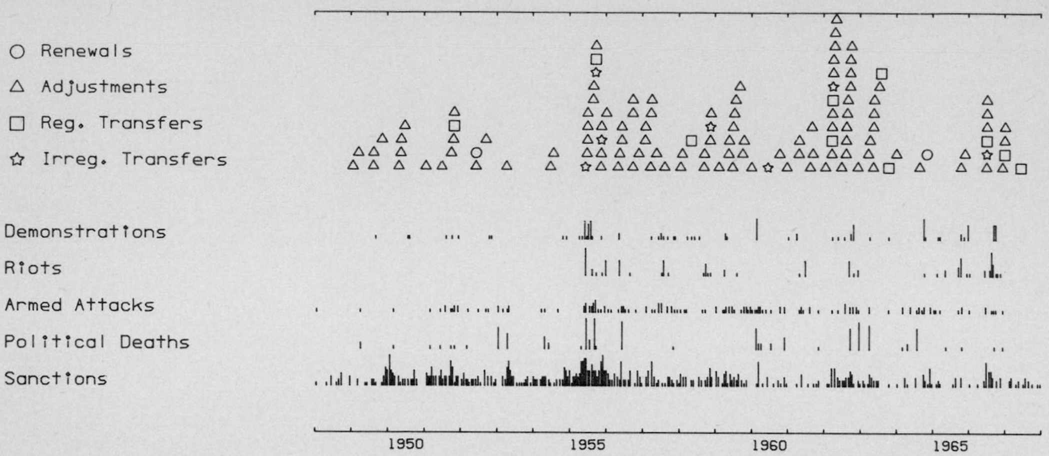

O Renewals
△ Adjustments
□ Reg. Transfers
☆ Irreg. Transfers

Demonstrations
Riots
Armed Attacks
Political Deaths
Sanctions

1950   1955   1960   1965

Australia

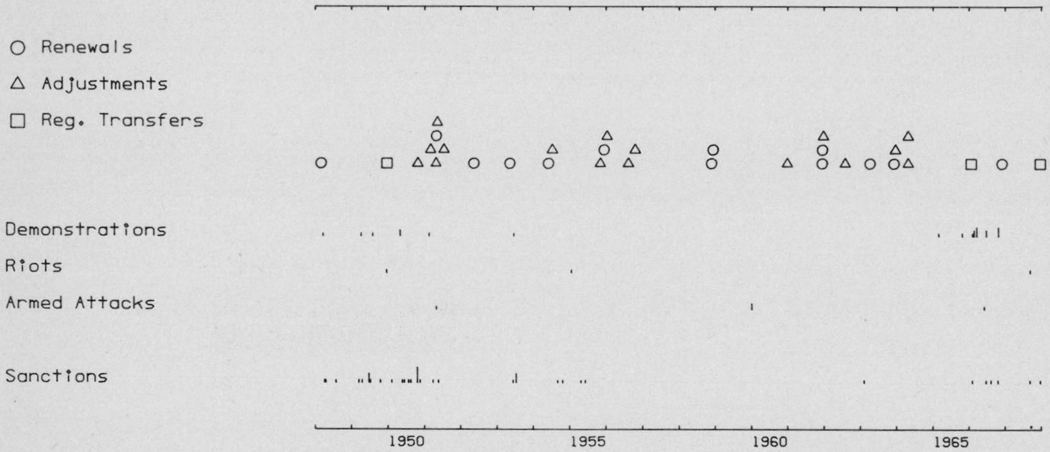

O Renewals
△ Adjustments
□ Reg. Transfers

Demonstrations
Riots
Armed Attacks

Sanctions

1950   1955   1960   1965

Austria

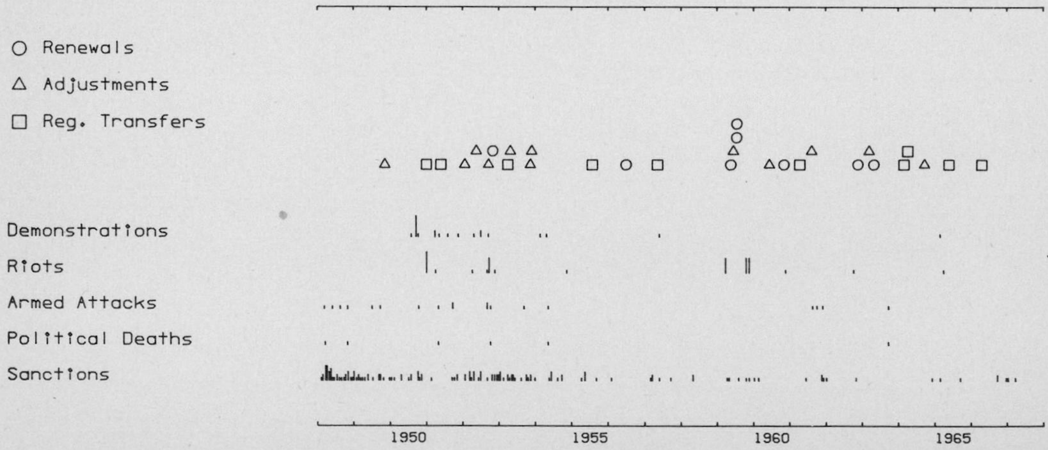

O Renewals
△ Adjustments
□ Reg. Transfers

Demonstrations
Riots
Armed Attacks
Political Deaths
Sanctions

1950   1955   1960   1965

156

Barbados

O Renewals

□ Reg. Transfers

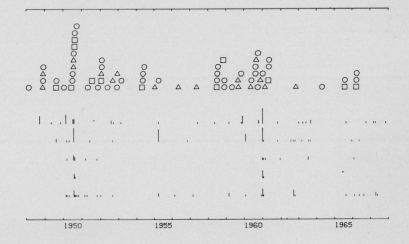

| 1950 | 1955 | 1960 | 1965 |

Belgium

O Renewals
△ Adjustments
□ Reg. Transfers

Demonstrations
Riots
Armed Attacks
Political Deaths
Sanctions

| 1950 | 1955 | 1960 | 1965 |

Bolivia

O Renewals
△ Adjustments
□ Reg. Transfers
☆ Irreg. Transfers

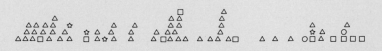

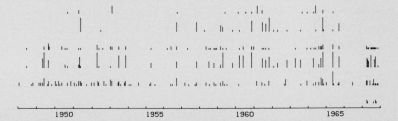

Demonstrations
Riots
Armed Attacks
Political Deaths
Sanctions
Interventions

| 1950 | 1955 | 1960 | 1965 |

Botswana

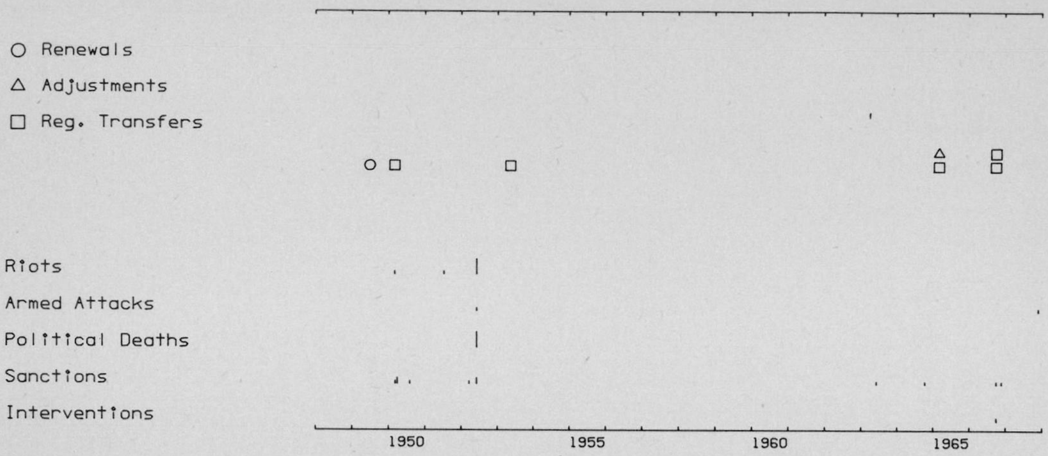

O Renewals
△ Adjustments
□ Reg. Transfers

Riots
Armed Attacks
Political Deaths
Sanctions
Interventions

1950   1955   1960   1965

Brazil

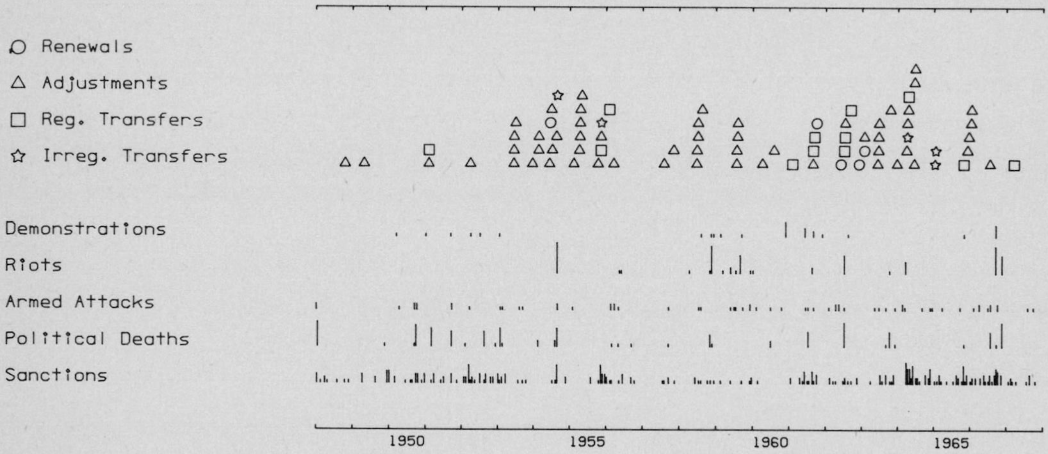

O Renewals
△ Adjustments
□ Reg. Transfers
☆ Irreg. Transfers

Demonstrations
Riots
Armed Attacks
Political Deaths
Sanctions

1950   1955   1960   1965

Bulgaria

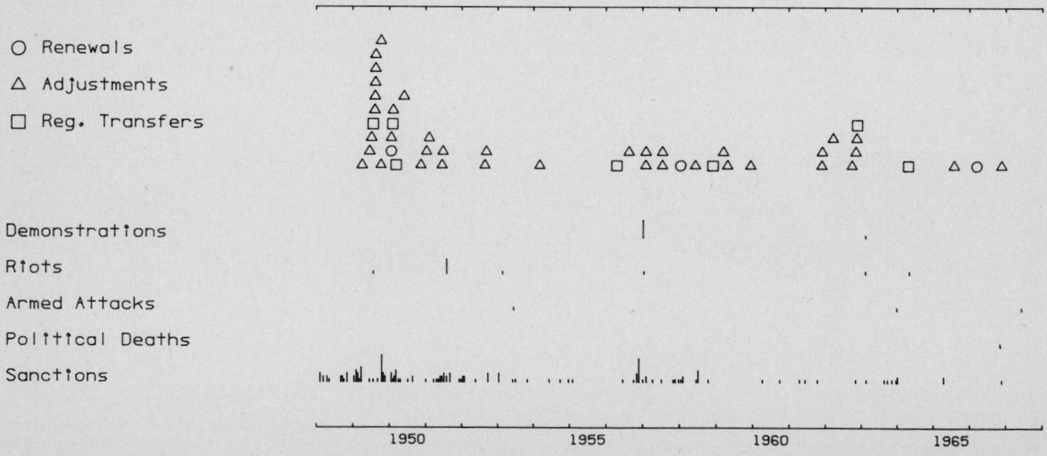

O Renewals
△ Adjustments
□ Reg. Transfers

Demonstrations
Riots
Armed Attacks
Political Deaths
Sanctions

1950   1955   1960   1965

158

Burma

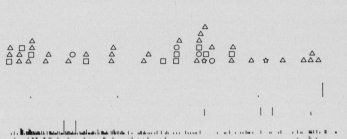

O Renewals
△ Adjustments
□ Reg. Transfers
☆ Irreg. Transfers

Demonstrations
Riots
Armed Attacks
Political Deaths
Sanctions
Interventions

1950   1955   1960   1965

Burundi

△ Adjustments
□ Reg. Transfers
☆ Irreg. Transfers

Armed Attacks
Political Deaths
Sanctions
Interventions

1950   1955   1960   1965

Cambodia

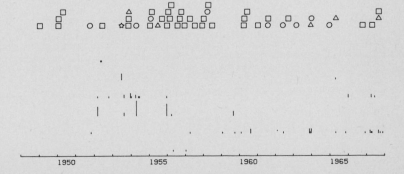

O Renewals
△ Adjustments
□ Reg. Transfers
☆ Irreg. Transfers

Demonstrations
Riots
Armed Attacks
Political Deaths
Sanctions
Interventions

1950   1955   1960   1965

Cameroon

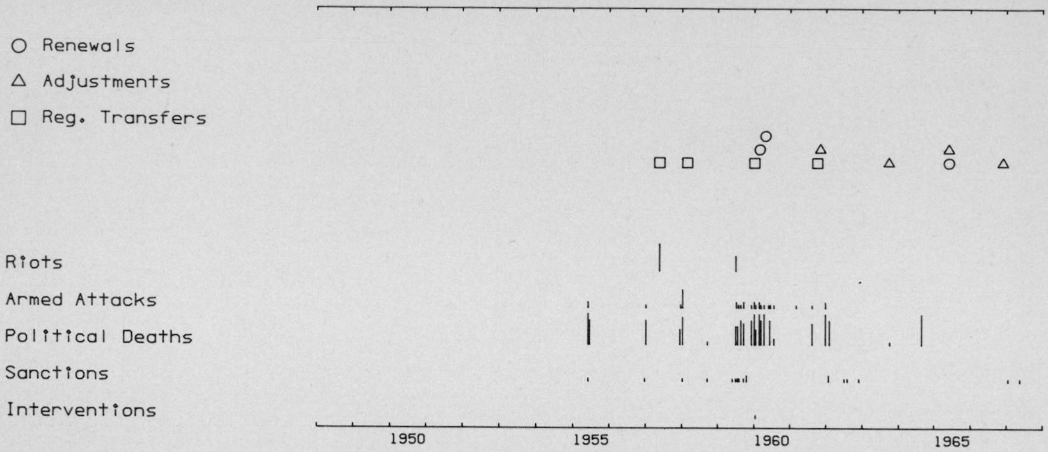

○ Renewals
△ Adjustments
□ Reg. Transfers

Riots
Armed Attacks
Political Deaths
Sanctions
Interventions

1950 1955 1960 1965

Canada

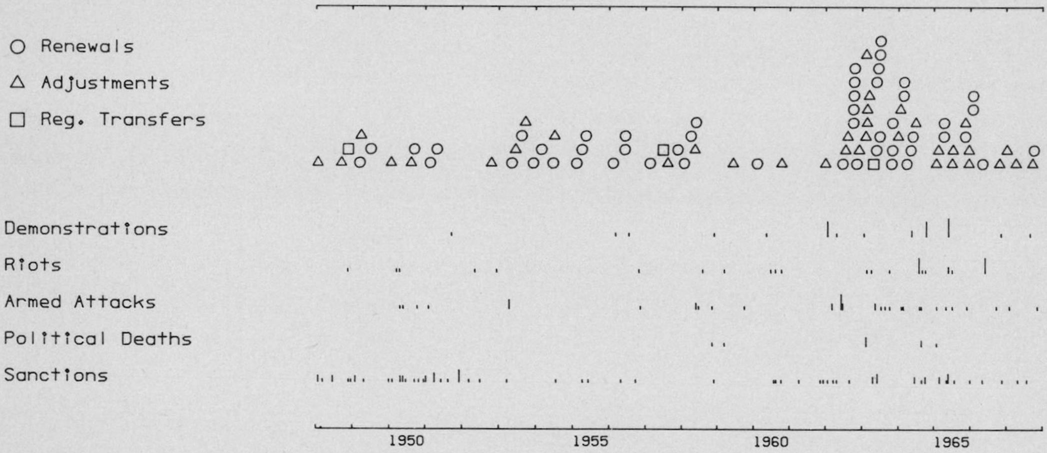

○ Renewals
△ Adjustments
□ Reg. Transfers

Demonstrations
Riots
Armed Attacks
Political Deaths
Sanctions

1950 1955 1960 1965

Central African Republic

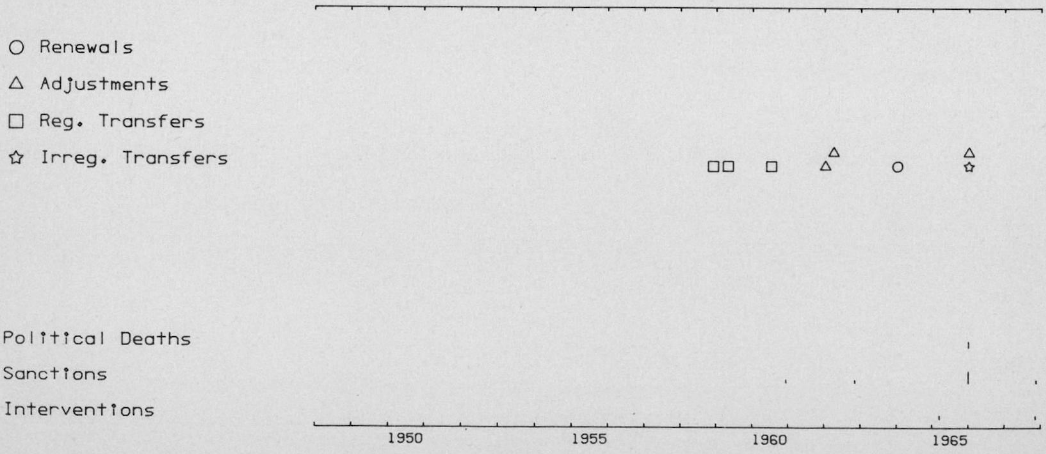

○ Renewals
△ Adjustments
□ Reg. Transfers
☆ Irreg. Transfers

Political Deaths
Sanctions
Interventions

1950 1955 1960 1965

160

Ceylon

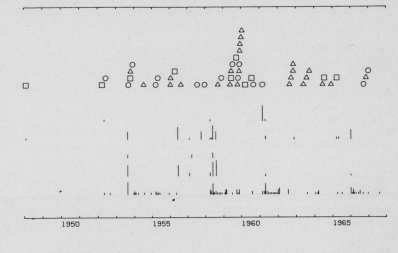

○ Renewals
△ Adjustments
□ Reg. Transfers

Demonstrations
Riots
Armed Attacks
Political Deaths
Sanctions

1950   1955   1960   1965

Chad

○ Renewals
△ Adjustments
□ Reg. Transfers

Demonstrations
Riots
Armed Attacks
Political Deaths
Sanctions
Interventions

1950   1955   1960   1965

Chile

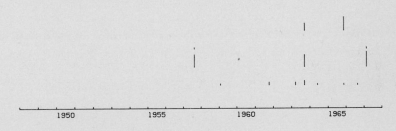

○ Renewals
△ Adjustments
□ Reg. Transfers

Demonstrations
Riots
Armed Attacks
Political Deaths
Sanctions

1950   1955   1960   1965

161

China

○ Renewals
△ Adjustments
□ Reg. Transfers
☆ Irreg. Transfers

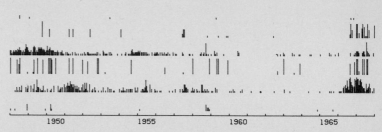

Demonstrations
Riots
Armed Attacks
Political Deaths
Sanctions
Interventions

1950   1955   1960   1965

Colombia

○ Renewals
△ Adjustments
□ Reg. Transfers
☆ Irreg. Transfers

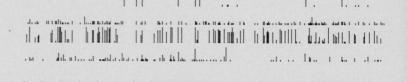

Demonstrations
Riots
Armed Attacks
Political Deaths
Sanctions

1950   1955   1960   1965

Congo – Brazzaville

○ Renewals
△ Adjustments
□ Reg. Transfers
☆ Irreg. Transfers

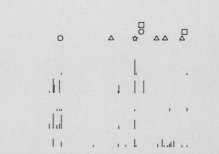

Demonstrations
Riots
Armed Attacks
Political Deaths
Sanctions
Interventions

1950   1955   1960   1965

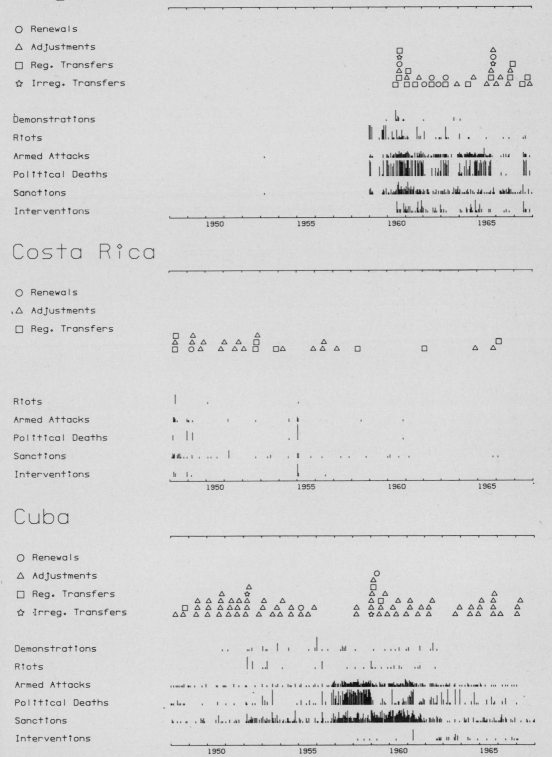

Congo — Kinshasa

O Renewals
△ Adjustments
□ Reg. Transfers
☆ Irreg. Transfers

Demonstrations
Riots
Armed Attacks
Political Deaths
Sanctions
Interventions

1950   1955   1960   1965

Costa Rica

O Renewals
△ Adjustments
□ Reg. Transfers

Riots
Armed Attacks
Political Deaths
Sanctions
Interventions

1950   1955   1960   1965

Cuba

O Renewals
△ Adjustments
□ Reg. Transfers
☆ Irreg. Transfers

Demonstrations
Riots
Armed Attacks
Political Deaths
Sanctions
Interventions

1950   1955   1960   1965

Cyprus

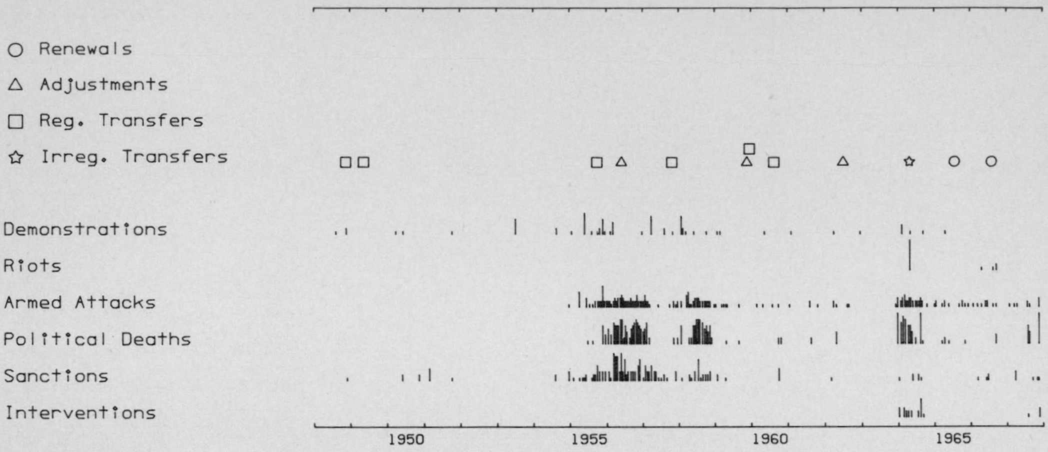

○ Renewals
△ Adjustments
□ Reg. Transfers
☆ Irreg. Transfers

Demonstrations
Riots
Armed Attacks
Political Deaths
Sanctions
Interventions

1950   1955   1960   1965

Czechoslovakia

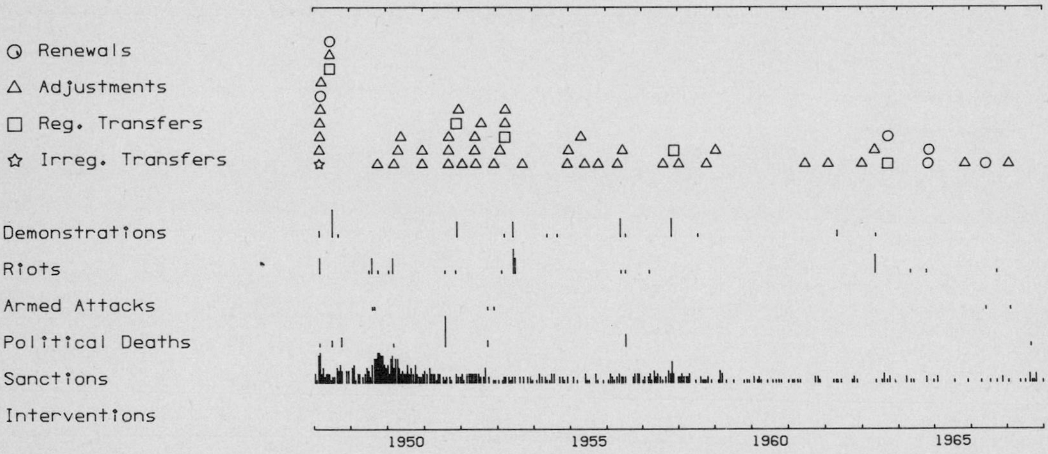

⊙ Renewals
△ Adjustments
□ Reg. Transfers
☆ Irreg. Transfers

Demonstrations
Riots
Armed Attacks
Political Deaths
Sanctions
Interventions

1950   1955   1960   1965

Dahomey

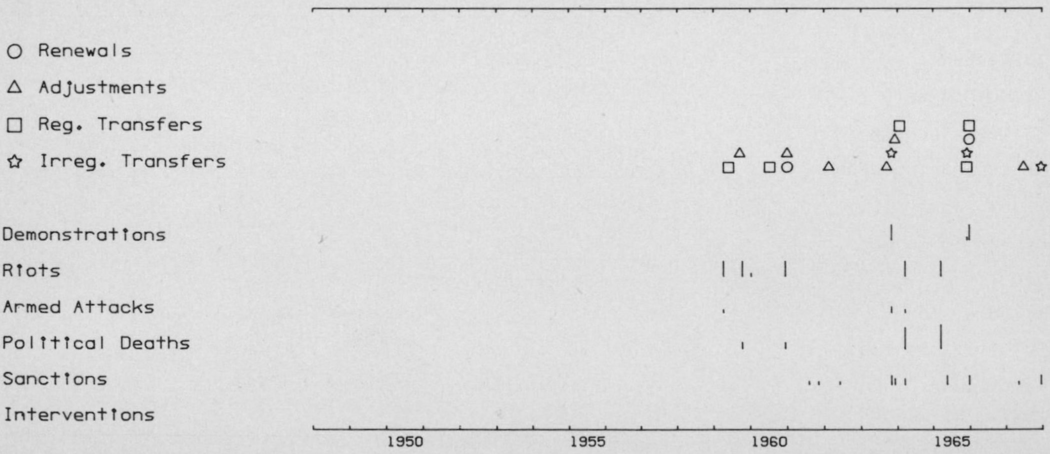

○ Renewals
△ Adjustments
□ Reg. Transfers
☆ Irreg. Transfers

Demonstrations
Riots
Armed Attacks
Political Deaths
Sanctions
Interventions

1950   1955   1960   1965

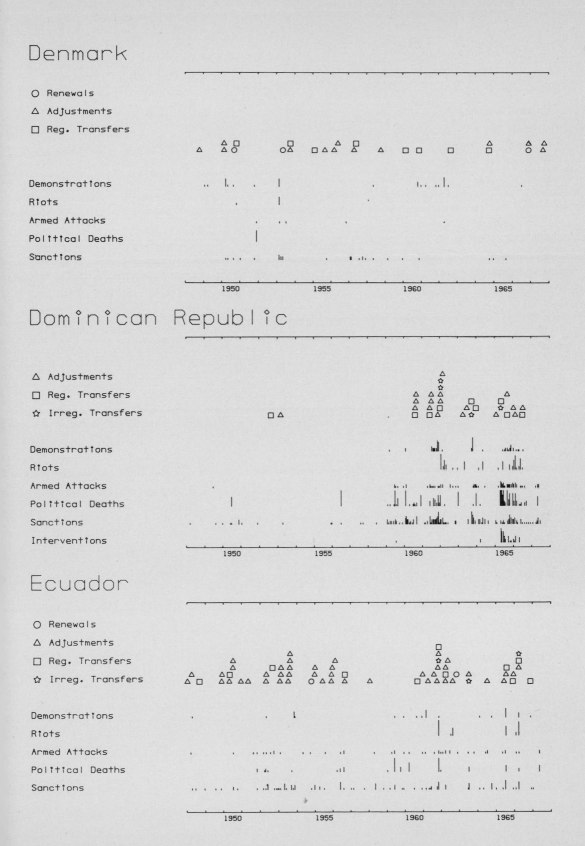

Denmark

O Renewals
△ Adjustments
□ Reg. Transfers

Demonstrations
Riots
Armed Attacks
Political Deaths
Sanctions

1950　　1955　　1960　　1965

Dominican Republic

△ Adjustments
□ Reg. Transfers
☆ Irreg. Transfers

Demonstrations
Riots
Armed Attacks
Political Deaths
Sanctions
Interventions

1950　　1955　　1960　　1965

Ecuador

O Renewals
△ Adjustments
□ Reg. Transfers
☆ Irreg. Transfers

Demonstrations
Riots
Armed Attacks
Political Deaths
Sanctions

1950　　1955　　1960　　1965

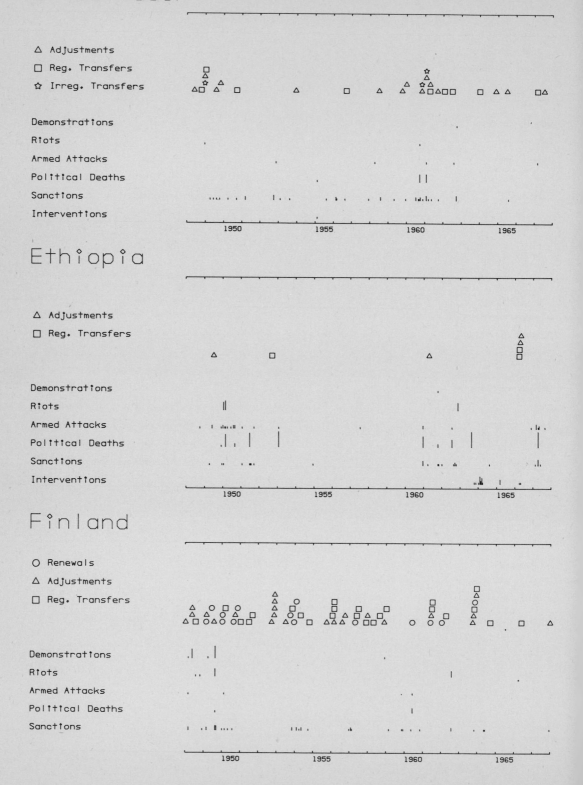

El Salvador

△ Adjustments
□ Reg. Transfers
☆ Irreg. Transfers

Demonstrations
Riots
Armed Attacks
Political Deaths
Sanctions
Interventions

1950   1955   1960   1965

Ethiopia

△ Adjustments
□ Reg. Transfers

Demonstrations
Riots
Armed Attacks
Political Deaths
Sanctions
Interventions

1950   1955   1960   1965

Finland

○ Renewals
△ Adjustments
□ Reg. Transfers

Demonstrations
Riots
Armed Attacks
Political Deaths
Sanctions

1950   1955   1960   1965

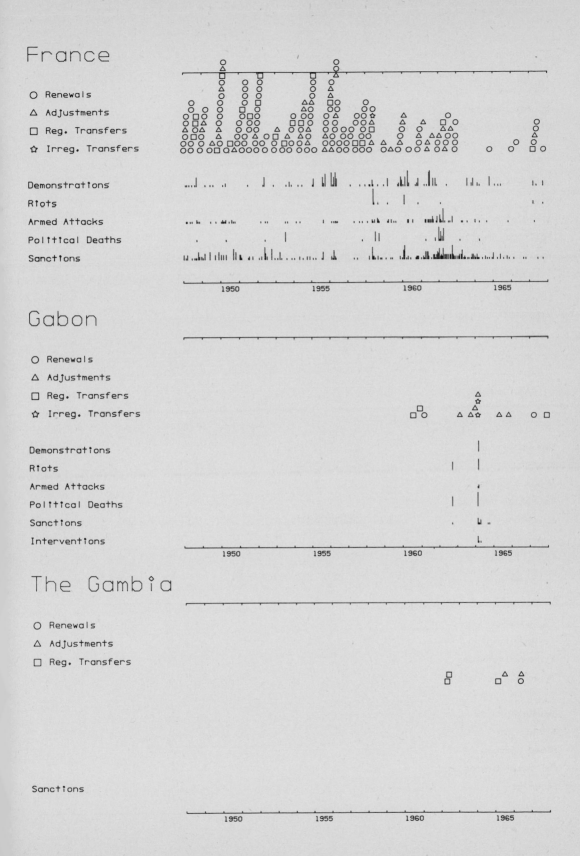

France

O Renewals
△ Adjustments
□ Reg. Transfers
☆ Irreg. Transfers

Demonstrations
Riots
Armed Attacks
Political Deaths
Sanctions

1950   1955   1960   1965

Gabon

O Renewals
△ Adjustments
□ Reg. Transfers
☆ Irreg. Transfers

Demonstrations
Riots
Armed Attacks
Political Deaths
Sanctions
Interventions

1950   1955   1960   1965

The Gambia

O Renewals
△ Adjustments
□ Reg. Transfers

Sanctions

1950   1955   1960   1965

East Germany

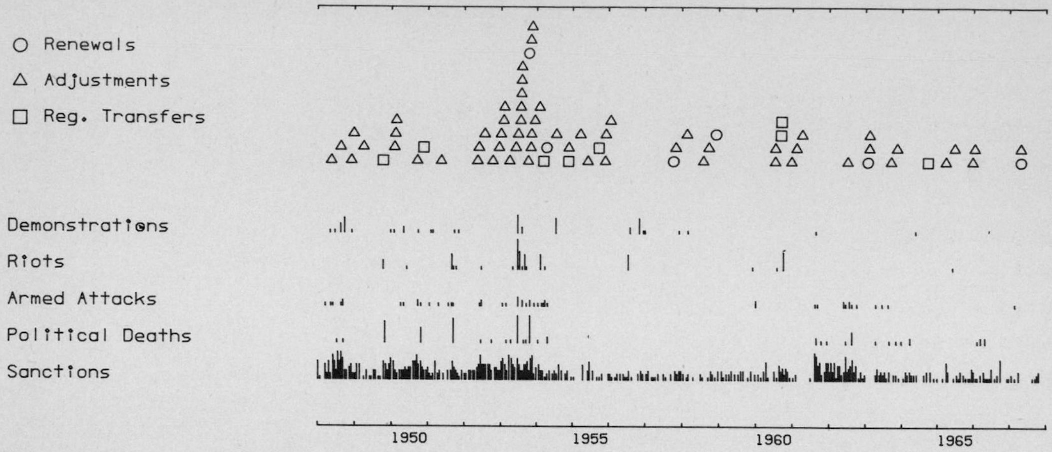

O Renewals
△ Adjustments
☐ Reg. Transfers

Demonstrations
Riots
Armed Attacks
Political Deaths
Sanctions

1950   1955   1960   1965

West Germany

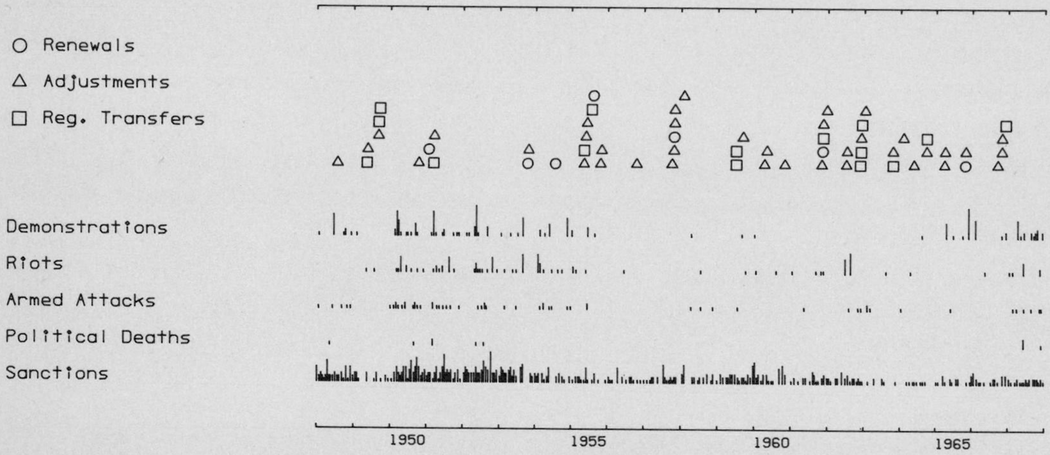

O Renewals
△ Adjustments
☐ Reg. Transfers

Demonstrations
Riots
Armed Attacks
Political Deaths
Sanctions

1950   1955   1960   1965

Ghana

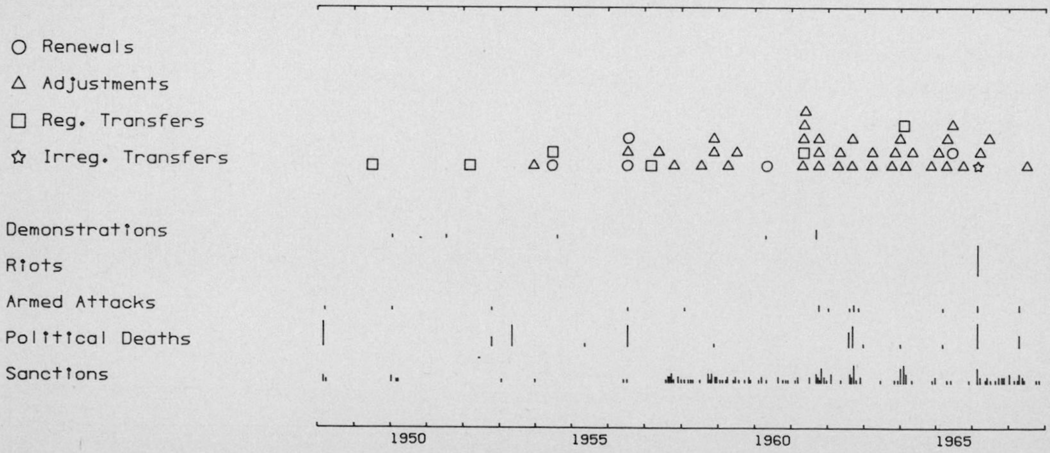

O Renewals
△ Adjustments
☐ Reg. Transfers
☆ Irreg. Transfers

Demonstrations
Riots
Armed Attacks
Political Deaths
Sanctions

1950   1955   1960   1965

168

Greece

○ Renewals
△ Adjustments
□ Reg. Transfers
☆ Irreg. Transfers

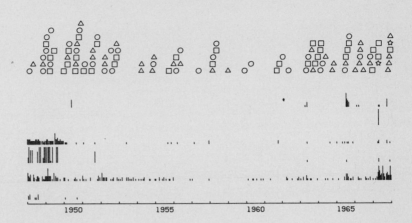

Demonstrations
Riots
Armed Attacks
Political Deaths
Sanctions
Interventions

1950   1955   1960   1965

Guatemala

△ Adjustments
□ Reg. Transfers
☆ Irreg. Transfers

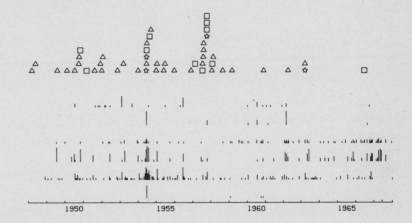

Demonstrations
Riots
Armed Attacks
Political Deaths
Sanctions
Interventions

1950   1955   1960   1965

Guinea

○ Renewals
△ Adjustments
□ Reg. Transfers

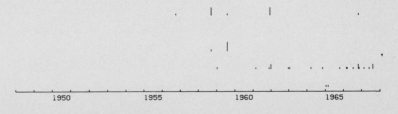

Riots

Political Deaths
Sanctions
Interventions

1950   1955   1960   1965

169

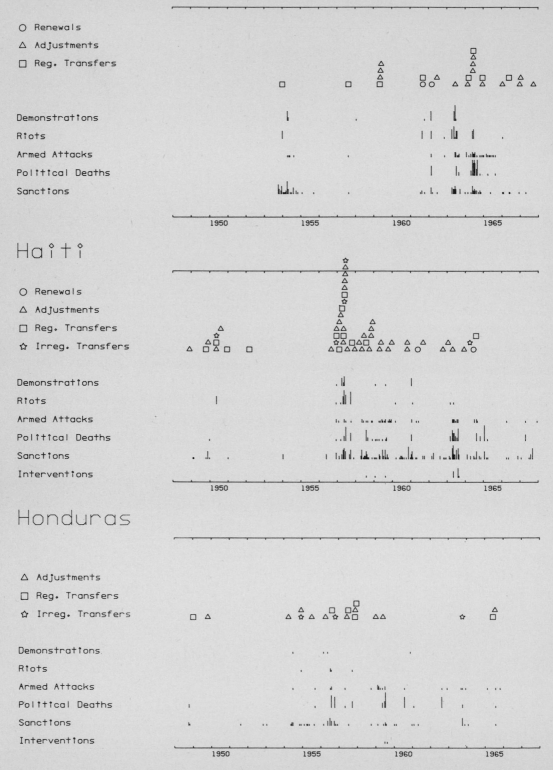

Guyana

O Renewals
△ Adjustments
□ Reg. Transfers

Demonstrations
Riots
Armed Attacks
Political Deaths
Sanctions

1950   1955   1960   1965

Haiti

O Renewals
△ Adjustments
□ Reg. Transfers
☆ Irreg. Transfers

Demonstrations
Riots
Armed Attacks
Political Deaths
Sanctions
Interventions

1950   1955   1960   1965

Honduras

△ Adjustments
□ Reg. Transfers
☆ Irreg. Transfers

Demonstrations
Riots
Armed Attacks
Political Deaths
Sanctions
Interventions

1950   1955   1960   1965

Hong Kong

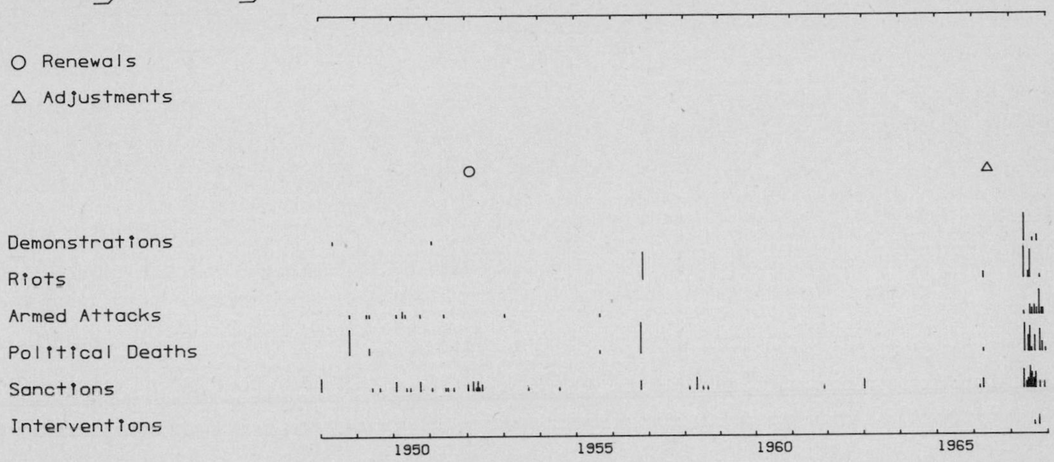

O Renewals
△ Adjustments

O

△

Demonstrations
Riots
Armed Attacks
Political Deaths
Sanctions
Interventions

1950   1955   1960   1965

Hungary

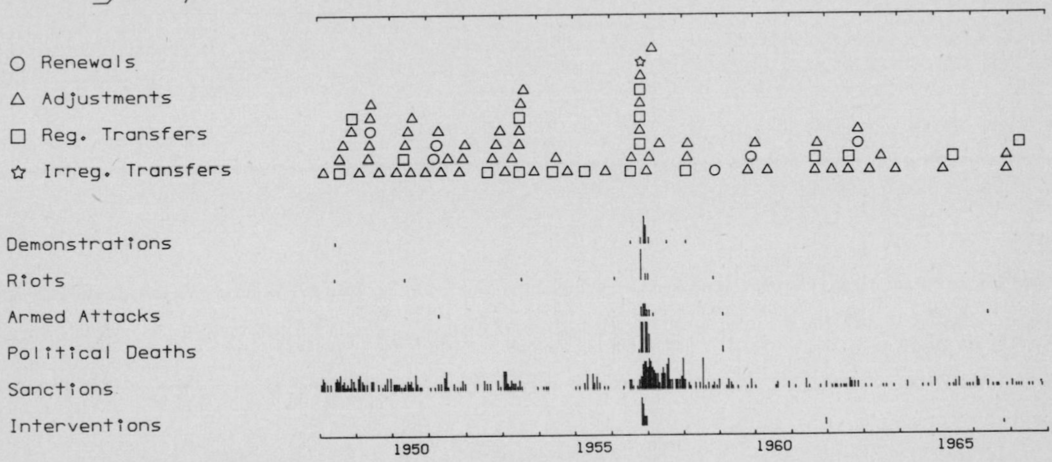

O Renewals
△ Adjustments
☐ Reg. Transfers
☆ Irreg. Transfers

Demonstrations
Riots
Armed Attacks
Political Deaths
Sanctions
Interventions

1950   1955   1960   1965

Iceland

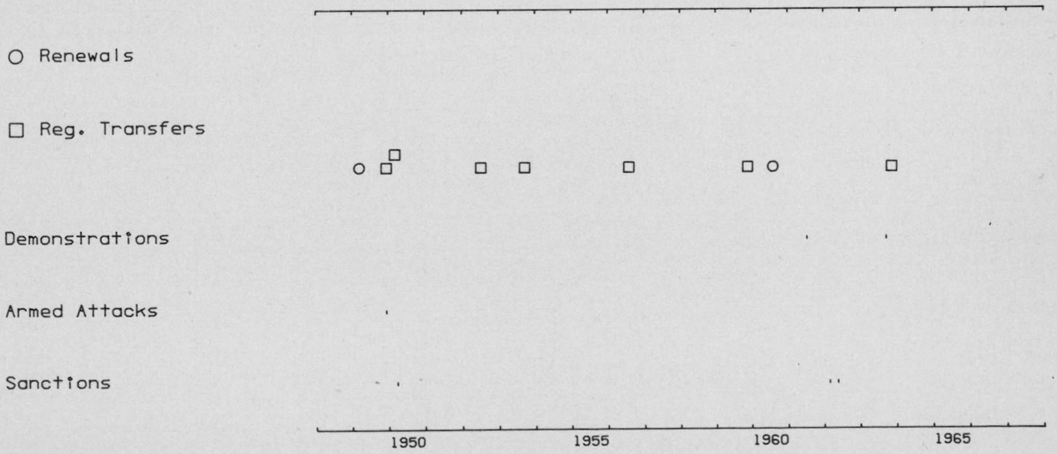

O Renewals

☐ Reg. Transfers

Demonstrations

Armed Attacks

Sanctions

1950   1955   1960   1965

171

India

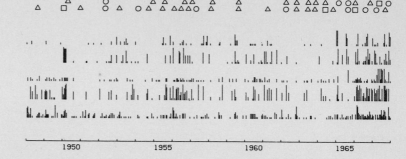

O Renewals
△ Adjustments
□ Reg. Transfers

Demonstrations
Riots
Armed Attacks
Political Deaths
Sanctions

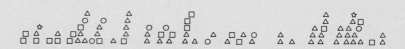

1950   1955   1960   1965

Indonesia

O Renewals
△ Adjustments
□ Reg. Transfers
☆ Irreg. Transfers

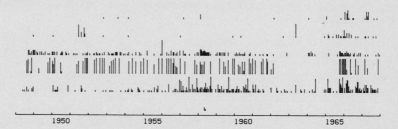

Demonstrations
Riots
Armed Attacks
Political Deaths
Sanctions
Interventions

1950   1955   1960   1965

Iran

O Renewals
△ Adjustments
□ Reg. Transfers
☆ Irreg. Transfers

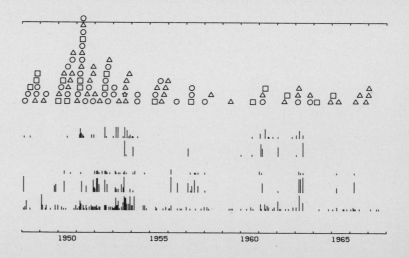

Demonstrations
Riots
Armed Attacks
Political Deaths
Sanctions

1950   1955   1960   1965

172

Iraq

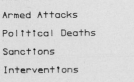

O Renewals
△ Adjustments
□ Reg. Transfers
☆ Irreg. Transfers

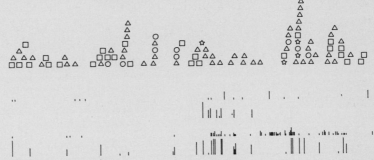

Demonstrations
Riots
Armed Attacks
Political Deaths
Sanctions
Interventions

1950 1955 1960 1965

Ireland

O Renewals
△ Adjustments
□ Reg. Transfers

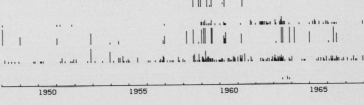

Demonstrations
Riots
Armed Attacks
Political Deaths
Sanctions

1950 1955 1960 1965

Israel

O Renewals
△ Adjustments
□ Reg. Transfers

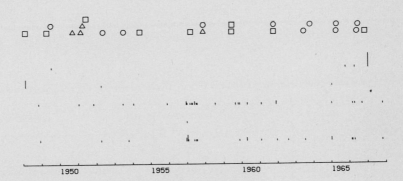

Demonstrations
Riots
Armed Attacks
Political Deaths
Sanctions

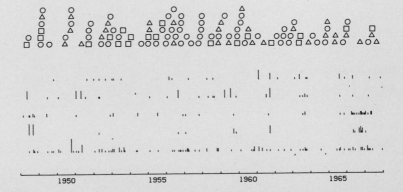

1950 1955 1960 1965

Italy

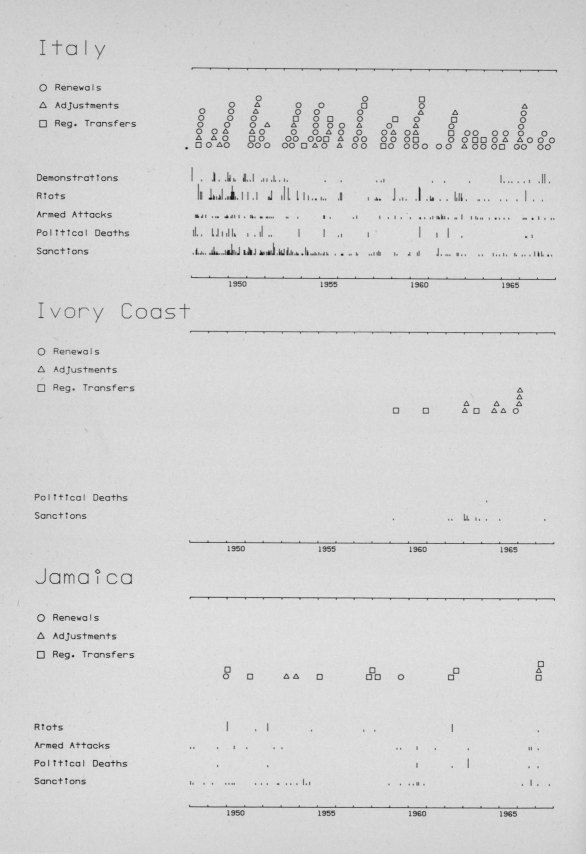

○ Renewals
△ Adjustments
□ Reg. Transfers

Demonstrations
Riots
Armed Attacks
Political Deaths
Sanctions

1950   1955   1960   1965

Ivory Coast

○ Renewals
△ Adjustments
□ Reg. Transfers

Political Deaths
Sanctions

1950   1955   1960   1965

Jamaica

○ Renewals
△ Adjustments
□ Reg. Transfers

Riots
Armed Attacks
Political Deaths
Sanctions

1950   1955   1960   1965

Japan

○ Renewals
△ Adjustments
□ Reg. Transfers

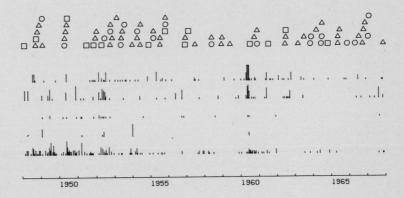

Demonstrations
Riots
Armed Attacks
Political Deaths
Sanctions

1950   1955   1960   1965

Jordan

○ Renewals
△ Adjustments
□ Reg. Transfers

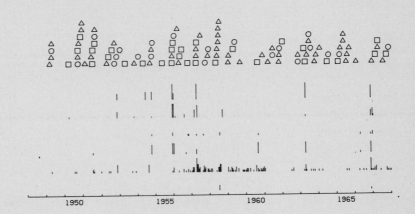

Demonstrations
Riots
Armed Attacks
Political Deaths
Sanctions
Interventions

1950   1955   1960   1965

Kenya

○ Renewals
△ Adjustments
□ Reg. Transfers

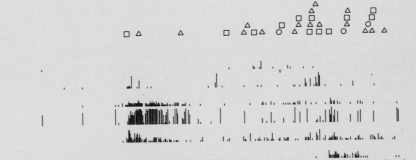

Demonstrations
Riots
Armed Attacks
Political Deaths
Sanctions
Interventions

1950   1955   1960   1965

North Korea

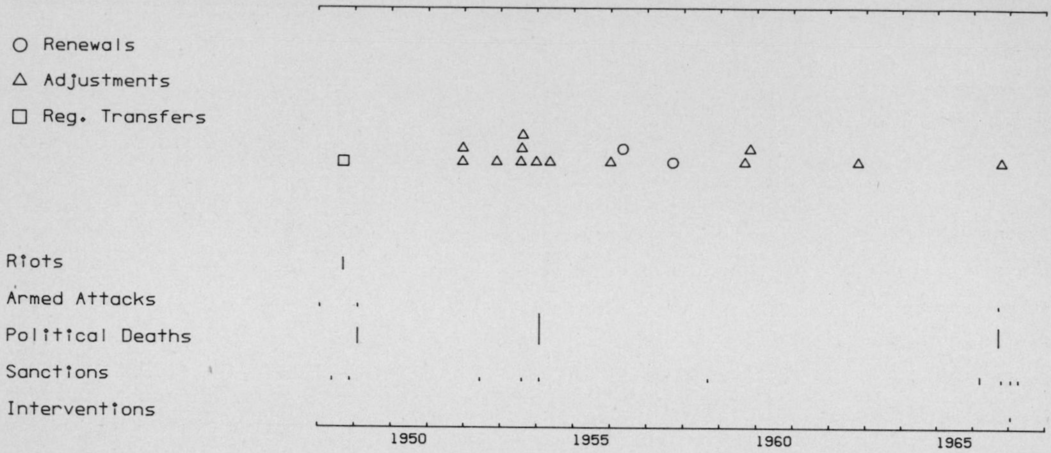

O Renewals
△ Adjustments
□ Reg. Transfers

Riots
Armed Attacks
Political Deaths
Sanctions
Interventions

1950   1955   1960   1965

South Korea

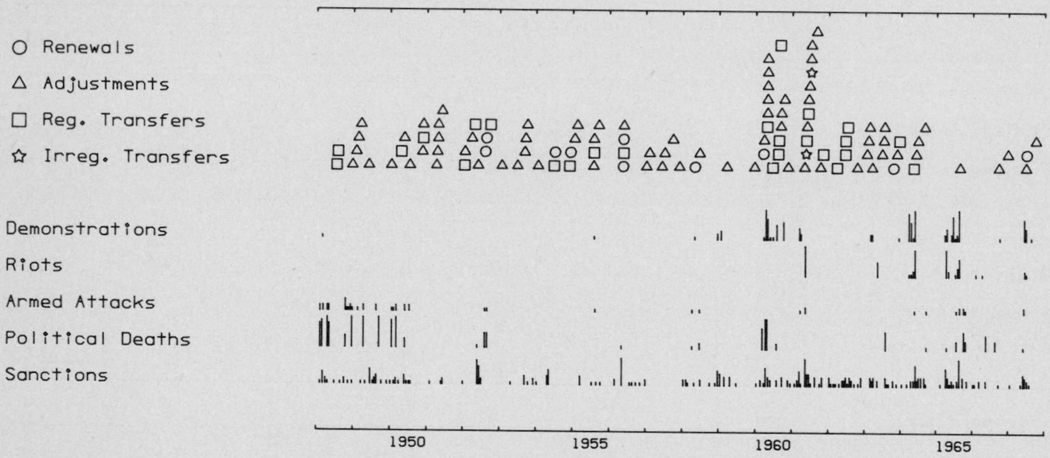

O Renewals
△ Adjustments
□ Reg. Transfers
☆ Irreg. Transfers

Demonstrations
Riots
Armed Attacks
Political Deaths
Sanctions

1950   1955   1960   1965

Kuwait

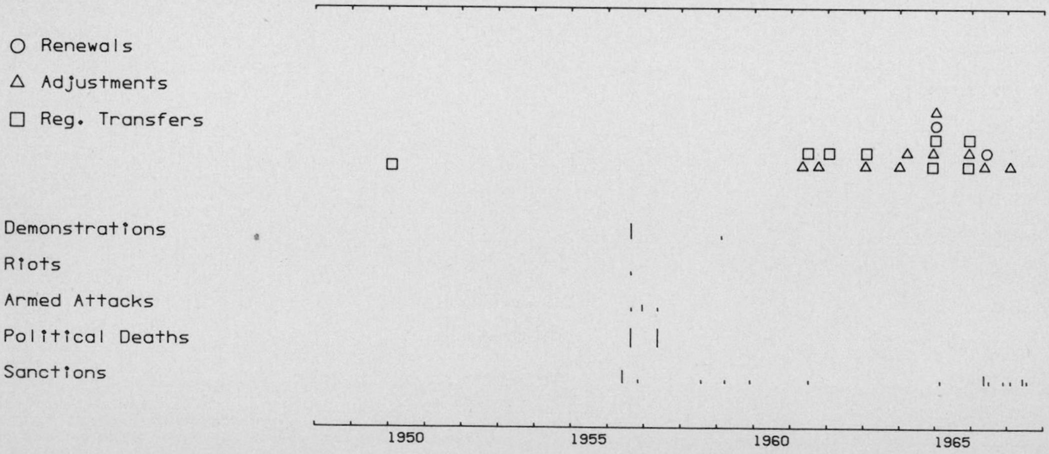

O Renewals
△ Adjustments
□ Reg. Transfers

Demonstrations
Riots
Armed Attacks
Political Deaths
Sanctions

1950   1955   1960   1965

Laos

O Renewals
△ Adjustments
□ Reg. Transfers
☆ Irreg. Transfers

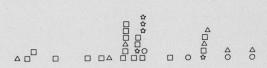

Riots
Armed Attacks
Political Deaths
Sanctions
Interventions

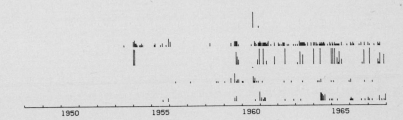

1950   1955   1960   1965

Lebanon

O Renewals
△ Adjustments
□ Reg. Transfers

Demonstrations
Riots
Armed Attacks
Political Deaths
Sanctions
Interventions

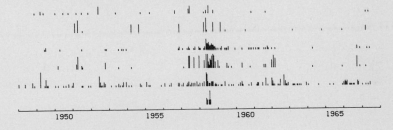

1950   1955   1960   1965

Lesotho

O Renewals
△ Adjustments
□ Reg. Transfers

Demonstrations
Riots
Armed Attacks
Political Deaths
Sanctions

1950   1955   1960   1965

Liberia

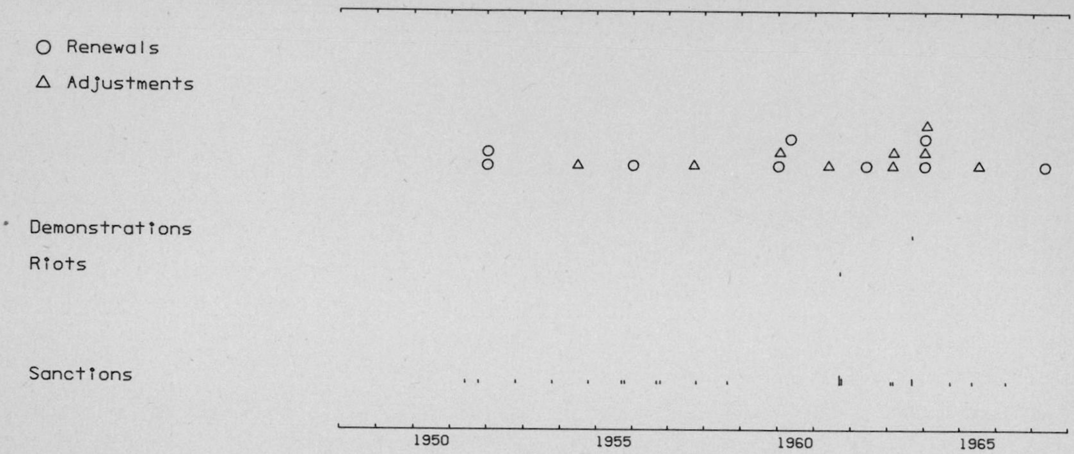

O Renewals
△ Adjustments

Demonstrations
Riots

Sanctions

1950   1955   1960   1965

Libya

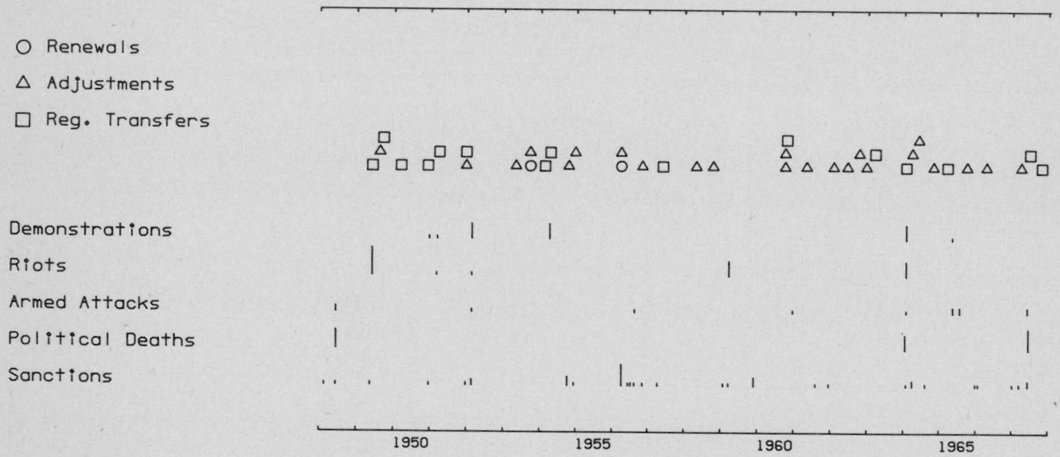

O Renewals
△ Adjustments
□ Reg. Transfers

Demonstrations
Riots
Armed Attacks
Political Deaths
Sanctions

1950   1955   1960   1965

Luxembourg

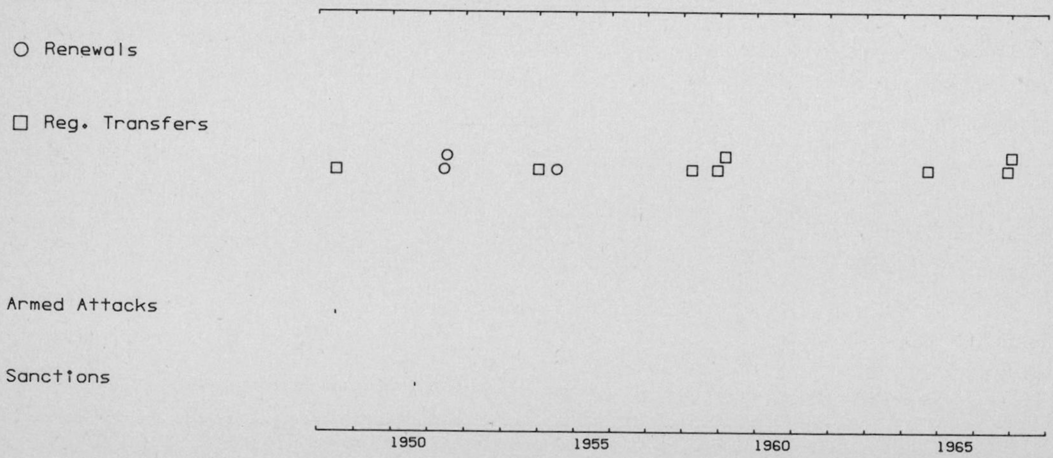

O Renewals

□ Reg. Transfers

Armed Attacks

Sanctions

1950   1955   1960   1965

Malagasy Republic

O Renewals
△ Adjustments
□ Reg. Transfers

Political Deaths

Sanctions

1950   1955   1960   1965

Malawi

O Renewals
△ Adjustments
□ Reg. Transfers

Demonstrations
Riots
Armed Attacks
Political Deaths
Sanctions
Interventions

1950   1955   1960   1965

Malaysia

O Renewals
△ Adjustments
□ Reg. Transfers

Demonstrations
Riots
Armed Attacks
Political Deaths
Sanctions
Interventions

1950   1955   1960   1965

179

Maldive Islands

☐ Reg. Transfers
☆ Irreg. Transfers

Demonstrations
Riots
Armed Attacks
Political Deaths
Sanctions
Interventions

1950   1955   1960   1965

Mali

△ Adjustments
☐ Reg. Transfers

Demonstrations
Riots
Armed Attacks
Political Deaths
Sanctions
Interventions

1950   1955   1960   1965

Malta

O Renewals

☐ Reg. Transfers

Demonstrations
Riots
Armed Attacks

Sanctions

1950   1955   1960   1965

180

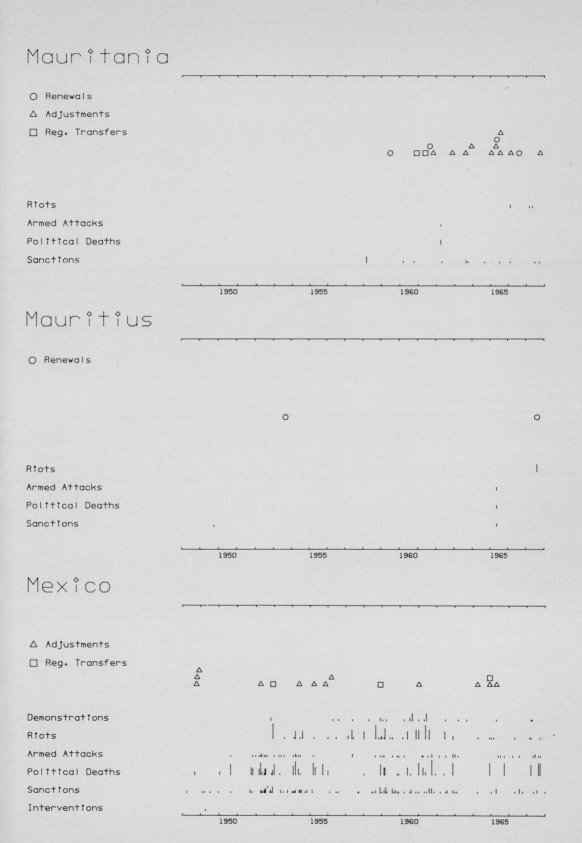

Mauritania

○ Renewals
△ Adjustments
□ Reg. Transfers

Riots
Armed Attacks
Political Deaths
Sanctions

1950   1955   1960   1965

Mauritius

○ Renewals

Riots
Armed Attacks
Political Deaths
Sanctions

1950   1955   1960   1965

Mexico

△ Adjustments
□ Reg. Transfers

Demonstrations
Riots
Armed Attacks
Political Deaths
Sanctions
Interventions

1950   1955   1960   1965

Mongolia

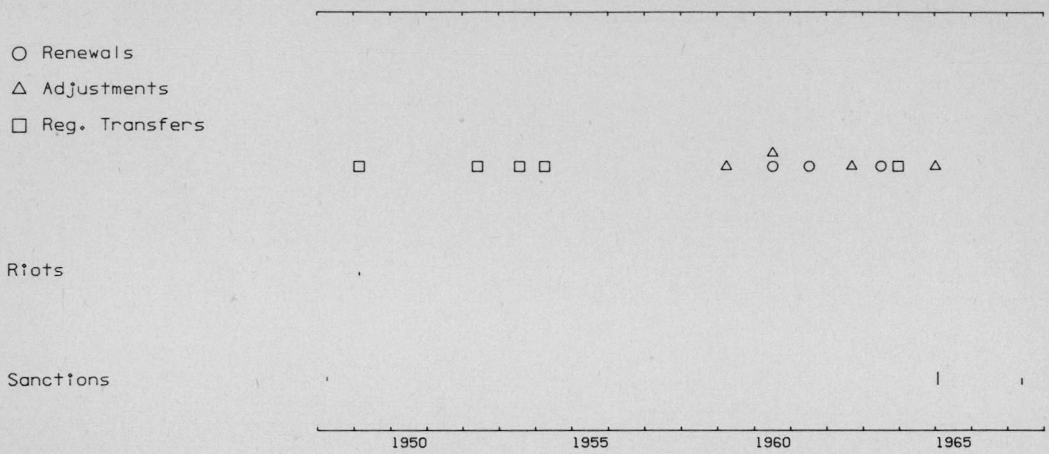

○ Renewals
△ Adjustments
□ Reg. Transfers

Riots

Sanctions

	1950	1955	1960	1965

Morocco

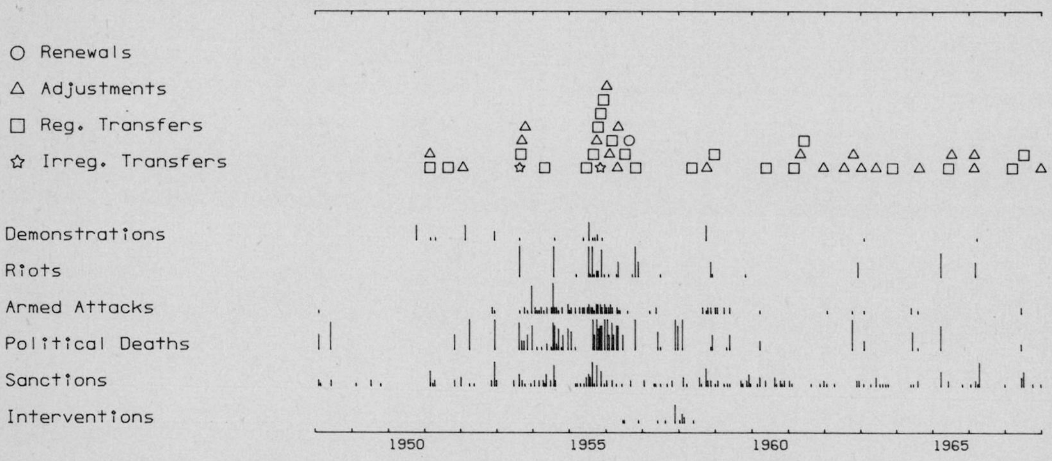

○ Renewals
△ Adjustments
□ Reg. Transfers
☆ Irreg. Transfers

Demonstrations
Riots
Armed Attacks
Political Deaths
Sanctions
Interventions

	1950	1955	1960	1965

Mozambique

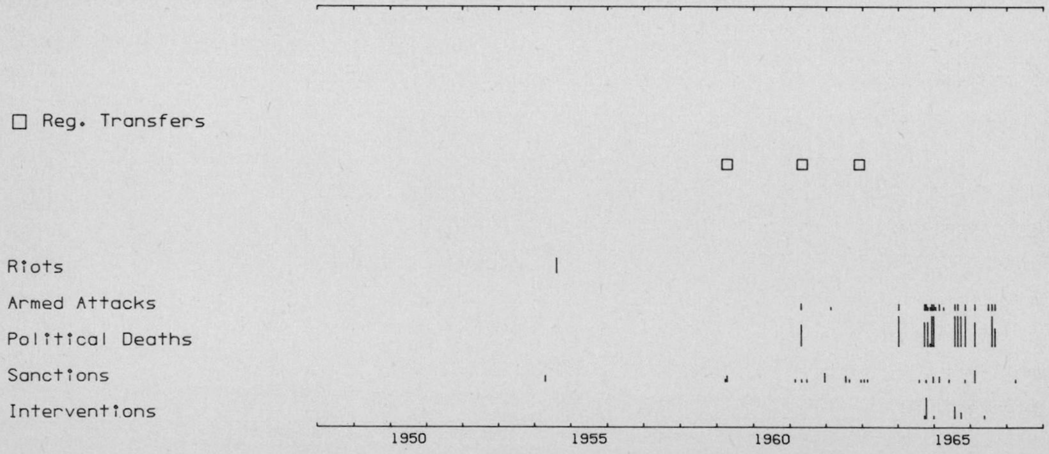

□ Reg. Transfers

Riots
Armed Attacks
Political Deaths
Sanctions
Interventions

	1950	1955	1960	1965

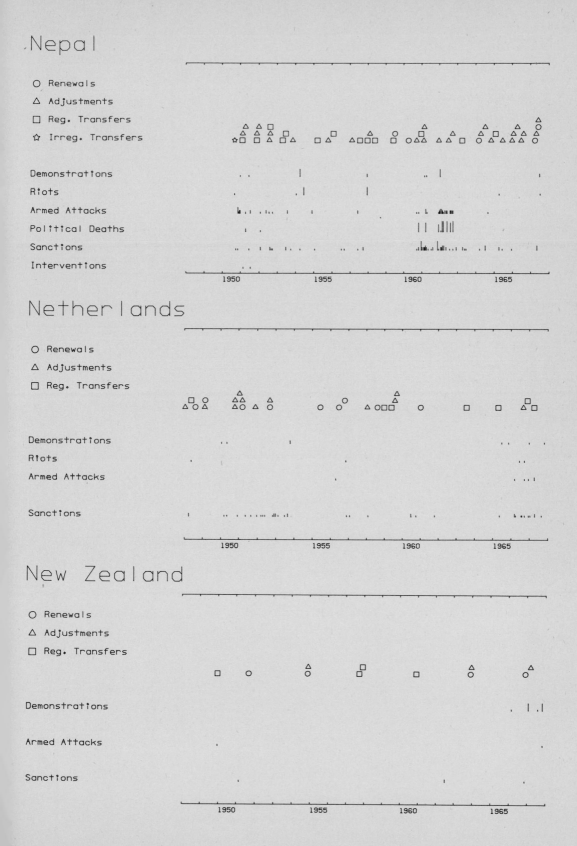

Nepal

O Renewals
△ Adjustments
□ Reg. Transfers
☆ Irreg. Transfers

Demonstrations
Riots
Armed Attacks
Political Deaths
Sanctions
Interventions

1950   1955   1960   1965

Netherlands

O Renewals
△ Adjustments
□ Reg. Transfers

Demonstrations
Riots
Armed Attacks

Sanctions

1950   1955   1960   1965

New Zealand

O Renewals
△ Adjustments
□ Reg. Transfers

Demonstrations

Armed Attacks

Sanctions

1950   1955   1960   1965

Nicaragua

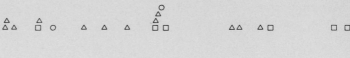

○ Renewals
△ Adjustments
□ Reg. Transfers

Demonstrations
Riots
Armed Attacks
Political Deaths
Sanctions
Interventions

1950   1955   1960   1965

Niger

△ Adjustments
□ Reg. Transfers

Armed Attacks
Political Deaths
Sanctions

1950   1955   1960   1965

Nigeria

○ Renewals
△ Adjustments
□ Reg. Transfers
☆ Irreg. Transfers

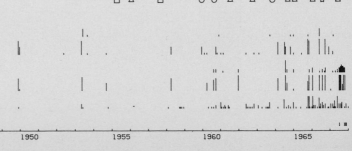

Demonstrations
Riots
Armed Attacks
Political Deaths
Sanctions
Interventions

1950   1955   1960   1965

Norway

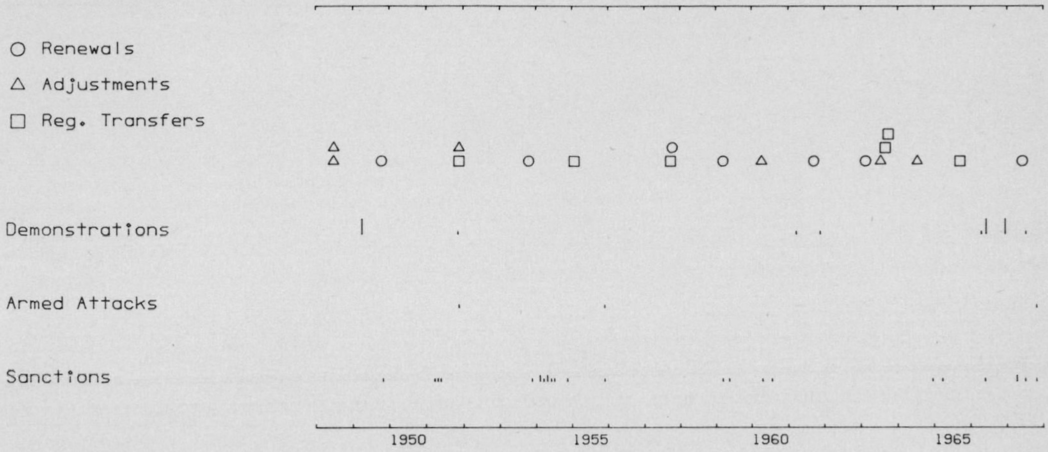

○ Renewals
△ Adjustments
□ Reg. Transfers

Demonstrations

Armed Attacks

Sanctions

1950   1955   1960   1965

Pakistan

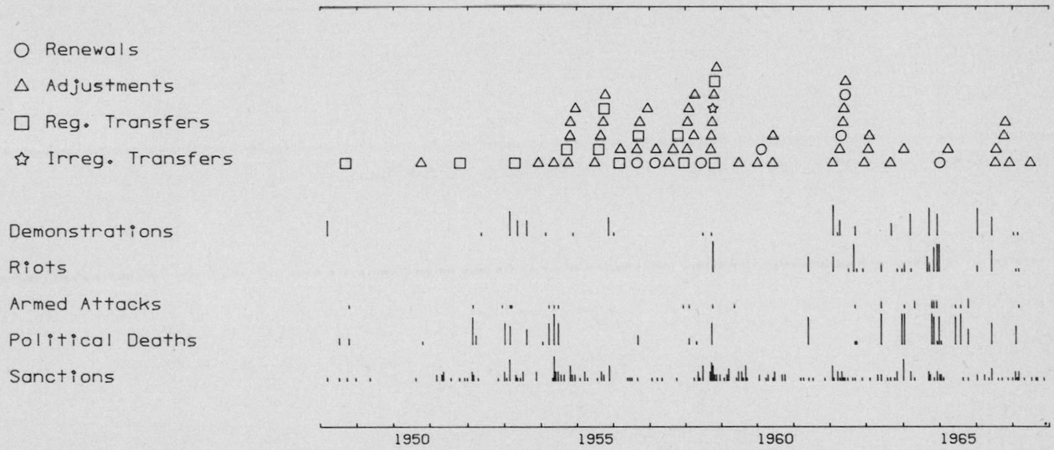

○ Renewals
△ Adjustments
□ Reg. Transfers
☆ Irreg. Transfers

Demonstrations
Riots
Armed Attacks
Political Deaths
Sanctions

1950   1955   1960   1965

Panama

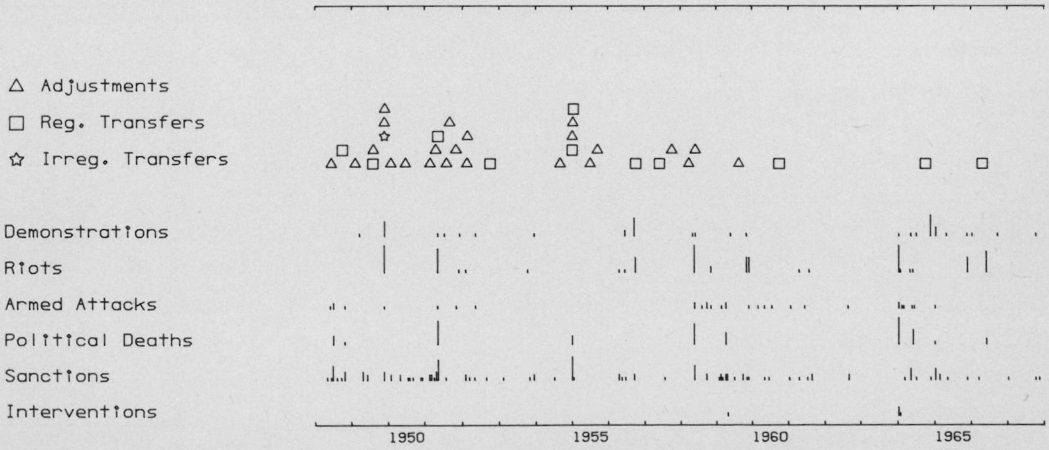

△ Adjustments
□ Reg. Transfers
☆ Irreg. Transfers

Demonstrations
Riots
Armed Attacks
Political Deaths
Sanctions
Interventions

1950   1955   1960   1965

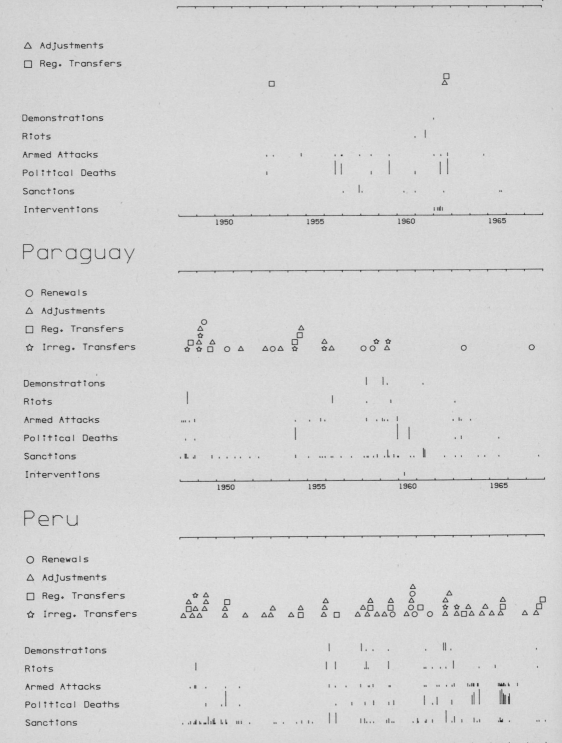

Papua / New Guinea

△ Adjustments
□ Reg. Transfers

Demonstrations
Riots
Armed Attacks
Political Deaths
Sanctions
Interventions

1950   1955   1960   1965

Paraguay

○ Renewals
△ Adjustments
□ Reg. Transfers
☆ Irreg. Transfers

Demonstrations
Riots
Armed Attacks
Political Deaths
Sanctions
Interventions

1950   1955   1960   1965

Peru

○ Renewals
△ Adjustments
□ Reg. Transfers
☆ Irreg. Transfers

Demonstrations
Riots
Armed Attacks
Political Deaths
Sanctions

1950   1955   1960   1965

186

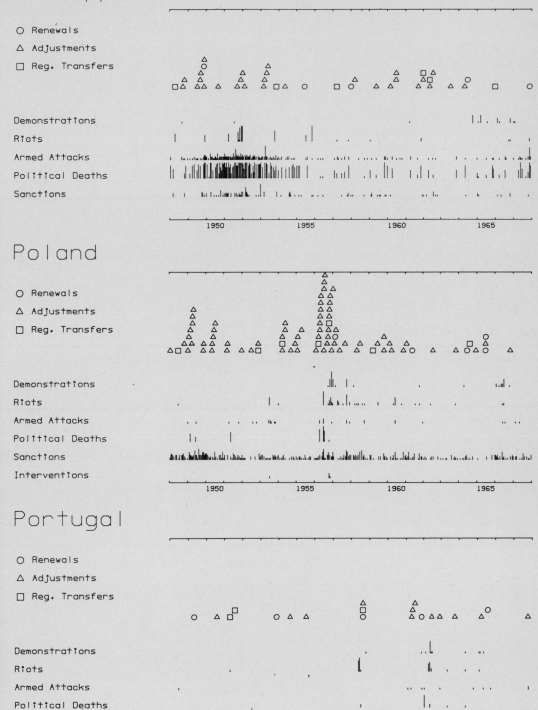

Philippines

○ Renewals
△ Adjustments
□ Reg. Transfers

Demonstrations
Riots
Armed Attacks
Political Deaths
Sanctions

1950　1955　1960　1965

Poland

○ Renewals
△ Adjustments
□ Reg. Transfers

Demonstrations
Riots
Armed Attacks
Political Deaths
Sanctions
Interventions

1950　1955　1960　1965

Portugal

○ Renewals
△ Adjustments
□ Reg. Transfers

Demonstrations
Riots
Armed Attacks
Political Deaths
Sanctions
Interventions

1950　1955　1960　1965

Puerto Rico

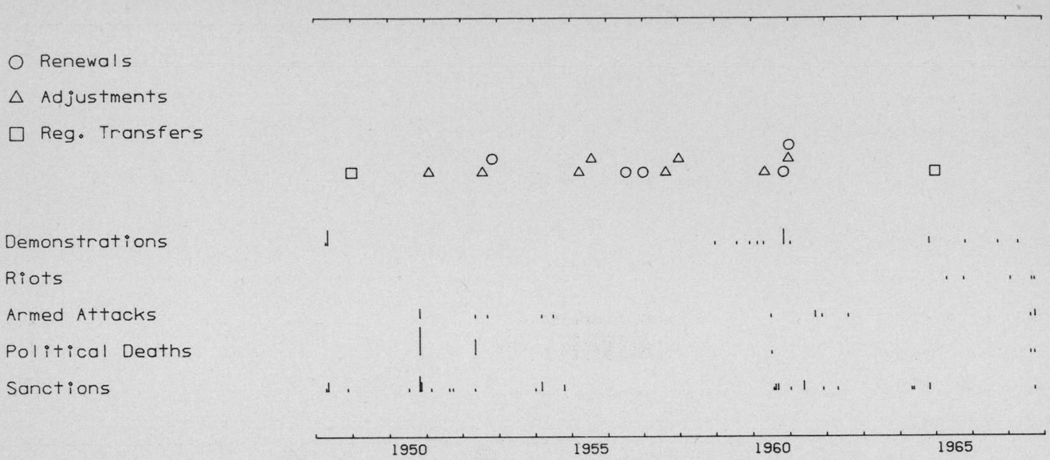

○ Renewals
△ Adjustments
□ Reg. Transfers

Demonstrations
Riots
Armed Attacks
Political Deaths
Sanctions

1950   1955   1960   1965

Rhodesia

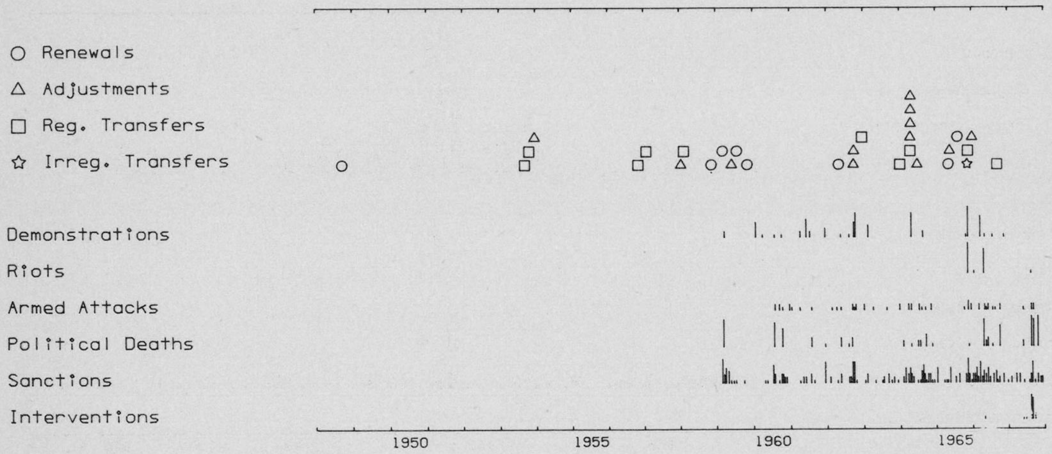

○ Renewals
△ Adjustments
□ Reg. Transfers
☆ Irreg. Transfers

Demonstrations
Riots
Armed Attacks
Political Deaths
Sanctions
Interventions

1950   1955   1960   1965

Romania

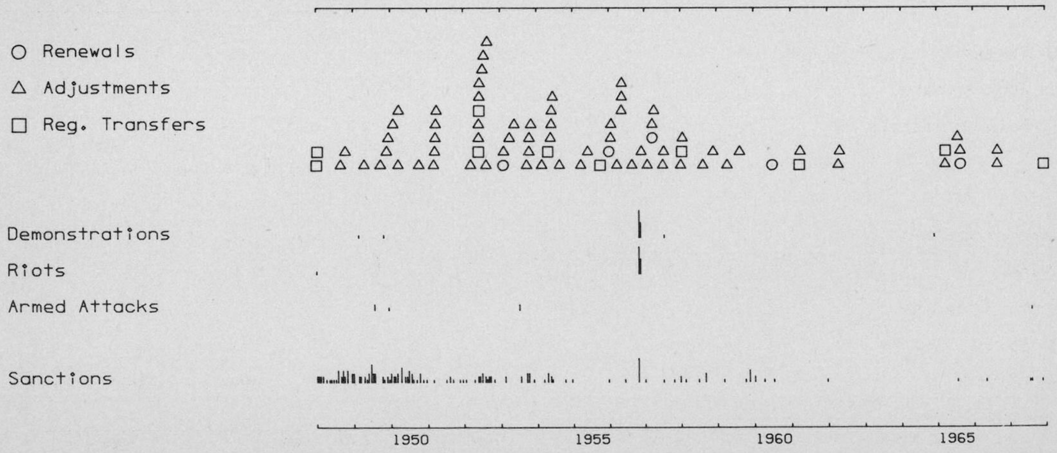

○ Renewals
△ Adjustments
□ Reg. Transfers

Demonstrations
Riots
Armed Attacks

Sanctions

1950   1955   1960   1965

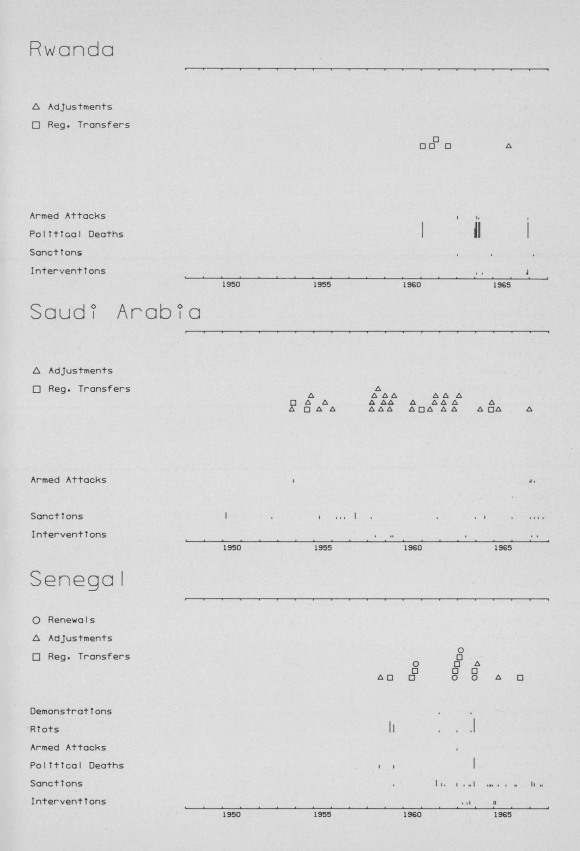

Rwanda

△ Adjustments
□ Reg. Transfers

Armed Attacks
Political Deaths
Sanctions
Interventions

1950　　　　1955　　　　1960　　　　1965

Saudi Arabia

△ Adjustments
□ Reg. Transfers

Armed Attacks

Sanctions
Interventions

1950　　　　1955　　　　1960　　　　1965

Senegal

○ Renewals
△ Adjustments
□ Reg. Transfers

Demonstrations
Riots
Armed Attacks
Political Deaths
Sanctions
Interventions

1950　　　　1955　　　　1960　　　　1965

Sierra Leone

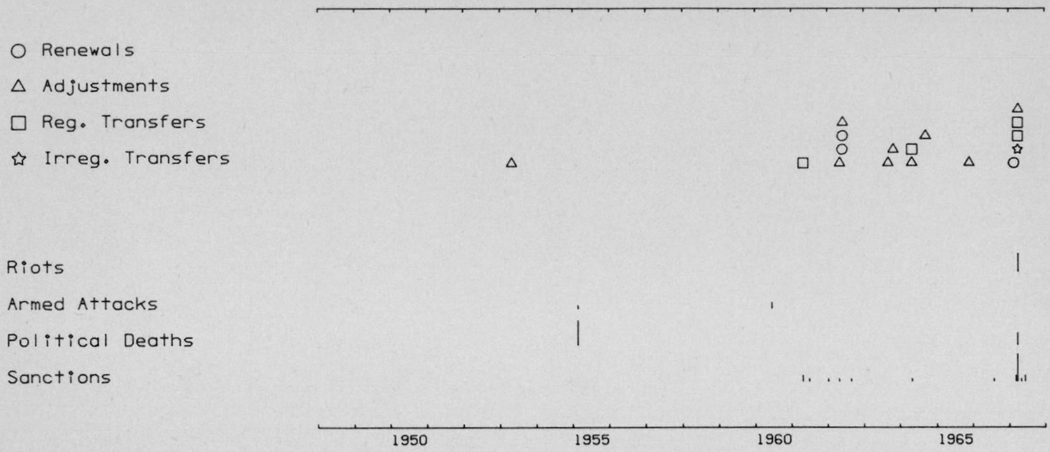

○ Renewals
△ Adjustments
□ Reg. Transfers
☆ Irreg. Transfers

Riots
Armed Attacks
Political Deaths
Sanctions

1950   1955   1960   1965

Singapore

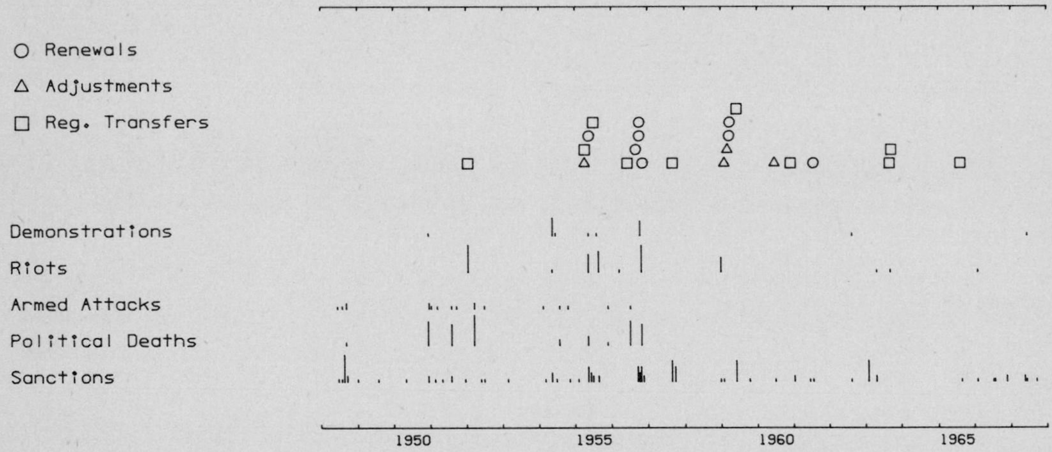

○ Renewals
△ Adjustments
□ Reg. Transfers

Demonstrations
Riots
Armed Attacks
Political Deaths
Sanctions

1950   1955   1960   1965

Somalia

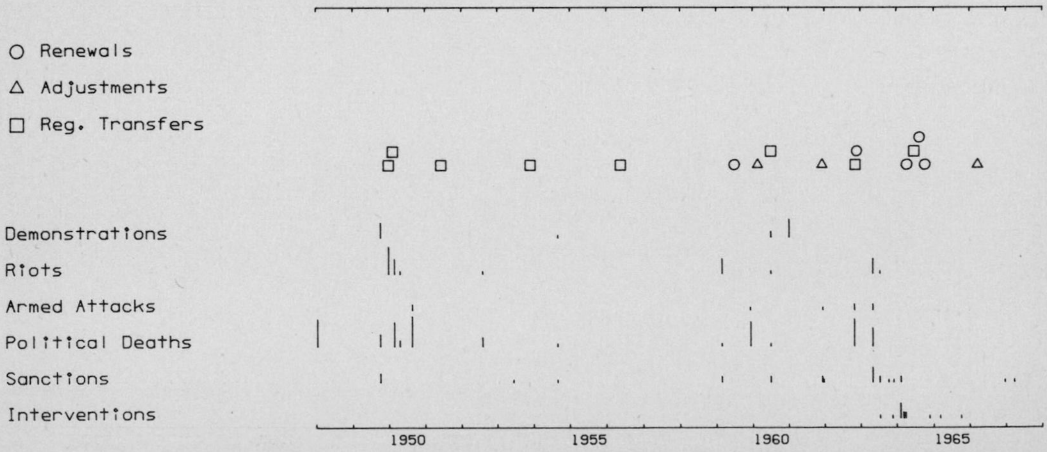

○ Renewals
△ Adjustments
□ Reg. Transfers

Demonstrations
Riots
Armed Attacks
Political Deaths
Sanctions
Interventions

1950   1955   1960   1965

South Africa

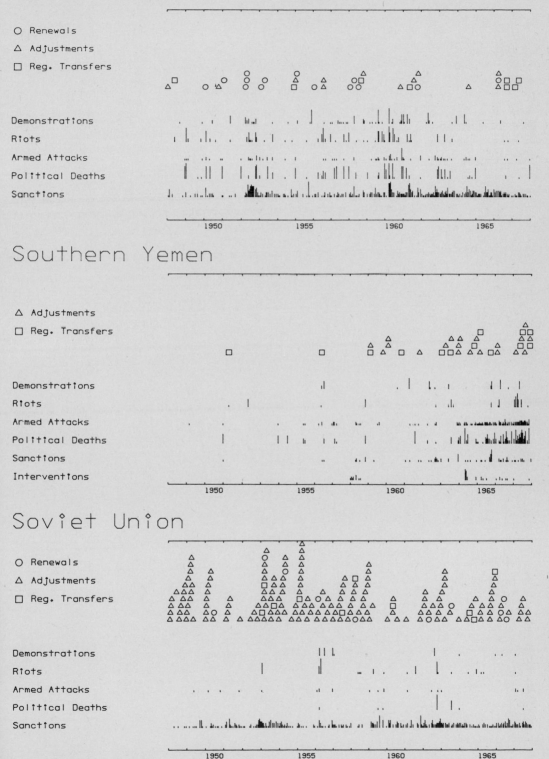

O Renewals
△ Adjustments
□ Reg. Transfers

Demonstrations
Riots
Armed Attacks
Political Deaths
Sanctions

1950　　1955　　1960　　1965

Southern Yemen

△ Adjustments
□ Reg. Transfers

Demonstrations
Riots
Armed Attacks
Political Deaths
Sanctions
Interventions

1950　　1955　　1960　　1965

Soviet Union

O Renewals
△ Adjustments
□ Reg. Transfers

Demonstrations
Riots
Armed Attacks
Political Deaths
Sanctions

1950　　1955　　1960　　1965

Spain

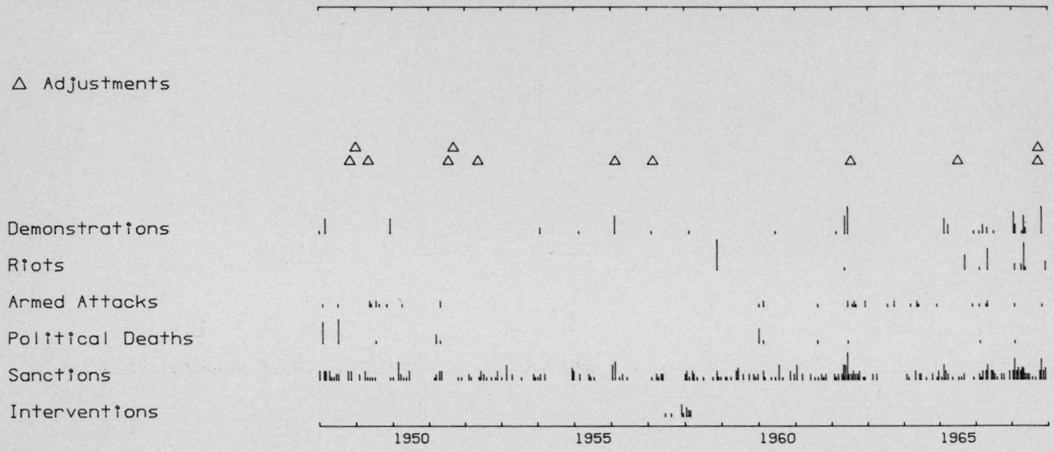

△ Adjustments

Demonstrations
Riots
Armed Attacks
Political Deaths
Sanctions
Interventions

1950   1955   1960   1965

Sudan

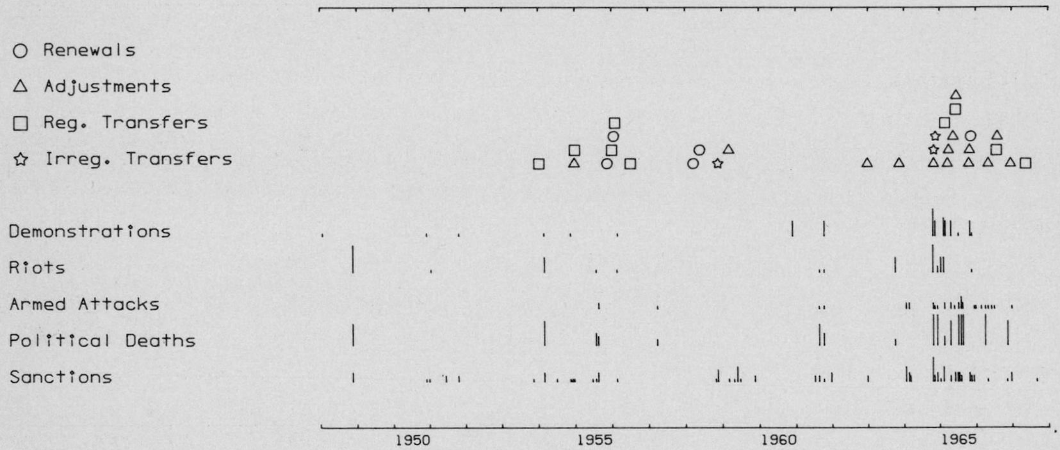

○ Renewals
△ Adjustments
□ Reg. Transfers
☆ Irreg. Transfers

Demonstrations
Riots
Armed Attacks
Political Deaths
Sanctions

1950   1955   1960   1965

Sweden

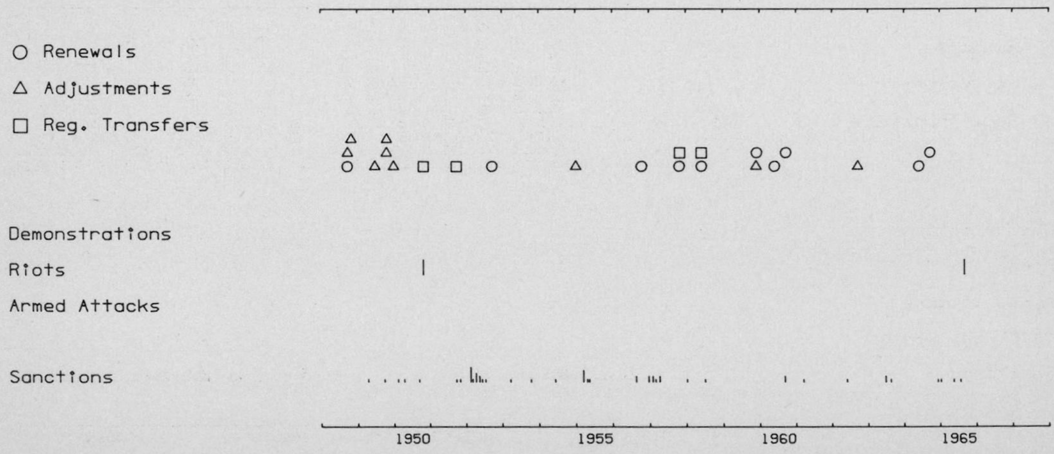

○ Renewals
△ Adjustments
□ Reg. Transfers

Demonstrations
Riots
Armed Attacks

Sanctions

1950   1955   1960   1965

Switzerland

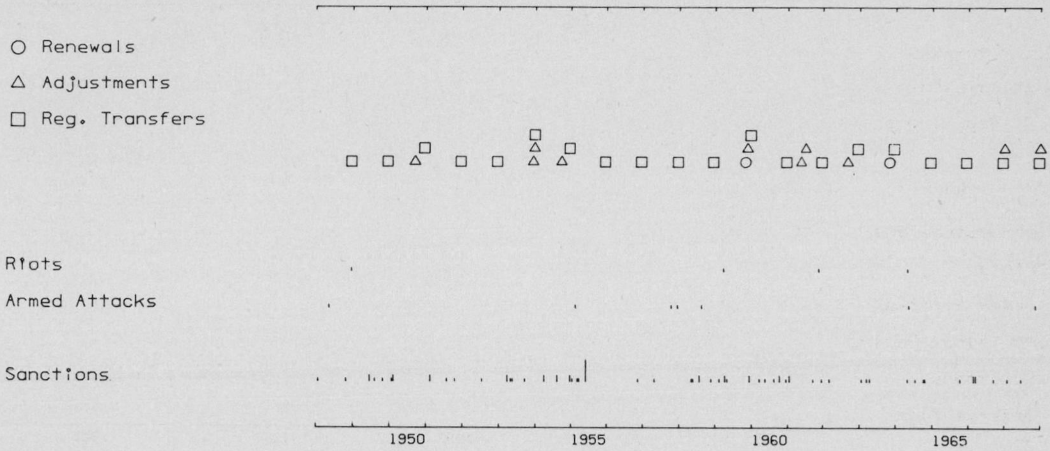

O Renewals
△ Adjustments
□ Reg. Transfers

Riots
Armed Attacks

Sanctions

1950　　　　　1955　　　　　1960　　　　　1965

Syria

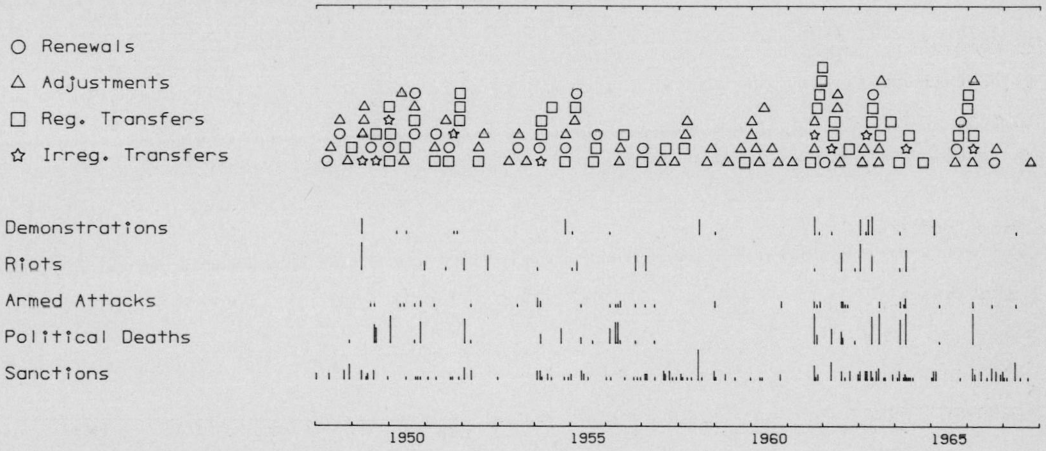

O Renewals
△ Adjustments
□ Reg. Transfers
☆ Irreg. Transfers

Demonstrations
Riots
Armed Attacks
Political Deaths
Sanctions

1950　　　　　1955　　　　　1960　　　　　1965

Taiwan

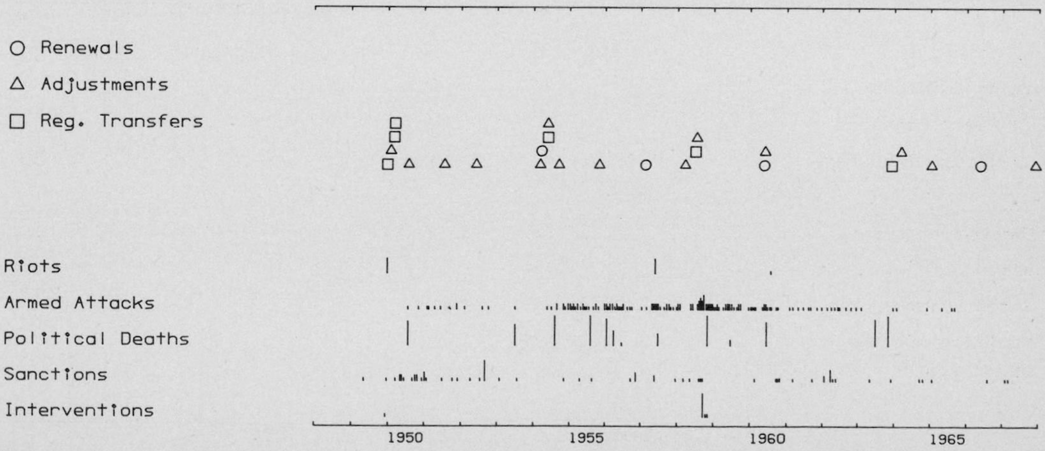

O Renewals
△ Adjustments
□ Reg. Transfers

Riots
Armed Attacks
Political Deaths
Sanctions
Interventions

1950　　　　　1955　　　　　1960　　　　　1965

193

Tanzania

○ Renewals
△ Adjustments
□ Reg. Transfers

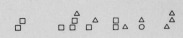

Demonstrations
Riots
Armed Attacks
Political Deaths
Sanctions
Interventions

1950   1955   1960   1965

Thailand

○ Renewals
△ Adjustments
□ Reg. Transfers
☆ Irreg. Transfers

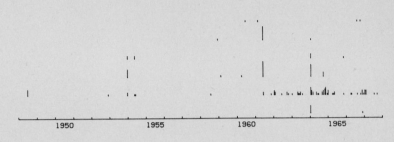

Demonstrations
Riots
Armed Attacks
Political Deaths
Sanctions
Interventions

1950   1955   1960   1965

Togo

○ Renewals
△ Adjustments
□ Reg. Transfers
☆ Irreg. Transfers

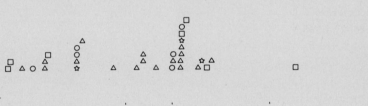

Demonstrations
Riots
Armed Attacks
Political Deaths
Sanctions

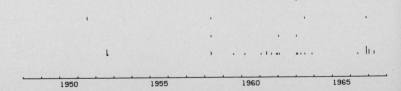

1950   1955   1960   1965

194

Trinidad and Tobago

○ Renewals

□ Reg. Transfers

Demonstrations
Riots
Armed Attacks
Political Deaths
Sanctions

1950   1955   1960   1965

Tunisia

○ Renewals
△ Adjustments
□ Reg. Transfers
☆ Irreg. Transfers

Demonstrations
Riots
Armed Attacks
Political Deaths
Sanctions
Interventions

1950   1955   1960   1965

Turkey

○ Renewals
△ Adjustments
□ Reg. Transfers
☆ Irreg. Transfers

Demonstrations
Riots
Armed Attacks
Political Deaths
Sanctions

1950   1955   1960   1965

195

Uganda

○ Renewals
△ Adjustments
□ Reg. Transfers
☆ Irreg. Transfers

Demonstrations
Riots
Armed Attacks
Political Deaths
Sanctions
Interventions

1950   1955   1960   1965

United Arab Republic

○ Renewals
△ Adjustments
□ Reg. Transfers
☆ Irreg. Transfers

Demonstrations
Riots
Armed Attacks
Political Deaths
Sanctions

1950   1955   1960   1965

United Kingdom

○ Renewals
△ Adjustments
□ Reg. Transfers

Demonstrations
Riots
Armed Attacks
Political Deaths
Sanctions

1950   1955   1960   1965

196

United States

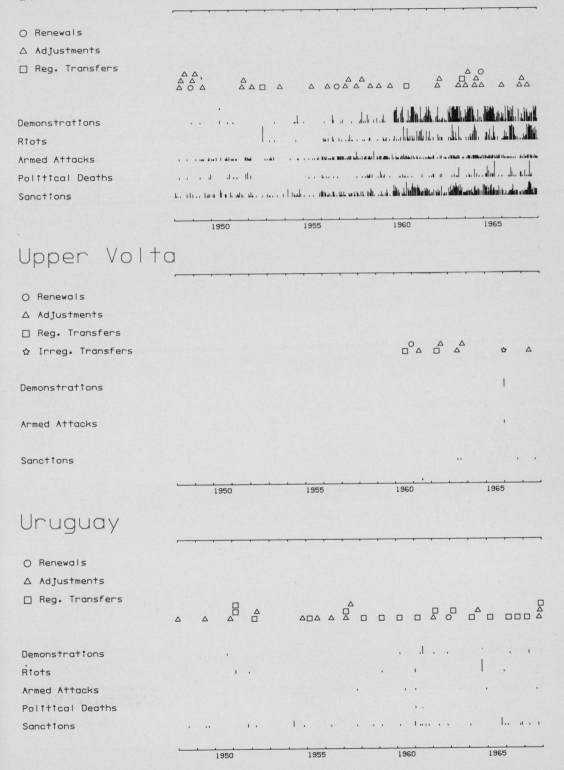

O Renewals
△ Adjustments
□ Reg. Transfers

Demonstrations
Riots
Armed Attacks
Political Deaths
Sanctions

1950　　1955　　1960　　1965

Upper Volta

O Renewals
△ Adjustments
□ Reg. Transfers
☆ Irreg. Transfers

Demonstrations

Armed Attacks

Sanctions

1950　　1955　　1960　　1965

Uruguay

O Renewals
△ Adjustments
□ Reg. Transfers

Demonstrations
Riots
Armed Attacks
Political Deaths
Sanctions

1950　　1955　　1960　　1965

Venezuela

○ Renewals
△ Adjustments
□ Reg. Transfers
☆ Irreg. Transfers

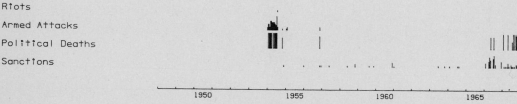

Demonstrations
Riots
Armed Attacks
Political Deaths
Sanctions
Interventions

1950   1955   1960   1965

North Viet Nam

○ Renewals
△ Adjustments
□ Reg. Transfers

Riots
Armed Attacks
Political Deaths
Sanctions

1950   1955   1960   1965

South Viet Nam

○ Renewals
△ Adjustments
□ Reg. Transfers
☆ Irreg. Transfers

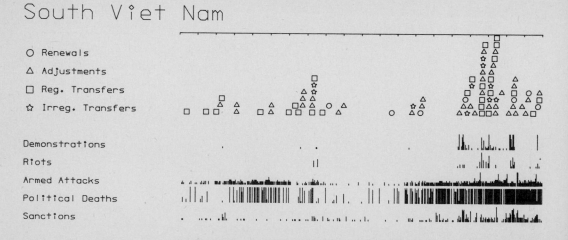

Demonstrations
Riots
Armed Attacks
Political Deaths
Sanctions

1950   1955   1960   1965

198

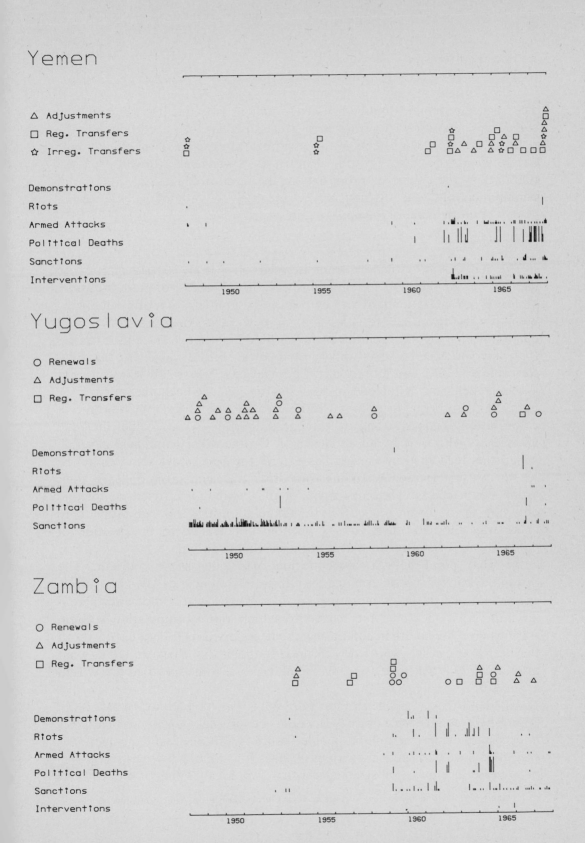

Yemen

△ Adjustments
□ Reg. Transfers
☆ Irreg. Transfers

Demonstrations
Riots
Armed Attacks
Political Deaths
Sanctions
Interventions

1950   1955   1960   1965

Yugoslavia

○ Renewals
△ Adjustments
□ Reg. Transfers

Demonstrations
Riots
Armed Attacks
Political Deaths
Sanctions

1950   1955   1960   1965

Zambia

○ Renewals
△ Adjustments
□ Reg. Transfers

Demonstrations
Riots
Armed Attacks
Political Deaths
Sanctions
Interventions

1950   1955   1960   1965

4 Social Patterns

The social, economic, and cultural environment is frequently assumed, and sometimes explicitly hypothesized, to influence the operation of the political system. Two aspects of the environment—size and level of economic development—are discussed in chapter 5. Social characteristics of the population—the degree of urbanization, the level of education, the type of communications, the distribution of income, the ethnolinguistic homogeneity, and the kind of religion—are presented here.

Urbanization

The movement of people from isolated or sparsely settled places into cities is one of the most prominent aspects of the process of modernization. Moreover, urbanization plays a key role in the politicization of modernizing people. City dwellers are subjected to new ideas that are more easily communicated by the facilities of urban life. Traditional ties and restraints that are integral parts of village and rural life dissolve in the city. Nevertheless, the concentration of populations into small spaces is not precisely the same as the end of parochialism and the beginning of the civic political culture—to use Almond and Verba's terminology.[1] At the time of colonization, Timbuktu and other large indigenous African cities included inhabitants who were hardly modernized. On the other hand, many "rural" Americans read the same magazines, attend the same movies and churches, see the same television programs, and drive the same automobiles as their urban counterparts. The concentration of population into cities, then, is only one means for breaking down the old relationships and commitments to make way for new ones. It is a phenomenon related to the creation of political and social awareness; it is not itself that creation.

At what point does a concentration of people become urban? The threshold cannot be determined by size; the boundaries of some urban agglomerations are much more precise than others. At the moment, there is no index that measures the degree to which various population concentrations give rise to urban conditions; the necessary data do not exist. About the best that can be expected with present data is that they can tell us what proportion of total population lives in all cities of some specified size within a country.

All definitional problems are not solved at this point. What is an appropriate cut-off for a "city"? Do 2,500 people make up an urban area? Is it necessary to have 1 million people before conditions really change? It is easy to believe that there are various changes for several particular thresholds of increase in population size and density. Empirical testing of propositions

1. Gabriel A. Almond and Sidney Verba, *The Civic Culture* (Princeton: Princeton University Press, 1963), pp. 17-19.

related to this point would be useful if the appropriate comparative information were available. Data below are limited to the proportion of population living in cities of 100,000 or more, however, because only these seem to meet our standards of reliability.[2] A city of 100,000 or more people has attained the status of a metropolitan area and surely by the time a concentration of population is that large, the quality of life for its inhabitants is different than that in smaller places. Nevertheless, the cut-off remains somewhat arbitrary.

A second, and more difficult, problem has to do with the comparability of the demarcation of cities in various countries or even within the same country. Some cities have a tremendous area that is not densely populated; e.g. the cities of Virginia Beach and Chesapeake in Virginia encompass the Dismal Swamp. Others, on the other hand, have legal limits that take in only a small fraction of the population in the relevant urban area; e.g. the London County Council, to say nothing of the City, is responsible for only a part of the population of the London metropolis. Ideally, one would wish for data on the people in each urbanized area, but the true limits of urbanized areas are constantly changing and most governments have neither the inclination nor the capability to be so fluid in their census taking. The 1966 United Nations *Demographic Yearbook* reports population in cities of 100,000 and more for 118 countries, but for only 38 of these does it give data by "urban agglomeration." Even for these 38 the United Nations Statistical Office has had to rely upon the noncomparable definitions used by the individual countries.[3]

Kinsley Davis and his International Population and Urban Research group have suggested the use of urbanized areas similar to the Standard Metropolitan Statistical Areas of the United States census. These consist of a central city and those administrative divisions contiguous to the city or to the continuous urban areas that are metropolitan in character, the whole of which has at least 100,000 people.[4] Error then tends to operate in one

2. On the tape deposited with the Consortium in Ann Arbor are two series giving percentages of total population living in cities of 20,000 or more inhabitants. One of these consists of data taken from the United Nations *Demographic Yearbooks* supplemented by a few special studies. The other reports data put together by Homer Hoyt of the Urban Land Institute and published in "World Urbanization: Expanding Population in a Shrinking World," *Technical Bulletin,* no. 43 (Washington: April 1962). Hoyt's estimates are based primarily on the population of localities given in the 1960 United Nations *Demographic Yearbook.*

3. We cannot, therefore, predict bias on the basis of those countries for which both types of data are available since there is no way of knowing—and no reason for suspecting—that this group of countries is representative of the way all governments handle census data.

4. Kingsley Davis, *The World's Metropolitan Areas* (Berkeley and Los Angeles: University of California Press, 1959) and *World Urbanization, 1950-1970; Volume 1: Basic Data for Cities and Regions,* Population Monograph Series, no. 4 (Berkeley: Institute of International Studies, University of California, 1969). These books contain excellent discussions of the problems of collecting comparable international urban data. They also have data for rural and urban populations, populations of individual cities of 100,000 or more people, and other useful information.

direction alone, i.e. a few rural people are added in the surrounding administrative districts but larger numbers of urban people are not left out. Working from this definition the International Population and Urban Research group has collected data on the metropolitan areas of the world for 1950, 1955, and 1960. The 1950 and 1960 data are reported in table 4.1.

The percentages of populations living in cities of 100,000 people or more indicate the degree to which the populations of countries are urbanized, but they do not measure the distribution or concentration of populations within countries. The 20 percent of a population living in cities of 100,000 or more may be in several separate cities or in one very large city. Hence, it is appropriate to take a measure of concentration:

$$C = \sum (P_i)^2$$

where P_i = the proportion of total population in the
    ith population concentration (city).

Table 4.2 reports concentrations for countries using this formula. Obviously, to get a very accurate measurement, one needs the populations of all the cities, towns, and villages of every country, but the nature of the index is such as to weigh the largest units much more heavily than the smallest.[5] Concentration is high enough in most countries so that the six or eight largest cities are sufficient to provide reasonable accuracy in the measure. If C' is calculated on the six or eight largest cities and the remainder of the population is assumed to be evenly divided into cities the size of the smallest for which data are collected, C' will be maximum value for C, given the known data. If C'' is calculated on the six or eight and the remainder of the population is assumed to be hermits, C'' will be a minimum value for C. In almost all cases the original difference between C' and C'' was less than .025, but when it was not additional data were collected.

These data, however, are also plagued by definitional differences. If urban agglomerations are generally larger than the populations within legal limits of the cities, then concentrations based upon the latter data will be biased downward as compared with the concentrations based upon the former. Nevertheless, without both sets of data, it seems impossible to measure the size of this bias. The very cautious scholar may wish to compare only countries using the same basic method.

Education

Mass education is usually thought to play a role in both economic modernization and the process of political change. A factory needs literate workers. A producing economy needs knowledgeable consumers. A democracy needs perceptive citizens. Educated people are likely to demand more of their government and to provide greater human resources for its

5. See section on exports in chapter 6 for fuller discussion of this measure.

operation. Several measures of education are available. Some of these, such as school enrollment ratios and proportion of population enrolled in institutions of higher education, indicate the current effort of the society to educate its younger population. Others, such as literacy and the proportions of adult population who have completed various levels of schooling, indicate the degree to which the society has educated its population in the past. Each kind of measure has its own theoretical use.

The Statistical Office of UNESCO collects educational data from most of the governments of the world. With some of these data, it has created a school enrollment ratio that relates the school enrollment at the first and second levels of education to the estimated population aged five to nineteen years, inclusive. Education at the first level is defined as that designed "to provide basic instruction in the tools of learning." The number of years devoted to these basic skills may vary from country to country and within countries. Education at the second level is defined as "based upon at least four years' previous instruction at the first level and providing general or specialized instruction, or both (e.g. at middle school, secondary school, high school, vocational school, teacher training school at this level)."[6] The number of years devoted to the second level may vary from country to country also.

Not all countries require or provide schooling for all children and adolescents between the ages of five and nineteen; therefore, UNESCO has also created a school enrollment ratio whose denominator is adjusted for the actual duration of schooling in each country. The unadjusted ratio might be considered a measure of how much total effort a country is devoting to primary and secondary education. The adjusted ratio better indicates how fully the government is providing mass education, given the goals it has set for itself. Unfortunately, of course, neither can measure the quality of education offered. The inexactitude of both ratios, moreover, is demonstrated by the fact that a few small countries have percentages in excess of 100 percent. (The UNESCO *Statistical Yearbook* notes that some of this discrepancy is the result of the occasional failure of the actual ages of pupils enrolled in primary and secondary schools to correspond to the arbitrary age groups selected.)

Enrollment data cover both public and private schools and refer to the beginning of the school year that starts in the year reported. (It must be remembered that not all children enrolled at the beginning of a year actually attend school throughout that year.) These data are given in table 4.3.

Education at the third level is defined by UNESCO as that "which requires, as a minimum condition of admission, the successful completion of education at the second level, or evidence of the attainment of an equivalent

6. UNESCO, *Statistical Yearbook, 1966* (Paris, 1968), p. 30.

level of knowledge."[7] Education at this level takes place, for example, in a university, a teachers' college, or a higher professional school. The data in table 4.4 includes enrollments of students in all such institutions, both public and private, whether or not they grant degrees. Generally, part-time students are included but persons enrolled in correspondence courses and auditors are not. Figures relate to enrollment at the beginning of the academic year that starts in the calendar year noted. Occasionally the data in table 4.4 differ slightly in their definitions and these differences, when known, are noted. The inequality of distribution, i.e. the degree to which one individual receives several years of schooling while another gets one or two, is unfortunately obscured here. The enrollment ratios do, however, provide one indication of the relative effort a society is making toward educating its population.

Literacy, on the other hand, is a measure of the degree to which a population has already been educated—or at least has been taught the rudiments of reading and writing. It measures the reservoir of talent available for learning modern technical skills, the potential force for precipitating social change, and the extent to which government may mobilize and control a population. By distinguishing only between those who have entered the world of the written word and those who have not, literacy tells little about how intellectually sophisticated the readers and writers are; yet, in the absence of more efficient measures for large numbers of countries, it is a very useful index in cross-national research.

Literacy figures must be qualified by the age group to which they refer. In modernizing societies, younger people are more likely to be able to read and write than are older people; mass education is relatively new. Data for most countries of the world are collected for populations aged fifteen and above. In table 4.5, data for only seven countries refer to other age groups. For many purposes, these latter may be used without adjustment. In the case of Italy, whose data are based upon the population aged six and above and which deviates most from the general definition, an adjustment based upon the conservative assumption that every Italian between the ages of six and fifteen is literate would adjust Italy's rate only from 92 percent to 90 percent.

Other kinds of error may easily account for that much variation. Each country takes its own census or sample survey and definitions vary somewhat from country to country.[8] In Japan, Sudan, Uganda, and Zambia, illiteracy is defined as never having attended school. To be counted literate in Tunisia, a person is required to be able to read but not necessarily to write. Most countries, however, cooperate with UNESCO in defining literacy

7. Ibid.

8. For a discussion of methods and definitions, see UNESCO, *World Illiteracy at Mid-Century* (Paris, 1957) and UNESCO, *Statistics of Illiteracy,* prepared for the World Congress of Illiteracy, Teheran (Paris, 1965).

as the ability both to read and to write. Persons whose literacy is unspecified are usually excluded from the calculations, but in a few countries, such as Botswana, El Salvador, and Jordan, the unknowns are placed with the illiterates, which possibly biases the literacy figure downward a bit. The United Arab Republic's exclusion of desert dwellers presumably inflates its literacy percentages. Panama's exclusion of both the Canal Zone and its Indian jungle population creates biases operating in each direction.

Table 4.a

Literacy, Circa 1950 and 1960

	Percentage, First Period	Percentage, Second Period	Annual Average Increase Percentage Points
Venezuela	52 (1950)	66 (1961)	1.3
Thailand	52 (1947)	68 (1960)	1.2
Brazil	49 (1950)	61 (1960)	1.2
Cyprus	60 (1946)	76 (1960)	1.1
Mauritius	52 (1952)	62 (1962)	1.0
Philippines	60 (1948)	72 (1960)	1.0
Ecuador	56 (1950)	67 (1962)	0.9
India	19 (1951)	28 (1961)	0.9
Libya	13 (1954)	22 (1964)	0.9
Nicaragua	38 (1950)	50 (1963)	0.9
Colombia	62 (1951)	73 (1964)	0.8
El Salvador	40 (1950)	49 (1961)	0.8
Mexico	57 (1950)	65 (1960)	0.8
Puerto Rico	73 (1950)	81 (1960)	0.8
Ceylon	68 (1953)	75 (1963)	0.7
Jamaica	77 (1953)	82 (1960)	0.7
Paraguay	66 (1950)	74 (1962)	0.7
Greece	74 (1951)	80 (1961)	0.6
Guatemala	29 (1950)	38 (1964)	0.6
Italy	86 (1951)	92 (1961)	0.6
Portugal	56 (1950)	62 (1960)	0.6
Turkey	32 (1950)	38 (1960)	0.6
Chile	80 (1952)	84 (1960)	0.5
Nepal	5 (1953)	9 (1961)	0.5
Spain	82 (1950)	87 (1960)	0.5
Argentina	86 (1947)	91 (1960)	0.4
Costa Rica	79 (1950)	84 (1963)	0.4
Yugoslavia	73 (1953)	76 (1961)	0.4
Iraq	11 (1947)	14 (1957)	0.3
Panama	70 (1950)	73 (1960)	0.3
Hungary	95 (1949)	97 (1960)	0.2
Poland	94 (1950)	95 (1960)	0.1
United States	97 (1950)	98 (1959)	0.1
Pakistan	19 (1951)	19 (1961)	0.0
United Arab Republic	20 (1947)	19 (1960)	−0.1

Sources: UNESCO, Statistical Yearbook, 1965; and UNESCO, Statistical Yearbook, 1967. (Not all data here correspond exactly with those in table 4.5 because of differences in dates.)

Changes in literacy over time are perhaps more important for the study of politics than are the percentage levels, but rates of change are more difficult to obtain. Change rates may be greatly affected by error margins of literacy figures, although frequently the same bias operates over time for a single country's figures so that change rates could be more reliable than the levels themselves. In any case relatively reliable data for more than one time period since 1945 are available for only a limited number of countries. (Estimates made by independent sources must be used with extreme caution since "change rates" may turn out to be essentially differences in judgment.) The countries for which we have reliable and comparable data are listed in table 4.a. It is possible to estimate change rates for other countries from the data in table 4.5. Little recent growth has occurred among the first 20 or 30 countries there; they have been developed for some time. Likewise, it is evident from the very low percentages that there has been little growth in the bottom 25 or 50 countries.

The measurement of literacy treats education as a dichotomy; either one has it or one does not. A more discriminating measure, built upon David McClelland's concept of "educational stock,"[9] is available for a few countries. A stock is the number of people in a country of a given age group who have attained some particular level of education. Like the others in this section, this measure does little to indicate the quality of education received, but by reporting the proportions of populations twenty-five years of age and above who have finished first, second, and third levels of education (see the early discussion in this section for definitions of levels), it maps out the relative educational sophistications of countries. Table 4.b lists the available data judged sufficiently comparable in definition and method of collection to offer a suitable series for statistical analysis. Although the countries included are few in number, the sample is not limited to Western Europe and North America but is representative of a wide range of countries.

Communications

Communications development is often identified as a source of political change. It is usually argued that more widespread information encourages in the population a desire for "the good things of life" to which a government must respond. Governmental instability may result if the revolution of rising expectations becomes a revolution of rising frustrations. Lucian Pye asserts that it was the pressure of communications development that brought the downfall of stable, traditional societies; until the peasant knew much about the outside world, he was unaware of the goods and services that he might demand of his government.[10] In his classic study of the Middle East, Daniel

9. David C. McClelland, "Does Education Accelerate Economic Growth?" *Economic Development and Cultural Change,* 14 (1966): 262.

10. Lucian W. Pye, *Communications and Political Development* (Princeton: Princeton University Press, 1963).

Table 4.b

Educational Stock

Percentage of Population
Which Has Completed

Rank	Country	4+ Years 1st Level	4+ Years 2nd Level	4+ Years 3rd Level	Date
2	Netherlands	100	12	1	1965
2	Norway	100	16	2	1965
2	Switzerland	100	31	9	1965
4	Czechoslovakia	99	17	2	1961
5	Japan	97	32	6	1965
6	United States	92	41	8	1965
7.5	Hungary	91	9	3	1963
7.5	Poland	91	20	3	1965
9	Canada	90	22	3	1961
10	Italy	78	7	2	1961
11	Jamaica	73	6	1	1965
12	Israel	72	24		1961
13	Yugoslavia	67	11	2	1961
14	Ceylon	62	15	0	1963
15.5	Chile	58	13	2	1965
15.5	Hong Kong	58	14	5	1966
17.5	Cyprus	57	10	1	1965
17.5	Peru	57	12	3	1961
19	Puerto Rico	56	15	4	1965
20	Portugal	55	5	1	1965
21	Philippines	50	11	4	1965
22	South Africa	49	13		1965
23	Greece	47	10	3	1961
24	Costa Rica	43	6		1963
25	South Korea	42	8	1	1965
26.5	France	41	10	2	1962
26.5	Uruguay	41	11	2	1963
28	Thailand	39	3	0	1965
29	Ecuador	36	9	1	1962
30	Mexico	26	3	1	1965
31	Indonesia	25	1	0	1961
32	Dominican Republic	24	2	1	1965
33	Jordan	19	3	1	1961
34	Mauritius	18	3	1	1962
35	Honduras	15	3	1	1961
36.5	Ghana	14	2	1	1965
36.5	Zambia	14	1		1963
38	Guatemala	13	2		1964
39	Iran	11	3		1966
40	Kenya	10	2	0	1962
41	India	9	3		1961
42	Liberia	6	6	1	1962
43	Syria	5	2	1	1965
44	Libya	3	3	0	1964

Source: UNESCO, *Statistical Yearbook, 1965* (Paris, 1967).

Lerner emphasizes that political and economic modernization are dependent upon the development of psychic mobility and empathy in individuals, once gained by physical mobility but now multiplied by mediated experience through the mass media.[11] Other scholars have drawn attention to the relation between a high level of communications development and mass participation and competitiveness. S. M. Lipset shows that the group means for several communications variables are highest for European stable democracies, somewhat lower for European unstable democracies and dictatorships, and lowest for Latin American stable dictatorships.[12] Phillips Cutright constructs an index of political development guided by the concept that the more complex and specialized the institutions of a nation are, the more politically developed it is. He finds the index to be highly related $(r = .81)$ to an index composed of newspaper circulation, newsprint consumption, telephones, and domestic mail.[13]

Communications development may be usefully thought to consist of the evolution of technical means for transmitting personal or business messages as well as the growth of mass media. Hence, table 4.6 presents domestic and foreign lettermail per capita and table 4.7 gives telephones per thousand population.[14] Measures of the mass media—newspaper circulation, radio receivers, and television sets per thousand population—are ranked on their sums for each country in table 4.8. This seems justified, given their high intercorrelations and the fact that any one is a possible substitute for the others in providing information.

Data on telephones refer to the number of public and private installations that can be connected to a central exchange. The series in table 4.7 is obtained by dividing the total number by population. Lettermail figures include letters (airmail, surface, and registered), postcards, printed matter, business papers, small merchandise samples, small packets, and phonopost packets. Mail without charge is included but ordinary packages and letters with a declared value are excluded. Foreign mail includes both that sent and that received. A newspaper is defined for the purposes of table 4.8 as a publication containing general news and appearing at least four times a week. No adjustment has been made for sales of newspapers across national

11. Daniel Lerner, *The Passing of Traditional Society: Modernizing the Middle East* (Glencoe, Ill.: Free Press, 1958), pp. 43-75.

12. Seymour Martin Lipset, *Political Man: The Social Basis of Politics* (Garden City, N.Y.: Doubleday, 1960), pp. 27-63.

13. Phillips Cutright, "National Political Development: Measurement and Analysis," *American Sociological Review,* 28 (1963): 253-64.

14. Telephones per population is often cited as an index of economic development—for example, K. Finsterbusch and T. Caplow, "A Matrix of Modernization" (Paper presented at the Annual Meeting of the American Sociological Association, 1964). Indeed, all of the variables listed here may be used as surrogates or, better, as supplements, for economic measures. The correlations among them are high (see Bruce M. Russett, *International Regions and the International System: A Study in Political Ecology* [Chicago: Rand McNally, 1967]).

boundaries but UNESCO believes this does not affect the results significantly. The size of newspaper may range from a single sheet to 100 or more pages. Radio data relate to all types of receivers including those connected to a redistribution system. They represent either the number of licenses issued or the estimated number of receivers in use. In many countries, one license may cover more than one receiver in the same household. Television data also refer either to the number of licenses or to estimated receivers in use. Radio and television data are marked R or L to distinguish the method used by the particular country. Adjustments to make the data more comparable were considered but were abandoned after we plotted receiver data against newspaper circulation, using R and L to identify the points. While newspapers and radios were related, no pattern developed with the Rs and Ls; the number of licenses, for example, do not seem to understate consistently the receivers in use.

Welfare

The well-being of their peoples is one of the first professed aims of almost all modern governments. However, they differ in their abilities and willingness to allocate resources to pay for the necessary facilities. Tables 4.9, 4.10, 4.11, and 4.12 demonstrate the variation among countries on several indicators of welfare. The political attitudes of people are determined, however, not so much by their objective well-being as by their perceptions of this well-being and especially by their comparison of their situations with those of people in their reference groups. Perceptions, of course, are difficult to measure by aggregate data and the cross-national surveys that have been done thus far are sufficient for comparisons among only a few countries. In this handbook, therefore, we are limited to measures of the inequality of income and land distribution, presented in tables 4.13 and 4.14. Although these get at the matter of perceptions indirectly, they may be of value for many purposes.

Vital statistics—crude birth rates and crude death rates—are reported in table 4.9. Rates are given as the number of live births and the number of deaths, excluding fetal deaths, per 1,000 people in a given year. The Statistical Office of the United Nations groups governmental vital statistics into those that are stated to cover at least 90 percent of events occurring during the year, those less reliable, and those whose reliability is unknown. Data that the Statistical Office marked as covering less than 90 percent of births or deaths were not used in this handbook. Estimates from other sources were gathered to supplement the more accurate data from the *Demographic Yearbooks*.

The accuracy of vital statistics is dependent upon the requirements and means provided for registration. Definitions also differ from country to country. Some countries require "breathing" to establish a live birth but others recognize any "signs of life." Some countries do not register as a live birth any infant dying within 24 hours or, occasionally, before registration. A few countries do not include deaths of newborn infants. It has been shown, however, that these variations make a difference of no more than 1 percent or so and, compared with other possible errors, are unimportant.[15] Finally, the comparability of data is affected by the fact that some governments report births and deaths not by year of occurrence but by year of registration. Such countries are noted when this fact is known.

Two kinds of error margins are associated with the data in table 4.9. For those taken from the United Nations *Demographic Yearbooks,* marked *C* for civil registration tabulated by date of occurrence or *D* for civil registration tabulated by date of registration, error operates essentially in one direction; inaccuracies are due to underregistration. Estimates made by scholars, which supplement the registration data, may be either too high or too low, probably by a margin of no more than 10 percent. Data from the United Nations marked with a "." are also estimates, usually based upon sample surveys.

Infant mortality, i.e. the number of deaths of infants under one year of age per 1,000 live births, is another and more direct measure of well-being. This rate is more easily affected by governmental policy and the development of the economy than are the crude birth and death rates. Especially if the rate is high, relatively small increments in health expenditure may bring drastic reduction in infant mortality. Rates have been declining in all parts of the world in the last decade or two but table 4.10 shows that the spread among countries is still rather severe. Problems of error are rather similar to those related to crude birth and death rates.

The United States Department of Agriculture reports that two-thirds of the world's people live in countries whose average national diets are nutritionally inadequate. These countries are those of Asia except for Japan and Israel, those of Africa except for the southern tip, and most of those in Central America and northern South America.[16]

Calories and grams of protein per capita per diem are reported in table 4.11. These data are estimated from total food production, trade, and movement in stocks. Appropriate deductions are made for the amounts used for animal feed, seed, and manufacture and for amounts wasted before they reach the retail level. Taking into account population, FAO estimates the caloric and protein value per capita of food supplies available in the retail market. Food balance sheets are put together by governments in collabora-

15. United Nations, Statistical Office, *Handbook of Vital Statistics Methods* ST/STAT/SER.F/7 (New York, 1954), pp. 46-53. Other sources of error and caveats on the use of crude birth and death rates are found in the United Nations, Statistical Office, *The Situation and Recent Trends of Mortality in the World,* Population Bulletin of the United Nations, no. 6 (New York, 1963).

16. United States, Department of Agriculture, Economic Research Service, Foreign Regional Analysis Division, *The World Food Budget, 1970,* Foreign Agriculture Economic Report, no. 19 (Washington: U.S. Government Printing Office, 1964).

tion with the FAO and, in the case of the European countries, the Organization for Economic Cooperation and Development. Some countries use split years and others use calendar years.

Data for physicians include those practicing privately or on hospital staffs, in laboratories or in public health services. Virtually every country requires that physicians be licensed so data are likely to be complete and reliable. Problems are more likely to arise because of differences in definitions. Generally data refer to persons fully qualified or certified from a medical school. Auxiliary personnel and assistant personnel are not included.

The quality of medical school personnel, of course, varies substantially from one country to another. This may result merely from differences in available resources; it may also be the consequence of deliberate public policy. Some underdeveloped countries have tried to maintain high standards even at the expense of drastically limiting the total number of physicians. Others have consciously relaxed standards on the grounds that the public good would be better served by quantity. Such countries will be at quite different positions in table 4.12 and the consequences of their policies will not be the same. Another problem of comparability stems from the concentration of medical personnel in many states. The disproportions between urban and rural services vary widely. In some countries a relatively modest ratio of inhabitants per physician may conceal a heavy concentration on the minority of the population involved in the modern sector. In other countries medical personnel may be concentrated on certain great estates. Plantation workers may be well cared for but other members of the native population neglected. For these reasons the physician-population ratio is less satisfactory than we would wish, but it seems important as one measure of well-being.

The Distribution of Wealth

Inequalities in income and land have long been thought to have major consequences for political stability, the nature of political regimes, and the incentives and availability of resources for investment. Unfortunately, the data on inequality have not been developed in as comparable a form for as many countries as is needed for extensive cross-national comparisons. Much income is not reported either because of deliberate tax evasion or because nonmonetary income is overlooked. Distributions before and after taxes, of course, will not be the same. Allowance should be made for differences in the size of income-receiving units; large families need more than small ones. The place of residence, the availability of state-provided medicine and education, and other similar factors affect the cost of living. Different types of goods may be required to satisfy the same level of need satisfaction in town and in country. Can a minimum level of need satisfaction be determined? Do the poor in an affluent society have psychological needs beyond their actual ones because of advertising?

Objections of these kinds to the simple measurement of inequality are not new. As early as 1920, Hugh Dalton published similar questions and Corrado Gini answered that his interest was "to estimate, not the inequality of economic welfare, but the inequality of incomes and wealth, independently of all hypotheses as to the functional relations between these quantities and economic welfare." [17] Gini had developed an index based upon the Lorenz curve, which depicts the distribution of a value over selected units within a society. (See pages 266 and 270 for examples of income and land distribution.) The curve is built with pairs of cumulative percentages. For example, if 25 percent of the households have 10 percent of the income, 50 percent have 20 percent, and 75 percent have 30 percent, then we have five points since none of the households have none of the income and all together have 100 percent. By drawing x and y axes to read from zero to 100 percent, we can plot the five points to obtain a distribution of income in our hypothetical economy. (By convention, the x values are placed to the left of the y axis to suit our notion of reading from left to right.) If our hypothetical economy had total equality, i.e. if 25 percent of the households had 25 percent of the income, 50 percent had 50 percent, 75 percent had 75 percent, and assuming the units of the two axes to be of the same length, the Lorenz curve would be a straight line at a 45° angle. The Gini index of inequality then is defined as the area between the Lorenz curve and the line of equality. It ranges from a value of zero representing perfect equality to unity representing maximum inequality (i.e. the richest single unit has all the income). [18]

Two qualities of the index need to be noted. The comparison is among kinds of distributions, not among levels of wealth. The households of the lowest decile in Sweden may be richer than those of a much higher decile in Costa Rica. The index also assumes that within a distribution, equal arithmetic differences are considered of equal importance. A $1,000 difference between starving and scraping is assumed the same as that between $100,000 and $101,000.

The most salient difficulty facing the scholar who wants to compare inequality of income over several national units, however, is the absence of sufficient data. Far more comparable data of distribution by economic sector are available than are those of distribution by household. Simon Kuznets calculated a Gini index based upon product per worker by dividing total domestic product and total labor force into identical sets of sectors. Since workers' incomes account for 75-90 percent of the product, gross

17. See Hugh Dalton, "Measurement of the Inequality of Income," *The Economic Journal,* 30 (1920): 348-61; and Corrado Gini, "Measurement of Inequality of Incomes," *The Economic Journal,* 31 (1921): 124-26.

18. For more explanation, see Hayward R. Alker and Bruce M. Russett, "Indices for Comparing Inequality," *Comparing Nations: The Use of Quantitative Data on Cross-National Research,* ed. Richard L. Merritt and Stein Rokkan (New Haven: Yale University Press, 1966).

domestic product per capita within sectors will measure approximately the average income received by the workers. However, it is very important to remember that *the variation within sectors is hidden and that total inequality will be understated unless there is no variation of income within the sectors.* The latter is difficult to assume for real countries. The kind of index does make a difference. The relative position of the United States in table 4.13 is much higher than in tables 71 and 72 of the first edition of the *World Handbook.* Some readers, therefore, may prefer the data for a smaller number of countries from that edition because they are more appropriate to the theoretical concerns of these readers. In any event *the series in table 4.13 must not be used as if it measured inequality of income among households;* it does not.

The distributions of intersectoral inequality relate quite well to economic development—the greater the development, the less the inequality among sectors—but for nine countries Kuznets found no significant relationship between Gini numbers based upon household data and Gini numbers based upon sectoral data. The sectoral numbers are much lower and range more widely than do the household numbers. In short, they are not including all of the variation of inequality in the economy. They do, however, get at the measurement of imbalance between the rural subsistence farming sector and the urban commercial and manufacturing sectors of a dual economy characteristic of an underdeveloped country. [19]

Kuznets's figures were published in the late 1950s. We have updated this work and enlarged somewhat the number of countries included. The results are reported in table 4.13 along with the smallest proportion of the population having half the total income. Following Kuznets, we have used the International Standard Industrial Classification employed by the International Labour Organization in its *Yearbook of Labour Statistics* and the Standard National Accounts categories of the United Nations Statistical Office employed in its *Yearbook of National Account Statistics.* These sectors are

> Agriculture, forestry, hunting, and fishing
> Mining and quarrying
> Manufacturing
> Construction
> Electricity, gas, water, and sanitary services

19. For a discussion of these problems, see Simon Kuznets, "Quantitative Aspects of the Economic Growth of Nations: VIII, Distribution of Income by Size," *Economic Development and Cultural Change,* 11 (1963): part II; and "Quantitative Aspects of the Economic Growth of Nations: II, Industrial Distribution of National Product and Labor Force," *Economic Development and Cultural Change,* 5 (1957): part II. See also Dan Usher, "Equalizing Differences in Income and the Interpretation of National Income Statistics," *Economica,* 32 (1965): 253-68; and Mary Jean Bowman, "A Graphical Analysis of Personal Income Distribution in the United States," *Readings in the Theory of Income Distribution,* The American Economic Association (Homewood, Ill.: Irwin, 1951), pp. 72-99.

Commerce (wholesale and retail trade, banking,
   insurance, and real estate)
Transportation, storage, and communication and services

Sometimes, it was impossible to obtain data for all eight sectors separately and two or more were lumped together. The number of combined sectors has been noted in the table. In our calculations data for males only were used whenever possible to enhance comparability. The treatment of unpaid females varies greatly from country to country. For three of the four cases in which data for males only were unavailable, we were able to use data on the labor force excluding unpaid family workers.

Recently, promising efforts have been made by the United Nations Research Institute for Social Development in the creation of an index on the level of living. First the "normal" correspondences between factors of development at various levels of development are determined. What level of a particular indicator normally corresponds to a given level of another indicator? The disproportionate development of certain indicators may reflect income maldistribution. For example, when indicators of affluence (automobiles) are relatively high but indicators of basic needs (health, nutrition) are relatively low, there is probably maldistribution of income. There are still a few difficulties with the analysis but limited comparisons show that the differences in ranks relate rather well to an income inequality coefficient for a few European countries. [20]

Distribution patterns of land ownership also vary greatly from country to country. In many less developed economies, a few landowners control large parts of the total acreage whereas in other countries peasant and small-farmer holdings account for a much larger share. Data on the number and acreage of farms with categories by size are available for some countries. By assuming a relationship between number of farms and number of owners, we were able to calculate measures of inequality. Category sizes and number are not the same for all countries. The major reason, of course, is that that is the way the data come, but these variations are at least partially justified in that a "big" farm in Belgium is something quite different from a "big" farm in Australia. The data refer to landholdings of which any part is used for agriculture. No provision is made for portions of the holdings that are not arable or for pasture only.

Ethnolinguistic Homogeneity

Political leaders have for a long time associated political stability with homogeneity of population. German princes of the sixteenth century sought to stabilize Central Europe by declaring some realms fully Catholic and some

20. Correspondence with Donald V. McGranahan, Director, United Nations Research Institute for Social Development, Geneva. For earlier work, see Jan Drewnowski and Wolf Scott, *The Level of Living Index,* United Nations Research Institute for Social Development, report no. 4 (Geneva, 1966).

fully Protestant. In the nineteenth and twentieth centuries, the concept of a homogeneous nation-state was and is a powerful force for irredentism, the dissolution of empires, and the unification of states. Many governments of Asia and Africa are striving to create nations from heterogeneous populations and are not finding the task easy.

Populations may be heterogeneous with regard to a number of phenomena and the reasons for cleavage in one society may not be those in another. Karl Deutsch insists that the unity of a people is "the complementarity of relative efficiency of communication among individuals—something that is in some ways similar to mutual rapport, but on a larger scale."[21] This communication may be impeded by any number of factors, but occasionally it persists in spite of some of the more obvious of them.

Among the obvious potential causes of cleavage in a society are differences in ethnicity, language, and religion. Religion is discussed in the next section. Language is frequently an indicant of ethnicity (e.g. Spanish-speaking Americans) but this is not always true (e.g. black Americans). One of the sources used below, *Atlas Narodov Mira,* published by the Department of Geodesy and Cartography of the State Geological Committee of the USSR (Academy of Sciences, Moscow), makes little distinction between ethnic and linguistic differences in its definition and collection of data. Groups are determined not by their physical characteristics but by their roles, their descent, and their relationships to others. The *Atlas* states on page 123:

> The language of a people is closely tied to their ethnic background. Giving up one's native language—the basic means of communication among people belonging to the same nation, the basic means of preserving and developing their cultures—although not equivalent to complete ethnic assimilation, does testify to a very significant development of assimilating processes.

An index of fractionalization calculated upon data from the *Atlas* does correlate highly with a similar index calculated upon linguistic data from other sources, but not quite highly enough to be considered the same variable. Since the two are measured in the same units, for the slope of a regression line to approximate unity, the intercept should be very near zero and the correlation coefficient should be at least .95 to account for nine-tenths of the variance. Instead

$$Y = .04 + .83 X_1 \quad (r = .82, n = 108)$$
$$Y = .08 + .89 X_2 \quad (r = .92, n = 51)$$

Where Y = ethnic fractionalization, X_1 and X_2 = linguistic fractionalization from the two sources reported in table 4.15. Although Y, X_1 and X_2 cannot

21. Karl W. Deutsch, *Nationalism and Social Communication* (New York: Wiley, 1953), p. 162.

in theory be considered the same, in practice either of the latter is a good estimate of Y.

Some introductory remarks in *Atlas Narodov Mira* may stimulate suspicions of bias in the data, but an examination of the residuals in the regressions reported above evince no particular patterns dividing Western and Eastern nations. The differences seem to be matters of interpretation on what precisely are the boundaries of a group. Do the Chinese speak Chinese or do they speak Mandarin, Wu, Cantonese, and so on? In spite of Soviet efforts to underplay ethnic differences within its boundaries, the USSR ranked high in the table. Somewhat surprising is the omission by the Russians of blacks in the United States; for this country the Soviet data have been adjusted to include nonwhites from the 1960 census and fractionalization was increased from .357 to .505.

The index of fractionalization used to measure ethnic and linguistic heterogeneity is that which we used in chapter 2 (from Rae and Taylor) for parties:

$$F = 1 - \sum_{i=1}^{n} \left(\frac{n_i}{N}\right)\left(\frac{n_i - 1}{N - 1}\right)$$

where n_i = the number of speakers of the ith language and N = the total number of people in the population. F varies from 0 to 1 and measures the probability that two randomly selected persons from one country will not speak the same language. It is quite similar to a measure for linguistic heterogeneity suggested more than a decade ago by Joseph H. Greenberg:[22]

$$A = 1 - \sum_{i=1}^{n} (P_i)^2$$

where P_i = the proportion of total population in the ith language group. The only difference, of course, is whether the individual is allowed to be selected twice randomly, a matter of small consequence when large populations are involved. Neither measure takes into account the distances among groups, i.e. all languages and dialects included are considered equally unalike. The weight of decision is, therefore, upon the selection of the mutually exclusive groups for which the data are orginally collected.[23] Greenberg suggests alternative indices that take into account varying differences among languages and dialects and which acknowledge the fact that some parts of the population speak more than one language. Data to calculate these indices

22. Joseph H. Greenberg, "The Measurement of Linguistic Diversity," *Language,* 32 (1956): 109-15.

23. This is no small matter. For example, the United Nations *Demographic Yearbook, 1963,* lists 113 tribal groups for Ghana but it divides Gabon's population simply between Africans and non-Africans. Comparing F's based upon these two sets of unedited data would be meaningless.

unfortunately do not exist for most countries.

Data employed to calculate the fractionalization measure are available from the Inter-University Consortium for Political Research in Ann Arbor, should scholars wish to develop other indexes.[24]

Religion

Religious diversity has had important—frequently tragic—political consequences in history, and for many countries it still is of political significance. Sometimes the relevant difference is between adherents of two major world religions; sometimes, however, it is among divisions of a religion or between clericals and anticlericals, all of whom share the same religious tradition.

Data, therefore, could be collected using world religions (for example, Christianity, Islam, Judaism), major divisions (for example, Roman Catholic, Mahayana, or Sunni), or even denominations as the basis for categorization. Indeed, it is conceivable that one might want a varying unit for collection from one study to another or from country to country; differences between Roman Catholics and Protestants in Northern Ireland are far more salient than differences between Buddhists and Christians in Hawaii.

Our original intention was to create a measure of religious fractionalization similar to the ethnolinguistic index, but the scarcity of data on non-Western religions make this inappropriate at this time. The next edition of the *World Christian Handbook* (cited in notes for table 4.16) will make this task much easier. In our handbook we present Moslems and Christians as percentages of total country populations. These two religions have adherents in sufficient numbers of countries to make them interesting series in a *world* handbook; moreover, these were the data that David Barrett, editor of the forthcoming *World Christian Handbook,* could make available to us at this date.

These data represent Barrett's judgment on a large number of individual national tables from varied sources. In many cases he has had to choose among two or three contradictory estimates. In some cases, the data are quoted from published sources that merely repeat earlier published estimates. In an effort to increase reliability, data were gathered in aggregate numbers and were divided by total populations appropriate to the date specific to the religious data. The assumption that percentages of adherents do not change over time seems substantially correct except among Christians in Africa, where Christianity is growing rapidly. Data for African Christians, however, are all for 1964 or 1965.

Adherents in tables 4.16 and 4.17 are defined to include the total community, children as well as adults. The data do not refer to the proportion of the population currently participating in religious activities;

24. One such index is defined as the standard deviation of the P_is divided by the largest possible standard deviation of P_is for a given N. It is developed in J. David Singer and James Ray, "Measuring Concentration and Distribution in a Large Social System," mimeographed.

they are more appropriate measures of the general religious-cultural characteristics of the countries. The data for Roman Catholics and Protestants are those
claimed by the churches themselves; government census figures are often
slightly higher. The number of distinct Christian denominations in a country
refers to the number of organizations. Baptists and Methodists or United and
Southern Presbyterians, for example, are counted as separate organizations
but all Roman Catholic dioceses are counted as one organization only.

Table 4.1
Urbanization

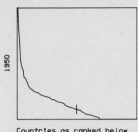

Countries as ranked below   Countries as ranked below

Mean	12.8	16.8
Standard Deviation	16.1	17.7
Median	8.7	13.3
Range	100.0	100.0
Skewness	2.33	1.98
Number of Countries	136	136

		Percentage of Population Living in Cities of 100,000 or More	
Rank	Country	1950	1960
1.5	Hong Kong	80.1	100.0
1.5	Singapore	100.0	100.0
3	United Kingdom	70.6	71.6
4	Australia	53.2	57.9
5	Argentina	45.6	54.3
6	Kuwait	.0	52.5
7	West Germany	48.4	51.5
8	United States	43.9	50.5
9	Canada	36.8	43.1
10	Japan	26.7	41.9
11	Israel	30.0	39.4
12	Netherlands	36.2	38.0
13	Uruguay	27.8	37.9
14	Austria	37.6	37.6
15	Denmark	33.5	34.2
16	France	26.2	34.0
17	New Zealand	32.9	33.8
18	Chile	26.5	31.5
19	Taiwan	24.0	30.0
20	Venezuela	20.3	29.4
21	Switzerland	24.6	29.1
22	Belgium	28.8	28.5
23	Puerto Rico	19.4	28.0
24	Spain	24.1	27.9
25.5	Cuba	24.2	27.5
25.5	Greece	21.7	27.5
27	Ireland	25.1	27.4
28	Lebanon	18.1	26.8
29	Poland	23.1	26.6
30	South Africa	23.6	26.5

Table 4.1 Urbanization—*Continued*

Rank	Country	Percentage of Population Living in Cities of 100,000 or More	
		1950	1960
31.5	Guyana	.0	26.4
31.5	Syria	22.5	26.4
33	United Arab Republic	20.8	26.2
34	Brazil	17.5	25.6
35	Sweden	21.4	25.1
36	Soviet Union	20.9	24.8
37	Panama	14.9	24.4
38	Colombia	17.4	24.3
39	Italy	20.2	24.2
40	Southern Yemen	15.4	23.5
41	Portugal	21.6	23.4
42	Jamaica	19.0	23.1
43	South Korea	15.2	22.8
44	Hungary	19.6	22.0
45	Costa Rica	17.4	21.9
47	East Germany	20.2	21.3
47	Iraq	15.0	21.3
47	Libya	11.4	21.3
49	Norway	19.8	20.3
50	Finland	16.4	20.1
51	Morocco	15.8	18.9
52	Mexico	15.1	18.6
53	Yugoslavia	11.7	18.0
54	Paraguay	16.3	17.8
55	Ecuador	14.6	17.6
56	Iran	14.1	17.4
57	Mongolia	.0	17.2
58.5	Algeria	12.0	16.4
58.5	Congo - Brazzaville	.0	16.4
60	Romania	10.0	16.2
61	North Korea	10.6	16.0
62	Tunisia	17.3	15.6
63	Peru	11.4	15.0
64	Czechoslovakia	13.9	14.4
65	Philippines	12.5	14.3
66.5	Bulgaria	9.1	14.0
66.5	Nicaragua	10.3	14.0
68	Jordan	.0	13.3
69	Guatemala	10.5	12.4
70	Turkey	8.3	12.2
71	Dominican Republic	8.5	12.1
72	Bolivia	9.9	11.6
73.5	Rhodesia	4.1	11.5
73.5	Senegal	8.9	11.5
75	Ghana	3.6	10.9
76	China	7.2	10.6
77	South Viet Nam	8.1	10.5
78.5	El Salvador	8.7	9.7
78.5	Indonesia	6.1	9.7
80	Ceylon	9.4	9.6
81	Malaysia	6.7	9.5
82	India	8.1	9.0
83	Albania	.0	8.4

Table 4.1 Urbanization—*Continued*

Rank	Country	Percentage of Population Living in Cities of 100,000 or More	
		1950	1960
84	Honduras	.0	8.2
85	Saudi Arabia	1.9	7.7
86	Pakistan	4.8	7.2
87	Thailand	5.9	6.5
88	Congo – Kinshasa	2.7	6.4
89	North Viet Nam	3.7	6.3
90	Cambodia	3.7	6.2
91	Haiti	4.3	6.0
92	Ivory Coast	.0	5.6
93	Burma	5.2	5.4
94.5	Kenya	2.2	5.3
94.5	Nigeria	4.3	5.3
96	Laos	.0	4.9
97	Sierra Leone	.0	4.8
98	Angola	3.4	4.7
99	Malagasy Republic	4.2	4.6
100	Guinea	.0	3.6
101	Cameroon	.0	3.3
102	Mali	.0	3.1
104.5	Afghanistan	1.8	2.7
104.5	Ethiopia	2.4	2.7
104.5	Mozambique	.0	2.7
104.5	Sudan	2.6	2.7
107	Nepal	1.5	2.2
108	Uganda	.0	2.0
109	Tanzania	.0	1.6

Notes: Countries that had no cities of 100,000 or more people in 1960 were Botswana, Barbados, Burundi, Central African Republic, Chad, Cyprus, Dahomey, Gabon, Iceland, Lesotho, Liberia, Luxembourg, Malawi, Maldive Islands, Malta, Mauritania, Mauritius, Niger, Papua/New Guinea, Rwanda, Somalia, The Gambia, Togo, Trinidad and Tobago, Upper Volta, Yemen, and Zambia.

These data were collected under the direction of Kingsley Davis and published by International Population and Urban Research, Institute of International Studies, University of California in *World Urbanization, 1950-1970, Volume I: Basic Data for Cities, Countries and Regions,* Population Monograph Series, no. 4 (Berkeley: University of California, 1969).

Table 4.2
Concentration of Population

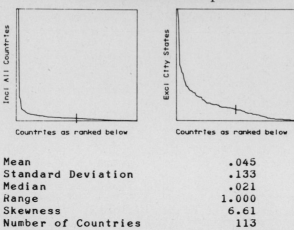

Countries as ranked below   Countries as ranked below

Mean	.045
Standard Deviation	.133
Median	.021
Range	1.000
Skewness	6.61
Number of Countries	113

Rank	Country	C	Date	Source
1.5	Hong Kong	1.000	1965	
1.5	Singapore	1.000	1965	
3	Uruguay	.210	1964	
4	Iceland	.188	1965	3
5	Australia	.104	1964	
6	Jordan	.099	1965	4
7	Lebanon	.090	1963	2
8	Luxembourg	.088	1966	
9	Chile	.076	1964	
10	South Viet Nam	.071	1964	
11.5	Austria	.064	1964	
11.5	New Zealand	.064	1965	
13	Puerto Rico	.060	1965	1
14	Greece	.057	1961	3
15	Israel	.056	1964	
16	Venezuela	.055	1965	
17	Cyprus	.053	1965	3
18.5	Dominican Republic	.052	1965	
18.5	Nicaragua	.052	1963	
20	Ireland	.047	1966	3
21	United Kingdom	.046	1964	
22	Hungary	.045	1964	
24	Canada	.044	1964	
24	Iraq	.044	1965	
24	Paraguay	.044	1962	2
26.5	Belgium	.039	1964	
26.5	Tunisia	.039	1966	4
28	Argentina	.037	1960	
29	Finland	.035	1965	2
31.5	Denmark	.033	1964	1
31.5	France	.033	1962	
31.5	Switzerland	.033	1965	

Table 4.2 Concentration of Population—*Continued*

Rank	Country	C	Date	Source
31.5	Syria	.033	1964	1
34.5	Costa Rica	.031	1965	4
34.5	Cuba	.031	1964	
37.5	Albania	.030	1964	3
37.5	Norway	.030	1965	1
37.5	Peru	.030	1965	4
37.5	Taiwan	.030	1964	
40.5	Senegal	.029	1960	
40.5	South Korea	.029	1964	
42.5	Trinidad and Tobago	.026	1960	2
42.5	United Arab Republic	.026	1962	
46	Colombia	.025	1964	
46	Ecuador	.025	1962	2
46	El Salvador	.025	1963	1
46	Guatemala	.025	1964	1
46	Japan	.025	1965	
50.5	Bolivia	.024	1965	4
50.5	Sweden	.024	1966	3
50.5	United States	.024	1964	
50.5	Zambia	.024	1964	
53.5	Iran	.023	1963	
53.5	Netherlands	.023	1964	
55.5	Botswana	.022	1964	1
55.5	Nepal	.022	1958	
57	South Africa	.021	1960	
59.5	Bulgaria	.020	1964	
59.5	East Germany	.020	1964	
59.5	Morocco	.020	1965	
59.5	Spain	.020	1964	
62	North Korea	.019	1962	
63.5	Gabon	.018	1965	1
63.5	Italy	.018	1965	3
65	Algeria	.017	1960	
66.5	Czechoslovakia	.015	1964	
66.5	Poland	.015	1964	
69.5	Honduras	.014	1966	4
69.5	Malaysia	.014	1957	1
69.5	Mexico	.014	1965	
69.5	West Germany	.014	1964	
72	Romania	.013	1964	
74	Brazil	.012	1960	
74	Ivory Coast	.012	1964	2
74	Portugal	.012	1960	2
77	Rhodesia	.011	1965	1
77	Saudi Arabia	.011	1963	4
77	Yugoslavia	.011	1965	3
79	Laos	.010	1966	4
80.5	North Viet Nam	.009	1960	1
80.5	Togo	.009	1963	1
82.5	Turkey	.008	1965	
82.5	Yemen	.008	1965	1
84.5	Cameroon	.007	1961	4
84.5	Ghana	.007	1960	4
87	Cambodia	.005	1962	2
87	Malagasy Republic	.005	1965	

Table 4.2 Concentration of Population—*Continued*

Rank	Country	C	Date	Source
87	Philippines	.005	1965	
90.5	Ceylon	.004	1963	2
90.5	Dahomey	.004	1963	2
90.5	Haiti	.004	1965	2
90.5	Thailand	.004	1965	4
96.5	Guinea	.003	1960	
96.5	Indonesia	.003	1961	
96.5	Mauritania	.003	1965	1
96.5	Nigeria	.003	1963	
96.5	Pakistan	.003	1961	
96.5	Sierra Leone	.003	1965	5
96.5	Soviet Union	.003	1965	
96.5	Upper Volta	.003	1965	3
104	Afghanistan	.002	1965	1
104	Burma	.002	1963	1
104	Chad	.002	1962	1
104	Kenya	.002	1962	1
104	Mali	.002	1963	
104	Somalia	.002	1964	1
104	Sudan	.002	1964	2
110	China	.001	1957	
110	Ethiopia	.001	1962	2
110	India	.001	1965	
110	Malawi	.001	1966	4
110	Tanzania	.001	1957	
113	Uganda	.000	1959	1

Notes: Data are missing for Angola, Barbados, Burundi, Central African Republic, Congo-Brazzaville, Congo-Kinshasa, Guyana, Jamaica, Kuwait, Lesotho, Liberia, Libya, Maldive Islands, Malta, Mauritius, Mongolia, Mozambique, Niger, Panama, Papua/New Guinea, Rwanda, Southern Yemen, and The Gambia.

Source, unless otherwise noted, is United Nations Statistical Office, *Demographic Yearbook, 1966* (New York, 1967).

1. *The Europa Yearbook, 1966* (London: Europa, 1966).

2. *The Statesman's Year-Book, Statistical and Historical Annual of the States of the World for the Year 1966-1967,* ed. S. H. Steinberg (London: Macmillan, 1966).

3. *The Europa Yearbook, 1967* (London: Europa, 1967).

4. *The Stateman's Year-Book, Statistical and Historical Annual of the States of the World for the Year 1967-1968,* ed. S. H. Steinberg (London: Macmillan, 1967).

5. *Hammond's Contemporary World Atlas* (New York: Doubleday, 1967).

Table 4.3
School Enrollment Ratios

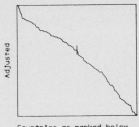 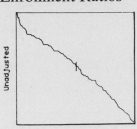

Countries as ranked below   Countries as ranked below

	Adjusted	Unadjusted
Mean	58	47
Standard Deviation	27	23
Median	64	49
Range	100	87
Skewness	−.33	−.17
Number of Countries	133	134

Rank	Country	Adjusted Ratio	Unadjusted Ratio	Bias	Date
1	Iceland	105	91		1963
2	East Germany	103	83		
3	United Kingdom	101	87		
4	Ireland	98	79	+1	
5	Puerto Rico	97	77	+1	
7	Belgium	93	81	+1	1964
7	Japan	93	74		
7	United States	93	87	+1	
9.5	Australia	92	80		
9.5	New Zealand	92	79	−1	
12	France	91	73		
12	Netherlands	91	73		
12	Norway	91	73		
15	Albania	90	66	+1	
15	Denmark	90	72		
15	West Germany	90	78		
17	Romania	89	71	+1	
19	Bulgaria	88	70		
19	Cyprus	88	71	−2	
19	Poland	88	71		
21	Guyana	86	74	−1	
23	Luxembourg	85	74		
23	Singapore	85	68		
23	Sweden	85	74		
25	Philippines	83	55		1964
27.5	Hungary	82	66		
27.5	Israel	82	66		
27.5	Soviet Union	82	72	+1	
27.5	Uruguay	82	66		
31.5	Austria	81	70		
31.5	Ceylon	81	65		

Table 4.3 School Enrollment Ratios—*Continued*

Rank	Country	Adjusted Ratio	Unadjusted Ratio	Bias	Date
31.5	Costa Rica	81	60	+1	
31.5	Greece	81	65		1964
34.5	Czechoslovakia	80	69		
34.5	Hong Kong	80	64		
36.5	Barbados	79	74	-1	1964
36.5	Yugoslavia	79	63		
39.5	Chile	77	61		
39.5	Cuba	77	61		
39.5	Panama	77	62		
39.5	Taiwan	77	61		
43.5	Canada	76	81		
43.5	Congo — Brazzaville	76	66		
43.5	Lesotho	76	61		1966
43.5	Trinidad and Tobago	76	71	-1	1963
47	Jamaica	75	55		
47	Malta	75	65		1964
47	Spain	75	55	-1	
49.5	Kuwait	74	59		
49.5	Venezuela	74	54		
51.5	Ghana	72	57	+1	
51.5	South Korea	72	58		
54	Finland	71	66	-1	
54	Peru	71	52		1964
54	South Africa	71	57		
56	Italy	70	61		
57	Cameroon	69	60		
59	Gabon	68	59		
59	Jordan	68	54		
59	Mauritius	68	59		1966
61.5	Ecuador	67	53		
61.5	Portugal	67	49		
63	Mexico	66	49		
65.5	Argentina	64	61		
65.5	Dominican Republic	64	51	+1	1966
65.5	Switzerland	64	56	-1	1964
65.5	Tunisia	64	51		
68	Paraguay	62	49		
69.5	Malaysia	59	51		
69.5	South Viet Nam	59	47		
71.5	China	58	46		1958
71.5	Lebanon	58	47		
73.5	Mongolia	57	30		1961
73.5	Rhodesia	57	42	-2	
75.5	Syria	54	43		
75.5	Turkey	54	39		1964
77	United Arab Republic	53	43		
79	Colombia	52	38	+1	
79	Congo — Kinshasa	52	42		
79	Iraq	52	38		
81.5	El Salvador	51	41	+1	
81.5	Libya	51	41		
83	Burma	50	30		1964
84.5	Bolivia	49	39		
84.5	Cambodia	49	42		

Table 4.3 School Enrollment Ratios—*Continued*

Rank	Country	Adjusted Ratio	Unadjusted Ratio	Bias	Date
86	Nicaragua	48	35		
87.5	Brazil	47	41		
87.5	Indonesia	47	38		1964
89.5	Honduras	46	33		
89.5	Papua / New Guinea	46	34		
91	Kenya	45	39	+1	
93.5	Botswana	44	33		
93.5	India	44	38		1963
93.5	Rwanda	44	38		1963
93.5	Thailand	44	38		
96	Zambia	42	33	+1	
97	Malagasy Republic	41	35		
98	Iran	40	32		1966
99	Algeria	39	34		
100	Morocco	38	27		
101.5	Central African Republic	35	30		
101.5	Guatemala	35	25		
103	Togo	33	29		
105	Ivory Coast	32	28		
105	Laos	32	27		
105	Uganda	32	23	-1	
107	Malawi	31	26	-1	1966
108	Liberia	30	24	+1	
109.5	Haiti	27	23	-1	
109.5	Pakistan	27	22		
111	Mozambique	26	19		1962
112	Nigeria	25	23		
113	Senegal	24	21		
114	Tanzania	23	20	-1	
115.5	Chad	20	17		
115.5	Dahomey	20	17		
117.5	Guinea	19	16		
117.5	Nepal	19	13	-1	
119.5	Burundi	18	14		
119.5	The Gambia	18	16		
121.5	Angola	16	12		1964
121.5	Sierra Leone	16	15		1964
123.5	Maldive Islands		15		
123.5	Saudi Arabia	15	12		
126	Mali	14	11		
126	Southern Yemen	14	13		1966
126	Sudan	14	11		
128	Afghanistan	11	9	-1	
130	Ethiopia	8	6		
130	Mauritania	8	7		1964
130	Upper Volta	8	7		
132.5	Niger	6	6		
132.5	Somalia	6	5		
134	Yemen	5	4		

Table 4.3 School Enrollment Ratios—*Continued*

Notes: Data are missing for North Korea and North Viet Nam.

Bias is indicated as follows:

—2 indicates high underestimate likely (e.g. significant portions of the population are excluded).

—1 indicates moderate underestimate likely (e.g. minor parts of the population excluded, for public education only, mission schools excluded or unaided private schools excluded).

+1 indicates moderate overestimate likely (e.g. preschool education, evening schools or special education included).

Blank indicates no known bias. See text for definition.

Date, unless otherwise noted, is 1965.

Source is UNESCO, *UNESCO Statistical Yearbook, 1967* (Paris, 1968).

Table 4.4
Enrollment in Higher Education

Countries as ranked below

Mean	4173
Standard Deviation	4898
Median	2020
Range	28394
Skewness	1.90
Number of Countries	121

Rank	Country	Students Per One Million Inhabitants	Bias	Date
1	United States	28400		
2	New Zealand	21000		
3	Soviet Union	16740	+1	
4	Canada	16510		
5	Puerto Rico	15300		
6	Philippines	14410		1964
7	Israel	14000		
8	Bulgaria	12200	+1	
9	Netherlands	12090		
10	Australia	11590		
11	Japan	11400		
12	Argentina	10890		
13	France	10420		
14	Denmark	10050		
15	Czechoslovakia	10010		
16	Yugoslavia	9480		
17	Sweden	9230		
18	Lebanon	8440		
19	Finland	8410		
20	Belgium	8050		1964
21	Poland	8000		
22	Ireland	7590		
23	Mongolia	7560		1963
24	Singapore	7400		
25	Taiwan	6870		
26	Romania	6860	+1	
27	Albania	6840	+1	
28	Austria	6810		
29	Panama	6585		
30	West Germany	6320		

Table 4.4 Enrollment in Higher Education—*Continued*

Rank	Country	Students Per One Million Inhabitants	Bias	Date
31	Greece	6260		1964
32	Uruguay	6100	-1	
33	Syria	6040	-2	
34	United Arab Republic	5980		
35	Italy	5830		
36	Switzerland	5540	-2	
37	Iceland	5490		1964
38	Venezuela	5370		
39	Norway	5250		
40	Chile	5080		
41	Costa Rica	5040		
42	Hungary	5030		
43	South Korea	5000		
44	United Kingdom	4857	-2	
45	East Germany	4660		
46.5	Malta	4230		
46.5	Peru	4230	-1	1963
48	Spain	4170		
49	Cuba	4000		
50	Bolivia	3630		
51	Portugal	3530		1964
52	Iraq	3470		
53	South Africa	3290	-1	
54	Mexico	3120		
55	Ecuador	2990		
56	Turkey	2930		1964
57	Hong Kong	2870		
58	India	2840		1963
59	Pakistan	2670		
60	Colombia	2140	-2	1964
61	Nicaragua	2020		
62	Brazil	1890		
63	Luxembourg	1860		
64	Dominican Republic	1820		
65	Guatemala	1730	-2	
66	Barbados	1710		
67	South Viet Nam	1680		
68	Thailand	1660		
69	Jordan	1620		
70	Tunisia	1410		
71	Malaysia	1367		
72	Cyprus	1330		
73	Ceylon	1290	-1	
74	El Salvador	1240		
75	China	1220		1962
76	Congo - Brazzaville	1210		
77.5	Cambodia	1200		
77.5	Libya	1200		
79	Honduras	1130		
80	Jamaica	1060	-1	
81	Iran	1050		
82	Indonesia	950	-2	1963
83	Trinidad and Tobago	930	-1	

Table 4.4 Enrollment in Higher Education—*Continued*

Rank	Country	Students Per One Million Inhabitants	Bias	Date
84	Burma	850		1964
85	Nepal	800		
86	Senegal	790		
87	Morocco	780		1964
88	Liberia	730		1966
89	Algeria	680		
90	Sudan	570		
91	Ghana	550	-1	
92	Malagasy Republic	480		
93	Ivory Coast	420		1964
94	Lesotho	410		1966
95.5	Guyana	390	-1	
95.5	Sierra Leone	390		
97	Haiti	370	-1	
98.5	Cameroon	300		
98.5	Kenya	300		
100	Papua / New Guinea	252		
101	Saudi Arabia	240		1964
102	Afghanistan	220		
103	Rhodesia	200	-1	
105.5	Congo - Kinshasa	160		1964
105.5	Guinea	160		
105.5	Nigeria	160		
105.5	Uganda	160		
108	Mauritius	130		
109	Gabon	120	-1	1964
110	Malawi	110		1966
111	Ethiopia	100		
113	Burundi	70		
113	Laos	70		
113	Mozambique	70		1964
115.5	Mali	50		
115.5	Tanzania	50		
117.5	Rwanda	40		
117.5	Togo	40		
119	Somalia	30		1964
120	Dahomey	20		
121	Upper Volta	6		

Notes: Data are missing for Angola, Botswana, Central African Republic, Chad, Kuwait, Maldive Islands, Mauritania, Niger, North Korea, North Viet Nam, Paraguay, Southern Yemen, The Gambia, Yemen, and Zambia.

Bias is indicated as follows:

—2 indicates high underestimate likely (e.g. only one major institution included, for universities or teacher training only, or teacher training excluded).

—1 indicates moderate underestimate likely (e.g. one or more universities excluded).

+1 indicates overestimate likely (e.g. correspondence courses included).

Blank indicates no known bias. See text for definition.

Date, unless otherwise noted, is 1965.

Source is UNESCO, *UNESCO Statistical Yearbook, 1967* (Paris, 1968).

Table 4.5
Literacy

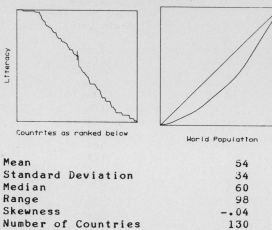

Mean	54
Standard Deviation	34
Median	60
Range	98
Skewness	-.04
Number of Countries	130

Rank	Country	Literacy	Age Base	Source
3.5	Denmark	100		2
3.5	Finland	100		2
3.5	Iceland	100		2
3.5	Norway	100		2
3.5	Sweden	100		2
3.5	Switzerland	100		2
13	Belgium	99		2
13	Canada	99		1
13	Czechoslovakia	99		1
13	East Germany	99		1
13	France	99		1
13	Luxembourg	99		1
13	Netherlands	99		1
13	New Zealand	99		1
13	Romania	99		2
13	Soviet Union	99		
13	United Kingdom	99		1
13	United States	99		
13	West Germany	99		1
22	Australia	98		4
22	Austria	98		2
22	Hungary	98		2
22	Japan	98		
22	Poland	98		2
25	Ireland	96		1
26	Barbados	95		1
27	Italy	92	6+	1
28	Argentina	91	14+	1
29.5	Israel	90		
29.5	Uruguay	90		1
31	Spain	87		1

Table 4.5 Literacy—*Continued*

Rank	Country	Literacy	Age Base	Source
32.5	Guyana	86		
32.5	Lebanon	86		
34.5	Bulgaria	85		1
34.5	Jamaica	85		
36.5	Chile	84		
36.5	Costa Rica	84		1
38	Greece	82		
39	Puerto Rico	81		1
41	Malta	80		2
41	Trinidad and Tobago	80		
41	Venezuela	80		
43	Yugoslavia	77		
44	Cyprus	76		
46	Ceylon	75		
46	Cuba	75		2
46	Taiwan	75		
48	Panama	73		
50	Albania	72	9+	1
50	Mongolia	72	8+	1
50	Philippines	72		
52.5	Hong Kong	71		
52.5	South Korea	71		
54	Thailand	70		
55	Paraguay	68		
56	Ecuador	67		
58.5	Colombia	65		2
58.5	Dominican Republic	65		3
58.5	Mexico	65		1
58.5	North Viet Nam	65	12+	1
61	Portugal	62		1
62.5	Brazil	61	10+	1
62.5	Peru	61	17+	
65	Burma	60		
65	Mauritius	60		
65	Singapore	60		
67.5	China	50		5
67.5	Nicaragua	50		1
69	El Salvador	49		
70	Kuwait	47		
71	Turkey	46		
72.5	Honduras	45		1
72.5	South Viet Nam	45		
74.5	Indonesia	43		
74.5	Malaysia	43		
76.5	Cambodia	41		3
76.5	Zambia	41	7+	
78	Guatemala	38		
81.5	Congo – Kinshasa	35		
81.5	Jordan	35		
81.5	Lesotho	35		
81.5	Malagasy Republic	35		
81.5	South Africa	35		
81.5	Syria	35		
85	Nigeria	33		

Table 4.5 Literacy—*Continued*

Rank	Country	Literacy	Age Base	Source
86	Bolivia	32	5+	
88	Libya	30		
88	Tunisia	30		
88	United Arab Republic	30		
90	India	28		
91	Uganda	25		
93.5	Congo – Brazzaville	23		
93.5	Ghana	23		
93.5	Iran	23		3
93.5	Kenya	23		
98	Botswana	20		
98	Iraq	20		
98	Ivory Coast	20		
98	Pakistan	20		
98	Rhodesia	20		
101	Tanzania	18		
103	Algeria	15		
103	Central African Republic	15		
103	Laos	15		
105.5	Morocco	13		
105.5	Sudan	13		
110	Cameroon	10		
110	Guinea	10		
110	Haiti	10		
110	Liberia	10		
110	Saudi Arabia	10		
110	Sierra Leone	10		
110	The Gambia	10		
117.5	Afghanistan	8		
117.5	Gabon	8		
117.5	Malawi	8		
117.5	Nepal	8		
117.5	Rwanda	8		
117.5	Senegal	8	14+	
117.5	Togo	8		
117.5	Upper Volta	8		
124	Chad	5		
124	Dahomey	5		
124	Ethiopia	5		
124	Mali	5		
124	Somalia	5		
128	Angola	3		
128	Mauritania	3		
128	Niger	3		
130	Mozambique	2		

Notes: Data are missing for Burundi, Maldive Islands, North Korea, Papua/New Guinea, Southern Yemen, and Yemen.

Age base, unless otherwise noted, is for population fifteen years old and above.

Source, unless otherwise noted, is United States, Agency for International Development, *A.I.D. Economic Data Books* (Washington, D.C.: U.S. Government Printing Office, 1967).

Table 4.5 Literacy—*Continued*

1. UNESCO, *UNESCO Statistical Yearbook, 1965* (Paris, 1967).
2. Moshe Y. Sachs, ed., *The Worldmark Encyclopedia of Nations* (New York: Harper & Row, 1967).
3. UNESCO, *UNESCO Statistical Yearbook, 1967* (Paris, 1968).
4. *Gallatin Business Intelligence* (New York: Copley International Corporation, 1967).
5. United States Congress, Joint Economic Committee, *Mainland China in the World Economy* (Washington, D.C.: U.S. Government Printing Office, 1967).

Table 4.6
Lettermail Per Capita

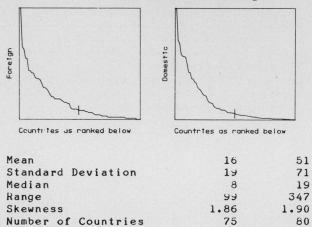

	Foreign	Domestic
Mean	16	51
Standard Deviation	19	71
Median	8	19
Range	99	347
Skewness	1.86	1.90
Number of Countries	75	80

Rank	Country	Foreign Mail Per Capita	Domestic Mail Per Capita	Bias	Date
1	United States	14	347		
2	Switzerland	62	246		
3	Belgium	41	237		
4	New Zealand		203		
5	United Kingdom	18	197		
6	Australia	28	196		
7	Netherlands	32	194		
8	Sweden	20	172		
9	France		147		
10	West Germany	18	146		
11	Luxembourg	99	127		
12	Denmark	20	126		
13	Norway	22	117		
14	Austria	41	114		
15	Italy	14	101		
16	Japan	2	95		
17	Ireland	54	92		
18	Finland	15	84		
19	Spain	18	77		
20	East Germany	9	75		
21	Israel	27	72		
22	Guyana		59		1963
23	Yugoslavia	7	53		
24	South Africa	10	52		
25	Hungary		51		
26	Portugal	18	41		
27	Malta	54	38		
28.5	Argentina	8	35		
28.5	Ceylon	2	35		
30	Iceland	25	34		
32	Greece		30		

Table 4.6 Lettermail Per Capita—*Continued*

Rank	Country	Foreign Mail Per Capita	Domestic Mail Per Capita	Bias	Date
32	Poland	2	30		
32	Taiwan	2	30		
34	Jamaica	37	27		
35	Barbados	43	23		
36.5	Cyprus	43	22		
36.5	Singapore	35	22		
38.5	Uruguay	2	21		1959
38.5	Venezuela	36	21		
40	Mexico	9	19		
41	South Korea	1	17		
42	Hong Kong	36	16		
43	Ghana	9	15		
44.5	Chile	1	14		1963
44.5	Rhodesia	9	14		
47	Brazil	15	13		
47	India	1	13		
47	Mauritius	8	13		
49.5	Malaysia	7	11		
49.5	Turkey	2	11		
51	Algeria	2	10	+1	
52.5	Lebanon	28	9		1964
52.5	United Arab Republic	3	9		
54	Zambia	8	8		
55	Iraq	6	7		1964
56.5	Malagasy Republic	8	6		
56.5	Pakistan	2	6		1964
60	Angola	1	5		
60	Jordan	6	5		1964
60	Morocco	6	5		1964
60	Southern Yemen	17	5	-1	
60	Syria	3	5		
63.5	Ivory Coast	5	4		1964
63.5	Libya	16	4		
68.5	Burma	0	3		
68.5	Colombia	2	3		1963
68.5	Kuwait	64	3		
68.5	Malawi	4	3		
68.5	Nigeria	1	3		
68.5	Saudi Arabia	4	3		
68.5	Sierra Leone	3	3		
68.5	South Viet Nam	2	3		
74.5	El Salvador	4	2		
74.5	Indonesia	0	2		
74.5	Paraguay	4	2		1964
74.5	Thailand	1	2		
78	Mozambique	3	1		
78	Niger	1	1		
78	Togo	2	1		
80	Laos	0	0		1959

Table 4.6 Lettermail Per Capita—*Continued*

Notes: Data are missing for Afghanistan, Albania, Bolivia, Botswana, Bulgaria, Burundi, Cambodia, Cameroon, Canada, Central African Republic, Chad, China, Congo-Brazzaville, Congo-Kinshasa, Costa Rica, Cuba, Czechoslovakia, Dahomey, Dominican Republic, Ecuador, Ethiopia, Gabon, Guatemala, Guinea, Haiti, Honduras, Iran, Kenya, Lesotho, Liberia, Maldive Islands, Mali, Mauritania, Mongolia, Nepal, Nicaragua, North Korea, North Viet Nam, Panama, Papua/New Guinea, Peru, Philippines, Puerto Rico, Romania, Rwanda, Senegal, Somalia, Soviet Union, Sudan, Tanzania, The Gambia, Trinidad and Tobago, Tunisia, Uganda, Upper Volta, and Yemen.

Bias is indicated as follows:

—1 indicates moderate underestimate likely.

+1 indicates moderate overestimate likely.

Blank indicates no known bias.

Date, unless otherwise noted, is 1965.

Source is United Nations, Statistical Office, *Statistical Yearbook, 1966* (New York, 1967).

Table 4.7
Telephones Per Thousand Population

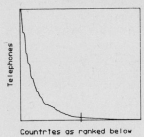

Countries as ranked below

Mean	54.4
Standard Deviation	95.7
Median	11.7
Range	481.2
Skewness	2.54
Number of Countries	126

Rank	Country	Telephones Per 000 Population	Date Source
1	United States	481.4	
2	Sweden	437.9	
3	Switzerland	380.0	
4	Canada	379.5	
5	New Zealand	364.6	
6	Iceland	290.6	
7	Denmark	286.7	
8	Australia	247.4	
9	Norway	243.9	
10	Luxembourg	240.9	
11	Netherlands	191.3	
12	Finland	181.2	
13	United Kingdom	181.0	
14	Belgium	164.6	
15	West Germany	149.1	
16	Austria	139.0	
17	Japan	125.1	
18	France	125.0	
19	Italy	116.0	
20	Czechoslovakia	105.3	
21	Israel	100.5	
22	East Germany	97.0	
23	Spain	87.7	
24	Puerto Rico	77.1	
25	Ireland	71.8	
26	Malta	68.9	
27	Hong Kong	68.7	
28	Uruguay	68.2	
29	Argentina	67.0	
30	Barbados	63.5	

Table 4.7 Telephones Per Thousand Population—*Continued*

Rank	Country	Telephones Per 000 Population	Date	Source
31	South Africa	63.4		
32	Portugal	59.8		
33	Greece	59.4		
34.5	Hungary	55.8		
34.5	Kuwait	55.8		
36	Cyprus	47.6		
37	Singapore	46.6		
38	Poland	41.1		
39	Lebanon	40.9		
40	Trinidad and Tobago	39.9		
41	Panama	35.7		
42	Bulgaria	34.0		
43	Venezuela	32.4		
44	Chile	30.7		
45	Cuba	30.3		
46	Jamaica	27.6		
47	Romania	24.9		
48	Colombia	24.5		
49	Rhodesia	23.8		
50	Yugoslavia	21.3		
51	Mexico	19.3		
52	Mauritius	18.4		
53	Guyana	16.5		
54	Brazil	16.1		
55	Costa Rica	15.2		
56	Syria	14.7		
57	Malaysia	14.0		
58	Taiwan	13.4		
59	Soviet Union	13.3	1961	2
60	Jordan	13.2		
61	Mongolia	12.3		
62	Algeria	11.8		
63	Peru	11.7		
64	Tunisia	11.4		
65	Turkey	11.3		
66	United Arab Republic	11.1		
67	Morocco	10.6		
68.5	Congo - Brazzaville	9.7		
68.5	South Korea	9.7		
70	Zambia	9.3		
71	Libya	9.1		
72	Iran	8.9		
73.5	Dominican Republic	8.6		
73.5	Ecuador	8.6		
75	Gabon	8.2		
76	Iraq	7.5		
77	Nicaragua	7.4		
78.5	Albania	7.2	1964	2
78.5	Senegal	7.2		
80.5	Paraguay	6.9		
80.5	Southern Yemen	6.9		
82.5	Bolivia	6.8		
82.5	El Salvador	6.8		

Table 4.7 Telephones Per Thousand Population—*Continued*

Rank	Country	Telephones Per 000 Population	Date	Source
84	Kenya	5.7		
85	Guatemala	5.6		
86	Philippines	5.1		
87	Papua / New Guinea	4.9		
88	Ivory Coast	4.6		
89	Ghana	4.5		
90	Saudi Arabia	4.1		
91	Honduras	3.9		
92	Ceylon	3.8		
93.5	Angola	3.0		
93.5	Malagasy Republic	3.0		
95.5	Mozambique	2.8		
95.5	The Gambia	2.8	1964	1
97	Sudan	2.7		
98	Uganda	2.6		
99	Thailand	2.5		
100	Sierra Leone	2.2		2
101.5	Central African Republic	2.1		
101.5	Tanzania	2.1		
103	Togo	1.9		
105	Dahomey	1.8		
105	Guinea	1.8		
105	Malawi	1.8		
107.5	India	1.6		
107.5	Indonesia	1.6		
109	South Viet Nam	1.4		
110.5	Congo - Kinshasa	1.3		
110.5	Pakistan	1.3		
112	Nigeria	1.2		
113	Ethiopia	1.1		
115	Chad	1.0		
115	Haiti	1.0		
115	Mali	1.0		
118.5	Burma	.8		
118.5	Cambodia	.8		
118.5	Cameroon	.8		
118.5	Mauritania	.8		1
121	Niger	.7		
123	Afghanistan	.6		
123	Burundi	.6		2
123	Lesotho	.6	1963	2
125	Upper Volta	.5		
126	Rwanda	.2	1964	1

Notes: Data are missing for Botswana, China, Laos, Liberia, Maldive Islands, Nepal, North Korea, North Viet Nam, Somalia, and Yemen.

Date, unless otherwise noted, is 1965.

Source, unless otherwise noted, is United Nations Statistical Office, *Statistical Yearbook, 1966* (New York, 1967).

1. *Gallatin Business Intelligence* (New York: Copley International Corporation, 1967).

2. Moshe Y. Sachs, ed., *The Worldmark Encyclopedia of Nations* (New York: Harper & Row, 1967).

Table 4.8
Mass Media

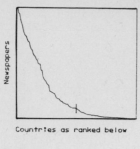

Newspapers

Countries as ranked below

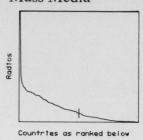

Radios

Countries as ranked below

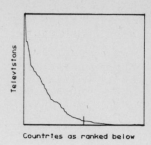

Televisions

Countries as ranked below

Mean	104
Standard Deviation	135
Median	42
Range	505
Skewness	1.39
Number of Countries	125

Rank	Country	Newspaper Circulation Per 000 Pop.	Bias	Date	Source
1	United States	310			
2	Sweden	505			
3	United Kingdom	479			
4	Canada	218	-1		1
5	West Germany	326	-1		
6	East Germany	421			1
7	Luxembourg	477			1
8	Denmark	347			
9	Finland	359			6
10	Japan	451			
11	Iceland	435			
12	Norway	384			
13	New Zealand	399		1964	
14	Belgium	285			
15	Australia	373			
16	Switzerland	376			
17	Uruguay	314		1963	
18	Netherlands	293			
19	Czechoslovakia	280			
20	France	246			1
21	Soviet Union	264			
22	Austria	249			
23	Kuwait	28		1964	
24	Ireland	246			
25	Panama	81	-1		
26	Singapore	268			
27	Argentina	148	-1		
28	Hungary	178			
29	Hong Kong	349			
30	Israel	188	-1	1966	1

142	52
155	75
100	13
1230	362
3.03	1.78
128	102

Radio Receivers Per 000 Pop.	Type	Date	Source	Television Receivers Per 000 Pop.	Type	Date	Source
1234	r			362	r		
382	l			270	l		
297	l			248	l		
519	r	1964		271	r		
440	r			193	l		
337	l	1964		188	l		
360	l			94	r		
334	l			228	l		
334	l			159	l		
209	l			183	l		
302	l			78	r		2
293	l			131	l		
244	l			156	l		
320	l			163	l		
222	l			172	l		
278	l			105	l		
339	r	1964		74	r		
252	l			172	l		
263	l			149	l		
314	l			131	l		
320	l			68	l		
297	l			98	l		
411	r	1964		141	r	1964	
212	r			115	r		
385	r			54	r		
214	l	1964		34	l		
295	r		1	72	r		
245	l			82	l		
139	r			13	l		
290	r		1	6	l		

Table 4.8 Mass Media—*Continued*

Rank	Country	Newspaper Circulation Per 000 Pop.	Bias	Date	Source
31	Malta				
32	Cyprus	217			
33	Bulgaria	172			
34	Italy	113	-1		
35	Southern Yemen				
36	Poland	167			
37	Iraq	12		1963	
38	Syria	21	-1	1964	
39	Spain	153		1963	
40	Mexico	116			
41	Cuba	88		1961	
42	Greece	121		1959	6
43	Venezuela	70	-1		
44	Romania	157			
45	Guyana	93		1964	
46	Trinidad and Tobago	102			
47	Barbados	112			
48	Mauritius	122			1
49	Jamaica	69			
50	Yugoslavia	90			
51	Mongolia	88		1963	
52	Bolivia	26			
53	Peru	47		1959	
54	Lebanon	77	-1		4
55	Chile	118	-1	1964	
56	Jordan	8			
57	Portugal	68			
58	The Gambia	5		1959	
59	Costa Rica	77	-1	1964	
60	El Salvador	47		1963	
61	Puerto Rico	64			
62	South Africa	45		1966	1
63	Colombia	52		1963	
64	Taiwan	64		1963	
65	Cambodia	7			
66	South Viet Nam	42			
67	Algeria	15			
68	Brazil	32		1964	
69	Ecuador	47			
70	Paraguay	37		1959	5
71	South Korea	64			
72	Turkey	51			6
73	Liberia	4		1964	
74	Nicaragua	49	-1		
75	Albania	47			
76	Malaysia	57		1964	
77	Mauritania				
78	Ghana	29			
79	Senegal	6			1
80	Guatemala	23		1961	2
81	Gabon	10		1961	3
82	Iran	15		1961	
83	Tunisia	18			

Radio Receivers Per 000 Pop.	Type	Date	Source	Television Receivers Per 000 Pop.	Type	Date	Source
232	l	1964		82	l		
219	r			24	l		
251	l			23	l		
208	l			117	l		
272	r			12	r		
179	l			66	l		
349	r		1	21	r		4
329	r			12	r		
144	r			55	r		
193	r			42	r		
181	r	1964		74	r	1964	
106	l						
190	r			75	r		
147	l			26	l		
124	r		1				
169	r			42	l	1964	4
176	r			25	r		
162	r			7	r		
196	r			14	r		
154	r			30	r		
142	r						
186	r	1964		18	r		
121	r	1964		53	r		
94	r	1959		6	r	1964	
136	l						
128	l			20	l		
133	r		1				
91	r			35	r		
135	r			12	r		
146	r			0	r	1967	2
118	r	1966	1	19	r		
102	l			5	l		4
158	r			1	r		
64	r	1964					
129	l	1963	1	13	r		
95	r	1964		29	r	1964	
100	r			8	r		
61	r	1959					
69	r			2	l		
79	l			0	r		
122	r			3	r		
63	r	1964		10	r		
70	r		1	1	r		
45	l			6	l		
34	r	1964					
74	l	1964		0	r		4
59	r	1964					
56	l			12	r		
78	r			3	r	1964	
67	r	1966	1	5	r		
67	l	1964		1	r		

Table 4.8 Mass Media—*Continued*

Rank	Country	Newspaper Circulation Per 000 Pop.	Bias	Date	Source
84	Malagasy Republic	13		1964	4
85	Honduras	19	-1	1964	
86	Dominican Republic	27	-1		
87	United Arab Republic	15		1963	
88	Ceylon	39			
89	Thailand	13	-1		
90	Morocco	17	-1	1963	
91	Philippines	17		1964	
92	Congo - Brazzaville	2			1
93	Libya	5	-1		1
94	Sierra Leone	7			
95	Burundi	0			6
96	Laos	5			
97	Kenya	7			
98	Lesotho	0			6
99	Cameroon	4		1964	
100	Angola	9		1964	
101	Togo	6		1964	
102	Uganda	8			1
103	Rhodesia	15			
104	Guinea	0		1959	6
105.5	Burma	10		1964	
105.5	Mozambique	6		1963	
107	Malawi				
108	Afghanistan	6	-1		
109.5	India	13	-1		1
109.5	Somalia	2		1964	
111	Dahomey	1		1964	
112	Pakistan	18			1
113	Central African Republic	0			6
114.5	Sudan	4		1961	2
114.5	Zambia	7			
116	Saudi Arabia	5			
117.5	Haiti	5			
117.5	Ivory Coast	3			
119	Nigeria	7	-1		
120	China				
121	Ethiopia	2	-1		
122	Upper Volta				
123	Indonesia	7	-1		
124.5	Congo - Kinshasa	1			6
124.5	Niger	0			6
126.5	Botswana	0			6
126.5	Tanzania	3		1962	
128	Nepal	3	-1		
129	Maldive Islands	3			4
130	Chad	0			6
131	Mali	1		1966	1

Radio Receivers Per 000 Pop.	Type	Date	Source	Television Receivers Per 000 Pop.	Type	Date	Source
44	r	1966	1				
59	r			4	r		
40	r	1966	1	14	r		
55	r			11	r		
39	l			0	r		1
54	r	1964		7	r		
53	l			3	l		
39	r	1964		4	r		
57	r	1964	2	1	r		3
31	l						
46	r			1	r		
31			3				
26	r	1964					
37	r			1	r		
30	r						
22	r		2				
16	l						
18	r						
27	r			1	l		
12	l		3	7	l		2
21	r						
11	l	1964					
15	l	1964					
20	r		1	0	r	1966	1
13	r						
11	l		1	0	r		
14	r						
15	r						
5	l	1964		0	r		
22	r			0	r		2
17	r	1964		1	r		
12	l		2	3	r		3
12	r	1959		5	r	1964	
14	r			1	r	1964	
16	r			2	r		4
11	l	1964		1	r		
12	l	1963		0	r		
15	r	1964		0			
11	r	1964		0	r		
8	r	1964	4	0	r		
13	l	1964		0	r		
14	r			1	r		4
9	l	1964					
11	r			0	r	1967	2
4	r		2				
8	r		1	0	r		1
4	r		1				

Table 4.8 Mass Media—*Continued*

Notes: Data are missing for North Korea, North Viet Nam, Papua/New Guinea, Rwanda, and Yemen.

This table is ranked on the basis of each country's average score for the three series.

Bias, for newspaper circulation, is coded as follows:

    —1 indicates moderate underestimate likely.

    Blank indicates no known bias.

Type, for radio and television receivers, is either *r* for data that refer to estimated number of receivers in us or *l* for data that refer to number of licenses issued or sets declared.

Date, unless otherwise noted, is 1965.

Source for all three series, unless otherwise noted, is United Nations, Statistical Office, *Statistical Yearbook, 1966* (New York, 1967).

Other sources for newspaper circulation include:

1. UNESCO, *UNESCO Statistical Yearbook, 1967* (Paris, 1968).
2. UNESCO, *UNESCO Statistical Yearbook, 1964* (Paris, 1966).
3. UNESCO, *UNESCO Statistical Yearbook, 1963* (Paris, 1964).
4. UNESCO, *UNESCO Statistical Yearbook, 1966* (Paris, 1968).
5. UNESCO, *UNESCO Statistical Yearbook, 1961* (Paris, 1962).
6. UNESCO, *UNESCO Statistical Yearbook, 1965* (Paris, 1967).

Other sources for radio and television receivers include:

1. UNESCO, *UNESCO Statistical Yearbook, 1967* (Paris, 1968).
2. UNESCO, *UNESCO Statistical Yearbook, 1966* (Paris, 1968).
3. *Gallatin Business Intelligence* (New York: Copley International Corporation, 1967).
4. Moshe Y. Sachs, ed., *The Worldmark Encyclopedia of Nations* (New York: Harper & Row, 1967).

Table 4.9
Vital Statistics

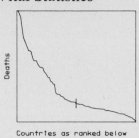

Mean	36	14
Standard Deviation	12	8
Median	40	10
Range	48	33
Skewness	−.33	1.30
Number of Countries	115	93

Rank	Country	Crude Birth Rate	Type	Bias	Source Date	Crude Death Rate	Type	Source Date
1	Rhodesia	53			1962 2			
2	Afghanistan	52			1959 5			
3.5	Iraq	51			1959 5			
3.5	Nigeria	51			1959 5			
5	Zambia	50			1963 2			
6	Ivory Coast	49			1959 5			
8	Chad	48	.		1			
8	Ecuador	48			1964 3			
8	Haiti	48	.		1			
10	Jordan	47	d		6			
11	Iran	46			1959 5			
12.5	North Korea	45	.		1			
12.5	South Viet Nam	45			1959 5			
15	Bolivia	44			1959 5			
15	Malaysia	44			1959 5			
15	Tunisia	44	d		1			
17.5	Burma	43			1959 5			
17.5	Malagasy Republic	43			1959 5			
19	Congo – Brazzaville	41	.		1			
20.5	Kuwait	40			1959 5			
20.5	Liberia	40			1962 2			
22	Angola					38		1950 2
23.5	Guinea	46			1955 2	37		1955 2
23.5	Mongolia	37			1959 5			
25	Upper Volta	49			2	36		2
26	Dahomey	49			1961 2	33		1961 2
27	Gabon	31			2			
28	Mali	61	.		1961 1	30	.	
29	Togo	56			1961 2	29	.	1961
30	Mauritania	45	.		1	28	.	

Table 4.9 Vital Statistics—*Continued*

Rank	Country	Crude Birth Rate	Type	Bias	Source Date	Crude Death Rate	Type	Source Date	
31	Niger	50			2	27	•		
33	Burundi	46	•		6	26	•		5
33	Congo – Kinshasa	45			1955 2	26		1957	2
33	Tanzania	46			1957 2	26		1957	2
35	Ghana	50			2	24	•		
37	Laos	47	•		1	23	•		
37	Lesotho	50			1959 5	23	•	1956	
37	Rwanda	52	•		1957 1	23		1957	2
39	Uganda	44			1959 2	22		1959	2
41.5	Indonesia	43	•		1962 1	21	•	1962	
41.5	Nepal	41	•		1961 1	21	•	1961	
41.5	Sudan	49			1955 2	21		1955	2
41.5	The Gambia	40			1963 2	21	•	1963	
44	Cambodia	41	•		1959 1	20	•	1959	
45.5	Morocco	46	•		1962 1	19	•	1962	
45.5	United Arab Republic	47	e		4	19	e		4
47.5	Kenya	48			1962 2	18		1962	2
47.5	Pakistan	43	•		1963 1	18	•		5
49.5	Guatemala	44	c		1966 1	17	c		
49.5	Senegal	49			2	17	•		
51.5	South Korea	41	e		4	16	•		
51.5	Turkey	43	•		1966 6	16	•	1966	5
54.5	Austria	18	c		1	13	c		
54.5	East Germany	17	c		1	13	c		
54.5	India	38	•		1964 1	13	•	1964	
54.5	Paraguay	44	•		1	13	•		
59	Belgium	16	c		1	12	c		
59	China	34	•		1957 1	12	•	1955	
59	Ireland	22	d		1	12	d		
59	Luxembourg	16	c		1	12	c		
59	United Kingdom	18	c		1	12	c		
65	Brazil	45			1959 5	11	•		5
65	Chile	33	c		1964	11	c		
65	El Salvador	45	c		1966 1	11	c		
65	France	18	c		1	11	c	1964	
65	Hungary	13	c		1	11	c		
65	Philippines	44	e		4	11	e		4
65	West Germany	18	c		1	11	c		
72.5	Colombia	39			1964 3	10		1964	3
72.5	Czechoslovakia	16	c		1	10	c		
72.5	Denmark	18	c		1	10	c		
72.5	Finland	17	c		1	10	c		
72.5	Italy	19	c		1	10	c		
72.5	Mexico	43	d		1966 1	10	d		
72.5	Portugal	23	c		1	10	c		
72.5	Sweden	16	c		1	10	c		
84	Albania	35	c		1	9	c		
84	Australia	20	d	-1	1	9	d		
84	Dominican Republic	36			4	9			4
84	Honduras	48			1964 3	9			4
84	Malta	18	c		1	9	c		
84	Mauritius	35	c		1	9	d		
84	New Zealand	23	d		1	9	d		

Table 4.9 Vital Statistics—*Continued*

Rank	Country	Crude Birth Rate	Type	Bias	Source	Date	Crude Death Rate	Type	Source	Date
84	Norway	18	c		1		9	c		
84	Peru	35			3	1963	9		3	1964
84	Romania	15	c		1		9	c		
84	Spain	21	c		1		9	c		
84	Switzerland	19	c		1		9	c		
84	Thailand	35			4		9		4	
84	United States	19	c		1		9	c		
84	Yugoslavia	21	c		1		9	c		
96.5	Argentina	22	c			1964	8	c		
96.5	Barbados	25	d		1	1966	8	d		
96.5	Bulgaria	15	c		1		8	c		
96.5	Canada	21	c		1		8	c		
96.5	Ceylon	33	d		6		8	d	5	
96.5	Costa Rica	41	c			1964	8	c		
96.5	Greece	18	c		1		8	c		
96.5	Guyana	40	d	−1			8	d		
96.5	Jamaica	39	d		1	1966	8	d		
96.5	Netherlands	20	c		1		8	c		
105.5	Iceland	25	c		1		7	c		
105.5	Japan	19	c		1		7	c		
105.5	Nicaragua	41			3		7		3	
105.5	Panama	39	c	−1			7		3	
105.5	Poland	17	c		1		7	c		
105.5	Puerto Rico	30	c		1		7	c		
105.5	Soviet Union	18	c		1		7	c		
105.5	Venezuela	43			3	1964	7		3	1964
112.5	Cuba	36			3	1964	6		3	1964
112.5	Cyprus	24	c		1		6	c		
112.5	Israel	26	c		1		6	c	5	
112.5	Singapore	31	c		1		6	d		
112.5	Taiwan	33	d		1		6	d		
112.5	Trinidad and Tobago	29	c		1	1966	6	c		
116	Hong Kong	28	d		1		5	d		

Notes: Data are missing for Algeria, Botswana, Cameroon, Central African Republic, Ethiopia, Lebanon, Libya, Malawi, Maldive Islands, Mozambique, North Viet Nam, Papua/New Guinea, Saudi Arabia, Sierra Leone, Somalia, South Africa, Southern Yemen, Syria, Uruguay, and Yemen.

Type refers to the manner of registration.

c indicates data from civil registration said to be relatively complete.

d indicates data from civil registration tabulated by year of registration rather than year of occurrence.

• indicates estimates usually based on sample surveys.

e indicates estimates of unknown reliability.

Blank indicates unknown quality.

Bias: Moderate underbias is indicated by −1 if certain parts of the population, e.g. jungle inhabitants, are excluded.

Date, unless otherwise noted, is 1965.

Source for crude birth rate, unless otherwise noted, is United Nations, Statistical Office, *Demographic Yearbook, 1965* (New York, 1966).

251

Table 4.9 Vital Statistics—*Continued*

1. United Nations, Statistical Office, *Demographic Yearbook, 1966* (New York, 1967).

2. William Brass et al., *The Demography of Tropical Africa* (Princeton: Princeton University Press, 1968).

3. Center for Latin American Studies, *Statistical Abstract of Latin America, 1967* (Los Angeles: University of California, 1967).

4. Nathan Keyfitz and Wilhelm Flieger, *World Population: An Analysis of Vital Data* (Chicago: University of Chicago Press, 1968).

5. Lee Jay Cho, "Estimated Refined Measures of Fertility for All Major Countries of the World," *Demography*, 1 (1964), 359-74.

6. United Nations, Statistical Office, *Demographic Yearbook, 1967* (New York, 1968).

Source for crude death rate, unless otherwise noted, is United Nations, Statistical Office, *Demographic Yearbook, 1966* (New York: 1967).

1. United Nations, Statistical Office, *Demographic Yearbook, 1960* (New York, 1961).

2. William Brass et al., *The Demography of Tropical Africa* (Princeton: Princeton University Press, 1968).

3. Center for Latin American Studies, *Statistical Abstract of Latin America, 1967* (Los Angeles: University of California, 1967).

4. Nathan Keyfitz and Wilhelm Flieger, *World Population: An Analysis of Vital Data* (Chicago: University of Chicago Press, 1968).

5. United Nations, Statistical Office, *Demographic Yearbook, 1967* (New York, 1968).

Table 4.10
Infant Mortality

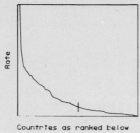

Countries as ranked below

Mean	87
Standard Deviation	87
Median	55
Range	487
Skewness	2.42
Number of Countries	102

Rank	Country	Rate	Type	Date	Source
1	Sweden	13			
2	Netherlands	14			
3	Iceland	15			
4	Norway	16		1964	
6.5	Australia	18	r		
6.5	Finland	18			
6.5	Japan	18			
6.5	Switzerland	18			
9.5	Denmark	19			
9.5	New Zealand	19	r		
11	United Kingdom	20			
12	France	22			
15.5	Belgium	24			
15.5	Canada	24			
15.5	East Germany	24			
15.5	Hong Kong	24	r		
15.5	Luxembourg	24			
15.5	West Germany	24			
20	Czechoslovakia	25			
20	Ireland	25	r		
20	United States	25			
22.5	Israel	26			1
22.5	Singapore	26	r		
24	Soviet Union	27			
25.5	Austria	28			
25.5	Cyprus	28			
27	Taiwan	30	r	1960	
28	Bulgaria	31			
29	Greece	34			
31	Cuba	35		1964	3
31	Malta	35			
31	Trinidad and Tobago	35		1964	

Table 4.10 Infant Mortality—*Continued*

Rank	Country	Rate	Type	Date	Source
34	Honduras	36			6
34	Italy	36			
34	South Viet Nam	36			1
36.5	Jamaica	37	r		
36.5	Spain	37			
38	Thailand	38		1963	1
39.5	Barbados	39	r		
39.5	Hungary	39			
41	Liberia	40		1963	1
42.5	Poland	42			
42.5	Uruguay	42		1963	1
44	Puerto Rico	43			
45	Rumania	44			
46	Panama	45			1
47	Venezuela	46			1
48	Jordan	48			1
49	Malaysia	50			1
50	Kuwait	51			1
51	Ceylon	53			4
52	Guyana	55		1963	1
53	Nicaragua	56			1
54	Argentina	60		1964	1
55	Mexico	61	r		
56	Mauritius	64	r		
57	Portugal	65			
58	Algeria	70		1963	1
60	El Salvador	71			
60	Philippines	71		1964	1
60	Yugoslavia	71			
62	Tunisia	74			1
63.5	Costa Rica	75			
63.5	Indonesia	75		1962	1
65	Malagasy Republic	76		1964	1
66	Colombia	82		1964	1
67	Paraguay	84			1
68	Albania	87			
69	Ecuador	90		1963	1
70	Peru	91		1964	1
71	Senegal	93		1961	1
72	Guatemala	95			
73	Dominican Republic	98		1960	6
74	Chile	107			
75	United Arab Republic	119			1
76	Mali	123		1961	1
77.5	Cambodia	127			1
77.5	Togo	127		1961	1
79	Burma	128		1964	1
80	India	139			1
81	Pakistan	142		1964	7
82	Ivory Coast	146		1964	1
83	Morocco	149		1962	1
84	Burundi	150			7
85	Ghana	156		1960	1
86	Chad	160		1964	1
87	Turkey	165			1

Table 4.10 Infant Mortality--*Continued*

Rank	Country	Rate	Type	Date	Source
88	Tanzania	170			1
89	Congo - Kinshasa	173		1957	5
90	Congo - Brazzaville	180		1961	1
92	Central African Republic	190		1960	1
92	Kenya	190		1964	1
92	Mauritania	190			1
94	Ethiopia	200		1964	1
95	Dahomey	206		1961	5
96	Niger	212		1960	5
97	Guinea	223		1955	5
98	Gabon	229		1961	1
99	Upper Volta	263		1961	5
100	Libya	300			1
101.5	Saudi Arabia	500		1964	1
101.5	Yemen	500			1

Notes: Data are missing for Afghanistan, Angola, Bolivia, Botswana, Brazil, Cameroon, China, Haiti, Iran, Iraq, Laos, Lebanon, Lesotho, Malawi, Maldive Islands, Mongolia, Mozambique, Nepal, Nigeria, North Korea, North Viet Nam, Papua/New Guinea, Rhodesia, Rwanda, Sierra Leone, Somalia, South Africa, Southern Yemen, South Korea, Sudan, Syria, The Gambia, Uganda, and Zambia.

Type refers to the manner of registration and r indicates that datum is determined by date of registration, not by date of occurrence.

Date, unless otherwise noted, is 1965.

Source, unless otherwise noted, is United Nations, Statistical Office, *Demographic Yearbook, 1966* (New York, 1967).

1. United States, Agency for International Development, *A.I.D. Economic Data Books* (Washington, D.C.: U.S. Government Printing Office, 1967).

2. Center for Latin American Studies, *Statistical Abstract of Latin America, 1967* (Los Angeles: University of California, 1967).

3. United Nations, Statistical Office, *Population and Vital Statistics Report*, Series A, vol. 20, no. 4 (New York, 1968).

4. William Brass et al., *The Demography of Tropical Africa* (Princeton: Princeton University Press, 1968).

5. Nathan Keyfitz and Wilhelm Flieger, *World Population: An Analysis of Vital Data* (Chicago: University of Chicago Press, 1968).

6. United Nations, Statistical Office, *Demographic Yearbook, 1967* (New York, 1968).

Table 4.11
Food Supply

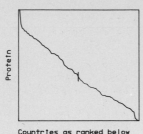 

Countries as ranked below   Countries as ranked below

Mean	68	2499
Standard Deviation	18	454
Median	65	2430
Range	72	2045
Skewness	.22	.17
Number of Countries	95	107

Rank	Country	Protein Grams Per Capita Per Diem	Date	Source	Calories Per Capita Per Diem	Date	Source
1.5	Ireland	91	1964		3460	1964	
1.5	New Zealand	110		1	3460		
3	Poland	93		1	3350		1
4	Denmark	93		1	3310		
5	United Kingdom	90		1	3250		
6	Yugoslavia	96	1964		3190		
7.5	Australia	92		1	3160		
7.5	Switzerland	88			3160		
9	United States	93		1	3140		1
10	Turkey	98		1	3110		1
11	Argentina	85	1964		3100	1964	
12	Canada	95		1	3090		1
13.5	Belgium	89			3080		
13.5	Czechoslovakia	72		2	3080		2
15	Hungary	96			3050		
16.5	Luxembourg	85		1	3040		1
16.5	Soviet Union	87		2	3040		2
18	Uruguay	95		1	3030		3
19	Romania	90	1963		3020	1963	
20	East Germany	70		2	3010		2
21	Sweden	83		1	3000		
22.5	France	101			2970		
22.5	Norway	82		1	2970		
24.5	Austria	87		1	2960		1
24.5	Greece	98	1963		2960		1
26.5	Brazil	71	1964		2950	1964	
26.5	Finland	91			2950		
28.5	Bulgaria	82		2	2930		2
28.5	United Arab Republic	84			2930		
30.5	Netherlands	78		1	2920		

Table 4.11 Food Supply—*Continued*

Rank	Country	Protein Per Capita Per Diem	Date	Source	Calories Per Capita Per Diem	Date	Source
30.5	West Germany	80		1	2920		1
32	Spain	79			2850		
33.5	Israel	86			2820		
33.5	South Africa	80		1	2820		1
35	Italy	82		1	2780		
37	Cuba	61		2	2730		2
37	Lebanon	74			2730		
37	Paraguay	74	1963		2730	1963	
39	Portugal	77		1	2640		
40	Cyprus	73		2	2630		2
41	Mexico	72		1	2580		3
42	Chile	81	1963		2560	1963	
43	South Viet Nam			1	2490		3
45	Ghana	47			2480		3
45	Malagasy Republic	48		1	2480		3
45	Niger			1	2480		3
47.5	Cameroon	55		2	2470		2
47.5	Trinidad and Tobago	63		2	2470		2
49	Senegal			1	2465		3
50.5	Congo – Kinshasa	44		2	2460		2
50.5	Costa Rica	54	1963	1	2460	1963	
52	Nigeria	51		2	2450		2
53	Tanzania	69		2	2440		2
54	Liberia	39		2	2430		2
55	Nicaragua	62			2420		
56	Malaysia	54		2	2400		2
57	Jordan	59	1964		2390	1964	
58	Kenya	64			2380		3
59	Congo – Brazzaville			1	2370		3
60	Syria	72	1963		2360	1963	
61	Japan	78			2350		
62	Taiwan	60		1	2340		1
63.5	Algeria	64		2	2330		3
63.5	Ivory Coast	53		2	2330		3
65	Dahomey			1	2325		3
66	Togo	59		2	2315		3
68	Angola	62		2	2310		2
68	Mauritius	49			2310		
68	Panama	59	1964		2310		1
70	Iraq	62		1	2280		3
71	Pakistan	51			2260		
72.5	Colombia	54	1964		2250	1964	
72.5	Jamaica	58	1958	1	2250	1958	1
74.5	Uganda	54		1	2240		1
74.5	Venezuela	60	1963		2240	1963	
76	Dominican Republic	53	1964		2230	1964	
77	Ceylon	38		1	2180		1
78.5	Burma	46		2	2170		2
78.5	Morocco	67		2	2170		3
80	Iran	60		1	2160		3
81	Peru	57	1963		2150	1963	
82	Mali			1	2125		3
83	Thailand	45		2	2120		2

Table 4.11 Food Supply—*Continued*

Rank	Country	Protein Per Capita Per Diem	Date	Source	Calories Per Capita Per Diem	Date	Source
84	India	54			2110		
85	Honduras	54		1	2080		1
86	Philippines	50			2070		
87.5	Afghanistan	68		1	2050		1
87.5	Guinea	46		2	2050		3
90	Ethiopia	69			2040		
90	Guatemala	54		1	2040		1
90	South Korea			1	2040		3
92	El Salvador	57		1	2030		1
93.5	Cambodia			1	2000		3
93.5	China	48		2	2000		4
95	Indonesia	38			1980		
96	Sudan	65	1964		1950	1964	
97	Mauritania			1	1920		3
98	Libya	50	1964		1910	1964	
99.5	Laos			1	1900		3
99.5	Tunisia	51		2	1900		2
101	Bolivia	49	1963		1860	1963	
102	Upper Volta			1	1840		3
103	Ecuador	44	1963		1830	1963	
104.5	Haiti	46		2	1780		2
104.5	Somalia	52			1780		
106	Saudi Arabia			1	1750		3
107	Sierra Leone	40		2	1415		3

Notes: Data are missing for Albania, Barbados, Botswana, Burundi, Central African Republic, Chad, Gabon, Guyana, Hong Kong, Iceland, Kuwait, Lesotho, Malawi, Maldive Islands, Malta, Mongolia, Mozambique, Nepal, North Korea, North Viet Nam, Papua/New Guinea, Puerto Rico, Rhodesia, Rwanda, Singapore, Southern Yemen, The Gambia, Yemen, and Zambia.

Date, unless otherwise noted, is 1965.

Source, unless otherwise noted, is Food and Agriculture Organization, *FAO Production Yearbook, 1966* (Rome, 1967).

1. Food and Agriculture Organization, *FAO Production Yearbook, 1965* (Rome, 1966).

2. United States, Department of Agriculture, Economic Research Service, Foreign Regional Analysis Division, *The World Food Budget, 1970*, Foreign Agriculture Economic Report, no. 19 (Washington, D.C.: U.S. Government Printing Office, 1964).

3. United States, Agency for International Development, *A.I.D. Economic Data Books* (Washington, D.C.: U.S. Government Printing Office, 1967).

4. United States Congress, Joint Economic Committee, *Mainland China in the World Economy* (Washington, D.C.: U.S. Government Printing Office, 1967).

Table 4.12
Physicians Per One Million Population

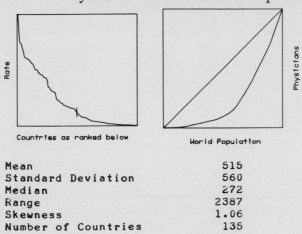

| Countries as ranked below | World Population |

Mean	515
Standard Deviation	560
Median	272
Range	2387
Skewness	1.06
Number of Countries	135

Rank	Country	Physicians Per One Million Population	Bias	Date	Source
1	Israel	2393		1964	
2	Soviet Union	2053		1964	
3	Hungary	1795	+1	1964	
4	Austria	1772	+1	1964	
5	Czechoslovakia	1754		1963	
6	Italy	1635	+1	1960	4
7	Bulgaria	1628		1964	
8	New Zealand	1493	+1	1964	
9	Argentina	1466		1960	4
10	Switzerland	1460		1964	
11	West Germany	1445		1964	
12	United States	1439	+1	1963	
13	Belgium	1425	+1	1963	
14	Greece	1408		1964	
15	Romania	1384	+1	1964	
16	Australia	1352		1964	
17	Iceland	1341		1963	
18	Denmark	1321		1963	
19	Kuwait	1279	+1	1964	
20	Spain	1215		1963	
21	Poland	1211		1964	
22	Norway	1202		1963	
23	United Kingdom	1200		1964	
24	East Germany	1142		1964	
25	Netherlands	1140		1963	
26	Canada	1110		1963	
27	North Korea	1100		1965	1
28	France	1095	+1	1964	
29	Japan	1082	+1	1963	
30	Ireland	1048		1961	

Table 4.12 Physicians Per One Million Population—*Continued*

Rank	Country	Physicians Per One Million Population	Bias	Date	Source
31	Sweden	1044		1963	
32	Mongolia	1032		1961	
33	Malta	1024		1960	4
34	Luxembourg	975		1963	
35	Yugoslavia	838		1965	
36	Portugal	830	+1	1964	
37	Cuba	807		1963	1
38	Venezuela	767		1963	
39	Puerto Rico	762		1964	
40	Lebanon	740	+1	1963	
41	Finland	739		1964	
42	Cyprus	722		1964	
43	Philippines	720		1964	
44	Dominican Republic	616		1964	
45	Paraguay	561	+1	1960	4
46.5	Chile	553		1965	1
46.5	Mexico	553		1961	
48	South Africa	526	+1	1963	
49	Panama	499	−1	1964	
50	Singapore	496		1964	
51	Jamaica	490		1964	
52	Uruguay	459		1960	4
53	Peru	448		1964	
54	Colombia	440		1963	
55	Albania	432	+1	1964	
56.5	Trinidad and Tobago	419		1960	2
56.5	United Arab Republic	419	+1	1964	
58	Taiwan	413		1964	
59	Costa Rica	391	−1	1963	
60	Barbados	390		1964	
61	Hong Kong	385	+1	1964	
62	Guyana	381	+1	1963	
63	Brazil	379		1965	1
64	Nicaragua	371		1965	
65	South Korea	351	+1	1964	
66	Turkey	316		1964	
67	Iran	297		1964	
68	Bolivia	272	−1	1963	
69	Guatemala	248		1964	
70	El Salvador	231		1964	
71	Ceylon	222		1960	4
72	Syria	196		1963	
73	Libya	194		1963	
74	Jordan	190		1964	
75	Ecuador	189		1964	
76	Iraq	186		1964	
77	India	173	+1	1962	
78	Gabon	172		1964	
79	Pakistan	156		1964	
80	Malaysia	145		1960	4
81.5	Rhodesia	132		1964	
81.5	Thailand	132		1963	
83	Honduras	113		1964	

Table 4.12 Physicians Per One Million Population—*Continued*

Rank	Country	Physicians Per One Million Population	Bias	Date	Source
84	Algeria	112		1964	
85	Burma	107		1963	
86	Tunisia	104		1963	
87	Kenya	103	+1	1963	
88	Morocco	101		1963	
89	Malagasy Republic	100		1964	
90	Congo - Brazzaville	93		1964	
91	North Viet Nam	91		1965	1
92	Southern Yemen	90		1963	
93	Liberia	87		1964	
94	Mauritius	83	-1	1964	
95	Saudi Arabia	82		1965	
96	Angola	76		1964	
97	Ghana	75	-1	1964	
98	Haiti	71		1965	
99	Papua / New Guinea	70		1964	
100	Tanzania	63	+1	1960	2
101	Mozambique	56		1964	
102	Ivory Coast	54		1964	
103.5	Senegal	52		1964	
103.5	Sierra Leone	52		1960	3
105	Lesotho	49		1964	
106	Botswana	48		1964	
107.5	The Gambia	46		1964	
107.5	Zambia	46		1964	
109	Cambodia	42		1964	
110	Cameroon	38		1965	
111	South Viet Nam	35		1965	1
112	Sudan	34		1963	
113	Somalia	33		1965	
114.5	Congo - Kinshasa	32		1965	
114.5	Nigeria	32	+1	1964	
116	Togo	28		1965	
117.5	Central African Republic	27		1960	4
117.5	Mauritania	27		1964	
119.5	Afghanistan	25	+1	1960	4
119.5	Mali	25		1964	
121.5	Indonesia	22		1960	4
121.5	Nepal	22		1965	
123.5	Guinea	21		1960	4
123.5	Uganda	21	-1	1964	
126	Dahomey	20		1960	4
126	Malawi	20		1965	
126	Maldive Islands	20		1965	1
128	Upper Volta	16		1964	
130	Ethiopia	15		1964	
130	Laos	15		1964	
130	Niger	15		1964	
132	Chad	14		1964	
133	Burundi	13		1963	
134	Rwanda	10		1964	
135	Yemen	6	-1	1965	

Table 4.12 Physicians Per One Million Population—*Continued*

Notes: Datum is missing for China.

Bias is indicated as follows:

—1 indicates moderate underestimate likely (e.g. data refer to personnel in government services only or to personnel in hospitals and clinics only).

+1 indicates moderate overestimate likely (e.g. data include stomatologists and odontologists).

Blank indicates no known bias. See text for definition.

Source, unless otherwise noted, is United Nations, Statistical Office, *Statistical Yearbook, 1966* (New York, 1967).

1. United Nations, Statistical Office, *Statistical Yearbook, 1965* (New York, 1966).
2. United Nations, Statistical Office, *Statistical Yearbook, 1964* (New York, 1965).
3. United Nations, Statistical Office, *Statistical Yearbook, 1963* (New York, 1964).
4. United Nations, Statistical Office, *Statistical Yearbook, 1962* (New York, 1963).

Table 4.13
Sectoral Income Distribution

Countries as ranked below

Mean	32.0	25.8
Standard Deviation	8.5	12.1
Median	32.4	24.7
Range	34.1	43.8
Skewness	-.18	.17
Number of Countries	52	52

Rank	Country	Size of Smallest Population with Half the Income	Gini Index	Notes	Date	Sources
1	Guatemala	21.2	48.8	8	1964	12
2.5	Jamaica	13.2	48.7	7		12
2.5	Venezuela	13.8	48.7	7	1963	12
4	Mexico	15.9	45.7	6		12
5	Thailand	24.8	43.0	8		12
6	Panama	21.6	40.5	8		12
7	Peru	20.8	39.8	7	1961	12
8	Jordan	23.9	38.7	7	1961	12
9	Philippines	24.8	37.9	8	1965	16
10	Cambodia	26.6	37.7	4	1962	12
11	El Salvador	28.3	37.4	7	1961	12
12	Chile	21.4	37.1	8		12
13	Nicaragua	27.7	37.0	7	1963	12
14	Brazil	24.7	36.4	5		12
15	South Africa	23.3	35.1	6		12
16	Trinidad and Tobago	24.9	33.1	6		12
17	Honduras	30.5	33.0	8	1961	12
18	Paraguay	30.0	31.9	8	1962	12
19	Puerto Rico	24.7	31.7	8		32
20	United Arab Republic	27.4	30.9	8		32
21.5	Costa Rica	29.0	29.3	4	1963	12
21.5	Ecuador	30.6	29.3	8	1962	12
23	Portugal	27.0	26.3	7		12
24	Cyprus	30.7	25.8	7		12
25	Finland	30.3	25.6	8		12
26.5	Ireland	32.1	24.7	4	1961	12
26.5	Turkey	33.1	24.7	8		12
28	Norway	32.4	23.7	8		12
29	India	35.0	22.5	5	1961	12
30	Italy	34.3	22.2	8	1965	14

Table 4.13 Sectoral Income Distribution—*Continued*

Rank	Country	Size of Smallest Population with Half the Income	Gini Index	Notes	Date	Sources
31	France	33.6	21.3	6	1962	12
32	Pakistan	37.2	21.2	8	1961	12
33	Canada	36.4	19.9	8	1961	32
34	Greece	32.9	19.5	8	1961	12
35	Mauritius	35.3	18.7	8	1962	12
36	Spain	37.4	18.6	b8	1965	12
37	South Korea	37.9	17.7	8	1965	15
38	Syria	39.1	16.9	6	1965	17
39	Austria	37.2	16.4	7	1961	12
40	Argentina	38.1	15.7	8		12
41	Denmark	39.1	15.4	8		12
42	Japan	40.0	14.9	7	1965	14
43	Uruguay	39.4	14.5	7	1963	12
44.5	United States	42.0	12.2	8	1965	14
44.5	West Germany	41.8	12.2	5	1965	14
46	Belgium	40.9	11.9	6	1961	12
47	Luxembourg	42.6	10.7	5		12
48	Netherlands	43.2	10.2	8		12
49	Australia	44.3	8.5	8	1961	12
50	Israel	46.2	5.7	b6	1965	12
51	Sweden	46.5	5.6	c6	1964	99
52	United Kingdom	47.3	5.0	b8	1964	82

Notes: Data are missing for Afghanistan, Albania, Algeria, Angola, Barbados, Bolivia, Botswana, Bulgaria, Burma, Burundi, Cameroon, Central African Republic, Ceylon, Chad, China, Colombia, Congo-Brazzaville, Congo-Kinshasa, Cuba, Czechoslovakia, Dahomey, Dominican Republic, East Germany, Ethiopia, Gabon, Ghana, Guinea, Guyana, Haiti, Hong Kong, Hungary, Iceland, Indonesia, Iran, Iraq, Ivory Coast, Kenya, Kuwait, Laos, Lebanon, Lesotho, Liberia, Libya, Malagasy Republic, Malawi, Malaysia, Maldive Islands, Mali, Malta, Mauritania, Mongolia, Morocco, Mozambique, Nepal, New Zealand, Niger, Nigeria, North Korea, North Viet Nam, Papua/New Guinea, Poland, Rhodesia, Romania, Rwanda, Saudi Arabia, Senegal, Sierra Leone, Singapore, Somalia, Southern Yemen, South Viet Nam, Soviet Union, Sudan, Switzerland, Taiwan, Tanzania, The Gambia, Togo, Tunisia, Uganda, Upper Volta, Yemen, Yugoslavia, and Zambia.

Under the *notes* column, a *b* indicates that data on the labor force include males and females but exclude unpaid family workers. A *c* indicates these data include total labor force. Otherwise, they include male labor force only. The digit listed in the same column reports the number of sectors used in the calculations.

Date, unless otherwise noted, is 1960.

Two *sources* are given for each country. The first refers to the source of the labor force data; the second, to that of the gross domestic product data. These sources are:

1. International Labour Organization, *Yearbook of Labour Statistics, 1966* (Geneva, 1967).

2. United Nations, Statistical Office, *Yearbook of National Account Statistics, 1965* (New York, 1966).

3. United Nations, Statistical Office, *Demographic Yearbook, 1964* (New York, 1965).

4. Organization of Economic Co-operation and Development, *National Account Statistics, 1956-1965* (Paris, 1967).

Table 4.13 Sectoral Income Distribution—*Continued*

5. Bank of Korea, Research Department, *Economic Statistics Yearbook* (Seoul, 1960–).

6. Philippines National Economic Council, Office of Statistical Co-ordination and Standards, *The Statistical Reporter* (Manila, April-June 1967).

7. Syria, Ministry of National Planning, Directory of Statistics, *Statistical Abstract, 1967.*

8. United Kingdom, Central Statistical Office, *Annual Abstract of Statistics, 1966* (London: HMSO, 1967).

9. Sweden, Central Bureau of Statistics, *Statistical Abstract of Sweden, 1966* (Stockholm, 1967).

Sample National Lorenz Curves of Sectoral Income Distribution

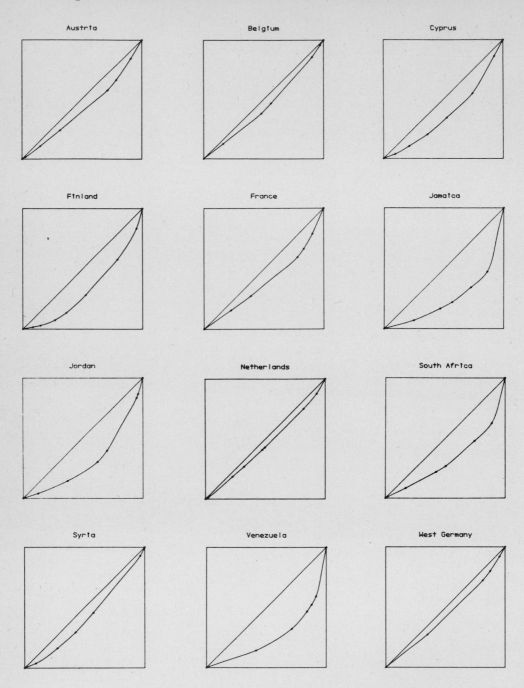

Table 4.14
Land Distribution

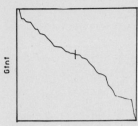

Countries as ranked below

Mean	9.4	67.0
Standard Deviation	7.8	15.2
Median	7.0	69.4
Range	27.7	58.2
Skewness	.57	-.23
Number of Countries	44	54

Rank	Country	Smallest Number of Farms with Half the Acreage	Gini Index	Notes	Date	Source
1	Peru	.3	93.3	11	1961	2
2	Venezuela		90.9		1956	7
3.5	Australia	3.5	88.2	10	1960	
3.5	Iraq	.7	88.2	11	1958	
5	Argentina	1.5	86.7	11	1960	
6.5	Colombia	1.2	86.4	14	1960	
6.5	Ecuador		86.4		1954	5
8	Guatemala		86.0		1950	5
9	Brazil	1.5	84.5	11	1960	2
10	El Salvador	1.3	82.7	11	1961	2
11	Uruguay	3.5	82.6	10	1961	
12	Dominican Republic	1.5	80.3	11	1960	
13	Nicaragua	3.3	80.1	11	1963	
14	Spain	1.6	79.7	04	1960	
15	Costa Rica	2.9	78.2	12	1963	
16	Jamaica	.4	77.0	05	1960	
17	Honduras		75.7		1952	5
18	Puerto Rico	3.4	73.8	06	1959	
19	Panama	4.8	73.5	14	1961	
20	New Zealand	3.6	73.4	09	1960	
21	Italy	4.1	73.2	13	1960	
22	United Kingdom	6.7	72.3	10	1960	
23	United States	3.9	71.0	08	1959	
24	Austria	4.5	70.7	08	1960	
25.5	Libya	7.0	70.0	b13	1960	
25.5	South Africa	8.9	70.0	10	1960	
27	Mexico		69.4		1960	6
28	Kenya	6.0	69.2	12	1960	3
29	Trinidad and Tobago	2.0	69.1	08	1963	2
30	Norway	12.4	67.6	10	1959	

Table 4.14 Land Distribution—*Continued*

Rank	Country	Smallest Number of Farms with Half the Acreage	Gini Index	Notes	Date	Source
31	United Arab Republic		67.4		1964	6
32	West Germany	8.2	66.8	07	1960	
33	Pakistan	9.9	65.0	b08	1960	
34	Luxembourg		63.8		1950	4
35	Iran	12.1	62.5	12	1960	
36	Belgium	13.1	60.4	b08	1959	
37	Ireland	14.1	59.4	09	1960	
38	Turkey	12.3	59.2	13	1963	
39	South Viet Nam	13.4	58.7	b11	1960	
40	Netherlands	15.7	57.9	b08	1959	
41	Philippines		53.4		1960	6
42	India		52.2		1955	1
43	Sweden	15.5	50.6	07	1961	
44	Malta	17.6	47.8	08	1960	
45	Mali	19.5	47.7	09	1960	
46	Malaysia	18.7	47.3	a12	1960	
47	Japan	18.5	47.0	12	1960	
48	Poland	22.3	46.5	c11	1960	
49	Taiwan	20.2	46.3	b09	1960	
50	Thailand	20.3	46.0	06	1963	
51	Denmark	20.7	45.8	07	1959	
52	Yugoslavia		43.7		1950	8
53	South Korea	23.7	38.7	08	1961	
54	Finland	28.0	35.1	10	1959	

Notes: Data are missing for Afghanistan, Albania, Algeria, Angola, Barbados, Bolivia, Botswana, Bulgaria, Burma, Burundi, Cambodia, Cameroon, Canada, Central African Republic, Ceylon, Chad, Chile, China, Congo-Brazzaville, Congo-Kinshasa, Cuba, Cyprus, Czechoslovakia, Dahomey, East Germany, Ethiopia, France, Gabon, Ghana, Greece, Guinea, Guyana, Haiti, Hong Kong, Hungary, Iceland, Indonesia, Israel, Ivory Coast, Jordan, Kuwait, Laos, Lebanon, Lesotho, Liberia, Malagasy Republic, Malawi, Maldive Islands, Mauritania, Mauritius, Mongolia, Morocco, Mozambique, Nepal, Niger, Nigeria, North Korea, North Viet Nam, Papua/New Guinea, Paraguay, Portugal, Rhodesia, Rumania, Rwanda, Saudi Arabia, Senegal, Sierra Leone, Singapore, Somalia, Southern Yemen, Soviet Union, Sudan, Switzerland, Syria, Tanzania, The Gambia, Togo, Tunisia, Uganda, Upper Volta, Yemen, and Zambia.

The *Notes* column qualifies the data base for the indexes:

a refers to Malaya only.

b indicates the inclusion of a category entitled "holdings without land."

c refers to private holdings only.

The two digits refer to the number of categories used in calculating the indexes.

Source, unless otherwise noted, is Food and Agricultural Organization, *Report on the 1960 World Census of Agriculture*, vols. 1-A and 1-B (Rome, 1967).

1. India, Central Statistical Organization, *Statistical Abstract, 1955-1956* (New Delhi, 1967), as reported in the first edition of the *World Handbook*.

2. Center for Latin American Studies, *Statistical Abstract for Latin America, 1967* (Los Angeles: University of California, 1967).

3. Food and Agricultural Organization *Report on the 1960 World Census of Agriculture*, Preliminary Report on vol. 1-C (Rome, 1967).

Table 4.14 Land Distribution—*Continued*

4. Food and Agricultural Organization, *Monthly Bulletin of Agricultural Statistics* (1953-63), as reported in the first edition of the *World Handbook.*

5. Center for Latin American Studies, *Statistical Abstract for Latin America, 1961* (Los Angeles: University of California, 1961) as reported in the first edition of the *World Handbook.*

6. Hung-chao Tai, *Land Reform in the Developing Conutries: Tenure Defects and Political Response,* preliminary draft, mimeographed (Cambridge: Center for International Affairs, Harvard University, 1967).

7. Albert O. Hirschmann, ed., *Latin American Issues* (New York: Twentieth Century Fund, 1961), as reported in the first edition of the *World Handbook.*

8. United Nations, Department of Economic Affairs, *Progress in Land Reform* (New York, 1954), as reported in the first edition of the *World Handbook.*

Sample National Lorenz Curves of Land Distribution

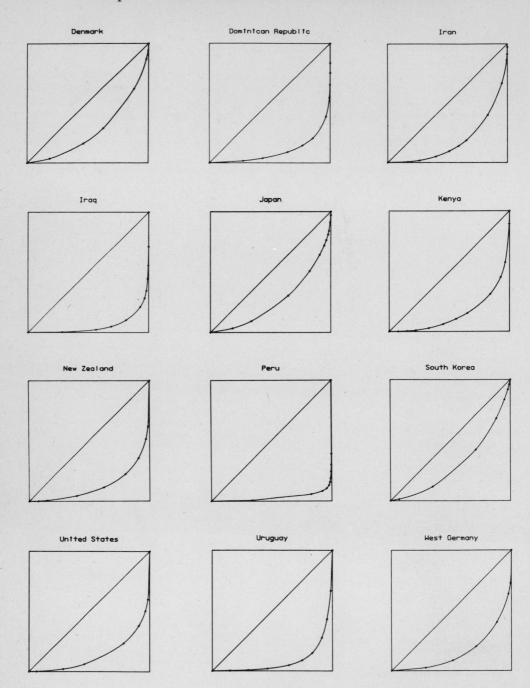

Table 4.15
Ethnic and Linguistic Fractionalization

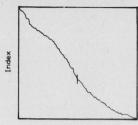

Countries as ranked below

	Roberts	Muller	Atlas Narodov Mira
Mean	.46	.39	.40
Standard Deviation	.32	.28	.29
Median	.50	.35	.36
Range	.90	.97	.92
Skewness	-.16	.36	.17
Number of Countries	55	111	129

Rank	Country	Roberts	Muller	Atlas Narodov Mira
1	Tanzania			.93
2.5	Congo - Kinshasa	.88	.89	.90
2.5	Uganda	.82	.92	.90
4.5	Cameroon		.89	.89
4.5	India	.75	.84	.89
6	South Africa	.84	.88	.88
7	Nigeria	.82	.91	.87
8	Ivory Coast	.77		.86
10	Chad	.64	.68	.83
10	Kenya	.90	.85	.83
10	Liberia	.85	.67	.83
12	Zambia	.81		.82
13.5	Angola	.77		.78
13.5	Mali	.84		.78
15	Sierra Leone	.77		.77
16.5	Indonesia	.71	.77	.76
16.5	Iran	.50	.66	.76
19	Canada		.48	.75
19	Guinea	.81	.83	.75
19	Yugoslavia		.43	.75
21	Philippines	.78	.82	.74
23	Niger	.83	.74	.73
23	Sudan	.49	.59	.73
23	The Gambia			.73
25.5	Malaysia			.72
25.5	Senegal	.78		.72
27.5	Ghana	.65		.71
27.5	Togo		.80	.71
29	Nepal		.48	.70
31	Central African Republic			.69

Table 4.15 Ethnic and Linguistic Fractionalization—*Continued*

Rank	Country	Roberts	Muller	Atlas Narodov Mira
31	Ethiopia	.70	.84	.69
31	Gabon			.69
33.5	Bolivia		.66	.68
33.5	Upper Volta	.66	.62	.68
35	Soviet Union		.63	.67
37	Afghanistan	.67	.71	.66
37	Congo - Brazzaville			.66
37	Thailand	.30	.46	.66
39	Mozambique	.89	.82	.65
40.5	Guatemala		.82	.64
40.5	Pakistan		.69	.64
42.5	Dahomey	.66	.84	.62
42.5	Malawi			.62
44	Laos		.43	.60
45	Peru		.65	.59
46.5	Guyana			.58
46.5	Mauritius			.58
48	Trinidad and Tobago		.39	.56
49	Belgium		.51	.55
50	Rhodesia		.70	.54
51.5	Ecuador		.35	.53
51.5	Morocco	.50	.38	.53
53	Botswana		.61	.51
54.5	Switzerland		.50	.50
54.5	United States		.25	.50
56	Czechoslovakia		.50	.49
57.5	Burma	.53	.43	.47
57.5	Ceylon	.41	.40	.47
59	Spain		.42	.44
60	Algeria	.48	.40	.43
62	Papua / New Guinea		.97	.42
62	Singapore	.41	.59	.42
62	Taiwan	.35	.42	
64	Mongolia	.01	.18	.38
65	New Zealand		.07	.37
66	Iraq	.39	.32	.36
67	Cyprus		.40	.35
68	Mauritania		.41	.33
69.5	Australia		.03	.32
69.5	United Kingdom		.04	.32
71	Argentina		.47	.31
72.5	Cambodia	.24	.30	.30
72.5	Mexico		.19	.30
74	Panama		.16	.28
75	North Viet Nam	.27		
76	France		.17	.26
77.5	Romania		.20	.25
77.5	Turkey	.16	.24	.25
79	Libya	.11	.35	.23
81.5	Barbados			.22
81.5	Bulgaria		.23	.22
81.5	Lesotho		.46	.22
81.5	Syria	.02	.29	.22

Table 4.15 Ethnic and Linguistic Fractionalization—*Continued*

Rank	Country	Roberts	Muller	Atlas Narodov Mira
84.5	Israel	.25	.67	.20
84.5	Uruguay			.20
86	South Viet Nam	.19		
88	Kuwait		.00	.18
88	Maldive Islands		.18	
88	Nicaragua		.11	.18
90	El Salvador		.07	.17
92	Finland		.35	.16
92	Honduras		.09	.16
92	Tunisia	.07	.22	.16
94	Luxembourg		.12	.15
96	Chile		.12	.14
96	Paraguay		.49	.14
96	Rwanda		.19	.14
98.5	Austria		.01	.13
98.5	Lebanon	.12	.18	.13
100	China	.52	.49	.12
101	Venezuela		.19	.11
103	Greece		.21	.10
103	Hungary		.19	.10
103	Netherlands		.04	.10
105	Albania		.01	.09
107	Malta		.52	.08
107	Somalia	.17	.26	.08
107	Sweden		.12	.08
109.5	Brazil		.17	.07
109.5	Costa Rica		.26	.07
112	Colombia		.25	.06
112	Malagasy Republic	.09	.29	.06
112	Saudi Arabia	.01	.00	.06
115.5	Denmark		.12	.05
115.5	Iceland		.54	.05
115.5	Jamaica		.00	.05
115.5	Jordan	.04	.11	.05
121.5	Burundi			.04
121.5	Cuba		.00	.04
121.5	Dominican Republic		.01	.04
121.5	Ireland		.44	.04
121.5	Italy		.09	.04
121.5	Norway		.19	.04
121.5	United Arab Republic	.00	.07	.04
121.5	Yemen	.04	.00	.04
126.5	Poland		.12	.03
126.5	West Germany			.03
129	East Germany			.02
129	Hong Kong	.04	.23	.02
129	Puerto Rico		.15	.02
132.5	Haiti		.35	.01
132.5	Japan	.01	.02	.01
132.5	Portugal		.00	.01
132.5	Southern Yemen		.01	
135.5	North Korea	.00		
135.5	South Korea	.00		

Table 4.15 Ethnic and Linguistic Fractionalization—*Continued*

Notes: There are no countries for which data are missing.

Dates are 1960-65.

Source for the first column is Janet Roberts, "Sociocultural Change and Communications Problems," *Study of the Role of Second Languages in Asia, Africa and Latin America,* ed. Frank A. Rice (Washington, D.C.: Center for Applied Linguistics of the Modern Language Association of America, 1962).

Source for the second column is Siegfried H. Muller, *The World's Living Languages: Basic Facts of Their Structure, Kinship, Location and Number of Speakers* (New York: Ungar, 1964).

Source for the third column is *Atlas Narodov Mira* (Moscow: The N. N. Miklukho-Maklaya Institute of Ethnography of the Academy of Sciences, Department of Geodesy and Cartography of the State Geological Committee of the USSR, 1964). United States data were adjusted by the official census as described in text. Barbados datum was added from Moshe Y. Sachs, ed., *Worldmark Encyclopedia of the Nations* (New York: Harper & Row, 1967).

Table 4.16
Christian Communities

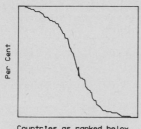

Countries as ranked below

Mean	20	13	29	47
Standard Deviation	23	24	35	39
Median	16	3	11	41
Range	204	100	100	100
Skewness	4.67	2.46	.90	.10
Number of Countries	136	136	136	136

		Percentage of Population			
Rank	Country	Protestant	Date	Catholic	Date	Christian
4	Brazil	10		90		100
4	El Salvador	3		97		100
4	Ireland	5	1946	94	1946	100
4	Norway	99		0		100
4	Romania	6		13		100
4	Spain	0		100		100
4	Sweden	100		0		100
9	Barbados	99		0		99
9	Bolivia	2		97		99
9	Malta	0		99		99
12	Dominican Republic	2		96		98
12	Finland	96		0		98
12	Guatemala	3		95		98
15.5	Austria	7		89		97
15.5	Denmark	97		1		97
15.5	Puerto Rico	8		89		97
15.5	West Germany	51	1950	45	1950	97
18	Luxembourg	2		94		96
21.5	Argentina	2		93		95
21.5	Belgium	1		93		95
21.5	Iceland	95		1		95
21.5	Panama	5		90		95
21.5	Paraguay	1		94		95
21.5	Portugal	0		94		95
25.5	Greece	0		1		94
25.5	Peru	1		93		94
27.5	East Germany	82	1950	11	1950	93
27.5	Poland	2		90		93
29	Italy	0		91		91
31.5	Chile	11		80		90

Table 4.16 Christian Communities—*Continued*

Rank	Country	Percentage of Population Protestant	Date	Catholic	Date	Christian
31.5	United States	48	1968	40	1968	90
31.5	Venezuela	1		89		90
31.5	Yugoslavia	1		31		90
34	Ecuador	0		88		89
35	Nicaragua	3		85		88
37	Colombia	1		86		87
37	Mexico	2		85		87
37	Switzerland	44		43		87
40	Australia	61		23		86
40	Bulgaria	0		0		86
40	Hungary	24		59		86
42	Cuba	4		81		85
44	France	2		82		84
44	Philippines	11		74		84
44	Uruguay	2		83		84
46.5	Canada	34		41		81
46.5	New Zealand	66		14		81
48	Haiti	12		67		79
49	Netherlands	38		40		78
50	Cyprus	0		1		76
51.5	Lesotho	30		39	1965	75
51.5	Trinidad and Tobago	39		36		75
54	Costa Rica	3		67		71
54	Honduras	3		68		71
54	United Kingdom	62		9		71
56	Gabon	18		51	1965	70
57	Czechoslovakia	14		49		66
58.5	Congo – Brazzaville	18		42	1965	62
58.5	South Africa	38		6	1965	62
60	Congo – Kinshasa	14		39	1965	59
61	Burundi	7		50	1965	58
62	Guyana	42	1960	15	1960	57
63	Uganda	21		33	1965	54
64	Jamaica	43		8		51
65	Papua / New Guinea	27		21		48
66	Lebanon	1		28		45
67	Angola	7		36	1965	43
68	Malagasy Republic	17		20	1965	41
69	Mauritius	2		35	1965	37
71	Ethiopia	1		0	1965	35
71	Rhodesia	14		8	1965	35
71	Rwanda	6		29	1965	35
73.5	Cameroon	14		19	1965	34
73.5	Malawi	17		16	1965	34
75	Albania	0		4		33
76.5	Kenya	9		12	1965	27
76.5	Tanzania	9		17	1965	27
78.5	Central African Republic	11		14	1965	25
78.5	Togo	6		19	1965	25
80.5	Soviet Union	1		1		24
80.5	Zambia	6		15	1965	24
82.5	Botswana	19		2	1965	22
82.5	Ghana	9		11	1965	22

Table 4.16 Christian Communities—*Continued*

Rank	Country	Percentage of Population Protestant	Date	Catholic	Date	Christian
84	Ivory Coast	3		10	1965	17
85	Liberia	12		2	1965	16
87	Dahomey	2		14	1965	15
87	Mozambique	2		12	1965	15
87	United Arab Republic	1		1	1965	15
89.5	Hong Kong	5		6		11
89.5	South Viet Nam	0		10		11
91.5	Nigeria	5		4	1965	10
91.5	Syria	0		5		10
93	South Korea	7		2		9
94	Singapore	3		6		8
95	Ceylon	1		7		7
97.5	Chad	3		3	1965	6
97.5	Indonesia	4		1		6
97.5	North Korea	4		2		6
97.5	Taiwan	4		2		6
102.5	Jordan	1		1		5
102.5	Malaysia	2		3		5
102.5	Senegal	0		5	1965	5
102.5	Sierra Leone	3		1	1965	5
102.5	Southern Yemen	0		4		5
102.5	Upper Volta	1		4	1965	5
109	Algeria	0		4	1965	4
109	Burma	3		1		4
109	Iraq	0		2		4
109	Israel	0		3		4
109	North Viet Nam	0		4		4
109	Sudan	1		2	1965	4
109	The Gambia	2		2	1965	4
113.5	India	1		1		3
113.5	Morocco	0		3	1965	3
115.5	Kuwait	1		1		2
115.5	Libya	0		2	1965	2
122	Cambodia	0		1		1
122	China	0		0	1949	1
122	Guinea	0		1	1965	1
122	Japan	1		0		1
122	Laos	0		1		1
122	Mali	0		1	1965	1
122	Mauritania	0		1	1967	1
122	Pakistan	1		0		1
122	Thailand	0		0		1
122	Tunisia	0		1	1965	1
122	Turkey	0	1948	0		1
132	Afghanistan	0		0		0
132	Iran	0		0		0
132	Maldive Islands	0		0		0
132	Mongolia	0		0		0
132	Nepal	0		0		0
132	Niger	0		0	1965	0
132	Saudi Arabia	0		0		0
132	Somalia	0		0	1965	0
132	Yemen	0		0		0

Table 4.16 Christian Communities—*Continued*

Notes: There are no missing data.

Date, unless otherwise noted, is 1964.

All data were compiled by David Barrett of the University of East Africa and Columbia University and were drawn from a variety of surveys, published and unpublished, many of which were presented in H. W. Coxill and K. G. Grubb, eds., *World Christian Handbook, 1968* (London: Macmillan, 1968). A more definitive survey, from which these data were taken, is underway and will be published by D. B. Barrett, et al., eds., *World Christian Handbook, 1971-2* (New York: Macmillan, 1972).

Table 4.17
Islamic Community

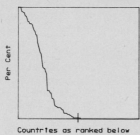

Countries as ranked below

Mean	20
Standard Deviation	33
Median	0
Range	100
Skewness	1.37
Number of Countries	135

Rank	Country	Muslims as % of Population	Date
2	Maldive Islands	100	
2	Saudi Arabia	100	1954
2	Yemen	100	1954
4	Somalia	96	
6	Iraq	95	1957
6	Kuwait	95	1957
6	Southern Yemen	95	1954
8.5	Afghanistan	92	1954
8.5	Libya	92	1954
10	Turkey	90	1954
11.5	Mauritania	87	1954
11.5	Pakistan	87	1961
14	Algeria	85	1954
14	Indonesia	85	1954
14	United Arab Republic	85	1954
16	Iran	84	1954
17	Morocco	81	1954
18	Jordan	79	1954
19	Tunisia	78	1954
20.5	Niger	75	
20.5	Senegal	75	
22	Syria	68	1954
23	Guinea	65	
24	Mali	62	
25.5	Chad	58	
25.5	Sudan	58	1954
27	Albania	52	1954
28	The Gambia	46	1954
29	Nigeria	45	
30	Malaysia	44	1954
31	Lebanon	42	1954

Table 4.17 Islamic Community—*Continued*

Rank	Country	Muslims as % of Population	Date
32	Ethiopia	40	
34	Liberia	25	
34	Tanzania	25	
34	Upper Volta	25	
36.5	Ivory Coast	23	
36.5	Sierra Leone	23	
38.5	Cameroon	18	
38.5	Cyprus	18	1946
40	Dahomey	17	
41	Mozambique	12	
43	Bulgaria	11	1954
43	Singapore	11	
43	Soviet Union	11	1954
46.5	Ghana	10	
46.5	India	10	1965
46.5	Kenya	10	
46.5	Yugoslavia	10	1954
49	Guyana	9	
50	Malawi	8	
51	Israel	7	1954
53.5	Ceylon	5	1954
53.5	Malagasy Republic	5	
53.5	Togo	5	
53.5	Uganda	5	
56.5	Central African Republic	4	
56.5	Thailand	4	
59	Burma	3	1954
59	Greece	3	1954
59	Philippines	3	1954
61	China	2	1954
64.5	Australia	1	1952
64.5	Burundi	1	
64.5	Congo - Kinshasa	1	
64.5	France	1	1954
64.5	Rwanda	1	
64.5	South Africa	1	
101.5	Angola	0	
101.5	Argentina	0	
101.5	Austria	0	
101.5	Barbados	0	
101.5	Belgium	0	
101.5	Bolivia	0	
101.5	Botswana	0	
101.5	Brazil	0	
101.5	Cambodia	0	
101.5	Canada	0	
101.5	Chile	0	
101.5	Colombia	0	
101.5	Congo - Brazzaville	0	
101.5	Costa Rica	0	
101.5	Cuba	0	
101.5	Czechoslovakia	0	
101.5	Denmark	0	
101.5	Dominican Republic	0	

Table 4.17 Islamic Community—*Continued*

Rank	Country	Muslims as % of Population	Date
101.5	East Germany	0	
101.5	Ecuador	0	
101.5	El Salvador	0	
101.5	Finland	0	1950
101.5	Gabon	0	
101.5	Guatemala	0	
101.5	Haiti	0	
101.5	Honduras	0	
101.5	Hong Kong	0	
101.5	Hungary	0	
101.5	Iceland	0	
101.5	Ireland	0	
101.5	Italy	0	
101.5	Jamaica	0	
101.5	Japan	0	1954
101.5	Laos	0	
101.5	Lesotho	0	
101.5	Luxembourg	0	
101.5	Malta	0	
101.5	Mauritius	0	
101.5	Mexico	0	
101.5	Nepal	0	
101.5	Netherlands	0	
101.5	New Zealand	0	
101.5	Nicaragua	0	
101.5	North Korea	0	1954
101.5	North Viet Nam	0	1954
101.5	Norway	0	
101.5	Panama	0	
101.5	Papua / New Guinea	0	
101.5	Paraguay	0	
101.5	Peru	0	
101.5	Poland	0	
101.5	Portugal	0	
101.5	Puerto Rico	0	
101.5	Rhodesia	0	
101.5	Rumania	0	1954
101.5	South Korea	0	1954
101.5	South Viet Nam	0	1954

Notes: There are no significant numbers of Moslems in Angola, Argentina, Austria, Barbados, Belgium, Bolivia, Botswana, Brazil, Cambodia, Canada, Chile, Colombia, Costa Rica, Cuba, Czechoslovakia, Denmark, Dominican Republic, East Germany, Ecuador, El Salvador, Finland, Guatemala, Haiti, Honduras, Hong Kong, Hungary, Iceland, Ireland, Italy, Jamaica, Japan, Laos, Lesotho, Luxembourg, Malta, Mauritius, Mexico, Nepal, Netherlands, New Zealand Nicaragua, North Korea, North Viet Nam, Norway, Panama, Papua/New Guinea, Paraguay, Peru, Poland, Portugal, Puerto Rico, Rhodesia, Romania, Singapore, South Korea, Spain, Sweden, Switzerland, Taiwan, Trinidad and Tobago, United Kingdom, United States, Uruguay, Venezuela, West Germany, and Zambia.

Datum is missing for Mongolia.

Date, unless otherwise noted, is 1960.

Table 4.17 Islamic Community—*Continued*

All data were compiled by David Barrett of the University of East Africa and Columbia University and were drawn from a variety of surveys, published and unpublished, many of which were presented in H. W. Coxill and K. G. Grubb, eds., *World Christian Handbook, 1968* (London: Macmillan, 1968). A more definitive survey, from which these data were taken, is underway and will be published by D. B. Barrett, et al., eds., *World Christian Handbook, 1971-2* (New York: Macmillan, 1972).

5 National Resources and Development

The operation of a polity is related to the kinds of society and of economy for which it is responsible. The resources—human, natural, man-made—that a polity has at its command help to determine its goals and its means toward these goals. Big states act differently than small states. Rich states behave in ways that poor states cannot. This chapter includes data on population, areal, and economic size and the relations among them, as well as data on economic development and on economic structure.

Population, Area, and Density

States range in size all the way from tiny Pitcairn with its 100 or so people to China with more than 700 million and from the Vatican's few square kilometers to the Soviet Union's 22,402,000. Size is one of the more obvious means of differentiation among states. In fact, it is so obvious that the question sometimes arises as to the admissibility of comparing units of such different size. We have answered this question in the affirmative, at least for certain types of inference (see the introduction). Nevertheless, this handbook does not include all of the more than 200 territorial units that make up the land area of the world. Our sample has been chosen on the dual criteria of population size and importance in international affairs (see the introduction and list of countries in appendix 2). Presumably, some very small states and territories are not quite the same kind of units as the larger ones and are inappropriate even for the types of inference discussed in the introduction. When the level of inference and the units are appropriate to each other, however, size may still be an important control or modifying variable.

One of the oldest and most widely used measures of size is total population. National censuses have existed since the end of the eighteenth century and have long been conducted in North America, Europe, and parts of Latin America. There has been a major increase in censuses in the rest of the world since World War II. Nevertheless, there are difficulties. Even in the United States, which has a long tradition of national enumerations, an estimated 5.7 million people were not counted in 1960.[1] The United Nations Statistical Office has developed a code to estimate the accuracy of population figures. In table 5.1, therefore, we have reported this code and error margins built upon it along with national populations for the 136 countries.

These midyear estimates for 1965 were based on the definition: "the total number of persons present in the country at the time of the census, *excluding* foreign military, naval, and diplomatic personnel and their families

---

1. "The Census—What's Wrong With It, What Can Be Done," *Trans-action: Social Science and Modern Society*, 5 (1968): 49-56.

located in the country but *including* military, naval, and diplomatic personnel of the country and their families located abroad and merchant seamen resident in the country but at sea at the time of the census."[2] Population may be defined as *de jure, de facto,* or modified *de facto.* The United Nations uses a modified *de facto* method of reporting but states that, although the terms have traditionally been accepted, they are so loosely used as to have lost international meaning.

Some countries do not include jungle tribes, aborigines, nomadic peoples, displaced persons, and refugees. Most of the cases in table 5.1 that deviate from the basic definition do so only by trivial amounts. Wherever underestimates because of exclusion would seem to reach 5 percent, we have adjusted the reported totals to conform with the definition if the necessary information was available to us. Countries for which minor parts of the population still are excluded have been noted in the table.

A much more serious source of inaccuracy stems from varying methods and periods of data collection. These sources of error in total population estimates can be identified: They are the nature of the base from which later annual estimates are calculated, the method of adjusting for population increase, and the length of time from the base date for which the adjustment is to be made. The base may be (1) a complete census of individuals taken at least decennially, taken sporadically, or taken one time only, (2) a census or survey based upon a sample of the population, (3) a partial census or registration, e.g. a count of dwellings or a count of voting or tax registers, or (4) conjecture. Adjustments may be made by a continuous population register of births and deaths, by calculations on the balance of births, deaths, and migration, or by an assumed rate of increase or estimate inferred from a regional rate of increase.

In the 1960 *Demographic Yearbook,* the United Nations Statistical Office published an essay entitled "How Well Do We Know the Present Size and Trend of the World's Population?" The essay stated that error ranges of approximately the following magnitudes (in percentages) appear typical:

For the data base
> 1.0 in censuses taken at least decennially
> 2.0 in censuses taken sporadically
> 3.5 in censuses taken for the first time
> 5.0 in data based upon sample survey
> 10.0 in data based upon an unconventional count
> 20.0 in data obtained by conjecture

For time adjustments
> 0.1 for adjustment by continuous population register
> with population balance adequately accounted for

2. United Nations, Statistical Office, *Demographic Yearbook, 1966* (New York, 1967), p.8.

> 0.2 for adjustment by continuous population register with population balance not determined
>
> 0.4 for adjustment by continuous population register with population balance inadequately accounted for
>
> 0.2 for adjustment based upon calculated balance of births, deaths, and migration with balance adequately accounted for
>
> 0.4 for adjustment based upon calculated balance of births, deaths, and migration with balance not determined
>
> 0.8 for adjustment based upon calculated balance of births, deaths, and migration with balance inadequately accounted for
>
> 0.6 for assumed rate of increase with two or more decennial censuses
>
> 0.8 for assumed rate of increase with two or more censuses taken at greater intervals
>
> 1.2 for assumed rate of increase with one census or none
>
> 1.6 for no adjustment
>
> 1.0 for adjustment derived from regional population estimates
>
> 1.2 for adjustment by methods unknown.

The percentages for data base are of estimated population. Those for time adjustment are of estimated population for each year adjusted.

The essay also suggested the formula:

$$E = B + T \cdot t$$

where E = range of percent error in the current estimate

B = range of percent error imputed to base data

T = range of annual percent error imputed to the method of time adjustment

t = the number of years since base data were established.[3]

These estimates and the formula were used in the calculation of the error margins printed in table 5.1.

We believe that these error ranges seem quite generous. While it is not possible to estimate the probability that the actual population total does fall within this error range, it would appear that the probability is high. The major exception occurs in some underdeveloped countries that have taken a decennial census. According to the United Nations code an error range of 1 percent should be assigned in such instances. This would often seem to be too narrow, but we lack the detailed information to judge particular cases.

---

3. United Nations, Statistical Office, *Demographic Yearbook, 1960* (New York, 1960), p.8.

Also, in a very few cases of the grossest conjecture, even a range of 20 percent may be too small.

Table 5.1 also includes two sets of growth rates. One is the average annual rate of change during the five-year period from 1960 to 1965; the other is the average annual rate of change over the fifteen-year period from 1950 to 1965. Both are calculated using the continuous growth rate formula

$$r = 100 \ \ln\left(\frac{V_2}{V_1}\right)/n$$

where V_1 = value at the first point in time
$\quad\ \ V_2$ = value at the second point in time
$\quad\ \ n\ $ = number of years between points in time.

Data on area and population density are given in table 5.2. Area figures "are assumed to represent total area, that is, they comprise the land area and inland waters, excluding only polar regions and some uninhabited islands. Inland waters are assumed to consist of major rivers and lakes."[4] Areas for the Netherlands and for Papua/New Guinea are land areas since territorial waters would inflate the figures beyond reasonable bounds. Area for Jammu-Kashmir has been added to India (137,400 square kilometers) and to Pakistan (80,900 square kilometers).[5]

The total area data are certainly among the most reliable in this book. In virtually all cases the error must be within the range of 1 or 2 percent. It is unlikely that there is any consistent bias toward either overstatement or understatement. Some small error may stem from the quality of surveys. Some figures are based on geodetic surveys carried out by modern scientific methods whereas others are based on less rigorous procedures. There are also some variabilities in the definition of "inland waters." Some countries include only major rivers and lakes; others include coastal bays, inlets, and gulfs. Error that results from either of these definitions is probably insignificant for most readers' purposes.

Population density, reported also in table 5.2, is obviously one measure of relative wealth in natural resources. A country may be too crowded, but on the other hand population sparseness may also be a handicap to economic development. A thinly spread population requires a greater investment in transportation and communications infrastructure per capita. Population density should be supplemented by other measures for many purposes. Data on urbanization and concentration of population are presented in chapter 4. Many of the economically most advanced states are among the most densely populated. A nation with limited area may have many other resources of a physical or human nature.

4. United Nations, Statistical Office, *Statistical Yearbook, 1965* (New York, 1966), p.5.

5. From *The Statesman's Year-Book, Statistical and Historical Annual of the States of the World for the Year, 1966-1967*, ed. S. H. Steinberg (London: Macmillan, 1969), p.385.

An overall measure of density will obscure some unequal distributions within countries. The United Arab Republic, for example, has a rather moderate overall density, but virtually all of its population is concentrated along the Nile River, and the large deserts are almost uninhabited. The United Arab Republic ranks much higher with regard to density upon agricultural land. Table 5.3 gives agricultural area and the population density of agricultural area. Data are essentially those reported by the Food and Agriculture Organization as arable land and land under permanent crops plus those reported as permanent meadows and pastures. Land under crops, lands temporarily fallow, meadows for mowing and pasture, land under market and kitchen gardens and land under fruit trees, vines, shrubs, and rubber plantations are all included. Double-cropped areas are counted only once. Unused but potentially productive land is excluded since variations in definition are far too numerous to allow comparability.

It is impossible to be very precise in assessing an error margin, but a few general observations may help. Data may be unreliable because national governments simply do not have adequate information, whatever definition they use. The major remaining source of incomparability stems from the definitional line, not always applied uniformly, between meadows and pastures on the one hand and forests and woodlands on the other. Though for some countries the proportion exceeds one-half, on the average about 30 percent of a nation's land is classified as forests and woodlands, with about an equal amount classified as agricultural land. It would seem very unlikely that area covered by scattered trees, and for that reason miscategorized, would exceed 20 percent of either the agricultural or the forest land of a country. Thus, in most cases, plus or minus 20 percent can be taken as a very approximate error margin. Given the wide range of data in table 5.3, even this much error would not cause a country to be too seriously misplaced from its proper ranking.

Economic and Technological Potential

The index most frequently employed to measure the production or total wealth and resources of a country is gross national product. Although several difficulties have been found with this index, it is probably as good an indicator as is available for aggregate national wealth. Gross national product is also sometimes used as a measure of power with the assumption that the ability of a country to force its will on another is directly related to its resources. There is a reasonably good fit between intuitive judgments on power and the rankings of table 5.4. Of course, the relationship is not exact, but if this index is used in conjunction with others such as scientific manpower, military manpower, and defense expenditure, it will provide a pretty good notion of relative national power.

Gross national product per capita is frequently employed as a measure of comfort or well-being. For some purposes this is useful, but certain cautions must be observed. The proportion of gross national product expended on private consumption is not the same in all countries. Certainly, the distribution of income is not equal in any country. If wealth is concentrated in the hands of a small minority, a high average income will not reflect the welfare of the majority of the population. Climate may also distort GNP per capita as an indicator of well-being. Warmer countries have certain advantages in ease of living that colder ones do not, although the costs of air conditioners may begin to cancel out the costs of furnaces at some stage in development.[6] GNP per capita, then, may be a better measure of production than of welfare. (Several welfare measures are reported in chapter 4.)

Estimates of gross national product are subject to substantial variation in accuracy. In some countries figures are put together from reliably reported components; in others, from rough estimates and guesses. Definitions vary as well although the United Nations Statistical Office has developed standards and guides to which an increasing number of governments are conforming.[7] No precise error margins are available but the degree of accuracy would clearly seem to be related to the development of the country.

There are also, of course, the difficulties of converting into comparative currency the data prepared in disparate national currencies. The events of late 1971 indicated that the dollar previously had been overvalued (and the yen and mark, undervalued) in the official exchange rates. Preferably, the exchange should be made in the components in terms of purchasing power for items commonly consumed. Unfortunately, the economists are not that far along in their work on national accounts. Several attempts have been made to convert GNPs in local currencies into United States dollar values more comparable to values in this country, but these have been limited to a few countries.[8] Except for the Communist countries, we report data that have been converted in the aggregate by official or alternative exchange

6. For an attempt to compare real income, see Wilfred Beckerman, *International Comparisons of Real Income* (Paris: Organization for Economic Co-operation and Development, 1966); Milton Gilbert and Irving B. Kravis, *An International Comparison of National Products and the Purchasing Power of Currencies: A Study of the United States, The United Kingdom, France, Germany and Italy* (Paris: The Organization of European Economic Co-operation, 1954); and Wilfred Beckerman and Robert Bacon, "International Comparison of Income Levels: A Suggested New Measure," *Economic Journal,* 76 (1966): 519-36.

7. See the United Nations, Statistical Office, "A System of National Accounts and Supporting Tables," Studies in Methods, Series F, No. 2, Rev. 2 (New York, 1964); and United Nations, Statistical Office, "National Accounting Practices in Sixty Countries," Studies in Methods, Series F, No. 11 (New York, 1964).

8. For example, see Milton Gilbert and Irving B. Kravis, *Comparative National Products and Price Levels, A Study of Western Europe and the United States* (Paris: Organization for Economic Co-operation and Development, 1958). A comparative cost of living index has been prepared for 84 cities based on 120 items by the United Nations Statistical Office but it measures prices only for professional people in major cities, not the costs of living for the average man. The use of these figures would still exaggerate the cost of living in underdeveloped countries. This index is reported in Lyman H. Long, ed., *The World Almanac and Book of Facts, 1971* (New York: Newspaper Enterprise Association, 1970), p. 59.

rates. The latter were used in our sources for countries of Latin America, Asia, and Africa when official rates yielded unrealistic dollar equivalents. The use of data based upon these rates exaggerates the poverty of underdeveloped countries although the rankings are probably not affected significantly.

The comparison of socialist and capitalist economies is made difficult by the differences between free market prices and those set by other methods. Though methods of adjustment have been developed, no thoroughly satisfactory solution exists. Comparison between socialist and other economies is made even more difficult by the different accounting methods used. In order to compare the gross material product of the Communist countries with the gross national product of others, a service component must be added to the former. Our source for the Warsaw Pact countries reported rough purchasing power equivalents of figures adjusted to the definition of gross national product.[9] We feel that these data are much more comparable to those of other developed countries than are data converted by exchange rates set for trading purposes.

National account data are available in a variety of sources. We attempted to choose the best among them but the pairwise correlations among the series from five sources were all .96 and higher. Gross national products are reported in table 5.4; gross national products per capita, in table 5.5.

Rates of growth for each of these series are also given in these tables. These growth rates are indices of change in whatever GNP and GNP per capita are employed to measure. Moreover, these rates, especially the one based upon GNP per capita, measure social change as do urbanization and literacy trends. Growth in GNP per capita has important consequences for a society's ability to meet the demands of various groups. Social change may involve less conflict if total wealth is growing rapidly enough to ensure that no major group suffers a decrease in at least its absolute level of income. It is even better if the growth in total wealth is substantial enough to mean that all groups find their conditions improved.

The growth rates may in some sense be more accurate than their base data since sectors of the economy whose production is overestimated or underestimated are likely to be erroneously estimated in a consistent fashion. Such errors should not seriously affect the growth rates unless the sectors are growing at substantially different rates. Unfortunately, this is precisely the case in a developing country. (See the discussion of intersectoral inequality on pages 212-14.) Agriculture that is underreported grows more slowly than industry; the result is a growth rate exaggeration.

National currencies in fixed prices were used frequently to calculate growth rates; error associated with exchange rates was avoided. We did not, therefore, use the data reported in the tables for this purpose. Most of these

9. For definitions of these and other national account terms, see the annual issues of the United Nations, Statistical Office, *Yearbook of National Account Statistics* (New York).

national accounts were stated in terms of gross national product but when more reliable series in gross domestic product or net material product were available, we used them instead. Rates were calculated by the continuous growth formula given on p. 286.

Development potential can also be measured by the size of the pool of scientific manpower and its output. Although the quality of journals, papers, and scientists varies from country to country and within countries, we may accept as the first crude measures of technological potential the number of scientific journals published in a country and the country's contribution to world scientific authorship. Derek de Solla Price observes that, while judging a scientist by the height of his reprint pile may be unjust, in the aggregate it becomes a good method for evaluating the scope of and investment in scientific research. The distribution of quality and per capita output, he states, can be shown not to differ widely from time to time or from country to country; therefore, a simple count of papers will give the same results as will one weighted by some complex measure of quality.[10] Likewise, not all journals are of equal worth nor do all scholars produce equal output—quantitatively or qualitatively. Moreover, the best journals and the most productive scholars probably are in the richest countries. Series based upon any of these will be biased towards these larger, more developed countries at the expense of the small and poor ones. As Derek Price points out, an author "may have been born in country A, educated and trained in countries B, C and D; he may have pursued his reported research in country E (with colleagues from F and G, money from H and equipment built in I) and only published in J."[11] Prestigious journals published in large countries will attract authors' works more readily than will local journals, but the universities, research institutes, and industry of these countries will also attract the authors themselves.

Whatever the difficulties may be, the kind of series that deals with authors and publications seems much easier to make comparable at the moment than do those based upon budget data. Dealing with the proportion of GNP spent on science involves a definitional morass. Many kinds of manpower data are also inadequate for international comparisons since standards for reporting differ greatly from country to country. One may take manpower to mean all those who have been trained in the appropriate disciplines, but the number of persons engaged in scientific research is only a small and variable part of this total. The number of journals published and the number of publishing scientists, therefore, may be the least inaccurate of several possible series.

The data entitled "Contribution to World Scientific Authorship" in table 5.6 refer to the proportion of all authors of scientific papers in the world living in particular countries. By "scientific" is meant the natural sciences;

10. Derek J. de Solla Price, "Nations Can Publish or Perish," *Science and Technology* (1967).

11. Derek J. de Solla Price, "The Distribution of Scientific Papers by Country and Subject—A Science Policy Analysis," mimeographed, p. 2.

the names of authors were taken from the *International Directory of Research and Development Scientists.* The percentages given in the table are generally averages of three separate percentages for the years 1967, 1968, and 1969. Exceptions are Congo-Brazzaville, Congo-Kinshasa, Gabon, Jamaica, Trinidad, North Vietnam, and South Vietnam. For these countries data were averaged only over 1967 and 1968. No data are available for China after 1967 and the percentage for this country is based upon that one year. Venezuela's percentage was derived only from 1967 and 1969. Angola, Barbados, Chad, Guyana, Ivory Coast, Laos, Mozambique, and Niger have authors listed in only one of the three years; their percentages were taken nevertheless over the three-year period. It proved too difficult to separate authors in East Germany from those in West Germany by their addresses as given in the original source and the total was listed under West Germany. Puerto Rican authors were incorporated with United States authors in the original sources and are included with this country in the table.

The data entitled "Scientific Journals" in table 5.6 refer to an unrestricted list of scientific and technical serials. They do not include promotional literature, technical reports, proceedings of international organizations, or translations and publishers' series but they do include almost everything else published with the intention of being continued indefinitely in the fields of natural, physical, and engineering sciences. Charles M. Gottschalk, one of the authors of the source of these data, suggests an error margin of plus or minus 10 percent.

Another alternative measure of development is energy consumption per capita. Aggregate energy consumption indicates industrial output and sheer economic size. These data, which are given in table 5.7, are expressed in terms of coal equivalents, i.e. the quantity of coal it would have taken to produce the heat value of oil, natural gas, or electricity.

Data refer to the gross inland consumption of commercial fuels and water power. Included are chiefly coal and lignite, gasoline (motor spirit), kerosene and fuel oils, natural gas, and hydroelectric power. Also included are derivatives of these such as briquettes, coke, manufactured gas, and thermal electric power. Natural gasoline, refinery gases, liquefied petroleum gases, and benzols have been included where possible. In calculating consumption from the data described, all duplications have been omitted for want of adequate data. These sources are believed to provide a major share of the energy supply in all but a few countries. The minimum amount of energy obtained from such sources is estimated as equivalent to about 0.25 tons of coal per capita per year for most countries. The figures have been computed mainly from production, trade, and processing data. Insofar as possible, changes in stocks and fuels loaded in vessels and aircraft have been taken into account.[12]

12. United Nations, Statistical Office, *Statistical Yearbook, 1969* (New York, 1970), p.40.

Also included in table 5.7 are growth rates for per capita energy consumption, calculated with the continuous growth rate formula given on p. 286. Rates are average annual rates based upon a five-year period and a fifteen-year period.

Economic Sectors

The economic and social structure of a country is at least partially indicated by the proportions of its population dependent upon agriculture and upon mining and manufacturing, by the product that arises from these sectors, and by the proportion of the labor force that has risen to professional and technical positions. Developed countries, even those that have large modernized agricultural sectors like Denmark and New Zealand, require fewer members of their labor forces in agriculture and more in industry than underdeveloped countries. Furthermore, as an economy develops a greater proportion of its product will be created in the industrial rather than in the agricultural sector.

The reliability of data on the economically active population and on proportions of it, as with all population statistics, depends upon the quality of the basic census or estimate. Other problems attend the figures, however. Many countries include in the economically active population only those persons who have reached some specified minimum age. Since this is a base for a proportion, variability becomes a problem only insofar as sectoral distribution is greatly affected by age range in the younger years. A much more serious problem involves the extent to which unpaid family workers, usually women, who assist in family enterprises are included in the enumerated economically active population. Since these family enterprises are usually farms and hence in the agricultural sector, differences in accounting for such workers may greatly affect the sectoral proportions. For this reason, we have chosen to use data based upon males only whenever possible in the belief that this eliminates many of the incomparabilities.

The economically active male population is the total number of employed males (including employers, own-account workers, salaried employees, wage earners, and, insofar as data are available, unpaid family workers). Data also include unemployed persons at the time of the census or survey. The economically active population does not include students, retired persons, persons living entirely on their own means, and persons wholly dependent upon others. The percentage of the economically active male population engaged in manufacturing, mining, and transportation is given for available countries in table 5.8. The percentages engaged in agriculture, forestry, or fishing are given in table 5.9. Data are reported on the basis of the nomenclature of the International Standard Industrial Classification of all Economic Activities and the International Standard Classification of Occupations. Deviations from the definition exist and are noted when known. More complete series were obtained by using data for total labor force when data for males only were not available; those have been duly marked.

Table 5.10 contains the percentage of the economically active male population occupied in professional and technical positions.

Table 5.11 includes the percentages of gross domestic product originating in agriculture and industry. The more developed the country the larger are the service sectors and the less the proportion of GNP accounted for in the table. The percentages for agriculture and for industry are equal to their contribution to gross domestic product, i.e. the compensation of employees, interest, net rent, profit, and consumption of fixed capital. The percentage can also be obtained by the addition of the value of sales at market prices plus the value of physical increase in stocks minus the market value of all current purchases, including imports, from other enterprises and all net indirect taxation. Goods or services produced for capital formation and for consumption by the owner or his employees are considered sales.[13] Deviations from the standard definitions are numerous; major differences are coded in the table.

Gross domestic capital formation refers to expenses related to the acquisition of capital goods. It includes the value of purchases and construction of fixed assets by enterprises (including households as house owners), private nonprofit institutions, and general government. Expenditure by general government for capital items in defense is not included in capital formation; also excluded are household expenditures on durable goods except for new dwellings. Included, however, are all expenses directly related to the acquisition of capital goods, such as transportation and installation charges, engineering fees, architectural, legal, and other services. Indirect costs are regarded as current expenditures.[14] This series is reported in table 5.12.

13. United Nations, Statistical Office, *Yearbook of National Account Statistics, 1968* (New York, 1969).
14. Ibid.

Table 5.1
Population and Population Growth Rates

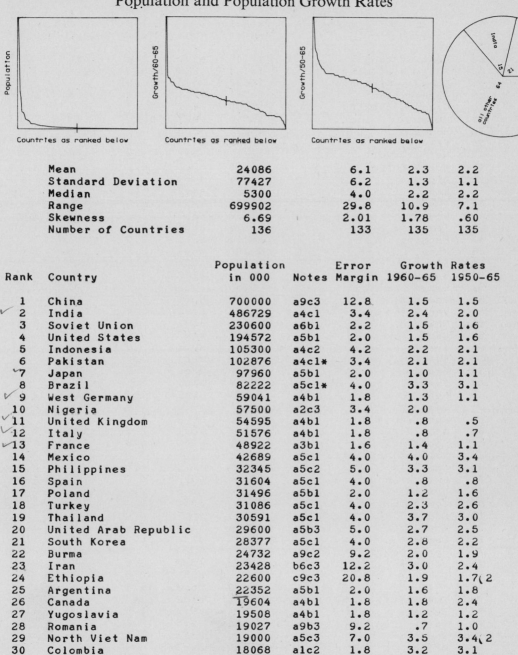

Mean	24086	6.1	2.3	2.2
Standard Deviation	77427	6.2	1.3	1.1
Median	5300	4.0	2.2	2.2
Range	699902	29.8	10.9	7.1
Skewness	6.69	2.01	1.78	.60
Number of Countries	136	133	135	135

Rank	Country	Population in 000	Notes	Error Margin	Growth Rates 1960-65	1950-65
1	China	700000	a9c3	12.8	1.5	1.5
2	India	486729	a4c1	3.4	2.4	2.0
3	Soviet Union	230600	a6b1	2.2	1.5	1.6
4	United States	194572	a5b1	2.0	1.5	1.6
5	Indonesia	105300	a4c2	4.2	2.2	2.1
6	Pakistan	102876	a4c1*	3.4	2.1	2.1
7	Japan	97960	a5b1	2.0	1.0	1.1
8	Brazil	82222	a5c1*	4.0	3.3	3.1
9	West Germany	59041	a4b1	1.8	1.3	1.1
10	Nigeria	57500	a2c3	3.4	2.0	
11	United Kingdom	54595	a4b1	1.8	.8	.5
12	Italy	51576	a4b1	1.8	.8	.7
13	France	48922	a3b1	1.6	1.4	1.1
14	Mexico	42689	a5c1	4.0	4.0	3.4
15	Philippines	32345	a5c2	5.0	3.3	3.1
16	Spain	31604	a5c1	4.0	.8	.8
17	Poland	31496	a5b1	2.0	1.2	1.6
18	Turkey	31086	a5c1	4.0	2.3	2.6
19	Thailand	30591	a5c1	4.0	3.7	3.0
20	United Arab Republic	29600	a5b3	5.0	2.7	2.5
21	South Korea	28377	a5c1	4.0	2.8	2.2
22	Burma	24732	a9c2	9.2	2.0	1.9
23	Iran	23428	b6c3	12.2	3.0	2.4
24	Ethiopia	22600	c9c3	20.8	1.9	1.7(2
25	Argentina	22352	a5b1	2.0	1.6	1.8
26	Canada	19604	a4b1	1.8	1.8	2.4
27	Yugoslavia	19508	a4b1	1.8	1.2	1.2
28	Romania	19027	a9b3	9.2	.7	1.0
29	North Viet Nam	19000	a5c3	7.0	3.5	3.4(2
30	Colombia	18068	a1c2	1.8	3.2	3.1
31	South Africa	17867	a5c1	4.0	2.3	2.4

Table 5.1 Population and Population Growth Rates—*Continued*

Rank	Country	Population in 000	Notes	Error Margin	Growth Rates 1960–65	Growth Rates 1950–65
32	East Germany	17100	a2..	3.4	-.1	-.4
33	South Viet Nam	16124	c9c3	20.8	2.7	3.0(2
34	Congo – Kinshasa	15627	b9c3*	15.8	2.0	2.2
35	Afghanistan	15051	d7..	28.4	1.7	1.5
36	Czechoslovakia	14159	a4b1	1.8	.7	.9
37	Sudan	13540	b9c3	15.8	2.8	2.8(2
38	Morocco	13323	a5c3	7.0	2.7	2.7
39	Taiwan	12429	a9a1	2.9	3.2	3.3
40	Netherlands	12292	a5a1	1.5	1.4	1.3
41	North Korea	12100	d5c3	26.0	2.6	2.8(2
42	Algeria	11871	a0c1	1.0	1.9	2.0
43	Peru	11650	a4c2*	4.2	3.0	2.5
44	Australia	11360	a4b1*	1.8	2.0	2.2
45	Ceylon	11232	a2b3	2.6	2.5	2.5
46	Tanzania	10515	a8c1	5.8	1.9	1.8
47	Hungary	10148	a5b1	2.0	.3	.6
48	Nepal	10100	a4..	5.8	1.9	1.6
49	Belgium	9464	a4b1	1.8	.7	.6
50	Malaysia	9403	a8b2	4.2	3.0	2.9
51	Kenya	9365	a3c2	3.4	2.9	2.9
52	Portugal	9199	a5b1	2.0	.8	.6
53	Venezuela	8722	a4c1*	3.4	3.4	3.7
54	Chile	8567	a5c1	4.0	2.2	2.3
55	Greece	8551	a4b2	2.6	.5	.8
56	Iraq	8262	a0..	1.0	4.4	3.1
57	Bulgaria	8200	a9b1	3.8	.8	.8
58	Ghana	7740	a5c2	5.0	2.7	2.7(4
59	Sweden	7734	a5a1	1.5	.7	.7
60	Cuba	7631	a9c2	9.2	2.2	2.2
61	Uganda	7551	a6c2	5.8	2.5	2.5
62	Austria	7255	a4b1	1.8	.6	.3
63	Mozambique	6956	a5c1	4.0	1.2	1.3
64	Saudi Arabia	6750	d9c3	30.8	2.2	.8
65	Malagasy Republic	6420	...		3.5	2.7
66	Cambodia	6115	a3..	4.6	2.3	2.7
67	Switzerland	5945	a5b1	2.0	2.1	1.6
68	Syria	5300	a5c3	7.0	3.0	3.1(4
69	Cameroon	5229	c0b2	10.0	2.1	2.2(3
70	Angola	5154	a5c1	4.0	1.4	1.5
71	Ecuador	5084	a3b3*	3.4	3.3	3.1
72	Yemen	5000	d5d	28.0	.0	.7
73	Upper Volta	4858	b5c3	11.0	2.4	2.5(4
74	Denmark	4758	a5a1	1.5	.8	.7
75	Finland	4612	a5b1	2.0	.8	.9
76	Mali	4576	b5c3	11.0	2.2	1.9
77	Guatemala	4438	a1b2	1.4	3.1	3.1
78	Tunisia	4414	a9c1	7.4	.8	1.4
79	Haiti	4396	a9c3	12.8	1.1	1.8
80	Rhodesia	4260	a3b3	3.4	3.1	3.2(2
81	Malawi	3940	a0c2	1.0	2.6	
82	Ivory Coast	3835	b8c3	14.6	3.4	2.7(1
83	Hong Kong	3804	a4b2	2.6	4.3	4.5(1
84	Norway	3723	a5b1	2.0	.8	.9
85	Zambia	3710	a2c3	3.4	2.9	2.8

Table 5.1 Population and Population Growth Rates—*Continued*

Rank	Country	Population in 000	Notes	Error Margin	Growth Rates 1960-65	Growth Rates 1950-65
86	Bolivia	3697	a9c3	12.8	1.4	1.4
87	Dominican Republic	3619	a5c2	5.0	3.5	3.5
88	Guinea	3500	c0b2	10.0	2.6	2.9
89	Senegal	3490	b5c3	11.0	2.3	2.3(3
90	Niger	3328	a6c3	8.2	3.3	3.1(1
91	Chad	3307	b2b2	5.8	1.2	
92	Burundi	3210	b0..	5.0	2.0	
93	Rwanda	3110	b9c3*	15.8	3.1	3.0(2
94	El Salvador	2928	a4b3	4.2	3.5	3.0
95	Ireland	2873	a0b2	1.0	.3	-.1
96	Uruguay	2715	a2c2	2.6	1.4	1.4
97	New Zealand	2640	a4b1	1.8	2.1	5.8
98	Puerto Rico	2633	a5b1	2.0	2.2	1.1
99	Lebanon	2565	c9c3	20.8	2.9	2.7(2
100	Israel	2563	a4b1	1.8	3.9	4.7
101	Somalia	2500	d0..	20.0	4.4	1.9
102	Dahomey	2365	b4c3	9.8	2.9	
103	Sierra Leone	2290	a2c3	3.4	2.1	.9
104	Honduras	2284	a4b3	4.2	3.3	3.1
105	Papua / New Guinea	2149	c0..	10.0	2.4	2.6
106	Paraguay	2030	a3c3	4.6	3.0	2.5
107	Laos	2000	c7c3	18.4	2.1	2.6
108	Jordan	1976	a4b3	4.2	3.1	2.9(1
109.5	Albania	1865	a5b2	3.0	3.0	2.9
109.5	Singapore	1865	a8b2	4.2	2.6	4.0
111	Jamaica	1788	a5b1	2.0	2.0	1.7
112	Nicaragua	1655	a2b3	2.6	3.2	3.0
113	Togo	1638	a7c3	9.4	2.6	2.7(3
114	Libya	1617	a1c1	1.6	3.6	3.6(2
115	Costa Rica	1433	a2b2	1.8	4.0	3.9
116	Central African Republic	1352	b6c3	12.2	1.9	1.5
117	Panama	1300	a5c1	4.0	3.3	2.7
118	Southern Yemen	1105	d1c3	21.2		
119	Mongolia	1104	a2..	3.4	3.3	2.7
120	Liberia	1070	a3c3	4.6	1.6	
121	Mauritania	1050	b0..	5.0	4.7	4.4
122	Trinidad and Tobago	975	a5b1	2.0	3.0	2.9
123	Congo - Brazzaville	840	b5c3	11.0	1.7	1.4
124	Lesotho	838	a0c1	1.0	4.0	2.3
125	Mauritius	741	a3b1	1.6	2.8	3.1
126	Guyana	647	a5b1	2.0	2.7	2.8
127	Cyprus	594	a5b2	3.0	.7	1.2
128	Botswana	559	a1..	2.2	2.9	2.8(1
129	Kuwait	467	...		10.4	6.7
130	Gabon	463	a5b2	3.0	.7	.8
131	Luxembourg	331	a5b2	3.0	1.1	.7
132	The Gambia	330	a2c3	3.4	2.0	1.5
133	Malta	319	a8b2	4.2	-.5	.1
134	Barbados	244	a5b1	2.0	.8	1.0
135	Iceland	192	a5a1	1.5	1.7	2.0
136	Maldive Islands	98	...		1.9	2.0(3

Table 5.1 Population and Population Growth Rates—*Continued*

Notes: No countries are missing from this table.
Date is midyear, 1965.
Under the column entitled *notes*, an asterisk indicates that minor parts of the population (e.g. jungle dwellers) have been excluded. These exclusions are thought to account for no more than 3 or 4 percent of the total population.

The coding system appearing in the same column is that of the United Nations Statistical Office; it indicates the methods used to derive the mid-1965 population estimates. The first letter refers to the nature of the original base data where

a = a complete census of individuals
b = a sample census or survey
c = a partial census or partial registration of individuals
d = conjecture
• = nature of base data undetermined

The digit immediately following indicates the number of years from the establishment of the base figure to 1965. The number "9" indicates that nine or more years elapsed between the two. The second letter and second digit refer to the method of adjustment, where

a = adjustment by continuous population register
b = adjustment based upon calculated balance of births, deaths, and migration
c = adjustment by assumed rate of increase
d = no adjustment; base figure held constant at least two consecutive years
• = method of adjustment not determined

and, if a or b above,

1 = population balance adequately accounted for
2 = adequacy of accounting for population balance not determined
3 = population balance not adequately accounted for

or, if c above,

1 = two or more censuses taken at decennial intervals or less
2 = two or more censuses taken, but latest interval exceeds a decennium
3 = one or no census taken

The *error margin* is calculated upon this information and data given in the text by use of the formula also reported there. (See p. 285).

Growth rates are given in percentages as annual average rates based upon the time periods indicated. For the continuous growth rate formula see the text, p. 286. Exceptions to the 1950-1965 standard time period are denoted as follows:

1. 1951-1965
2. 1955-1965
3. 1956-1965
4. 1957-1965

Source is United Nations, Statistical Office, *Statistical Yearbook, 1966* (New York, 1967). Data for the growth rates came from several editions of the *Demographic Yearbooks* published annually by the Statistical Office of the United Nations.

Table 5.2
Area and Population Density

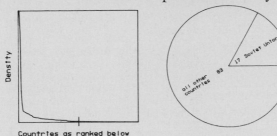

Density

Countries as ranked below

Mean	964.2	126.8
Standard Deviation	2537.1	430.2
Median	255.8	28.9
Range	22401.9	3803.3
Skewness	5.64	7.12
Number of Countries	136	136

Rank	Country	Area in 000 Km(2)	Persons Per Km(2)
1	Hong Kong	1.0	3804.0
2	Singapore	.6	3108.3
3	Malta	.3	1063.3
4	Barbados	.4	610.0
5	Mauritius	1.9	390.0
6	Netherlands	33.6	365.8
7	Taiwan	36.0	345.3
8	Maldive Islands	.3	326.7
9	Belgium	30.5	310.3
10	Puerto Rico	8.9	295.8
11	South Korea	98.4	288.4
12	Japan	369.7	265.0
13	Lebanon	10.4	246.6
14	West Germany	248.5	237.6
15	United Kingdom	244.0	223.8
16	Trinidad and Tobago	5.1	191.2
17.5	Ceylon	65.6	171.2
17.5	Italy	301.2	171.2
19	Jamaica	11.0	162.5
20	Haiti	27.8	158.1
21	East Germany	108.3	157.9
22	India	3183.6	152.9
23	Switzerland	41.3	143.9
24	El Salvador	21.4	136.8
25	Luxembourg	2.6	127.3
26	Israel	20.7	123.8
27	North Viet Nam	158.8	119.6
28	Rwanda	26.3	118.3
29	Burundi	27.8	115.5
30.5	Czechoslovakia	127.9	110.7
30.5	Denmark	43.0	110.7

Table 5.2 Area and Population Density—*Continued*

Rank	Country	Area in 000 Km(2)	Persons Per Km(2)
32	Hungary	93.0	109.1
33	Philippines	300.0	107.8
34	Poland	312.5	100.8
35	North Korea	120.5	100.4
36	Pakistan	1027.6	100.1
37	Portugal	92.0	100.0
38	South Viet Nam	170.8	94.4
39	France	547.0	89.4
40	Austria	83.8	86.6
41	Romania	237.5	80.1
42	Yugoslavia	255.8	76.3
43	Dominican Republic	48.7	74.3
44	Bulgaria	110.9	73.9
45	China	9561.0	73.2
46	Nepal	140.8	71.7
47	Indonesia	1491.6	70.6
48	Cuba	114.5	66.6
49	Albania	28.7	65.0
50	Greece	131.9	64.8
51	Cyprus	9.3	63.9
52	Spain	504.7	62.6
53	Nigeria	923.8	62.2
54	Thailand	514.0	59.5
55	Ireland	70.3	40.9
56	Guatemala	108.9	40.8
57	Turkey	780.6	39.8
58	Burma	678.0	36.5
59	Cambodia	181.0	33.8
60	Malawi	119.3	33.0
61	Ghana	238.5	32.5
62	Uganda	236.0	32.0
63	Sierra Leone	71.7	31.9
64	Morocco	445.1	29.9
65	United Arab Republic	1000.0	29.6
66.5	Kuwait	16.0	29.2
66.5	The Gambia	11.3	29.2
68	Togo	56.6	28.9
69	Syria	185.2	28.6
70.5	Costa Rica	50.7	28.3
70.5	Malaysia	332.6	28.3
72	Lesotho	30.3	27.7
73	Tunisia	164.2	26.9
74	Yemen	195.0	25.6
75	Afghanistan	647.5	23.2
76	Mexico	1972.5	21.6
77	Dahomey	112.6	21.0
78	United States	9363.4	20.8
79	Honduras	112.1	20.4
80	Jordan	97.7	20.2
81	Ethiopia	1221.9	18.5
82	Iraq	448.7	18.4
83	Ecuador	283.6	17.9
84	Senegal	196.2	17.8
85	Upper Volta	274.2	17.7

Table 5.2 Area and Population Density—*Continued*

Rank	Country	Area in 000 Km(2)	Persons Per Km(2)
86.5	Panama	75.7	17.2
86.5	Sweden	449.8	17.2
88	Kenya	582.6	16.1
89	Colombia	1138.3	15.9
90	South Africa	1221.0	14.6
91	Uruguay	186.9	14.5
92.5	Guinea	245.9	14.2
92.5	Iran	1648.0	14.2
94	Finland	337.0	13.7
95	Ivory Coast	322.5	11.9
96	Nicaragua	139.7	11.8
97	Norway	324.2	11.5
98	Chile	756.9	11.3
99	Tanzania	939.7	11.2
100	Cameroon	475.4	11.0
101.5	Malagasy Republic	587.0	10.9
101.5	Rhodesia	389.4	10.9
103	Soviet Union	22402.2	10.3
104	New Zealand	268.7	9.8
105	Brazil	8512.0	9.7
106.5	Liberia	111.4	9.6
106.5	Venezuela	912.1	9.6
108	Peru	1285.2	9.1
109	Mozambique	783.0	8.9
110	Laos	236.8	8.4
111	Argentina	2776.7	8.0
112	Congo - Kinshasa	2345.4	6.7
113	Sudan	2505.8	5.4
114.5	Algeria	2381.7	5.0
114.5	Paraguay	406.8	5.0
116	Zambia	752.6	4.9
117	Papua / New Guinea	461.7	4.7
118	Angola	1246.7	4.1
119	Somalia	637.7	3.9
120.5	Mali	1201.6	3.8
120.5	Southern Yemen	287.7	3.8
122	Bolivia	1098.6	3.4
123.5	Guyana	215.0	3.0
123.5	Saudi Arabia	2253.3	3.0
125.5	Chad	1284.0	2.6
125.5	Niger	1267.0	2.6
127	Congo - Brazzaville	342.0	2.5
128	Central African Republic	623.0	2.2
129	Canada	9976.2	2.0
130	Iceland	103.0	1.9
131	Gabon	267.7	1.7
132	Australia	7686.8	1.5
133.5	Botswana	569.6	1.0
133.5	Mauritania	1030.7	1.0
135	Libya	1759.5	.9
136	Mongolia	1535.0	.7

Table 5.2 Area and Population Density—*Continued*

Notes: No countries are missing from this table.

Areas are given in thousand square kilometers. One square mile equals 2.589988 square kilometers.

Data are for the period circa 1964.

For definition and qualifications to it for a few countries see the text, p. 286.

Source is United Nations, Statistical Office, *Demographic Yearbook, 1965* (New York, 1966) except in the case of Bulgaria, where the source was Food and Agriculture Organization, *FAO Production Yearbook, 1965* (Rome, 1966).

Table 5.3
Agricultural Area and Density

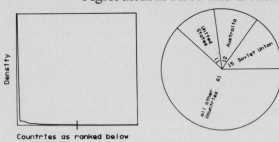

Mean	303.7	672.5
Standard Deviation	828.7	3690.7
Median	59.5	133.3
Range	5999.7	38038.6
Skewness	4.95	8.87
Number of Countries	130	130

Rank	Country	Agricultural Area in 000 km(2)	Source	Persons Per Km(2)
1	Hong Kong	.1		38040.0
2	Singapore	.1		18650.0
3	Malta	.2		1595.0
4	Japan	69.9		1401.4
5	Taiwan	8.9		1396.5
6	Kuwait	.2	1	1335.0
7	South Korea	21.5		1319.9
8	Papua / New Guinea	1.7		1264.1
9	United Arab Republic	25.0		1184.0
10	North Viet Nam	20.2		940.6
11	Lebanon	2.8		916.1
12	Barbados	.3		813.3
13	Mauritius	1.2		617.5
14	Indonesia	177.0		594.9
15	Ceylon	18.9		594.3
16	Belgium	16.7		566.7
17	Nepal	18.3		551.9
18	Trinidad and Tobago	1.8		541.7
19	Netherlands	22.7		541.5
20	Yemen	9.8	2	510.2
21	Haiti	8.7		505.3
22	Puerto Rico	6.1		431.6
23	West Germany	141.3		417.8
24	Pakistan	257.6		399.4
25	Norway	10.2		365.0
26	Jamaica	4.9		364.9
27	Gabon	1.3		356.2
28	Thailand	106.0		288.6
29	Philippines	112.1		288.5
30	Dominican Republic	12.6		287.2
31	United Kingdom	196.6		277.7

Table 5.3 Agricultural Area and Density—*Continued*

Rank	Country	Agricultural Area in 000 km(2)	Source	Persons Per Km(2)
32	India	1770.6		274.9
33	Switzerland	21.7		274.0
34	South Viet Nam	59.5		271.0
35	El Salvador	10.9		268.6
36	East Germany	64.5		265.1
37	Nigeria	218.0		263.8
38	Italy	204.6		252.1
39	China	2873.5		243.6
40	Luxembourg	1.4		236.4
41	Malawi	16.8		234.5
42	Israel	11.1		230.9
43	Portugal	41.3		222.7
44	Guatemala	20.5		216.5
45	Czechoslovakia	68.2		207.6
46	Cambodia	29.8		205.2
47	Sweden	38.3		201.9
48	Uganda	37.9		199.2
49	Austria	39.8		182.3
50	Jordan	11.4		173.3
51	Malaysia	56.2		167.3
52	Kenya	56.2		166.6
53	Rwanda	18.7		166.3
54	The Gambia	2.0		165.0
55	Finland	28.2		163.5
56	Burma	152.9		161.8
57	Burundi	19.9		161.3
58	Poland	201.3		156.5
59	Denmark	30.7		155.0
60	Albania	12.3		151.6
61	Ghana	53.1		145.8
62	Hungary	69.8		145.4
63	France	341.1		143.4
64	Bulgaria	57.7		142.1
65	Congo — Brazzaville	6.3		133.3
66	Yugoslavia	147.7		132.1
67	Iran	180.0		130.2
68	Cuba	58.7		130.0
69	Romania	147.4		129.1
70	Laos	16.0		125.0
71	Afghanistan	122.3		123.1
72	Dahomey	19.9		118.8
73	Cyprus	5.3		112.1
74	Ecuador	50.9		99.9
75	Upper Volta	49.0		99.1
76	Greece	89.9		95.1
77	Costa Rica	15.4		93.1
78	Panama	14.0		92.9
79	Nicaragua	17.9		92.5
80	Colombia	196.5		91.9
81	Spain	351.9		89.8
82	Morocco	155.1		85.9
83	Togo	23.6		69.4
84	Chile	129.6		66.1
85	Brazil	1267.3		64.9

Table 5.3 Agricultural Area and Density—*Continued*

Rank	Country	Agricultural Area in 000 km(2)	Source	Persons Per Km(2)
86	Rhodesia	66.9		63.7
87	Senegal	55.0		63.5
88	Ireland	46.6		61.7
89	Peru	201.0		58.0
90	Turkey	543.8		57.2
91	Honduras	42.4		53.9
92	Iraq	156.7		52.7
93	Venezuela	191.8		45.5
94	Tunisia	99.9		44.2
95	United States	4413.7		44.1
96	Sudan	311.0		43.5
97.5	Mexico	1029.1		41.5
97.5	Syria	127.6		41.5
99	Sierra Leone	58.7		39.0
100	Soviet Union	5999.8		38.4
101	Cameroon	165.9		31.5
102	Canada	628.5		31.2
103	Congo - Kinshasa	514.3		30.4
104	Lesotho	28.5		29.4
105	Ethiopia	788.9		28.6
106	Liberia	40.9		26.2
107	Algeria	454.7		26.1
108	Bolivia	144.1		25.7
109	Guyana	27.3		23.7
110.5	Central African Republic	60.0		22.5
110.5	Tanzania	466.4		22.5
112	New Zealand	136.3		19.4
113	Paraguay	107.8		18.8
114	Niger	179.0		18.6
115	Malagasy Republic	367.5		17.5
116	South Africa	1024.5		17.4
117	Angola	299.0		17.2
118	Uruguay	161.0		16.9
119	Argentina	1378.3		16.2
120	Mozambique	460.0		15.1
121	Libya	112.9		14.3
122	Zambia	303.0		12.2
123	Southern Yemen	93.2		11.9
124	Somalia	215.3		11.6
125	Iceland	22.8		8.4
126	Saudi Arabia	853.6		7.9
127	Chad	520.0		6.4
128	Mauritania	395.1		2.7
129	Australia	4793.5		2.4
130	Botswana	412.8		1.4

Notes: Data are missing for Guinea, Ivory Coast, Maldive Islands, Mali, Mongolia, and North Korea.

Areas are given in thousand square kilometers. One square mile equals 2.589988 square kilometers.

Data are for the period circa 1950-1965.

Source, unless otherwise noted, is Food and Agriculture Organization, *FAO Production Yearbook, 1965* (Rome, 1966).

1. United States, Agency for International Development, *A.I.D. Economic Data Books* (Washington, D.C.: U.S. Government Printing Office, 1967).

2. *Gallatin Business Intelligence* (New York: Copley International Corporation, 1967).

Table 5.4
Gross National Product and Growth Rates

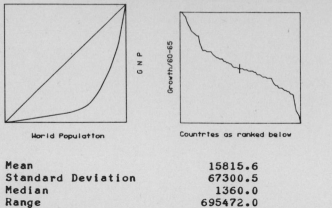

World Population   Countries as ranked below

Mean	15815.6	5.1
Standard Deviation	67300.5	2.0
Median	1360.0	4.9
Range	695472.0	9.2
Skewness	8.32	.22
Number of Countries	135	84

Rank	Country	GNP in $m	Date Source	Growth Rate- Recent Period	Dates
1	United States	695500	1	4.6	1960-65
2	Soviet Union	313000	2	6.4	1960-65
3	West Germany	112232	1	4.7	1960-65
4	United Kingdom	99260	1	3.3	1960-65
5	France	94125	1	5.0	1960-65
6	Japan	84347	1	9.2	1960-65
7	China	76000	2		
8	Italy	56947	1	5.0	1960-65
9	India	49220		3.0	1960-65
10	Canada	48473	1	5.3	1960-65
11	Poland	30800	2	6.0	1960-65
12	Australia	22739	1	4.8	1960-65
13	Czechoslovakia	22100	2	2.0	1960-65
14	Brazil	21970		4.3	1960-65
15	East Germany	21546	5		
16	Sweden	19714	1	4.9	1960-65
17	Mexico	19432	1	5.8	1960-65
18	Netherlands	19106	1	4.9	1960-65
19	Spain	17743	1	8.0	1960-65
20	Argentina	17204	1	3.3	1960-65
21	Belgium	17071	1	4.7	1960-65
22	Romania	14800	2	8.5	1960-64
23	Switzerland	13869	1	5.1	1960-65
24	Pakistan	11160		5.5	1960-65
25	Hungary	11100	2	4.4	1960-65
26	South Africa	10911	1	5.7	1960-65
27	Indonesia	10450			
28	Denmark	10088	1	4.7	1960-65
29	Austria	9336	1	4.1	1960-65

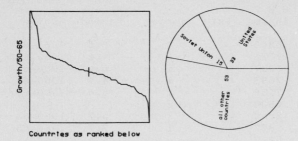

Growth/50-65

Countries as ranked below

4.9
1.7
4.8
9.7
.70
85

Growth Rate-Longer Period	Dates	Source	Rates Calculated on the Basis of	at Fixed Prices of
3.7	1950-65	1	gnp	1963
6.2	1953-65	1	nmp	1958
6.6	1950-65		gnp	1965
2.9	1950-65	1	gnp	1958
4.6	1950-65	1	gnp	1959
8.8	1952-65	1	gnp	1960
5.4	1950-65		gnp	1965
3.7	1950-65		gnp	1965
4.4	1950-65	1	gnp	1957
6.6	1953-65	1	nmp	1961
4.1	1950-65		gnp	1965
5.1	1953-65	1	nmp	1960
5.2	1950-65		gnp	1965
3.8	1950-65	1	gnp	1959
5.9	1950-65	1	gnp	1950
4.8	1950-65	1	gnp	1958
6.0	1950-65		gnp	1965
3.1	1950-65	1	gnp	1960
3.6	1950-65		gnp	1965
9.5	1950-64	1	nmp	1950
4.6	1950-65	1	gnp	1958
3.6	1950-65		gnp	1965
5.7	1958-65	1	nmp	1959
4.7	1953-65	1	gnp	1958
3.5	1951-59	1	gdp	1955
3.7	1950-65	1	gnp	1955
5.0	1950-65	1	gnp	1954

307

Table 5.4 Gross National Product and Growth Rates—*Continued*

Rank	Country	G N P in $m	Date	Source	Growth Rate- Recent Period	Dates
30	Yugoslavia	8800		2	8.3	1960-64
31	Turkey	8776		1	4.2	1960-65
32	Finland	8067		1	5.4	1960-65
33	Venezuela	7692		1	4.9	1960-65
34	Norway	7038		1	5.4	1960-65
35	Bulgaria	6800		2		
36	Iran	5889		1	5.7	1960-65
37	Greece	5677		1	7.7	1960-65
38	New Zealand	5227			4.4	1960-64
39	Philippines	5172		1	4.7	1960-65
40	Colombia	5103			4.2	1960-65
41	Nigeria	4852			4.8	1960-65
42	Chile	4842		1	4.1	1960-65
43	United Arab Republic	4700			6.4	1960-64
44	Peru	4277		1	6.4	1960-65
45	Thailand	3930		1	6.7	1960-65
46	Portugal	3731		1	6.3	1960-65
47	Israel	3645		1	9.5	1960-65
48	Puerto Rico	3038		1	7.6	1960-65
49	Cuba	3000		2		
50	South Korea	2973		1	7.6	1960-65
51	Malaysia	2875		1	6.1	1960-65
52	Taiwan	2820		1	9.6	1960-65
53	Ireland	2814		1	3.8	1960-65
54	Algeria	2630				
55	Morocco	2605		1	3.1	1960-65
56	North Korea	2500		2		
57	South Viet Nam	2413		1	5.0	1960-65
58	Ghana	2207			2.8	1960-65
59	Iraq	1909			6.3	1960-65
60	North Viet Nam	1900		2	2.7	1960-63
61	Burma	1760			2.8	1960-65
62	Ceylon	1622		1	3.1	1960-65
63	Hong Kong	1600				
64	Kuwait	1583		1		
65	Uruguay	1555			.4	1960-65
66	Saudi Arabia	1521				
67	Guatemala	1410		1	6.3	1960-65
68	Sudan	1360		1	4.1	1960-64
69	Congo - Kinshasa	1273				
70	Afghanistan	1250				
71	Syria	1125			8.8	1960-65
72	Lebanon	1120				
73	Ecuador	1096		1	4.2	1960-65
74	Rhodesia	1021		1	3.3	1960-64
75	Ethiopia	1020		1	3.5	1961-65
76	Ivory Coast	963				
77	Dominican Republic	960			1.4	1960-65
78	Tunisia	945		1	4.9	1960-65
79	Singapore	933				
80	Jamaica	889		1	5.5	1960-65
81	Libya	876				

Growth Rate— Longer Period	Dates	Source	Rates Calculated on the Basis of	at Fixed Prices of
8.9	1952-64	1	nmp	1960
5.1	1950-65		gnp	1965
5.0	1950-65	1	gnp	1954
6.8	1950-65		gnp	1965
4.1	1950-65	1	gnp	1963
5.3	1959-65	1	gnp	1959
6.6	1950-65	1	gnp	1958
4.0	1954-64	1	gnp	1954
5.2	1950-65	1	gnp	1955
4.5	1950-65		gnp	1965
4.8	1960-65		gnp	1965
3.7	1950-65		gnp	1965
5.8	1950-64	1	gdp	1959
5.5	1950-65	1	gnp	1963
5.9	1951-65	1	gdp	1962
4.8	1950-65		gnp	1965
10.1	1950-65	1	gnp	1964
6.1	1950-65	1	gnp	1963
5.7	1953-65	1	gnp	1960
6.1	1960-65		gnp	1965
7.9	1953-65	1	gnp	1964
2.4	1950-65	1	gnp	1958
2.1	1951-65	.	gnp	1965
5.0	1960-65	1	gdp	1960
2.8	1960-65		gnp	1965
6.3	1960-65		gnp	1965
4.3	1957-63	1	nmp	1957
5.0	1950-65		gnp	1965
3.7	1958-65	1	gnp	1958
.4	1960-65		gnp	1965
4.6	1950-65	1	gnp	1958
4.6	1955-64	1	gnp	1961
5.6	1953-65	1	gnp	1956
4.6	1950-65	1	gnp	1960
4.9	1955-64	1	gnp	1954
3.5	1961-65		gnp	1965
4.4	1950-65		gnp	1965
4.9	1960-65		gnp	1965
6.5	1953-65	1	gnp	1960

Table 5.4 Gross National Product and Growth Rates—*Continued*

Rank	Country	GNP in $m	Date	Source	Growth Rate- Recent Period	Dates
82	Kenya	846			4.1	1960-65
83	Cambodia	830				
84	El Salvador	794		1	6.3	1960-65
85	Zambia	792		1	5.8	1960-65
86	Tanzania	751			3.0	1960-65
87	Nepal	736				
88	Albania	700e	1966	4	7.0	1960-64
89	Senegal	680				
90	Cameroon	670				
91	Uganda	658			3.5	1960-65
92	Luxembourg	655		1	3.6	1960-65
93.5	Panama	630		1	7.8	1960-65
93.5	Trinidad and Tobago	630			5.9	1960-65
95	Bolivia	605		1	4.8	1960-65
96	Costa Rica	592		1	4.4	1960-65
97	Malagasy Republic	578				
98	Nicaragua	567		1	7.9	1960-65
99.5	Angola	515		2		
99.5	Mozambique	515		3		
101	Jordan	505		1	9.3	1960-65
102	Honduras	504		1	3.2	1960-65
103	Mongolia	500		2		
104	Yemen	489				
105	Iceland	474		1	5.3	1960-65
106	Paraguay	443			4.6	1960-65
107	Cyprus	413		1	5.7	1960-65
108	Sierra Leone	353		1		
109	Haiti	327				
110	Mali	297				
111.5	Guinea	257				
111.5	Upper Volta	257				
113	Niger	250				
114	Chad	237				
115	Liberia	213				
116	Guyana	198		1		
117	Mauritius	194		1		
118	Malawi	185		1	1.0	1960-63
119	Laos	173				
120	Dahomey	165				
121	Malta	160		1	1.2	1960-65
122	Togo	156				
123	Rwanda	155				
124	Somalia	150				
125	Burundi	140				
126.5	Congo - Brazzaville	138				
126.5	Southern Yemen	138		3		
128	Gabon	130				
129	Mauritania	127				
130	Central African Republic	122				
131	Barbados	91		3		
132	Papua / New Guinea	82				
133	Lesotho	49				

Growth Rate– Longer Period	Dates	Source	Rates Calculated on the Basis of	at Fixed Prices of
4.1	1960–65		gnp	1965
4.9	1950–65		gnp	1965
4.7	1950–65	1	gnp	1954
3.0	1960–65	1	gdp	1960
6.9	1955–64	1	nmp	1960
3.5	1960–65		gnp	1965
2.7	1950–65		gnp	1965
5.8	1950–65		gnp	1965
5.9	1960–65		gnp	1965
4.1	1958–65	1	gnp	1963
5.4	1950–65		gnp	1965
6.0	1950–65		gnp	1965
9.3	1960–65		gnp	1965
4.3	1950–65	1	gnp	1948
4.7	1950–65	1	gnp	1960
3.3	1950–65		gnp	1965
3.8	1950–65	1	gnp	1958
2.9	1954–63	1	gnp	1954
2.7	1954–65	1	gnp	1954

Table 5.4 Gross National Product and Growth Rates—*Continued*

Rank	Country	G N P in $m	Date	Source	Growth Rate- Recent Period	Dates
134	Botswana	34				
135	The Gambia	28				

Notes: Data are missing for Maldive Islands.

GNP figures are reported in millions of United States dollars.

An e indicates that GNP figure is gross estimate.

Date for GNP, unless otherwise noted, is 1965.

Source, unless otherwise noted, is United States, Agency for International Development, Office of Program Co-ordination, Statistics and Reports Division, *Gross National Product: Growth Rates and Trend Data by Region and Country,* RC-W-138 (Washington, D.C.: U.S. Government Printing Office, 1967), supplemented by United States, Agency for International Development, Office of Program and Policy Co-ordination, Statistics and Reports Division, *Selected Economic Data for the Less Developed Countries,* W-136 (Washington, D.C.: Government Printing Office, 1967).

1. United Nations, Statistical Office, *Yearbook of National Account Statistics, 1966* (New York, 1967).

2. United States, Arms Control and Disarmament Agency, Economics Bureau, *World-Wide Defense Expenditures and Selected Economic Data, Calendar Year, 1965.* Research Report 66-1 (Washington, D.C.: U.S. Government Printing Office, 1966).

3. Dittoed sheets from the Statistical Office of the United Nations (July 1967). Very rough estimates of GNP per capita that we multiplied by population.

4. United States, Arms Control and Disarmament Agency, Economics Bureau, *World Military Expenditures and Related Data, Calendar Year 1966 and Summary Trends, 1962-1967,* Research Report 68-52 (Washington, D.C.: U.S. Government Printing Office, 1968).

5. International Bank for Reconstruction and Development, *World Bank Atlas* (New York, 1967).

Growth rates are given in percentages as annual average rates for the time periods indicated. For the continuous growth rate formula, see p. 286.

Source for data on which growth rates were based, unless otherwise noted, is United States, Agency for International Development, Office of Program Co-ordination, Statistics and Reports Division, *Gross National Product: Growth Rates and Trend Data By Region and Country,* RC-W-138 (Washington, D.C.: U.S. Government Printing Office, 1967).

1. United Nations, Statistical Office, *Yearbook of National Account Statistics, 1966* (New York, 1967).

Most rates were calculated on the basis of GNP but some were of necessity based upon other aggregates. Notation is made of this fact in the next to last column. There,

nmp refers to net material product

gdp refers to gross domestic product

The last column gives the date upon which prices were fixed.

Growth Rate- Longer Period	Dates	Source	Rates Calculated on the Basis of	at Fixed Prices of

Table 5.5
Gross National Product Per Capita and Growth Rates

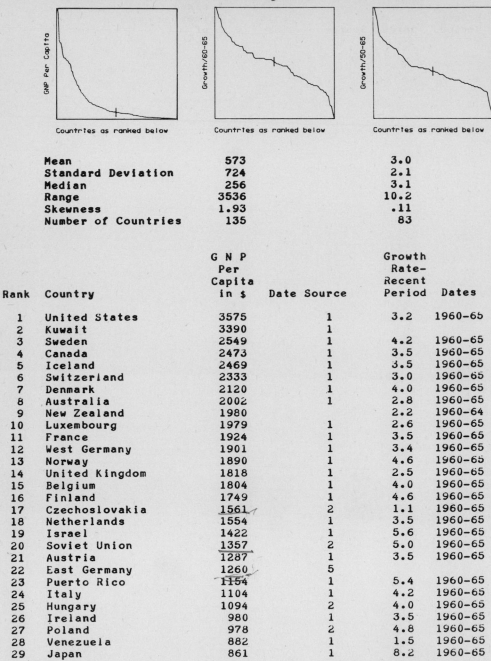

Mean	573	3.0	
Standard Deviation	724	2.1	
Median	256	3.1	
Range	3536	10.2	
Skewness	1.93	.11	
Number of Countries	135	83	

Rank	Country	GNP Per Capita in $	Date Source	Growth Rate-Recent Period	Dates
1	United States	3575	1	3.2	1960-65
2	Kuwait	3390	1		
3	Sweden	2549	1	4.2	1960-65
4	Canada	2473	1	3.5	1960-65
5	Iceland	2469	1	3.5	1960-65
6	Switzerland	2333	1	3.0	1960-65
7	Denmark	2120	1	4.0	1960-65
8	Australia	2002	1	2.8	1960-65
9	New Zealand	1980		2.2	1960-64
10	Luxembourg	1979	1	2.6	1960-65
11	France	1924	1	3.5	1960-65
12	West Germany	1901	1	3.4	1960-65
13	Norway	1890	1	4.6	1960-65
14	United Kingdom	1818	1	2.5	1960-65
15	Belgium	1804	1	4.0	1960-65
16	Finland	1749	1	4.6	1960-65
17	Czechoslovakia	1561	2	1.1	1960-65
18	Netherlands	1554	1	3.5	1960-65
19	Israel	1422	1	5.6	1960-65
20	Soviet Union	1357	2	5.0	1960-65
21	Austria	1287	1	3.5	1960-65
22	East Germany	1260	5		
23	Puerto Rico	1154	1	5.4	1960-65
24	Italy	1104	1	4.2	1960-65
25	Hungary	1094	2	4.0	1960-65
26	Ireland	980	1	3.5	1960-65
27	Poland	978	2	4.8	1960-65
28	Venezuela	882	1	1.5	1960-65
29	Japan	861	1	8.2	1960-65

2.9
1.8
2.7
9.9
.61
85

Growth Rate- Longer Period	Dates	Source	Rates on the Basis of	Calculated at Fixed Prices of
2.0	1950–65	1	gnp	1963
3.1	1950–65	1	gnp	1959
2.0	1950–65	1	gnp	1957
2.7	1950–65	1	gnp	1960
3.0	1950–65	1	gnp	1958
3.0	1950–65	1	gnp	1955
1.9	1950–65		gnp	1965
1.9	1954–64	1	gnp	1954
2.0	1950–65		gnp	1965
3.6	1950–65	1	gnp	1959
5.5	1950–65		gnp	1965
3.2	1950–65	1	gnp	1963
2.4	1950–65	1	gnp	1958
2.9	1950–65		gnp	1965
4.1	1950–65	1	gnp	1954
4.2	1953–65	1	nmp	1960
3.5	1950–65	1	gnp	1958
5.4	1950–65	1	gnp	1964
4.9	1953–65	1	nmp	1958
4.7	1950–65	1	gnp	1954
5.0	1950–65	1	gnp	1963
4.7	1950–65		gnp	1965
5.3	1958–65	1	nmp	1959
2.6	1950–65	1	gnp	1958
5.1	1953–65	1	nmp	1961
3.1	1950–65		gnp	1965
7.8	1952–65	1	gnp	1960

Table 5.5 Gross National Product Per Capita and
Growth Rates—*Continued*

Rank	Country	GNP Per Capita in $	Date	Source	Growth Rate– Recent Period	Dates
30	Bulgaria	829		2		
31	Romania	778		2	7.7	1960–64
32	Argentina	770		1	1.7	1960–65
33	Cyprus	695		1	5.0	1960–65
34	Greece	687		1	7.1	1960–65
35	Trinidad and Tobago	646			3.0	1960–65
36	South Africa	611		1	3.4	1960–65
37	Uruguay	573			-.9	1960–65
38	Chile	565		1	1.9	1960–65
39	Spain	561		1	7.2	1960–65
40	Libya	542				
41	Malta	502		1	1.8	1960–65
42	Singapore	500				
43	Jamaica	497		1	3.5	1960–65
44	Panama	485		1	4.6	1960–65
45	Mexico	455		1	1.8	1960–65
46	Mongolia	453		2		
47	Yugoslavia	451		2	5.9	1960–64
48	Lebanon	437				
49	Hong Kong	421				
50	Costa Rica	413		1	.4	1960–65
51	Portugal	406		1	5.5	1960–65
52	Cuba	393		2		
53	Barbados	373		3		
54	Peru	367		1	3.4	1960–65
55	Albania	366e	1966	4	4.0	1960–64
56	Nicaragua	343		1	4.7	1960–65
57	Guatemala	318		1	3.3	1960–65
58	Guyana	306		1		
59	Malaysia	306		1	3.1	1960–65
60	Ghana	285			.1	1960–65
61	Colombia	282			1.0	1960–65
62	Turkey	282		1	1.9	1960–65
63	Gabon	281				
64	El Salvador	271		1	2.8	1960–65
65	Brazil	267			1.0	1960–65
66	Dominican Republic	265			-2.0	1960–65
67	Mauritius	262		1		
68	Jordan	256		1	6.2	1960–65
69	Iran	251		1	2.8	1960–65
70	Ivory Coast	251				
71	Rhodesia	240		1	.0	1960–64
72	Iraq	231			1.9	1960–65
73	Taiwan	227		1	6.4	1960–65
74	Saudi Arabia	225				
75	Algeria	222				
76	Honduras	221		1		1960–65
77	Paraguay	218			1.6	1960–65
78	Ecuador	216		1	.9	1960–65
79	Tunisia	214		1	4.0	1960–65
80	Zambia	214		1	2.9	1960–65
81	Syria	212			5.8	1960–65

Growth Rate- Longer Period	Dates	Source	Rates on the Basis of	Calculated at Fixed Prices of
8.4	1950-64	1	nmp	1950
1.3	1950-65	1	gnp	1960
2.6	1950-65	1	gnp	1958
5.7	1950-65	1	gnp	1958
3.0	1960-65		gnp	1965
2.3	1953-65	1	gnp	1958
-.9	1960-65		gnp	1965
1.4	1950-65		gnp	1965
5.1	1950-65		gnp	1965
2.7	1954-65	1	gnp	1954
4.8	1953-65	1	gnp	1960
3.1	1950-65		gnp	1965
2.4	1950-65	1	gnp	1950
7.2	1952-64	1	nmp	1960
1.6	1950-65		gnp	1965
4.2	1950-65		gnp	1965
2.9	1950-65	1	gnp	1963
3.8	1955-64	1	nmp	1960
3.0	1950-65		gnp	1965
1.5	1950-65	1	gnp	1958
3.1	1960-65		gnp	1965
.1	1960-65		gnp	1965
1.3	1950-65		gnp	1965
2.5	1950-65		gnp	1965
1.9	1950-65		gnp	1965
2.1	1950-65		gnp	1965
.9	1950-65		gnp	1965
6.2	1960-65		gnp	1965
2.4	1959-65	1	gnp	1959
1.6	1955-64	1	gnp	1954
1.9	1960-65		gnp	1965
4.5	1953-65	1	gnp	1964
1.3	1950-65	1	gnp	1948
.8	1950-65		gnp	1965
1.4	1950-65	1	gnp	1960
4.0	1960-65		gnp	1965
1.9	1950-65	1	gnp	1954
5.8	1960-65	1	gnp	1956

Table 5.5 Gross National Product Per Capita and
Growth Rates—*Continued*

Rank	Country	G N P Per Capita in $	Date Source	Growth Rate–Recent Period	Dates
82	North Korea	207	2		
83	Liberia	199			
84	Morocco	196	1	.4	1960-65
85	Senegal	195			
86	Congo - Brazzaville	164			
87	Bolivia	164	1	3.4	1960-65
88	Philippines	160	1	1.4	1960-65
89	United Arab Republic	159		3.6	1960-64
90	Sierra Leone	154	1		
91	South Viet Nam	150	1	2.2	1960-65
92	Ceylon	144	1	.6	1960-65
93	Cambodia	136			
94	Thailand	129	1	2.9	1960-65
95	Cameroon	128			
96	Southern Yemen	125	3		
97	Mauritania	121			
98	China	109	2		
99	Pakistan	109		3.4	1960-65
100	South Korea	105	1	4.7	1960-65
101	India	101		.6	1960-65
102	Sudan	100	1	1.2	1960-64
103	North Viet Nam	100	2	-.8	1960-63
104	Angola	100	2		
105	Indonesia	99			
106	Yemen	98			
107	Togo	95			
108	Kenya	90		1.2	1960-65
109	Central African Republic	90			
110	Malagasy Republic	90			
111	Uganda	87		1.0	1960-65
112	Laos	87			
113	The Gambia	85			
114	Nigeria	84		2.8	1960-65
115	Afghanistan	83			
116	Congo - Kinshasa	82			
117	Niger	75			
118	Haiti	74			
119	Mozambique	74	3		
120	Guinea	73			
121	Nepal	73			
122	Chad	72			
123	Tanzania	71		1.1	1960-65
124	Burma	71		.7	1960-65
125	Dahomey	70			
126	Mali	65			
127	Botswana	61			
128	Somalia	60			
129	Lesotho	59			
130	Upper Volta	53			
131	Rwanda	50			
132	Malawi	47	1	-1.5	1960-63
133	Ethiopia	45	1	1.6	1961-65

Growth Rate-Longer Period	Dates	Source	Rates Calculated on the Basis of	at Fixed Prices of
-.5	1951-65		gnp	1965
2.7	1958-65	1	gnp	1963
2.1	1950-65	1	gnp	1955
3.3	1950-64	1	gdp	1959
2.2	1960-65	1	gdp	1960
1.2	1958-65	1	gnp	1958
2.9	1951-65	1	gdp	1962
1.5	1950-65		gnp	1965
2.9	1955-65	1	gnp	1960
1.7	1950-65		gnp	1965
1.7	1955-64	1	gnp	1961
.9	1957-63	1	nmp	1957
1.8	1951-59	1	gdp	1955
1.2	1960-65		gnp	1965
1.0	1960-65		gnp	1965
2.8	1960-65		gnp	1965
1.1	1960-65	1	gdp	1960
3.1	1950-65		gnp	1965
-1.5	1960-63	1	gnp	1954
1.6	1961-65		gnp	1965

Table 5.5 Gross National Product Per Capita and

Growth Rates—*Continued*		G N P Per Capita in $	Date	Source	Growth Rate- Recent Period	Dates
Rank	Country					
134	Burundi	44				
135	Papua / New Guinea	38				

Notes: Data are missing for Maldive Islands.

GNP per capita figures are reported in United States dollars.

An "e" indicates that the GNP per capita figure is a gross estimate.

Date for GNP per capita, unless otherwise noted, is 1965.

Source, unless otherwise noted, is United States, Agency for International Development, Office of Program Co-ordination, Statistics and Reports Division, *Gross National Product: Growth Rates and Trend Data by Region and County,* RC-W-138 (Washington, D.C.: U.S. Government Printing Office, 1967); supplemented by United States, Agency for International Development, Office of Program and Policy Co-ordination, Statistics and Reports Division, *Selected Economic Data for the Less Developed Countries,* W-136 (Washington, D.C.: U.S. Government Printing Office, 1967).

1. United Nations, Statistical Office, *Yearbook of National Account Statistics, 1966* (New York, 1967).

2. United States, Arms Control and Disarmament Agency, Economics Bureau, *World-Wide Defense Expenditures and Selected Economic Data, Calendar Year, 1965,* Research Report 66-1 (Washington, D.C.: U.S. Government Printing Office, 1966).

3. Dittoed sheets from the Statistical Office of the United Nations (July, 1967). Very rough estimates of GNP per capita that we multiplied by population.

4. United States, Arms Control and Disarmament Agency, Economics Bureau, *World Military Expenditures and Related Data, Calendar Year 1966 and Summary Trends, 1962-1967,* Research Report 68-52 (Washington, D.C.: U.S. Government Printing Office, 1968).

5. International Bank for Reconstruction and Development, *World Bank Atlas* (New York, 1967).

Growth rates are given in percentages as annual average rates for the time periods indicated. For the continuous growth rate formula, see p. 286.

Source for data on which growth rates were based, unless otherwise noted, is U.S., Agency for International Development, Office of Program Co-ordination, Statistics and Reports Division, *Gross National Product: Growth Rates and Trend Data By Region and Country,* RC-W-138 (Washington, D.C.: U.S. Government Printing Office, 1967).

1. United Nations, Statistical Office, *Yearbook of National Account Statistics, 1966* (New York, 1967).

Most rates were calculated on the basis of GNP per capita but some were of necessity based upon other aggregates. Notation is made of this fact in the next to last column. There,

nmp refers to net material product per capita

gdp refers to gross domestic product per capita

The last column gives the date upon which prices were fixed.

Growth Rate- Longer Period	Dates	Source	Rates on the basis of	Calculated at Fixed Prices of

Table 5.6
Scientific Capacity

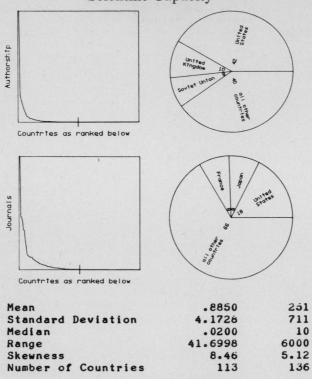

Mean		.8850	251
Standard Deviation		4.1728	711
Median		.0200	10
Range		41.6998	6000
Skewness		8.46	5.12
Number of Countries		113	136

Rank	Country	Contribution to World Scientific Authorship	Scientific Journals
1	United States	41.7000	6000
2	Japan	4.2200	2820
3	France	5.4400	2780
4	West Germany	6.8900	2560
5	Soviet Union	8.2000	2100
6	United Kingdom	10.1700	2090
7	Italy	1.9800	1530
8	Belgium	.7300	1260
9	Switzerland	1.3500	810
10	Poland	.9500	750
11	Sweden	1.2800	710
12	India	2.2600	670
13.5	China	.0290	660
13.5	Netherlands	1.0800	660
15	Brazil	.1600	650
16	East Germany		550
17	Canada	3.3700	540

Table 5.6 Scientific Capacity—*Continued*

Rank	Country	Contribution to World Scientific Authorship	Scientific Journals
18	Austria	.5300	490
19	Australia	1.8000	460
20	Czechoslovakia	1.2900	420
21.5	Denmark	.5700	400
21.5	Yugoslavia	.2300	400
23	Spain	.2600	320
24	Argentina	.2400	310
25	South Africa	.2600	295
26	Finland	.3600	280
27.5	Hungary	.7600	250
27.5	Portugal	.0370	250
29	Norway	.3700	240
30	Mexico	.1100	225
31	Taiwan	.0580	200
32	Romania	.4400	170
33	New Zealand	.2300	160
34.5	Bulgaria	.2700	150
34.5	Chile	.0960	150
36	Uruguay	.0230	135
37	Peru	.0200	125
38	Philippines	.0250	110
39.5	Cuba	.0040	100
39.5	South Korea	.0180	100
42.5	Indonesia	.0080	90
42.5	Pakistan	.0550	90
42.5	Turkey	.0450	90
42.5	Venezuela	.0610	90
45	Colombia	.0220	75
46	United Arab Republic	.2100	70
47.5	Greece	.1100	60
47.5	North Korea		60
49.5	Ireland	.1300	50
49.5	Thailand	.0330	50
51	Puerto Rico		45
54	Burma	.0030	30
54	Ecuador	.0020	30
54	Iceland	.0080	30
54	Israel	.8600	30
54	Luxembourg	.0020	30
58.5	Algeria	.0180	20
58.5	Ceylon	.0150	20
58.5	Lebanon	.0430	20
58.5	South Viet Nam	.0040	20
64	Bolivia	.0020	15
64	Costa Rica	.0070	15
64	El Salvador	.0008	15
64	Guatemala	.0050	15
64	Honduras	.0020	15
64	Paraguay	.0010	15
64	Tunisia	.0060	15
72	Albania		10
72	Cyprus	.0010	10

Table 5.6 Scientific Capacity—*Continued*

Rank	Country	Contribution to world Scientific Authorship	Scientific Journals
72	Dominican Republic		10
72	Haiti		10
72	Iran	.0430	10
72	Iraq	.0220	10
72	Nicaragua	.0004	10
72	North Viet Nam	.0020	10
72	Panama		10
106.5	Botswana		0
106.5	Afghanistan	.0020	0
106.5	Angola	.0002	0
106.5	Barbados	.0004	0
106.5	Burundi		0
106.5	Cambodia	.0010	0
106.5	Cameroon	.0040	0
106.5	Central African Republic		0
106.5	Chad	.0002	0
106.5	Congo - Brazzaville	.0005	0
106.5	Congo - Kinshasa	.0070	0
106.5	Dahomey		0
106.5	Ethiopia	.0110	0
106.5	Gabon	.0040	0
106.5	Ghana	.0190	0
106.5	Guinea		0
106.5	Guyana	.0002	0
106.5	Hong Kong	.0300	0
106.5	Ivory Coast	.0010	0
106.5	Jamaica	.0370	0
106.5	Jordan	.0010	0
106.5	Kenya	.0320	0
106.5	Kuwait	.0006	0
106.5	Laos	.0002	0
106.5	Lesotho		0
106.5	Liberia	.0020	0
106.5	Libya	.0020	0
106.5	Malagasy Republic	.0080	0
106.5	Malawi	.0020	0
106.5	Malaysia	.0380	0
106.5	Maldive Islands		0
106.5	Mali	.0004	0
106.5	Malta	.0080	0
106.5	Mauritania		0
106.5	Mauritius		0
106.5	Mongolia		0
106.5	Morocco	.0090	0
106.5	Mozambique	.0004	0
106.5	Nepal	.0009	0
106.5	Niger	.0002	0
106.5	Nigeria	.0740	0
106.5	Papua / New Guinea	.0010	0
106.5	Rhodesia	.0170	0
106.5	Rwanda		0
106.5	Saudi Arabia	.0080	0

Table 5.6 Scientific Capacity—*Continued*

Rank	Country	Contribution to World Scientific Authorship	Scientific Journals
106.5	Senegal	.0130	0
106.5	Sierra Leone	.0030	0
106.5	Singapore	.0330	0
106.5	Somalia		0
106.5	Southern Yemen		0
106.5	Sudan	.0250	0
106.5	Syria	.0010	0
106.5	Tanzania	.0110	0
106.5	The Gambia	.0006	0
106.5	Togo		0
106.5	Trinidad and Tobago	.0120	0
106.5	Uganda	.0420	0
106.5	Upper Volta		0
106.5	Yemen		0
106.5	Zambia	.0060	0

Notes: No countries are missing from this table.

Date for the first column is 1967-69; for the second it is 1961.

Source for contributions to world scientific authorship is Derek J. de Solla Price, Department of History of Science, Yale University, who used the *International Directory of Research and Development Scientists* to make his calculations.

Source for number of scientific journals is Charles M. Gottschalk and Winifred F. Desmond, "Worldwide Census of Scientific and Technical Serials," *American Documentation*, 14 (1963), 188-94 and further correspondence with Mr. Gottschalk.

Table 5.7
Energy Consumption

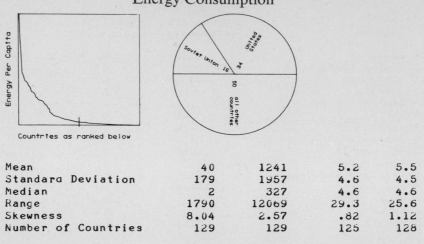

Mean	40	1241	5.2	5.5
Standard Deviation	179	1957	4.6	4.5
Median	2	327	4.6	4.6
Range	1790	12069	29.3	25.6
Skewness	8.04	2.57	.82	1.12
Number of Countries	129	129	125	128

Rank	Country	Aggregate in Million Metric Tons	Per Capita in Kilograms	Per Capita Growth Rates 1960-65	Per Capita Growth Rates 1950-65
1	Kuwait	6	12077		19.8**
2	United States	1790	9201	2.7	1.2
3	Canada	150	7653	6.0	1.1
4	Czechoslovakia	80	5676	3.5	4.3
5	East Germany	93	5460	3.2	3.4**
6	United Kingdom	282	5151	1.0	1.0
7	Australia	54	4795	4.0	2.9
8	Belgium	45*	4727	3.6	2.0
9	Luxembourg	2*	4653	2.8	1.7
10	Sweden	35	4506	5.1	2.2
11	West Germany	250	4234	2.8	3.1
12	Denmark	20	4172	7.8	4.6
13	Iceland	1	3963	2.3	2.8
14	Soviet Union	833	3611	4.9	4.9**
15	Norway	13	3588	5.4	-1.3
16	Poland	110	3504	2.5	2.3
17	Trinidad and Tobago	3	3482	11.7	5.8
18	Netherlands	40	3271	3.9	3.4
19	Venezuela	26	2974	2.5	9.0
20	France	144	2951	4.0	2.5
21	Hungary	29	2812	6.0	7.0
22	South Africa	54	2716	3.0	2.4
23	Finland	12	2679	9.7	5.5
24	Switzerland	16	2668	6.4	1.5
25	Austria	19	2630	4.0	3.6
26	Bulgaria	21	2571	13.7	14.3
27	New Zealand	7	2530	4.4	.3
28	Ireland	7	2284	4.3	4.9
29	Israel	6	2239	11.8	6.9
30	Puerto Rico	6	2125	7.6	9.9

Table 5.7 Energy Consumption—*Continued*

Rank	Country	Aggregate in Million Metric Tons	Per Capita in Kilograms	Per Capita Growth Rates 1960-65	1950-65
31	Romania	39	2035	7.4	9.9
32	Italy	92	1787	9.1	7.0
33	Japan	175	1783	8.5	5.5
34	Argentina	30	1341	4.2	3.8
35	Panama	2	1292	14.8	5.4**
36	Yugoslavia	23	1192	6.2	7.1
37	Chile	9	1089	5.2	2.4
38	Spain	32	1023	4.4	3.9
39	Mexico	42	977	1.3	3.3
40	Cuba	7	950	2.3	4.6
41.5	Cyprus	1	916	2.3	8.1
41.5	Uruguay	2	916	1.5	2.4
43	Jamaica	2	887	10.6	13.3
44	Guyana	1	811	7.2	6.2
45	Greece	7	784	11.4	8.5
46	Lebanon	2	747	7.2	4.5**
47	Malta	0	727	7.8	4.6**
48	Taiwan	8	654	4.9	5.4**
49	Rhodesia	3	651		-.5
50	Hong Kong	2	603	5.3	3.9**
51	Peru	7	588	3.5	7.5
52	Iraq	5	581	1.8	7.8
53	Singapore	1	578	-.9	-1.2**
54	Colombia	10	532	.6	4.5
55	Portugal	5	521	6.4	4.6
56	Zambia	2	487		1.1
57	China	338	461	-6.1	10.6**
58	South Korea	13	445	10.7	11.7**
59	Barbados	0	422	3.1	5.0
60	Iran	9	391	2.6	6.7**
61	Malaysia	3	357	4.9	1.7**
62	Turkey	11	348	6.9	1.9
63.5	Albania	1	347	2.6	8.0**
63.5	Brazil	29	347	.6	3.0
65	Libya	1	327	3.0	5.8**
66	Saudi Arabia	2	311	5.8	3.4**
67	Costa Rica	0	306	7.1	1.6
68	Syria	2	303	3.0	4.6**
69	United Arab Republic	9	301	.7	2.1
70	Algeria	4	300	3.1	4.2
71	Jordan	1	291	8.4	9.4**
72	Liberia	0	259	23.2	17.1
73	Gabon	0	240	4.9	
74	Nicaragua	0	234	4.3	6.4
75	Ecuador	1	212	2.6	3.8
76	Philippines	7	209	7.6	5.6
77	Tunisia	1	200	3.7	1.9
78	Dominican Republic	1	194	4.1	5.1
79	Bolivia	1	185	3.9	4.8
80	Guatemala	1	182	1.4	1.7
81	Mauritius	0	179	7.8	1.6
82	India	84	172	4.1	3.6
83	El Salvador	0	168	5.4	4.2

Table 5.7 Energy Consumption—*Continued*

Rank	Country	Aggregate in Million Metric Tons	Per Capita in Kilograms	Per Capita Growth Rates 1960-65	Per Capita Growth Rates 1950-65
84	Morocco	2	153	1.9	1.1
85	Ivory Coast	1	152	15.8	
86	Honduras	0	151	-1.2	.0
87	Congo - Brazzaville	0	148	.8	
88	Senegal	1	145	8.2	
89	Paraguay	0	126	7.4	12.3
90	Kenya	1	124	-2.4	3.2
91	Angola	1	117	6.9	11.8
92	Ceylon	1	114	.7	2.4
93	Indonesia	12	111	-3.8	4.1
94	Thailand	3	110	11.5	11.4
95	Mozambique	1	106	-1.1	3.8
96	Ghana	1	104	1.0	1.0
97	Guinea	0	98	7.9	
98	Pakistan	9	90	5.6	5.4
99	Congo - Kinshasa	1	83	-.2	-.5
100	Papua / New Guinea	0	74	7.1	5.9**
101	South Viet Nam	1	73	6.8	6.8**
102	Cameroon	0	71	2.4	5.7
103	Sudan	1	69	6.0	5.6
104	Sierra Leone	0	68	7.4	5.5
105	Tanzania	1	55	2.3	2.9**
106	Mauritania	0	48	19.6	
107	Burma	1	47	-2.4	5.7
108	Cambodia	0	45	5.0	8.1**
109	Nigeria	3	44	8.3	.6
110	Laos	0	43	13.4	18.2**
112	Malagasy Republic	0	42	2.5	2.2
112	Malawi	0	42		
112	Uganda	0	42	5.4	5.6
114	Togo	0	41	11.6	9.4
115	The Gambia	0	39	4.6	4.1**
116	Central African Republic	0	38	.5	
117	Haiti	0	33	-2.8	3.3
118	Dahomey	0	30	-5.8	
119	Somalia	0	27	4.1	5.2**
120	Afghanistan	0	25	10.2	10.2**
121	Mali	0	21	6.7	
122.5	Chad	0	15	8.1	
122.5	Rwanda	0	15	6.2	
124	Niger	0	13	19.1	
125	Burundi	0	12	1.7	
127	Ethiopia	0	10	4.5	15.4
127	Upper Volta	0	10	7.1	
127	Yemen	0	10	10.2	
129	Nepal	0	8	13.9	

Notes: Data are missing for Botswana, Lesotho, Maldive Islands, Mongolia, North Korea, North Viet Nam, and Southern Yemen.

Date for the aggregate and per capita figures is 1965.

*Data for Luxembourg and Belgium were reported together in the source.

**For these countries, annual average rates of growth are based upon the years 1955-65.

Data for Southern Yemen refers to Aden only.

For growth rate formula, see p. 286.

Source is United Nations, Statistical Office, *Statistical Yearbook, 1965* (New York, 1966).

Table 5.8
Distribution of Male Labor Force: Percentage in Mining and Manufacturing

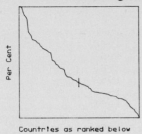

Countries as ranked below

Mean	17.4
Standard Deviation	10.5
Median	14.2
Range	42.7
Skewness	.76
Number of Countries	91

Rank	Country	Per Cent	Notes	Bias	Date	Source
1	West Germany	43.7	b		1965	1
2	Luxembourg	43.5			1966	2
3	Switzerland	41.7			1960	
4	Belgium	40.3	c		1964	1
5	United Kingdom	39.8			1961	2
6	Sweden	38.8		-1	1960	
7	Netherlands	34.0			1960	
8	Austria	33.2			1961	
9	Hong Kong	32.6			1966	2
10	Czechoslovakia	31.0	t		1950	2
11	Denmark	30.9			1960	
12	Hungary	30.7	c		1963	
13	France	30.4	b		1962	
14.5	Australia	29.7		-1	1961	
14.5	United States	29.7	c		1965	1
16	Italy	28.7	b		1965	1
17	Canada	28.2	c	-1	1965	
18	Norway	27.6			1960	
19	Israel	27.4			1965	1
20	Japan	27.1	b		1965	1
21	South Africa	26.9	b		1960	1
22	New Zealand	26.4		-1	1961	
23	Argentina	26.1	b		1960	
24	Spain	25.9	b		1965	1
25	Malta	23.1			1966	2
26	Finland	22.9			1960	
27	Chile	22.5			1960	
28	Trinidad and Tobago	21.4			1960	
29	Iceland	21.3			1950	1
30	Uruguay	20.6	b		1963	
31	Bulgaria	20.0		+1	1956	2

Table 5.8 Distribution of Male Labor Force: Percentage in
Mining and Manufacturing—*Continued*

Rank	Country	Per Cent	Notes	Bias	Date	Source
32	Bolivia	19.9		-1	1950	
33	Guyana	19.7			1965	2
34	Portugal	19.5			1960	
35	Barbados	17.6			1960	
36	Cuba	16.8			1953	
37.5	Burma	16.6	b		1953	4
37.5	Ireland	16.6			1961	
39	Mauritius	16.4			1962	
40	Cyprus	15.9		+1	1960	1
41	Mexico	15.5			1960	
42	Syria	15.4	b		1965	1
43	Yugoslavia	15.2			1961	2
44	Peru	14.7		-1	1961	
45	Greece	14.5		-1	1961	
46	Singapore	14.2			1957	
47	Puerto Rico	13.9	b		1960	
48	Kuwait	13.8			1965	2
49	Sierra Leone	13.6			1963	1
50	Venezuela	13.4	b		1961	
51	Colombia	13.1			1964	2
52	Taiwan	13.0			1956	
53	Jamaica	12.3			1960	
54	Ecuador	12.2		-1	1962	1
55	Turkey	11.3			1965	2
56	Nicaragua	11.1			1963	
57	Brazil	10.9		+1	1960	
58.5	Costa Rica	10.8			1963	
58.5	Ghana	10.8	b		1960	
60	India	10.7		-1	1961	
61.5	El Salvador	10.5			1961	
61.5	South Korea	10.5	c		1965	1
63	Paraguay	10.4	b		1962	
64	Malagasy Republic	10.3		-1	1951	3
65	Iran	10.2			1956	
66	Guatemala	10.1	b		1964	1
67	Jordan	10.0			1961	
68	United Arab Republic	9.8		-1	1960	
69.5	Ceylon	9.4			1963	2
69.5	Iraq	9.4			1957	
71	Malaysia	9.3			1957	
72.5	Gabon	9.2	c		1963	
72.5	Libya	9.2		-1	1964	
74	Congo - Kinshasa	8.7	b		1957	
75.5	Pakistan	8.4		-1	1961	
75.5	Philippines	8.4	b	-1	1965	1
77	Liberia	8.3		-1	1962	
78	Tunisia	8.2	b		1956	
79	Dominican Republic	7.9	b		1960	1
80	Morocco	7.7			1960	
81	Panama	7.4	a	-1	1960	
82	Honduras	6.7			1961	
83	Algeria	6.2	a	-1	1954	
84	Mozambique	5.2	a		1950	
85	Indonesia	4.9	b		1961	

Table 5.8 Distribution of Male Labor Force: Percentage in
Mining and Manufacturing—*Continued*

Rank	Country	Per Cent	Notes	Bias	Date	Source
86	Thailand	4.4			1960	
87	Haiti	4.2			1950	
88	Cambodia	3.2			1962	
89	Botswana	2.8			1964	1
90	Nepal	2.3			1965	2
91	Ivory Coast	1.0	t		1964	2

Notes: Data are missing for Afghanistan, Albania, Angola, Burundi, Cameroon, Central African Republic, Chad, China, Congo-Brazzaville, Dahomey, East Germany, Ethiopia, Guinea, Kenya, Laos, Lebanon, Lesotho, Malawi, Maldive Islands, Mali, Mauritania, Mongolia, Niger, Nigeria, North Korea, North Viet Nam, Papua/New Guinea, Poland, Rhodesia, Romania, Rwanda, Saudi Arabia, Senegal, Somalia, Southern Yemen, South Viet Nam, Soviet Union, Sudan, Tanzania, The Gambia, Togo, Uganda, Upper Volta, Yemen, and Zambia.

Notes are indicated as follows:

a indicates data from actual enumeration of population.

b indicates data from sample survey or sample census returns.

c indicates data are official estimates.

Blank denotes unknown method of collection.

t indicates that data are based on total population rather than males only.

Bias is indicated as follows:

—1 indicates moderate underestimate expected (e.g. tribal populations or unemployed are excluded).

+1 indicates moderate overestimate expected (e.g. inmates of institutions or armed forces stationed abroad—neither normally included in economically active population—are included here).

Blank indicates no known bias.

Source, unless otherwise noted, is International Labour Organization, *ILO Yearbook of Labour Statistics, 1965* (Geneva, 1966).

1. International Labour Organization, *ILO Yearbook of Labour Statistics, 1966* (Geneva, 1967).

2. International Labour Organization, *ILO Yearbook of Labour Statistics, 1967* (Geneva, 1968).

3. International Labour Organization, *ILO Yearbook of Labour Statistics, 1959* (Geneva, 1959).

4. International Labour Organization, *ILO Yearbook of Labour Statistics, 1957* (Geneva, 1957).

Table 5.9
Distribution of Male Labor Force: Percentage in Agriculture

Countries as ranked below

Mean	47
Standard Deviation	25
Median	49
Range	96
Skewness	-.02
Number of Countries	106

Rank	Country	Per Cent	Bias/ Notes	Date	Source
1	Niger	97		1965	
2	Nepal	92		1961	2
3.5	Laos	90	t	1953	3
3.5	Malawi	90	t	1949	3
6	Botswana	87		1964	1
6	Haiti	87		1965	
6	Sudan	87		1956	
8	Ivory Coast	86	t	1964	2
9	Afghanistan	85	t	1954	3
10	Thailand	78		1965	
12	Cambodia	76		1962	
12	Gabon	76		1963	
12	Honduras	76		1961	
14	Liberia	74		1962	
16	Guatemala	73		1964	1
16	Mozambique	73		1965	
16	Pakistan	73		1961	
18.5	Albania	72	t	1955	3
18.5	Congo - Kinshasa	72		1965	
20.5	El Salvador	71		1961	
20.5	Mongolia	71	t	1955	3
22	Nicaragua	70		1963	
23.5	China	69	t	1950	3
23.5	Indonesia	69		1961	
26	Algeria	68		1954	
26	Dominican Republic	68		1965	1
26	India	68		1961	
28.5	Philippines	67		1965	1
28.5	Sierra Leone	67		1963	1
30	Ecuador	63		1965	4
31	Paraguay	61	-2	1962	

Table 5.9 Distribution of Male Labor Force: Percentage in
Agriculture—*Continued*

Rank	Country	Per Cent	Bias/ Notes	Date	Source
32	Ghana	60		1965	
34.5	Mexico	59		1965	
34.5	Nigeria	59	t	1950	3
34.5	Romania	59		1956	
34.5	Tunisia	59		1956	
39	Costa Rica	58		1963	
39	Iran	58		1956	
39	Morocco	58		1965	
39	Turkey	58		1965	2
39	United Arab Republic	58	-2	1965	
43	Brazil	57		1965	
43	Panama	57	-2	1965	
43	Yugoslavia	57		1961	
45	Colombia	56		1964	2
47	Bulgaria	55		1956	
47	Malaysia	55		1957	4
47	Peru	55		1961	
49	Bolivia	53		1965	
50	Jamaica	52		1965	
51	South Korea	51		1965	1
52	Lebanon	50	t	1955	6
53.5	Iraq	49		1957	
53.5	Taiwan	49		1956	
55.5	Greece	48		1961	
55.5	Portugal	48		1965	
57.5	Cuba	47		1953	
57.5	Syria	47		1965	1
59	Ceylon	46		1963	2
60	Ireland	42		1961	
61	Poland	39		1965	
63.5	Czechoslovakia	38		1966	
63.5	Finland	38		1965	
63.5	Rhodesia	38		1951	4
63.5	Venezuela	38	-2	1961	
67	Iceland	37		1965	
67	Libya	37		1964	1
67	Mauritius	37		1962	
70	Guyana	36		1965	2
70	Jordan	36		1961	
70	Spain	36		1965	1
72	South Africa	35		1965	
73.5	Chile	34		1965	
73.5	Soviet Union	34	-1	1959	
75	Hungary	32		1963	1
76	Cyprus	28		1965	
77.5	Barbados	25		1965	
77.5	France	25		1962	
80	Italy	24		1965	1
80	Norway	24		1965	
80	Puerto Rico	24		1965	1
83.5	Argentina	23		1965	
83.5	Denmark	23		1965	
83.5	Uruguay	23		1963	
83.5	Zambia	23		1951	4

Table 5.9 Distribution of Male Labor Force: Percentage in
Agriculture—*Continued*

Rank	Country	Per Cent	Bias/Notes	Date	Source
86	Trinidad and Tobago	22		1965	1
87	Japan	21		1965	1
89.5	Austria	18		1961	
89.5	East Germany	18		1961	
89.5	New Zealand	18		1961	
89.5	Sweden	18		1965	
92	Switzerland	15		1965	
94	Australia	13	-2	1961	4
94	Israel	13		1965	1
94	Netherlands	13		1965	
96.5	Burma	12		1953	5
96.5	Canada	12		1965	1
98	Luxembourg	10		1966	2
100	Malta	8		1966	2
100	United States	8		1965	1
100	West Germany	8		1965	1
102.5	Belgium	7		1964	1
102.5	Singapore	7		1957	
104.5	Hong Kong	5		1966	2
104.5	United Kingdom	5		1961	2
106	Kuwait	1		1965	2

Notes: Data are missing for Angola, Burundi, Cameroon, Central African Republic, Chad, Congo-Brazzaville, Dahomey, Ethiopia, Guinea, Kenya, Lesotho, Malagasy Republic, Maldive Islands, Mali, Mauritania, North Korea, North Viet Nam, Papua/New Guinea, Rwanda, Saudi Arabia, Senegal, Somalia, Southern Yemen, South Viet Nam, Tanzania, The Gambia, Togo, Uganda, Upper Volta, and Yemen.

In *notes* column, t indicates data are based upon total population rather than males only.

Bias is indicated as follows:

—2 indicates high underestimate expected (e.g. portions of the population are excluded or data relate only to persons living on agricultural holdings).

—1 indicates moderate underestimate expected (e.g. forestry and fishing—normally included in agriculture—are excluded; or persons living in collective dwellings, part-time employees or unpaid family workers are excluded).

Blank indicates no known bias.

Source, unless otherwise noted, is Food and Agriculture Organization, *FAO Production Yearbook, 1965* (Rome, 1966).

1. International Labour Organization, *ILO Yearbook of Labour Statistics, 1966* (Geneva, 1967).

2. International Labour Organization, *ILO Yearbook of Labour Statistics, 1967* (Geneva, 1968).

3. Norton Ginsburg, *Atlas of Economic Development* (Chicago: University of Chicago Press, 1961) as reported in the first edition of the *World Handbook*.

4. Food and Agriculture Organization, *FAO Production Yearbook, 1964* (Rome, 1965).

5. Food and Agriculture Organization, *FAO Production Yearbook, 1959* (Rome, 1960).

6. United States Congress, Senate, Special Committee to Study the Foreign Aid Program, *Foreign Aid Program,* 86th Congress, 1st Session (Washington, D.C.: U.S. Government Printing Office, 1957) as reported in the first edition of the *World Handbook*.

Table 5.10
Percentage of Economically Active Male Population Engaged in Professional and Technical Occupations

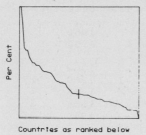

Per Cent

Countries as ranked below

Mean	6.5
Standard Deviation	4.3
Median	5.1
Range	22.9
Skewness	1.35
Number of Countries	72

Rank	Country	Per Cent	Notes	Bias	Date	Source
1	United States	23.1	b			
2	Canada	19.7	c	−1		2
3	Australia	14.6		−1	1961	
4.5	New Zealand	14.1		−1	1961	
4.5	Sweden	14.1		−1	1960	
6	Malta	12.7		−1	1957	
7	West Germany	12.0			1961	
8.5	France	11.5			1962	1
8.5	United Kingdom	11.5	b		1961	
10.5	Austria	11.0			1961	
10.5	Netherlands	11.0			1960	
12	Hong Kong	10.9			1966	1
13	Norway	10.4			1960	
14	Colombia	9.9		−1	1951	
15.5	Hungary	9.7	c		1963	
15.5	Switzerland	9.7			1960	
17	Belgium	9.6			1961	
18	Finland	9.5			1960	
19	Israel	9.4	b	−1		1
20	Japan	9.0	b			
21	Trinidad and Tobago	8.5			1960	
22	Denmark	7.9			1960	
23	Cuba	7.7			1953	
24	Luxembourg	7.6		−1	1960	
25.5	Guyana	7.4			1960	
25.5	Kuwait	7.4				1
27	Brazil	7.3	t	−1	1960	1
28	Barbados	7.2			1960	
29	Yugoslavia	6.5			1961	
30	Ireland	6.1			1961	
31	Singapore	5.8			1957	

335

Table 5.10 Percentage of Economically Active Male Population
Engaged in Professional and Technical Occupations—*Continued*

Rank	Country	Per Cent	Notes	Bias	Date	Source
32	Chile	5.3			1960	
33.5	Cyprus	5.2			1960	
33.5	Syria	5.2	b			
36	Cambodia	5.1			1962	
36	Puerto Rico	5.1	b	-1	1960	1
36	Uruguay	5.1	b		1963	
38	Libya	5.0			1964	
40.5	Panama	4.9	a	-1	1960	
40.5	Philippines	4.9	b	-1		
40.5	Taiwan	4.9			1956	
40.5	Venezuela	4.9	b	-1	1961	
43	Italy	4.6	b	-1		1
44	Mauritius	4.5			1962	
45	Greece	4.4		-1	1961	
46	Ceylon	4.3			1963	1
48	Costa Rica	4.1			1963	
48	Malaysia	4.1		-1	1957	
48	Spain	4.1	t		1966	1
50	South Africa	4.0	b		1960	
51	Mexico	3.7			1960	
53	Ghana	3.6	b		1960	
53	Jordan	3.6			1961	
53	United Arab Republic	3.6		-1	1960	
55	India	3.5		-1	1961	
56	Morocco	3.4			1960	
57	South Korea	3.3				1
58	Guatemala	3.2		-1	1964	1
59.5	Jamaica	3.1			1960	
59.5	Portugal	3.1			1960	
61	Liberia	2.9		-1	1962	
62	Turkey	2.7		-1		1
63	Paraguay	2.5	b	-1	1962	
64	Ecuador	2.4		-1	1962	
66.5	Dominican Republic	1.9	b		1960	
66.5	Iran	1.9			1956	
66.5	Pakistan	1.9		-1	1961	
66.5	Thailand	1.9			1960	
69.5	Honduras	1.8			1961	
69.5	Nicaragua	1.8			1963	
71	El Salvador	1.7			1961	
72	Sierra Leone	.2			1963	

Notes: Data are missing for Afghanistan, Albania, Algeria, Angola, Argentina, Bolivia, Botswana, Bulgaria, Burma, Burundi, Cameroon, Central African Republic, Chad, China, Congo-Brazzaville, Congo-Kinshasa, Czechoslovakia, Dahomey, East Germany, Ethiopia, Gabon, Guinea, Haiti, Iceland, Indonesia, Iraq, Ivory Coast, Kenya, Laos, Lebanon, Lesotho, Malagasy Republic, Malawi, Maldive Islands, Mali, Mauritania, Mongolia, Mozambique, Nepal, Niger, Nigeria, North Korea, North Viet Nam, Papua/New Guinea, Peru, Poland, Rhodesia, Romania, Rwanda, Saudi Arabia, Senegal, Somalia, Southern Yemen, South Viet Nam, Soviet Union, Sudan, Tanzania, The Gambia, Togo, Tunisia, Uganda, Upper Volta, Yemen, and Zambia.

Table 5.10 Percentage of Economically Active Male Population
Engaged in Professional and Technical Occupations—*Continued*

Notes are indicated as follows:
    a indicates data from actual enumeration of population.
    b indicates data from sample survey or sample census returns.
    c indicates data are official estimates.
    Blank denotes unknown method of collection.
    t indicates data are based on total population rather than males only.
Bias is indicated as follows:
    —1 indicates moderate underestimate expected (e.g. tribal populations or unemployed are excluded).
    Blank indicates no known bias.
Date, unless otherwise indicated, is 1965.
Source, unless otherwise indicated, is International Labour Organization, *ILO Yearbook of Labour Statistics, 1966* (Geneva, 1967).
    1. International Labour Organization, *ILO Yearbook of Labour Statistics, 1967* (Geneva, 1968).
    2. *International Labour Organization, ILO Yearbook of Labour Statistics, 1965* (Geneva, 1966).

Table 5.11
Agricultural and Industrial Shares of Gross Domestic Product

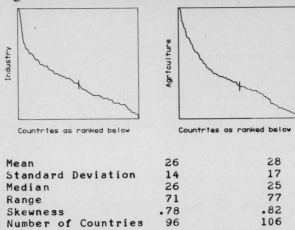

Countries as ranked below   Countries as ranked below

Mean	26	28
Standard Deviation	14	17
Median	26	25
Range	71	77
Skewness	.78	.82
Number of Countries	96	106

Rank	Country	Industry	Bias	Agriculture	Bias	Base Date	Source
1	Niger	3		80			4
2	Afghanistan	6		78			4
3	Upper Volta			69		1959	4
4	Nepal			66			4
5	Ethiopia	7		65		1963	
6	Yemen			60			2
7.5	Nigeria	9		59		1963	
7.5	Uganda	12		59			
9	North Viet Nam			57		1961	4
10	Tanzania	7		55			
11	Sudan	6		54		1964	
12	India	18	+1	51	ndp	1964	
13	Indonesia	13		50		1964	4
14.5	Haiti			49		1962	1
14.5	Togo	11	+1	49		1964	
16	Pakistan	12		48		1964	
17	Malawi	7	-1	47		1963	
18.5	Ceylon	8		44			2
18.5	Honduras	17		44			
20	Albania			43		1958	4
21.5	Cambodia	12		41		1963	
21.5	South Korea	21		41			
23	China	18		40			3
24.5	Kenya	13		38			
24.5	Paraguay	16		38			
26.5	Malagasy Republic			37		1960	4
26.5	Syria	13		37	ndp	1964	
28	Turkey	18		36			
29	Nicaragua	16		35			
31	Bulgaria	45		34	nmp		
31	Ecuador	21		34			

Table 5.11 Agricultural and Industrial Shares of Gross Domestic
Product—*Continued*

Rank	Country	Industry	Bias	Agricul- ture	Bias	Base	Date	Source
31	Philippines	20	-1	34		y		
33.5	Burma	16		33	+1		1964	
33.5	Thailand	15		33	-1			
36.5	Colombia	22		32				
36.5	El Salvador	16		32			1964	
36.5	Morocco	22		32				
36.5	South Viet Nam	13		32			1964	
40	Costa Rica	15	-1	31			1964	
40	Iran	30		31				
40	Sierra Leone	26		31			1964	
43	Malaysia	19		30			1964	
43	Rumania	48	-1	30		nmp		
43	United Arab Republic			30			1960	
45.5	Brazil	28	+1	29		ndp	1964	
45.5	Yugoslavia	38	-1	29		nmp		
48.5	Congo - Kinshasa	26		28			1959	1
48.5	Guatemala	16		28				
48.5	Liberia	30		28			1964	
48.5	Venezuela	40		28	+1		1963	
51.5	Barbados	9	-1	26	+1		1964	
51.5	Taiwan	24		26				
55	Greece	19		25				
55	Guyana	31	-1	25				
55	Jordan	10	-1	25			1964	
55	Libya			25			1959	
55	Mauritius	18		25				
58.5	Dominican Republic	18		24			1964	
58.5	Panama	18		24				
61.5	Bolivia	28	-1	23				
61.5	Congo - Brazzaville	17	+1	23			1963	2
61.5	Poland	51	-1	23		nmp		
61.5	Senegal	13		23				4
66	Cyprus	22		22				
66	Ireland	32	+1	22				
66	New Zealand	23		22				4
66	Soviet Union	52		22		nmp		
66	Tunisia	18	+1	22	-1			
69.5	Portugal	37		21				
69.5	Spain	30		21			1964	
72	Algeria	18		20				5
72	Hungary	58	-1	20		nmp		
72	Peru	25		20			1964	
74	Rhodesia	29	-1	19				
75.5	Finland	29		18				
75.5	Lebanon	12		18			1964	
77.5	Argentina	37		17				
77.5	Mexico	32		17				
79.5	Iraq	47	-1	16	-1		1963	
79.5	Uruguay	26		16			1964	
82	Czechoslovakia	65		13		nmp		
82	East Germany	74	-1	13		nmp		
82	Italy	31		13				
85	Australia	34		12			1964	
85	Jamaica	26		12				

Table 5.11 Agricultural and Industrial Shares of Gross Domestic
Product—*Continued*

Rank	Country	Industry	Bias	Agriculture	Bias	Base	Date	Source
85	Japan	29	-1	12		ndp		
87	Denmark	32	-1	11	+1			
89.5	Chile	26		10		ndp		
89.5	South Africa	37	-1	10		ndp		
89.5	Trinidad and Tobago	45	-1	10			1963	
89.5	Zambia	48	-1	10				
93	Austria	41		9				
93	Israel	35		9		ndp		
93	Norway	31		9				
96	France	38		8				
96	Malta	29	+1	8				
96	Netherlands	41	+1	8				
99	Luxembourg	44		7			1963	
99	Puerto Rico	27		7				
99	Sweden	37		7			1963	4
101.5	Belgium	35		6				
101.5	Canada	34		6				
103	West Germany	45		5				
104.5	Singapore			4				5
104.5	United States	34		4		ndp		
106	United Kingdom	41	-1	3				

Notes: Data are missing for Angola, Botswana, Burundi, Cameroon, Central African Republic, Chad, Cuba, Dahomey, Gabon, Ghana, Guinea, Hong Kong, Iceland, Ivory Coast, Kuwait, Laos, Lesotho, Maldive Islands, Mali, Mauritania, Mongolia, Mozambique, North Korea, Papua/New Guinea, Rwanda, Saudi Arabia, Somalia, Southern Yemen, Switzerland, and The Gambia.

Bias is indicated as follows:

−1 indicates moderate underestimate likely.

+1 indicates moderate overestimate likely.

Blank indicates no known bias.

Base is normally gross domestic product but may be:

ndp = net domestic product

nmp = net material product

y = national income.

For relationships among these, see discussions in U.N., Statistical Office, *Yearbooks of National Account Statistics.*

Date, unless otherwise noted, is 1965.

Source, unless otherwise noted, is United Nations, Statistical Office, *Yearbook of National Account Statistics, 1966* (New York, 1967).

1. Moshe Y. Sachs, ed., *The Worldmark Encyclopedia of Nations* (New York: Harper & Row, 1963).

2. United States, Agency for International Development, *A.I.D. Economic Data Books* (Washington, D.C.: U.S. Government Printing Office, 1967).

3. United States, Congress, Joint Economic Committee, *Mainland China in the World Economy.* Report No. 348 (Washington, D.C.: U.S. Government Printing Office, 1967).

4. Moshe Y. Sachs, ed., *The Worldmark Encyclopedia of Nations* (New York: Harper & Row, 1967).

5. *Gallatin Business Intelligence* (New York: Copley International Corporation, 1967).

Table 5.12
Gross Fixed Domestic Capital Formation as Percentage of Gross National Product

Countries as ranked below

Mean	18
Standard Deviation	5
Median	17
Range	23
Skewness	42
Number of Countries	88

Rank	Country	%	Base	Bias	Date	Source
1	Japan	31				
2.5	Luxembourg	29				
2.5	Norway	29				
4.5	Australia	28				
4.5	Switzerland	28				
8.5	Iceland	27				
8.5	Israel	27				
8.5	Trinidad and Tobago	27			1964	
8.5	Tunisia	27				
8.5	West Germany	27				
8.5	Yugoslavia	27	gmp	-1		
12	Austria	26				
13.5	Finland	25				
13.5	Puerto Rico	25				
15	New Zealand	24				
18.5	China	23				1
18.5	Greece	23				
18.5	Netherlands	23				
18.5	South Africa	23		+1		
18.5	Sweden	23				
18.5	Thailand	23				
22.5	Denmark	22				
22.5	France	22				
27	Barbados	21			1964	
27	Belgium	21				
27	Cuba	21	gmp			
27	Guyana	21				
27	Malta	21				
27	Venezuela	21		+1		
27	Zambia	21				
32.5	Canada	20				
32.5	Jamaica	20				

Table 5.12 Gross Fixed Domestic Capital Formation as Percentage of
Gross National Product—*Continued*

Rank	Country	%	Base	Bias	Date Source
32.5	Kuwait	20			
32.5	Peru	20			
36	Ireland	19			
36	Italy	19			
36	Syria	19			1963
39.5	Argentina	18			
39.5	Costa Rica	18			
39.5	Iran	18			
39.5	United Kingdom	18			
46.5	Bolivia	17			
46.5	Cambodia	17			1963
46.5	Dominican Republic	17			1964
46.5	East Germany	17	nmp		
46.5	Ghana	17			
46.5	Malaysia	17			1964
46.5	Mauritius	17			
46.5	Pakistan	17			1964
46.5	Poland	17	nmp		
46.5	United States	17		-1	
56	Burma	16			1964
56	Colombia	16			
56	Cyprus	16			
56	Hungary	16	nmp		
56	Mexico	16			
56	Nicaragua	16			
56	Panama	16			
56	Portugal	16			
56	Taiwan	16			
63.5	Bulgaria	15	nmp		
63.5	El Salvador	15			
63.5	Sierra Leone	15			
63.5	South Korea	15			
63.5	Soviet Union	15	nmp		
63.5	Togo	15			1964
69.5	Brazil	14			1964
69.5	Congo - Kinshasa	14			1964
69.5	Iraq	14			1964
69.5	Philippines	14			
69.5	Tanzania	14			
69.5	Turkey	14			
75.5	Ceylon	13			
75.5	Chile	13			
75.5	Honduras	13			
75.5	Jordan	13			
75.5	Malawi	13			
75.5	Rhodesia	13			
80	Ecuador	12			
80	Ethiopia	12			1963
80	Guatemala	12			
83.5	Cameroon	11			1963
83.5	Chad	11			1963
83.5	Morocco	11			
83.5	Uruguay	11			1964
86.5	Lesotho	10			
86.5	Sudan	10			

Table 5.12 Gross Fixed Domestic Capital Formation as Percentage of Gross National Product—*Continued*

Rank	Country	%	Base	Bias	Date	Source
88	South Viet Nam	8				

Notes: Data are missing for Afghanistan, Albania, Algeria, Angola, Botswana, Burundi, Central African Republic, Congo-Brazzaville, Czechoslovakia, Dahomey, Gabon, Guinea, Haiti, Hong Kong, India, Indonesia, Ivory Coast, Kenya, Laos, Lebanon, Liberia, Libya, Malagasy Republic, Maldive Islands, Mali, Mauritania, Mongolia, Mozambique, Nepal, Niger, Nigeria, North Korea, North Viet Nam, Papua/New Guinea, Paraguay, Romania, Rwanda, Saudi Arabia, Senegal, Singapore, Somalia, Southern Yemen, Spain, The Gambia, Uganda, United Arab Republic, Upper Volta, and Yemen.

Base is normally gross national product but may be:

gmp = gross material product

nmp = net material product

For relationships among these, see discussions in United Nations, Statistical Office, *Yearbook of National Account Statistics.*

Bias is indicated as follows:

−1 indicates moderate underestimate expected.

+1 indicates moderate overestimate expected.

Blank indicates no known bias.

Date, unless otherwise noted, is 1965.

Qualifications: Datum for Malaysia is for Malaya only. Datum for Tanzania is for Tanganyika only. Datum for South Africa includes South West Africa, Swaziland, Botswana, and Lesotho.

Source, unless otherwise noted, is United Nations, Statistical Office, *Monthly Bulletin of Statistics,* 21 (1967).

1. United States, Congress, Joint Economic Committee, *Mainland China in the World Economy,* Report No. 348 (Washington, D.C.: U.S. Government Printing Office, 1967).

6 External Relations

Most of our attention in this handbook has been devoted to cross-national comparative politics. We have reserved this data chapter, however, for some new tables dealing with relations among states. A country's orientation to the rest of the world may be directly related to its internal political profile. Activities of groups within its population may have significant effects upon foreign policy, but a country's status in the world, its geographic location, its degree of communication with other countries, and its dependence upon them for development resources and for normal commercial relations all may have consequences on the internal political configuration.

The location of a country helps to determine its role in the world. The strategic positions of Singapore and Panama have given these countries far more prominence in international politics than other countries of their size and level of development possess. The distance of a country from the world centers of power may be useful in predicting some kinds of political behavior. At the same time, the ease with which one can travel from a country to the major city of one of the two superpowers is a function both of distance and of politics. Table 6.1 reports air fares from the capital of each country to New York and to Moscow. Data are in United States dollars and refer to the costs of round-trip economy class international air tickets as of spring 1967. Relative distance was defined as the angle between the X-axis and a line drawn from the origin to a country's point in the plot accompanying table 6.1. This plot was drawn by placing the logarithmic transformations of the fares to Moscow along the X-axis and the logarithmic transformations of those to New York along the Y-axis. The measure is reported in whole degrees ranging from 0 to 90.

Countries are related to the outside world through official governmental ties as well. Chadwick F. Alger and Steven J. Brams observe that participation in international organizations provides most nations with much greater access to the outside world than do diplomatic ties. Whereas only one-eighth of all countries have representatives in more than half of the world's capitals, seven-eighths have organizational ties with more than half of all other countries. International organizations are far more numerous than the United Nations and its specialized agencies; Alger and Brams mention such exotic groups as the International Tea Committee in London, the Administrative Center for Social Security for Rhine Boatmen in Strasbourg, and the Desert Locust Control Organization for Eastern Africa in Nairobi.[1] Nevertheless, diplomatic exchanges and organizational affiliations are related to each other and both indicate the degree to which countries maintain formal channels for activity outside their borders.

1. Chadwick F. Alger and Steven J. Brams, "Patterns of Representation in National Capitals and Intergovernmental Organizations," *World Politics,* 19 (1967): 646-63.

Tables 6.2 and 6.3 report data on membership in international organizations and diplomatic representation abroad. Not all international organizations seemed to us of equal importance. In a small attempt to weight their importance, we separated the United Nations and its affiliated organizations from the others, but many scholars may prefer to use the totals given in the table or to consult particular cases in our source.[2] The 16 United Nations organizations are

United Nations
International Labor Organization
Food and Agriculture Organization
World Health Organization
United Nations
    Educational, Scientific and Cultural Organization
International Monetary Fund
International Bank
    for Reconstruction and Development
International Finance Corporation
International Development Association
General Agreement on Tariffs and Trade
International Atomic Energy Agency
International Civil Aviation Organization
International Telecommunication Union
Universal Postal Union
Inter-Governmental
    Maritime Consultative Organization
World Meteorological Organization

Only full memberships are counted; associates, observers, "participating countries," and corresponding members are not reflected in our table.

In table 6.3 "missions abroad" refers to the total number of countries to which a state sends accredited representatives. Diplomats sent and received refer to the numbers of these representatives. Honorary representatives and nonprofessional support staff were excluded. Also excluded were foreign economic and military aid personnel. However, all specialists, including military, who were listed as attachés to embassies and legations and all consuls living in national capitals were included. Some smaller countries send a single representative to several neighboring countries; these representatives were counted only once each for the country in which they were physically located. Alger and Brams collected these data mostly from official publications. Receiving lists of host governments were more fully available than sending lists but as many of the latter as possible were used to check

2. Moshe Y. Sachs, ed., *The Worldmark Encyclopedia of Nations, Volume I: United Nations* (New York: Harper & Row, 1967).

upon reliability. Alger and Brams estimate that their tally is over 90 percent complete.

The dependence of a country on another for trade or aid may have certain consequences on its foreign policy. A country is likely to treat messages from other countries, or concerning other countries, as more salient the greater its proportion of foreign trade to GNP or the more concentrated that trade is with a few countries or in a few commodities. A country may give special attention to countries from which it receives aid. The salience of a message, of course, only determines the attention given to it; the response may be friendly or hostile.

Data on American and Soviet foreign aid are given in table 6.4. Soviet data refer to Soviet economic credits and grants to countries in the period from 1954 to 1965. American data refer to grants and loans in the period from 1958 to 1965. American data are reported both including and excluding military aid. For a few countries, those listed at the bottom of the table, the data on military aid are classified and therefore not reported in our source.

Countries vary widely in the degree to which they approach autarky. In the past some countries (Czarist Russia, for example) have attempted to be as self-sufficient as possible in order to avoid the dangers of foreign contact and dependence. Others, like Britain, accepted wholeheartedly the arguments of comparative advantage and free trade. Whether it results from choice or circumstances, the level of a country's foreign trade is an indication of its dependence upon the outside world for its economic well-being. Also important is the composition of a country's foreign trade. A country whose exports consist chiefly of one commodity is dependent upon the fluctuating supply and demand of that commodity; a country that sends its exports primarily to one country is dependent upon markets in that one country.

Most economic theoreticians have emphasized the short-term export instability that arises out of narrow markets and limited commodities, an instability to which underdeveloped economies are especially vulnerable. These analyses have become a contributing factor in a number of proposals designed to dampen the effects of these fluctuations. Some recent literature, however, has begun to cast doubt on this explanation for export instability. Alasdair I. MacBean has presented evidence that concentration of commodities or of receiving countries in a country's export pattern is not related to instability in export earnings. According to MacBean, fluctuations in any event do not inflict significant damage on the growth of most under-developed countries due to the relatively low value of the foreign trade multiplier in most of them and to the usual pattern of distributed lags in response to changes in exporters' incomes.[3] In any event, however, the

3. Alasdair I. MacBean, *Export Instability and Economic Development* (London: Allen and Unwin, 1966), pp. 32, 41. See also Joseph D. Coppock, *International Economic Instability: The Experience After World War II* (New York: McGraw-Hill, 1962); Benton F. Massell,

economic dependence of a country upon others is likely to have political consequences. Three indexes of external dependence follow. The first measure, reported in table 6.5, is one of concentration of commodities within a country's exports. The second, presented in table 6.6, is a measure of concentration in the countries to which a country sends these exports. The third, given in table 6.7, is total trade as a percentage of gross national product.

Perhaps the measure for concentration used most frequently is one developed by Albert O. Hirschman during World War II. Hirschman insisted that an efficient measure would take into account both the distribution of value over the units (i.e. the amounts by various commodities or to various countries) and the number of units (i.e. the number of commodities actually exported or countries exported to). Concentration is a direct function of the relative inequality of dispersion but a reciprocal function of the number of units. Several indexes can meet these criteria, but the one proposed by Hirschman and used by a number of economists since is the square root of the sum of the square of the elements in the series stated as proportion of the total:

$$C = \sqrt{\sum_{1}^{n} \left(\frac{x_i}{x}\right)^2}$$

where x_i is the value for the particular unit and x is the sum of all the units.[4] This measure is independent of the absolute sum of the units and is a function of the relative shares. For example, the United States and the Netherlands could have the same coefficient value regardless of the fact that the trade of one is several times that of the other. It theoretically ranges from 0 to 1, with unity obtained when exports are entirely accounted for by one commodity or one receiving country and zero approached when each dollar of exports is in a separate commodity. In practice, the lower limit is set by $1/n$ if n = the largest number of exports that can possibly be exported.

The Hirschman index is clearly superior to various concentration ratios that have been used in social science (for example, the percentage of the total accounted for by the largest or the four largest or the twenty largest) because it takes into account the size of all the units. The two countries in the following hypothetical example have the same concentration ratio, based upon the first and second units, but different concentration coefficients, based upon all of them.

"Export Concentration and Fluctuations in Export Earnings: A Cross-Section Analysis," *The American Economic Review,* 65 (1964): 47-63; and Michael Michaely, *Concentration in International Trade* (Amsterdam: North-Holland, 1962).

4. Albert O. Hirschman, *National Power and the Structure of Foreign Trade* (Berkeley and Los Angeles: University of California Press, 1945), pp. 157-62. Hirschman multiplies his results by 100 to obtain percentages.

	Country a	Country b
Largest	40	40
Second largest	30	30
Third "	10	30
Fourth "	5	—
Fifth "	5	—
Sixth "	4	—
Seventh "	4	—
Eighth "	2	—

Marshall Hall and Nicolaus Tideman have suggested an alternative to the Hirschman measure. Weighting by squaring implies that the relative sizes of units are more important than the absolute number of them. Hall and Tideman have proposed weighting by rank to give more importance to the number involved.[5] Their formula is:

$$TH = \frac{1}{\left[2\sum_i \left(\frac{x_i}{x}\right)\right] - 1}$$

where i = the rank.

For export commodities and export-receiving countries, however, it seems best to use the measure that concentrates primarily on dispersion and secondarily takes account of number since the number of possible commodities is fixed by definition and the number of countries is set by international law. Each country has, at least potentially, the same number of units; what varies primarily among them is the dispersion over the units.

Once the index has been chosen the identification of receiving countries is straightforward. Defining "commodities" requires more effort. The Standard International Trade Classification, which is promoted by the United Nations Statistical Office, divides commodities into 10 sections, 52 divisions, 177 groups, and 1, 312 items.[6] Michael Michaely used the groups in his studies of international trade since, he said, at a finer level commodities that are very close substitutes in production and/or consumption would be defined as separate goods. As with all dispersion measures, all units are assumed equidistant. On the other hand, selecting too coarse a division would group together goods that really should be kept separate. Presumably, one would really like to make his decision at the country level or even at the commodity level within the country but this would make replication difficult. One other factor that was considered in choosing among levels of the Standard International Trade Classification was the availability of data.

5. Marshall Hall and Nicolaus Tideman, "Measures of Concentration," *Journal of the American Statistical Association,* 62 (1967): 162-68.

6. United Nations, Statistical Office, *Standard International Trade Classification, Revised,* United Nations Statistical Papers, Series M, No. 34 (New York, 1960).

The coarser classifications are available for many more countries than are the finer ones. The coefficients in table 6.5 are, therefore, based upon the 52 divisions. It was not necessary to collect the data for the entire number of commodities or for all the possible receiving nations; five to eight were usually sufficient for the accuracy reported. See p. 202 for discussion of the problem.

Table 6.7 reports trade as a percentage of gross national product and foreign mail as a percentage of total mail. These series are designed to show whether the country has an inward or outward orientation and the degree of that orientation. Do cour.tries that trade a great deal also communicate frequently? For definitions relating to mail see p. 208.

Countries differ as to their trade accounting systems. Some consider trade to consist of imports for domestic consumption *and* imports into bonded warehouses and free zones; exports *and* reexports. Others consider trade only to be imports for domestic consumption and withdrawals from bonded warehouses and free zones for domestic consumption and exports, excluding reexports, from these warehouses and zones. Still others include all imports less reexports plus exports of national produce. Trade systems of countries are marked in table 6.7 with a G (general trade) for the first system, an S (special trade) for the second system, and an M (modified special trade) for the third. A blank indicates that the system is unknown. It is difficult to estimate how much effect this variation has upon the comparability of the data since reexports vary greatly from country to country.

A second problem of comparability arises when imports or exports of foreign aid have been included in a country's reports on trade. In many ways aid can be considered closer either to services or to capital accounts than to transfers of merchandise. Those few countries that report foreign aid as part of trade are marked in table 6.7. Also noted are data that do not include trade with neighboring areas (usually within a customs union). The exclusion of these data may bring a serious downward bias to the data on these countries; however, for example, trade within former French Equatorial Africa is probably a small proportion of total trade of each of these states since markets for most of their products are in Europe and North America.

Data on exports and imports have been collected for a very long time for customs purposes and have therefore perhaps less error attached to them than any other kind of economic data. "Error" is primarily a function of differences in definition rather than of inaccuracies.

Table 6.1
Air Fares from the Two Super Powers

Mean	766	768	46
Standard Deviation	343	334	17
Median	770	819	47
Range	1468	1633	90
Skewness	-.00	-.11	-.62
Number of Countries	136	136	136

Rank	Country	Air Fares in Dollars from Capitals to New York	to Moscow	Relative Distance Measure
1	Soviet Union	730	0	90
3	Finland	580	173	74
3	Iran	946	274	74
3	Poland	593	174	74
5	Romania	643	218	71
6	Afghanistan	1016	371	70
8	Bulgaria	642	255	69
8	Hungary	567	220	69
8	Sweden	536	212	69
10	Yugoslavia	571	232	68
11	Austria	526	226	67
12.5	Albania	645	305	65
12.5	China	1387	657	65
14	North Korea	1432	703	64
16	Cyprus	739	395	62
16	Czechoslovakia	526	278	62
16	India	1128	592	62
19.5	Denmark	479	268	61
19.5	Lebanon	798	443	61
19.5	Norway	479	268	61
19.5	Pakistan	1128	617	61
24	East Germany	501	289	60
24	Italy	544	313	60
24	Mongolia	966	551	60
24	Nepal	1180	687	60
24	Turkey	722	406	60
27	West Germany	479	289	59
29	Burma	1255	768	58
29	Maldive Islands	1180	754	58
29	Switzerland	479	297	58
31.5	North Viet Nam	1468	967	57
31.5	United Arab Republic	798	523	57
35	Belgium	441	304	56
35	Luxembourg	456	310	56
35	Netherlands	441	302	56
35	Tunisia	544	359	56
35	Yemen	1157	793	56
38.5	Malta	558	386	55
38.5	Sudan	942	660	55
42.5	Cambodia	1226	896	54
42.5	France	441	316	54
42.5	Israel	789	583	54

Table 6.1 Air Fares from the Two Super Powers—*Continued*

| Rank | Country | Air Fares in Dollars from Capitals | | Relative Distance Measure |
		to New York	to Moscow	
42.5	Jordan	798	583	54
42.5	Somalia	1162	835	54
42.5	Syria	798	583	54
46.5	Indonesia	1379	1031	53
46.5	Southern Yemen	1045	793	53
49.5	Algeria	533	419	52
49.5	Ethiopia	1045	825	52
49.5	Iraq	894	701	52
49.5	Uganda	1045	819	52
53	Kenya	1045	851	51
53	Niger	937	769	51
53	Rwanda	1137	911	51
57	Greece	691	567	50
57	Hong Kong	1131	965	50
57	Lesotho	1145	964	50
57	Malagasy Republic	1226	1048	50
57	Papua / New Guinea	1416	1193	50
63	Burundi	1045	920	49
63	Ceylon	1180	1022	49
63	Libya	596	519	49
63	Mozambique	1092	947	49
63	South Africa	1156	1020	49
63	Tanzania	1045	899	49
63	United Kingdom	399	352	49
67	Mali	751	670	48
74	Dahomey	779	745	47
74	Ghana	779	745	47
74	Guinea	750	697	47
74	Malaysia	1226	1165	47
74	Mauritania	758	715	47
74	Mauritius	1383	1274	47
74	Nigeria	779	745	47
74	Philippines	1112	1045	47
74	Saudi Arabia	904	830	47
74	Singapore	1226	1165	47
74	Thailand	1226	1149	47
74	Togo	779	745	47
74	Upper Volta	887	826	47
85	Congo – Brazzaville	883	846	46
85	Congo – Kinshasa	884	846	46
85	Gabon	884	841	46
85	Ivory Coast	770	745	46
85	Liberia	751	724	46
85	Malawi	1045	1007	46
85	Morocco	466	463	46
85	Sierra Leone	750	724	46
85	South Viet Nam	1207	1160	46
91.5	Chad	849	843	45
91.5	Laos	1226	1220	45
91.5	Senegal	656	665	45
91.5	The Gambia	687	687	45
95.5	Botswana	1045	1070	44
95.5	Angola	956	1004	44

Table 6.1 Air Fares from the Two Super Powers—*Continued*

Rank	Country	Air Fares in Dollars from Capitals to New York	to Moscow	Relative Distance Measure
95.5	Taiwan	1112	1126	44
95.5	Zambia	1045	1080	44
99	Central African Republic	884	939	43
99	Ireland	369	401	43
99	Rhodesia	1045	1123	43
101	New Zealand	1216	1346	42
102	Spain	441	512	41
103	Portugal	399	476	40
104.5	Cameroon	834	1035	39
104.5	Kuwait	946	1160	39
106	Australia	1269	1633	38
107	Japan	998	1447	35
108	South Korea	1055	1576	34
109	Iceland	286	450	33
110	Brazil	618	1056	30
112	Argentina	630	1157	29
112	Paraguay	629	1157	29
112	Uruguay	630	1157	29
114	Chile	599	1243	26
115	Peru	521	1146	24
116	Bolivia	529	1243	23
117	Guyana	346	1013	19
119	Colombia	352	1070	18
119	Ecuador	352	1085	18
119	Venezuela	330	1013	18
122	Costa Rica	313	1030	17
122	Panama	325	1043	17
122	Trinidad and Tobago	304	1013	17
125.5	El Salvador	296	1030	16
125.5	Guatemala	290	1030	16
125.5	Honduras	296	1030	16
125.5	Nicaragua	296	1030	16
128	Barbados	285	1013	15
129	Mexico	254	975	14
130.5	Haiti	225	933	13
130.5	Jamaica	225	933	13
132.5	Cuba	195	897	12
132.5	Dominican Republic	198	920	12
134	Puerto Rico	122	880	8
135	Canada	58	730	5
136	United States	0	763	0

Notes: No data are missing in this table.

Date is spring 1967.

Data in United States dollars refer to the cost of a round-trip economy class international air ticket. For information on the calculation of the relative distance measure, see p. 344.

Source is Pan American World Airways, New York.

Table 6.1 Air Fares from the Two Super Powers—*Continued*

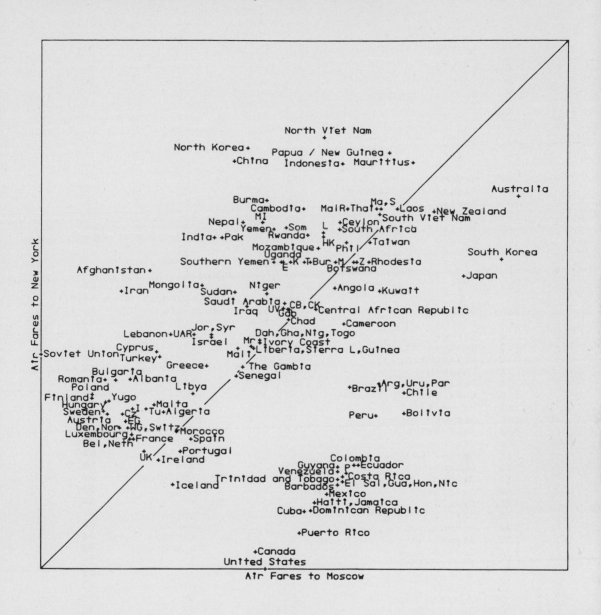

Air Fares to New York (vertical axis)

Air Fares to Moscow (horizontal axis)

North Viet Nam

North Korea
Papua / New Guinea
China Indonesia Mauritius

Australia

Burma
Cambodia MaIR+That Ma,S +Laos +New Zealand
MI South Viet Nam
Nepal +Ceylon
Yemen +Som L +South Africa
India+ +Pak Rwanda +Taiwan
Mozambique+ HK Phil
Uganda South Korea
Southern Yemen +E+K +Bur+M +Z+Rhodesia +Japan
E Botswana

Afghanistan+
Mongolia Niger
+Iran Sudan+ +Angola +Kuwait
Saudi Arabia +CB,CK
Iraq UV Central African Republic
Gab
+Chad +Cameroon
Jor,Syr
Lebanon+UAR Dah,Gha,Nig,Togo
Israel Mr+Ivory Coast
Cyprus +Liberia,Sierra L,Guinea
+Soviet Union Mali
Turkey+
Greece+ The Gambia
Bulgaria +Senegal
Romania+ +Albania Libya
Poland +Brazil Arg,Uru,Par
Finland+ +Yugo +Chile
Hungary+ +Malta
Sweden+ +C+I +Tu+Algeria Peru+ +Bolivia
Austria +EG
Den,Nor +WG,Switz +Morocco
Luxembourg+ France +Spain
Bel,Neth
+Portugal
UK +Ireland
Colombia
Guyana+ p++Ecuador
Venezuela+ +Costa Rica
+Iceland Trinidad and Tobago+ +El Sal,Gua,Hon,Nic
Barbados+
+Mexico
+Haiti,Jamaica
Cuba+ +Dominican Republic

+Puerto Rico

+Canada
United States

Abbreviations

Arg	= Argentina	I	= Italy	Phil	= Philippines
Bel	= Belgium	Jor	= Jordan	Sierra L	= Sierra Leone
Bur	= Burundi	K	= Kenya	Som	= Somalia
CB	= Congo – Brazzaville	L	= Lesotho	Switz	= Switzerland
CK	= Congo – Kinshasa	M	= Malawi	Syr	= Syria
Cz	= Czechoslovakia	Ma,S	= Malaysia, Singapore	T	= Tanzania
Dah	= Dahomey	MaIR	= Malagasy Republic	That	= Thailand
Den	= Denmark	MI	= Maldive Islands	Tu	= Tunisia
E	= Ethiopia	Mr	= Mauritania	UAR	= United Arab Republic
EG	= East Germany	Neth	= Netherlands	UK	= United Kingdom
El Sal	= El Salvador	Nic	= Nicaragua	Uru	= Uruguay
Gab	= Gabon	Nig	= Nigeria	UV	= Upper Volta
Gha	= Ghana	Nor	= Norway	WG	= West Germany
Gua	= Guatemala	P	= Panama	Yugo	= Yugoslavia
HK	= Hong Kong	Pak	= Pakistan	Z	= Zambia
Hon	= Honduras	Par	= Paraguay		

Table 6.2
Memberships in International Organizations

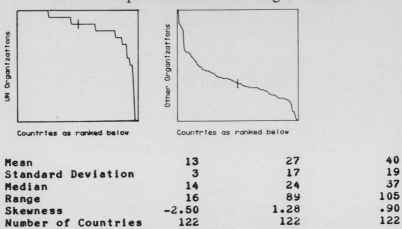

Mean	13	27	40
Standard Deviation	3	17	19
Median	14	24	37
Range	16	89	105
Skewness	-2.50	1.28	.90
Number of Countries	122	122	122

Rank	Country	United Nations Organizations	Memberships in Other International Organizations	All International Organizations
1	France	16	91	107
2	Netherlands	16	78	94
3	United Kingdom	16	77	93
4	Belgium	16	75	91
5	Italy	16	73	89
6	West Germany	15	73	88
7	Denmark	16	55	71
8	Norway	16	52	68
10	Austria	15	52	67
10	Spain	16	51	67
10	United States	16	51	67
12	Luxembourg	15	51	66
13	Sweden	16	49	65
14	Switzerland	11	52	63
15	Brazil	16	46	62
16	Mexico	15	46	61
17	Greece	16	44	60
18.5	Argentina	15	43	58
18.5	India	16	42	58
20.5	Portugal	12	43	55
20.5	Turkey	16	39	55
23	Canada	16	37	53
23	Ecuador	15	38	53
23	Japan	16	37	53
25	United Arab Republic	16	35	51
27	Finland	16	34	50
27	Peru	15	35	50
27	Yugoslavia	15	35	50
30.5	Australia	14	35	49

Table 6.2 Memberships in International Organizations—*Continued*

Rank	Country	United Nations Organizations	Memberships in Other International Organizations	All International Organizations
30.5	Chile	15	34	49
30.5	Pakistan	16	33	49
30.5	Venezuela	13	36	49
33.5	Colombia	14	34	48
33.5	Guatemala	14	34	48
36	Ireland	14	33	47
36	Nicaragua	15	32	47
36	Nigeria	16	31	47
38	Dominican Republic	16	30	46
39	Morocco	15	30	45
40.5	Panama	14	30	44
40.5	Uruguay	13	31	44
43.5	Costa Rica	14	29	43
43.5	Honduras	15	28	43
43.5	Ivory Coast	16	27	43
43.5	Senegal	16	27	43
48.5	Cameroon	15	27	42
48.5	El Salvador	14	28	42
48.5	Iceland	16	26	42
48.5	Israel	16	26	42
48.5	Poland	12	30	42
48.5	Tunisia	16	26	42
53	Haiti	16	25	41
53	New Zealand	15	26	41
53	Paraguay	14	27	41
55.5	Ghana	16	24	40
55.5	Romania	11	29	40
57.5	Bolivia	14	25	39
57.5	Czechoslovakia	11	28	39
59.5	Niger	13	25	38
59.5	Soviet Union	9	29	38
62.5	Kenya	15	22	37
62.5	Tanzania	14	23	37
62.5	Thailand	14	23	37
62.5	Upper Volta	13	24	37
65	Uganda	14	22	36
67	Ceylon	15	20	35
67	Congo – Brazzaville	13	22	35
67	Cyprus	15	20	35
70.5	Dahomey	13	21	34
70.5	Hungary	8	26	34
70.5	Lebanon	14	20	34
70.5	Malagasy Republic	16	18	34
77	Algeria	15	18	33
77	Bulgaria	9	24	33
77	Chad	13	20	33
77	Gabon	14	19	33
77	Iran	15	18	33
77	Malaysia	14	19	33
77	Mauritania	13	20	33
77	Philippines	15	18	33
77	Sudan	14	19	33

Table 6.2 Memberships in International Organizations—*Continued*

Rank	Country	United Nations Organizations	Memberships in Other International Organizations	All International Organizations
82.5	Cuba	12	20	32
82.5	Sierra Leone	15	17	32
85.5	Central African Republic	13	18	31
85.5	Indonesia	12	19	31
85.5	Togo	14	17	31
85.5	Trinidad and Tobago	13	18	31
89	Congo – Kinshasa	14	16	30
89	Mali	14	16	30
89	South Korea	13	17	30
91	South Africa	13	16	29
92	Taiwan	13	15	28
93.5	Libya	13	14	27
93.5	South Viet Nam	12	15	27
96.5	Iraq	14	12	26
96.5	Malawi	13	13	26
96.5	Rwanda	13	13	26
96.5	Syria	15	11	26
99.5	Burma	16	9	25
99.5	Jamaica	14	11	25
101	Ethiopia	14	10	24
104.5	Burundi	12	11	23
104.5	Guinea	11	12	23
104.5	Jordan	14	9	23
104.5	Liberia	14	9	23
104.5	Malta	9	14	23
104.5	Zambia	13	10	23
109	Cambodia	11	11	22
109	Kuwait	16	6	22
109	Laos	12	10	22
111.5	Afghanistan	14	7	21
111.5	Saudi Arabia	13	8	21
113	Somalia	13	7	20
114	Nepal	13	6	19
115	Albania	8	9	17
116	Yemen	8	3	11
117.5	Mongolia	6	4	10
117.5	Rhodesia	3	7	10
119	East Germany	0	5	5
120	North Viet Nam	0	3	3
121.5	China	0	2	2
121.5	North Korea	0	2	2

Notes: Date for all data is 1965. In that year, the following countries were not independent and, therefore, this series does not apply to them: Angola, Barbados, Botswana, The Gambia, Hong Kong, Lesotho, Maldive Islands, Mauritius, Mozambique, Papua/New Guinea, Puerto Rico, Singapore, and Southern Yemen.

These series are put together on the basis of data published in Moshe Y. Sachs, ed., *The Worldmark Encyclopedia of Nations* (New York: Harper & Row, 1967).

Table 6.3
Diplomatic Representation

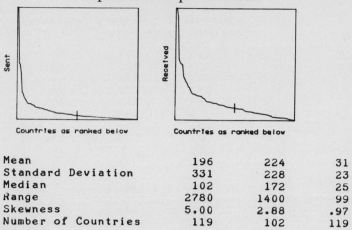

Mean	196	224	31
Standard Deviation	331	228	23
Median	102	172	25
Range	2780	1400	99
Skewness	5.00	2.88	.97
Number of Countries	119	102	119

Rank	Country	Diplomats Sent	Diplomats Received	Missions Abroad
1	United States	2782	1418	100
2	France	1152	716	98
3	United Kingdom	1403	1305	96
4	West Germany	671	778	88
5	Italy	511	707	87
6	Netherlands	352	258	74
7	Belgium	279	473	72
8	Japan	638	494	71
9	Switzerland	240	315	70
10	United Arab Republic	550	559	67
11	Soviet Union	1345	732	65
13	India	467	530	64
13	Israel	292	229	64
13	Sweden	237	287	64
15.5	Argentina	301		60
15.5	Brazil	300	431	60
17	Spain	306	342	59
18	Denmark	201	231	58
19.5	Czechoslovakia	422	321	57
19.5	Yugoslavia	280	324	57
21.5	Canada	388	383	55
21.5	Poland	386	301	55
23	Turkey	392	353	54
24	Austria	162	420	53
25	Finland	139	182	48
26.5	Bulgaria	247	209	47
26.5	Indonesia	348	339	47
28	Taiwan	268	120	46
29.5	Chile	161	214	44
29.5	Mexico	186	315	44
32	Greece	218	245	43

Table 6.3 Diplomatic Representation—*Continued*

Rank	Country	Diplomats Sent	Diplomats Received	Missions Abroad
32	Pakistan	188	321	43
32	Portugal	137	175	43
35.5	Ghana	212	242	42
35.5	Hungary	264	209	42
35.5	Lebanon	91	127	42
35.5	Norway	156	240	42
38	Cuba	216	201	41
39	Romania	360	228	40
40.5	China	389		38
40.5	Venezuela	133	174	38
42.5	Iran	248	246	36
42.5	Uruguay	106	206	36
44.5	Colombia	127	162	35
44.5	Peru	131	203	35
46	Australia	280	190	34
47	Morocco	129		32
48	Panama	103	172	31
49	Thailand	191	286	29
50	Tunisia	99		28
52.5	Bolivia	82		27
52.5	Ecuador	102	122	27
52.5	Iraq	140	249	27
52.5	Sudan	93	153	27
55.5	Nigeria	151	223	26
55.5	Philippines	154	180	26
58.5	Ethiopia	81	129	25
58.5	Saudi Arabia	155	125	25
58.5	South Korea	155	95	25
58.5	Syria	118	179	25
61.5	Algeria	102	339	24
61.5	Haiti	53	58	24
64	Dominican Republic	82		23
64	Liberia	54	99	23
64	Senegal	72	163	23
67.5	Ceylon	66	158	22
67.5	Costa Rica	77	88	22
67.5	Guatemala	67	108	22
67.5	Jordan	82	165	22
70	South Viet Nam	107	173	21
72	Afghanistan	83	109	20
72	Burma	85	230	20
72	El Salvador	70	104	20
75	Malta	37	18	19
75	Nicaragua	78	51	19
75	South Africa	163	98	19
78	Mali	55	115	18
78	North Korea	111		18
78	Paraguay	50	95	18
81	Guinea	63	158	17
81	Libya	68		17
81	North Viet Nam	81		17
83.5	East Germany	153	186	16
83.5	Ireland	46	57	16
85.5	Albania	56	59	15

Table 6.3 Diplomatic Representation—*Continued*

Rank	Country	Diplomats Sent	Diplomats Received	Missions Abroad
85.5	Yemen	49		15
87	Malaysia	65	140	14
89	Cambodia	53	132	13
89	Honduras	34	75	13
89	Kuwait	56	49	13
91.5	Ivory Coast	39		12
91.5	New Zealand	91	88	12
94	Laos	46	125	11
94	Mongolia	43		11
94	Nepal	31	52	11
97	Cameroon	41	80	10
97	Somalia	39	92	10
97	Upper Volta	33		10
99	Congo - Brazzaville	22	60	9
102	Dahomey	19		8
102	Iceland	18	35	8
102	Luxembourg	17	32	8
102	Niger	15		8
102	Sierra Leone	35	50	8
106	Central African Republic	16	29	7
106	Congo - Kinshasa	33	158	7
106	Cyprus	34	109	7
108	Chad	16	40	6
111	Burundi	11		5
111	Mauritania	11	26	5
111	Rwanda	8		5
111	Togo	16	45	5
111	Trinidad and Tobago	18	44	5
115	Gabon	10	23	4
115	Jamaica	25	50	4
115	Malagasy Republic	19	51	4
117	Tanzania	9	104	3
118	Uganda	6	52	2
119	Kenya	2	75	1

Notes: Dates for all data are 1963-64. In that year, the following countries were not independent and, therefore, this series does not apply to them: Angola, Barbados, Botswana, Guyana, Hong Kong, Lesotho, Malawi, Maldive Islands, Mauritius, Mozambique, Papua/New Guinea, Puerto Rico, Rhodesia, Singapore, Southern Yemen, The Gambia and Zambia.

Source is Chadwick F. Alger and Steven J. Brams, "Patterns of Representation in National Capitals and Intergovernmental Organizations," *World Politics*, 19 (1967), 646-63.

Table 6.4
Foreign Aid

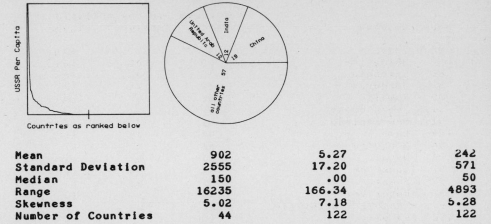

Mean	902	5.27	242
Standard Deviation	2555	17.20	571
Median	150	.00	50
Range	16235	166.34	4893
Skewness	5.02	7.18	5.28
Number of Countries	44	122	122

Rank	Country	Total Soviet Aid in $m	Soviet Aid Per Capita in $	Source	Total U. S Economic Aic in $m
1	Jordan		.00		414
2	Israel		.00		532
3	Liberia		.00		189
4	Iceland		.00		30
5	Laos	36	1.80	2	284
6	Tunisia	28	6.34		430
7	South Viet Nam		.00		1554
8	Chile		.00		826
9	Libya		.00		145
10	Panama		.00		108
11	Bolivia		.00		283
12	South Korea		.00		1819
13	Costa Rica		.00		88
14	Taiwan		.00		692
15	Dominican Republic		.00		188
16	Nicaragua		.00		83
17	Yugoslavia	232	1.19	1	917
18	Turkey	210	6.76		1393
19	Trinidad and Tobago		.00		43
20	Greece	84	9.82		358
21	Morocco		.00		454
22	Ecuador		.00		165
23	Cyprus		.00		19
24	Colombia		.00		579
25	United Arab Republic	1011	34.16		945
26	Venezuela		.00		275
27	Paraguay		.00		62
28	El Salvador		.00		88
29	Peru		.00		335

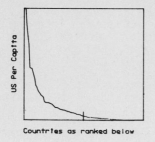

US Per Capita

Countries as ranked below

Pakistan

India

17

all other countries 75

22.86	262	27.41
39.68	497	43.46
6.75	68	10.60
209.46	3331	226.32
2.90	3.52	2.57
122	115	115

U. S. Economic Aid Per Capita in $	Total U. S. Economic and Military Aid in $m	U. S. Economic and Military Aid Per Capita in $
209.46	447	226.32
207.49	551	215.06
176.36	192	179.53
157.81	30*	157.81
142.05		
97.49	450	101.88
96.40		
96.39	905	105.68
89.92	153	94.87
83.23	110	84.31
76.63	294	79.47
64.10	3331	117.39
61.20	89	62.25
55.68	1702	136.91
51.92	196	54.02
49.85	89	53.53
47.00	951	48.74
44.80	2567	82.59
44.00	43*	44.00
41.89	1058	123.75
34.04	472	35.41
32.36	193	37.94
32.15	19*	32.15
32.07	631	34.92
31.92	945*	31.92
31.56	341	39.11
30.30	66	32.66
29.95	91	31.15
28.78	415	35.58

Table 6.4 Foreign Aid—*Continued*

Rank	Country	Total Soviet Aid in $m	Soviet Aid Per Capita in $	Source	Total U. S. Economic Aid in $m
30	Guatemala		.00		120
31	Uruguay		.00		68
32	Spain		.00		732
33	Pakistan	94	.91		2360
34	Honduras		.00		52
35	Cambodia	21	3.43		136
36	Ghana	89	11.50		164
37	Guinea	70	20.00		69
38	Congo — Kinshasa		.00		299
39	Jamaica		.00		34
40	Iran	330	14.09		428
41	Somalia	57	22.80		45
42	Brazil		.00		1476
43	Lebanon		.00		43
44	Argentina	115	5.14		362
45	Syria	150	28.30		82
46	Mexico		.00		651
47	Afghanistan	552	36.68		219
48	Algeria	230	19.37		161
49	Norway		.00		50
50	Philippines		.00		421
51	Portugal		.00		119
52	Sierra Leone	28	12.23		27
53	Haiti		.00		52
54	Gabon		.00		5
55	India	1022	2.10		4893
56	Italy		.00		515
57	Austria		.00		70
58	Thailand		.00		278
59	Yemen	92	18.40		39
60	Nepal	20	1.98		76
61	Ivory Coast		.00		26
62	Ceylon	30	2.67		74
63	Sudan	22	1.62		89
64	Togo		.00		10
65	Ethiopia	102	4.51		116
66	Cameroon	8	1.53		25
67	Senegal	7	2.01		17
68	United Kingdom		.00		252
69	Iraq	184	22.27		37
70	Japan		.00		439
71	Tanzania		.00		44
72	Indonesia	372	3.53		411
73	Saudi Arabia		.00		26
74	Malaysia		.00		36
75	Dahomey		.00		9
76	Kenya	44	4.70		31
77	Finland		.00		15
78	Mali	55	12.02		14
79	Congo — Brazzaville	9	10.71		2
80	Burma	14	.57		68
81	Nigeria		.00		157

U. S. Economic Aid Per Capita in $	Total U. S. Economic and Military Aid in $m	U. S. Economic and Military Aid Per Capita in $
26.93	127	28.62
25.19	92	33.89
23.17	1053	33.30
22.94		
22.90	55	24.26
22.24	179	29.21
21.24	164	21.24
19.83	69	19.83
19.10	306	19.58
19.02	35	19.35
18.29	907	38.72
18.00	45*	18.00
17.95	1648	20.04
16.80	50	19.34
16.19	414	18.54
15.45	82	15.45
15.25	661	15.48
14.53	221	14.69
13.56	161*	13.56
13.43	326	87.43
13.00	580	17.92
12.97	197	21.43
11.88	27*	11.88
11.81	55	12.47
10.37	5*	10.37
10.05		
9.99	1233	23.90
9.59		
9.09		
7.84	39	7.84
7.52		
6.75	26	6.78
6.62	74*	6.62
6.59	89	6.59
5.98	10*	5.98
5.11	189	8.35
4.74	25	4.78
4.73	19	5.39
4.62	579	10.60
4.51	59	7.15
4.48	1061	10.83
4.21	44*	4.21
3.91	475	4.51
3.82	110	16.31
3.80	36	3.80
3.68	9	3.72
3.31	31*	3.31
3.25	15*	3.25
2.95	15	3.30
2.86	2*	2.86
2.75	68*	2.75
2.74	158	2.75

Table 6.4 Foreign Aid—*Continued*

Rank	Country	Total Soviet Aid in $m	Soviet Aid Per Capita in $	Source	Total U. S. Economic Aid in $m
82	Niger		.00		9
83	Poland	2986	9.48	1	76
84	Cuba	1226	16.07	1	18
85	Burundi		.00		7
86	Uganda	16	2.12		17
87	Malawi		.00		8
88	Central African Republic		.00		3
89	Mauritania		.00		1
90	Chad		.00		4
91	Malagasy Republic		.00		8
92	Upper Volta		.00		5
93	West Germany		.00		61
94	Zambia		.00		3
95	Rwanda		.00		2
96	Rhodesia		.00		2
97	South Africa		.00		6
98	Netherlands		.00		3
99	France		.00		9
100	Australia		.00		2
101	New Zealand		.00		0
102.5	Belgium		.00		1
102.5	Luxembourg		.00		1
113	Albania	293	15.76	1	0
113	Bulgaria	5197	63.39	1	0
113	Canada		.00		0
113	China	16242	2.32	1	0
113	Czechoslovakia	552	3.90	1	0
113	Denmark		.00		0
113	East Germany	763	4.46	1	0
113	Hungary	1214	11.97	1	0
113	Ireland		.00		0
113	Kuwait		.00		0
113	Malta		.00		0
113	Mongolia	1836	166.34	1	0
113	North Korea	752	6.22	1	0
113	North Viet Nam	1123	5.91	1	0
113	Romania	2181	11.46	1	0
113	Sweden		.00		0
113	Switzerland		.00		0

Notes: Dates for United States aid are 1958-65; for Soviet aid dates are 1954/5-65.

The following countries were not independent in 1965 and the series were judged inapplicable to them: Angola, Barbados, Botswana, Guyana, Hong Kong, Lesotho, Maldive Islands, Mauritius, Mozambique, Papua/New Guinea, Puerto Rico, Singapore, Southern Yemen and The Gambia. The United States and the Soviet Union were, of course, also omitted from the table.

Soviet data refer to economic credits and grants. American data refer to grants and loans in which distinction is made between economic and military aid. Countries receiving no military aid from the United States are marked with an asterisk (*) in the column of total United States aid. No data are reported there for Austria, India, Laos, Nepal, Pakistan, South Viet Nam, and Thailand because military aid figures for these countries are classified.

U. S. Economic Aid Per Capita in $	Total U. S. Economic and Military Aid in $m	U. S. Economic and Military Aid Per Capita in $
2.58	9	2.61
2.43	76*	2.43
2.32	21	2.80
2.31	7*	2.31
2.25	17*	2.25
2.06	8*	2.06
2.00	3*	2.00
1.33	1*	1.33
1.30	4*	1.30
1.25	8*	1.25
1.09	5	1.11
1.03	399	6.75
.75	3*	.75
.55	2*	.55
.49	2*	.49
.34	6*	.34
.24	272	22.15
.18	449	9.18
.13	84	7.37
.11	5	1.82
.10	186	19.02
.10	186	19.02
.00	0	.00
.00	0	.00
.00	9	.46
.00	0	.00
.00	0	.00
.00	210	44.16
.00	0	.00
.00	0	.00
.00	0	.00
.00	0	.00
.00	0	.00
.00	0	.00
.00	0	.00
.00	0	.00
.00	0	.00
.00	0	.00
.00	0	.00

Source for data on United States aid is United States, Agency for International Development, *U.S. Overseas Loans and Grants and Assistance from International Organizations, July 1, 1945-June 30, 1965,* Special Report Prepared for the House Foreign Affairs Committee (Washington, D.C.: U.S. Government Printing Office, 1966).

Source for data on Soviet aid, unless otherwise noted, is United States, Department of State, Director of Intelligence and Research, *Research Memorandum*, RSB-50 (Washington, 1966).

1. Marshall I. Goldman. *Soviet Foreign Aid* (New York: Praeger, 1967), p. 28.

2. Kurt Muller, *The Foreign Aid Programs of the Soviet Bloc and Communist China*, trans. Richard H. Weber and Michael Roloff (New York: Walker, 1966), p. 219.

Table 6.5
Concentration of Export Commodities

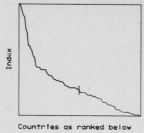

Countries as ranked below

$$C = \sum_i p_i^2$$

where p_i = proportion of total value of exports accounted for by ith commodity.

Mean	.30
Standard Deviation	.21
Median	.25
Range	.93
Skewness	1.36
Number of Countries	101

Rank	Country	C	Date
1	Libya	.99	
2	Mauritius	.96	1964
3	Zambia	.92	
4	Mauritania	.89	1964
5	Kuwait	.88	
6	Iran	.78	1964
7	Cuba	.75	
8.5	Barbados	.64	
8.5	Trinidad and Tobago	.64	
10	Chad	.61*	
11	Liberia	.59	
12	South Viet Nam	.55	
13	Ghana	.54	
14	Ethiopia	.47	
16	Ceylon	.46	
16	Chile	.46	1963
16	Sierra Leone	.46	
20	Burma	.44	1962
20	Cambodia	.44	
20	Colombia	.44	
20	Congo – Kinshasa	.44	
20	Rwanda	.44	
23	Iceland	.41	
24	The Gambia	.40	
26	Ecuador	.39	1964
26	Ivory Coast	.39	
26	Niger	.39	
28	United Arab Republic	.37	
29.5	Panama	.36	
29.5	Uganda	.36*	
32	Central African Republic	.35*	
32	Dominican Republic	.35	1964

Table 6.5 Concentration of Export Commodities—*Continued*

Rank	Country	C	Date
32	Upper Volta	.35	1964
35	Congo - Brazzaville	.34*	
35	Dahomey	.34	
35	Pakistan	.34	
37	Togo	.33	
38.5	Cameroon	.31	1964
38.5	El Salvador	.31	
40.5	Jordan	.30	
40.5	Somalia	.30	
44.5	Gabon	.29*	
44.5	Guatemala	.29	
44.5	Guyana	.29	
44.5	Indonesia	.29	1963
44.5	Jamaica	.29	
44.5	Sudan	.29	
48.5	Senegal	.28*	
48.5	Syria	.28	
50	Costa Rica	.27	
53	Brazil	.25	
53	Honduras	.25	
53	Malagasy Republic	.25	
53	Malawi	.25	
53	Nicaragua	.25	1964
56	Afghanistan	.24	
58.5	Kenya	.23*	
58.5	Malaysia	.23	
58.5	Tanzania	.23*	
58.5	Thailand	.23	
62	Argentina	.22	
62	Cyprus	.22	
62	New Zealand	.22	
64.5	Greece	.21	
64.5	Mali	.21	
67	Israel	.20	
67	Malta	.20	
67	Morocco	.20	1964
69	Nigeria	.18	
71	India	.17	
71	Peru	.17	1963
71	Turkey	.17	
73	Finland	.16	
75	Hong Kong	.15	
75	Philippines	.15	
75	Rhodesia	.15	
78	Australia	.14	
78	Spain	.14	
78	Tunisia	.14	
80	Taiwan	.12	
82	Ireland	.11	
82	Singapore	.11	
82	Switzerland	.11	
84.5	Denmark	.10	
84.5	West Germany	.10*	
88.5	Japan	.09	
88.5	Mexico	.09	

Table 6.5 Concentration of Export Commodities—*Continued*

Rank	Country	C	Date
88.5	Portugal	.09	
88.5	South Korea	.09*	
88.5	Sweden	.09	
88.5	United Kingdom	.09	
93	Canada	.08	
93	Norway	.08	
93	United States	.06	
97	Austria	.07	
97	Hungary	.07	
97	Italy	.07	
97	South Africa	.07	
97	Yugoslavia	.07	
100.5	France	.06	
100.5	Netherlands	.06	

Notes: Data are missing for Albania, Algeria, Angola, Belgium, Bolivia, Botswana, Bulgaria, Burundi, China, Czechoslovakia, East Germany, Guinea, Haiti, Iraq, Laos, Lebanon, Lesotho, Luxembourg, Maldive Islands, Mongolia, Mozambique, Nepal, North Korea, North Viet Nam, Papua/New Guinea, Paraguay, Poland, Puerto Rico, Romania, Saudi Arabia, Southern Yemen, Soviet Union, Uruguay, Venezuela, and Yemen.

*Total exports do not include those to certain surrounding countries (usually in a customs union).

South Africa includes Lesotho, Botswana, and Swaziland. Panama excludes the Canal Zone. The United States includes Puerto Rico.

Date, unless otherwise noted, is 1965.

Source of data used in constructing the index is United Nations, Statistical Office. *Yearbook of International Trade Statistics, 1965* (New York, 1967). Original data are on the archive tape.

Table 6.6
Concentration of Export Receiving Countries

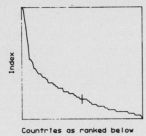

Countries as ranked below

$$c = \sum p_i^2$$

where p_i = proportion of total value of exports going to i^{th} country.

Mean	.19
Standard Deviation	.12
Median	.16
Range	.62
Skewness	1.75
Number of Countries	118

Rank	Country	C	Date
1	Dominican Republic	.67	
2	Senegal	.65	
3	Mauritius	.60	
4	Algeria	.56	
5	Ireland	.50	
6	Sierra Leone	.46	
7.5	Bolivia	.38	
7.5	Niger	.38	
9	The Gambia	.37	1964
10	Canada	.36	
11.5	Honduras	.33	
11.5	Malawi	.33	
13	Dahomey	.32	
14	Mexico	.31	
16	Costa Rica	.30	
16	Philippines	.30	
16	Somalia	.30	1964
18.5	Bulgaria	.29	
18.5	Ecuador	.29	
21	Congo - Kinshasa	.28	
21	Gabon	.28	
21	Malagasy Republic	.28	
23.5	Ethiopia	.27	1964
23.5	New Zealand	.27	
27.5	Cameroon	.25	
27.5	Chad	.25	
27.5	Colombia	.25	
27.5	Cuba	.25	
27.5	Haiti	.25	
27.5	Jamaica	.25	
31.5	Panama	.24	
31.5	Togo	.24	

Table 6.6 Concentration of Export Receiving Countries—*Continued*

Rank	Country	C	Date
33.5	Central African Republic	.23	
33.5	Upper Volta	.23	1964
37	Angola	.22	
37	Congo - Brazzaville	.22	
37	Libya	.22	
37	Morocco	.22	
37	Venezuela	.22	
40	East Germany	.21	
43	Barbados	.20	
43	Ivory Coast	.20	
43	Mozambique	.20	
43	Nigeria	.20	
43	South Korea	.20	
48	Guatemala	.19	
48	Liberia	.19	
48	Mauritania	.19	
48	Nicaragua	.19	
48	South Africa	.19	
52	Rumania	.18	
52	South Viet Nam	.18	
52	Taiwan	.18	
55.5	Czechoslovakia	.17	
55.5	El Salvador	.17	
55.5	Guyana	.17	
55.5	Peru	.17	
61	Chile	.16	
61	Indonesia	.16	
61	Kuwait	.16	
61	Mali	.16	
61	Paraguay	.16	
61	Rhodesia	.16	
61	Trinidad and Tobago	.16	
66.5	Afghanistan	.15	
66.5	Cyprus	.15	
66.5	Hungary	.15	
66.5	Poland	.15	
69.5	Belgium	.14	
69.5	Jordan	.14	
72.5	Brazil	.13	
72.5	Netherlands	.13	
72.5	Tunisia	.13	
72.5	Zambia	.13	1964
78.5	Austria	.12	
78.5	Guinea	.12	
78.5	Hong Kong	.12	
78.5	Iraq	.12	
78.5	Malaysia	.12	
78.5	Malta	.12	
78.5	Saudi Arabia	.12	
78.5	Uganda	.12	
84	Denmark	.11	
84	Ghana	.11	
84	Thailand	.11	
89	Ceylon	.10	
89	Finland	.10	

Table 6.6 Concentration of Export Receiving Countries—*Continued*

Rank	Country	C	Date
89	Iceland	.10	
89	India	.10	
89	Lebanon	.10	
89	Norway	.10	
89	Uruguay	.10	
98	Australia	.09	
98	Burma	.09	
98	Cambodia	.09	
98	Greece	.09	
98	Japan	.09	
98	Kenya	.09	
98	Portugal	.09	
98	Sweden	.09	
98	Syria	.09	
98	Tanzania	.09	
98	Turkey	.09	
106	Argentina	.08	
106	France	.08	
106	Italy	.08	
106	Spain	.08	
106	United Arab Republic	.08	
112.5	Iran	.07	
112.5	Israel	.07	
112.5	Soviet Union	.07	
112.5	Sudan	.07	
112.5	Switzerland	.07	
112.5	United States	.07	
112.5	West Germany	.07	
112.5	Yugoslavia	.07	
117	Pakistan	.06	
118	United Kingdom	.05	

Notes: Data are missing for Albania, Botswana, Burundi, China, Laos, Lesotho, Maldive Islands, Mongolia, Nepal, North Korea, North Viet Nam, Papua/New Guinea, Puerto Rico, Rwanda, Southern Yemen, and Yemen. Data for Belgium and Luxembourg are combined under Belgium; and Malaysia includes Singapore.

Date, unless otherwise noted, is 1965.

Source is International Monetary Fund and International Bank for Reconstruction and Development, *Direction of Trade: A Supplement to International Financial Statistics, 1961-1965* (Washington, 1966), supplemented by United Nations, Statistical Office, *Yearbook of International Trade Statistics, 1966* (New York, 1968). Original data are on the archive tape.

Table 6.7
Foreign Trade and Mail

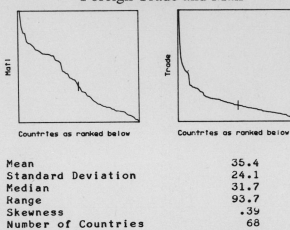

Countries as ranked below   Countries as ranked below

Mean	35.4
Standard Deviation	24.1
Median	31.7
Range	93.7
Skewness	.39
Number of Countries	68

Rank	Country	Foreign Mail as % of Total Mail	Date
1	Singapore	61.4	
2	Hong Kong	69.2	
3	Trinidad and Tobago		
4	Libya	81.7	
5	Gabon		
6	Barbados	65.0	
7	Liberia		
8	Saudi Arabia	57.3	
9	Zambia	51.2	
10	The Gambia		
11	Guyana		1963
12	Congo – Brazzaville		
13	Sierra Leone		
14	Rhodesia	38.8	
15.5	Angola	10.3	
15.5	Southern Yemen	76.7	
17	Malta	58.6	
18.5	Belgium	14.6	
18.5	Luxembourg	43.8	
20	Mauritius	38.3	
21	Netherlands	14.0	
22	Iraq	44.4	1964
23	Bulgaria		
24	Kuwait	95.4	
25	Algeria	14.0	
26	Malaysia		
27	Ireland	36.9	
28	Somalia		
29	Jamaica	58.1	
30	Mauritania		

46.9
33.9
38.7
232.4
2.36
124

Trade as % of G N P	Notes	System Type	Date
238.4		g	
169.5		g	
139.2		s	
127.5		g	
121.5	c	s	
116.5		g	
112.2		s	
110.2			
108.2	fob	g	
107.1		g	
101.5		s	
81.2	c	s	
80.5		g	
79.4	fob	g	
76.7		s	
76.2		g	
74.7		s	
74.7		s	
73.7		g	
72.6		s	
69.8		s	
67.5	fob	g	
67.2	fob	g	
66.5		s	1963
64.9		g	
59.2		g	
58.7	fob	s	
57.0		g	
56.4		s	1964

Table 6.7 Foreign Trade and Mail—*Continued*

Rank	Country	Foreign Mail as % of Total Mail	Date
31	Iceland	42.5	
32	Mozambique	67.6	
33	Nicaragua		
34.5	Ivory Coast	57.3	1964
34.5	Venezuela	62.5	
36.5	Cyprus	66.3	
36.5	Malawi	58.6	
38	Honduras		
39	Norway	15.8	
40	Cuba		
41	Lebanon	76.2	1964
42.5	Congo - Kinshasa		
42.5	Denmark	13.6	
44	El Salvador	62.1	
45	Costa Rica		
46	Switzerland	20.2	
47	Czechoslovakia		
48	Kenya		
49	Togo	67.9	
50	Panama		
51	Uganda		
52.5	Central African Republic		
52.5	Ceylon	6.5	
54	Cameroon		
55	Senegal		
56	Sweden	10.5	
57	Tanzania		
58	Portugal	30.1	
59	Hungary		
60	Malagasy Republic	59.0	
61	Austria	26.3	
62	New Zealand		
63	Guinea		
64	Tunisia		
65	Finland	14.9	
66	Bolivia		
67	Iran		
68	Jordan	52.7	1964
69	South Africa	16.6	
70	Taiwan	5.6	
71	Canada		
72	Thailand	23.3	
73.5	Morocco	53.8	1964
73.5	Syria	34.7	
75.5	Ghana	37.3	
75.5	Israel	27.0	
77	United Arab Republic	26.8	
78	Peru		
79	Romania		
80	Philippines		
81	West Germany	10.9	
82	Nigeria	22.2	
83	Sudan		

Trade as % of G N P	Notes	System Type	Date
56.1		s	
54.8		s	
54.5		g	
53.4		s	
53.4	fob	g	
53.0		g	
53.0	fob	g	
52.2	fob	s	
51.9		g	
51.7		s	
51.6		s	1964
51.0		s	
51.0		g	
49.1		s	
49.0		s	
48.0		s	
47.1	fob	g	
46.6	c	g	
46.2		s	
45.6	fob	s	
44.5	c	g	
44.3	c	s	
44.3		g	
43.4		s	
42.9		s	
42.3		g	
42.1	c	g	
40.2		s	
39.9		g	
39.8		s	
39.6		s	
39.4		g	
38.7		g	1964
38.6		s	
38.1		g	
37.9		s	
36.7		s	
36.0		s	
35.9		g	
35.7	b	s	
34.8	fob	g	
34.4		g	
33.8		s	
33.8		s	
33.5		g	
33.5		s	
32.7		s	
32.5		s	
32.2	fob	g	
32.1		g	
31.5		s	
31.4		g	
29.7		s	

Table 6.7 Foreign Trade and Mail—*Continued*

Rank	Country	Foreign Mail as % of Total Mail	Date
84	Guatemala		
85.5	Dahomey		
85.5	United Kingdom	8.5	
87	Ecuador		
88	Yugoslavia	10.9	
89	Burma	7.4	
90	Chile		1963
91	Ethiopia		
92	East Germany	10.8	
93	Italy	12.4	
94	Niger	58.8	
95	Cambodia		
96	Greece		
97	Chad		
98	Upper Volta		
99	Albania		
100	Paraguay	60.3	1964
101	Dominican Republic		
102	Rwanda		
103	Spain	19.0	
104.5	Haiti		
104.5	Uruguay		
106	France		
107	South Korea	7.2	
108	Poland		
109	Mali		
110.5	Japan	1.7	
110.5	Laos		
112	Colombia		1963
113	Indonesia	10.0	
114	South Viet Nam	42.0	
115	Afghanistan		
116	Argentina	18.1	
117	Australia	12.3	
118	Pakistan	23.5	1964
119	Mexico	31.7	
120	Brazil	53.2	
121	Turkey	16.7	
122	Soviet Union		
123	India	3.8	
124	United States	3.8	
125	China		

Notes: Data are missing for Botswana, Burundi, Lesotho, Maldive Islands, Mongolia, Nepal, North Korea, North Viet Nam, Papua/New Guinea, Puerto Rico, and Yemen.

Foreign mail is the sum of that sent and that received. Total mail includes domestic mail as well. See table 4.6.

Date for mail and trade, unless otherwise noted, is 1965.

Notes for trade are as follows:

b indicates imports or exports of foreign aid have been included.

c indicates trade with neighboring areas has been excluded (e.g. trade within former French Equatorial Africa).

e indicates estimated data.

fob indicates imports were reported F.O.B. rather than C.I.F. and were adjusted upwards by ten percent.

Trade as % of GNP	Notes	System Type	Date
29.5		g	
29.1		s	
29.1		m	
28.7	fob	g	
27.0		s	
26.9		g	
26.7		s	
26.3		g	
25.9	cfob	g	
25.5		s	
25.2		s	
25.1		s	
24.9		s	
24.6	c	s	
24.2		s	1964
24.0	e		1964
23.7	fob	m	
23.3	fob	g	
22.6		s	
22.5		s	
22.0		m	
22.0		s	
21.7		s	
21.0	b	s	
20.5	fob	g	
19.9		s	
19.7		g	
19.7		s	
19.5		s	
18.2		s	1964
16.3		s	
16.1	b	g	
15.7		s	
14.4	fob	g	
14.1		g	
13.9		g	
12.3		m	
11.8		s	
9.8	fob	g	
9.1		g	
7.3	fob	m	
6.0	c	m	

System type is coded:

G = general trade, which includes imports both directed for domestic consumption and for bonded warehouses or free zones and which includes both national exports and re-exports.

S = special trade, which includes imports directly for domestic consumption with withdrawals from bonded warehouses or free zones for domestic consumption and which considers exports to consist only of merchandise originating within the nation.

M = modified special trade, which considers imports to be general imports less all re-exports and exports to be exports of national produce.

Blank = system unknown.

Source for mail data is United Nations, Statistical Office, *Statistical Yearbook, 1966* (New York, 1967). For trade data, it is United Nations, Statistical Office, *Yearbook of International Trade Statistics, 1965* (New York, 1967). See table 5.4 for sources of GNP data.

7 A Note on Analysis

One hundred pages of the first edition of the *World Handbook* were devoted to suggestive, preliminary analyses and "fishing expeditions" into the data. The authors began with a long table of simple linear correlations designed to show the basic bivariate relationships among the data series. They continued with illustrations of "a variety of more complex analytical techniques as applied to some of the material" (p. 12). One of these categorized countries by level of development as measured by gross national product per capita and then showed the distributions of several social, economic, and political variables for the categories. Two other illustrations were of curvilinear and multiple regression and a third analyzed relationships within regions. A final chapter projected into the future those series for which the authors had growth rates.

Suggestive analyses of cross-national aggregate data are needed less in 1972 than they were in 1964. In the eight years that separates the publications of the two editions, there have been innumerable examples of both good and bad aggregate data analysis. Even in the mid-1960s, reviewers paid much less attention to the handbook's analytical illustrations than to its data collection.[1] As stated in the introduction to this edition, we have chosen to concentrate on the gathering, cleaning, and presentation of data in this volume. Our analyses are being published in the journals and elsewhere. Likewise, we have chosen not to give projections of series; we believe that future scores of countries on series are likely to be functions of more than past growth rates. The projection of series into the future is a research project in its own right,[2] but our data will be helpful in such an enterprise if other scholars wish to use them in that manner.

Our position on data summary is a bit more difficult. With the presentation of such a large dataset (and the archiving of an even larger one), it would appear no more than courteous to provide the reader with some kind of data reduction or other handle with which to manage the bulk. The custom of our field is to do so. But there are serious difficulties in providing the usual correlation matrix and/or factor analysis, even if one stays with the

We are thankful to Lutz Erbing for his exhaustive suggestions with the factor analysis in this chapter.

1. See Charles L. Taylor, "Further Problems: A Consideration of Other Views," *Aggregate Data Analysis: Political and Social Indicators in Cross-National Research,* ed. Charles Lewis Taylor (Paris: Mouton, 1968), pp. 115-38.
2. The authors of the first edition certainly agree. See, for example, Bruce M. Russett, "The Ecology of Future International Politics," *International Studies Quarterly,* 11 (1967): 12-31. See also the work of Kingsley Davis and his staff in *World Urbanization, 1950-1970; Volume I: Basic Data for Cities and Regions,* Population Monograph Series, no. 4 (Berkeley: Institute of International Studies, University of California, 1969).

modest claim that they give a quick summary of the internal structure of the dataset. These difficulties are not limited to the usual problems of missing data cells, the surfeit of series for the number of observations, or the competing solutions for the method.

First, of course, is the obvious point that since not all readers of the book will have the same purpose, they will not need the same summary. No one can deny that a summary is appropriate only if it summarizes that in which one is interested. If one wishes to use countries' scores on a factor in further analysis, for example, one will need to think carefully about which variables are to be allowed to load on the factor. Selecting concepts occurs *before* as well as after the analysis because what comes out is obviously dependent upon what goes in. Hence, factors found in cross-national data are not objective statements of the way in which the world is organized but are statements of the interlinear correlations among the particular series selected. We hope that each of our series will find useful service by some scholar, but we doubt that all or most of them can be profitably employed at one time by one scholar.

More important to the argument against including a correlation matrix and factor analysis of all the data is the point made by all elementary texts in statistics. We should look at the data that we are attempting to analyze since a linear correlation coefficient taken alone does not indicate the nature of the relationship between two variables; it may in fact cover up a functional relationship that is not linear or that is linear only after some appropriate transformation. The three scatterplots in figure 7.1 show sets of data for which the relationships between X and Y are widely divergent.

Figure 7.1a.

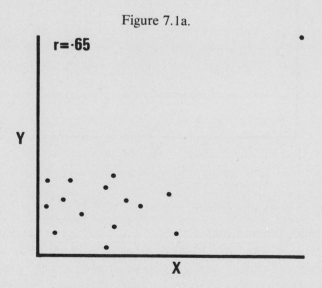

Figure 7.1b.

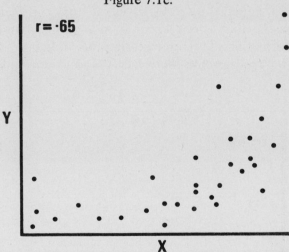

Figure 7.1c.

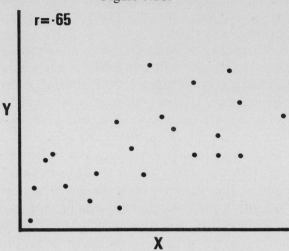

Edward Tufte, who prepared them, explains:

> The first plot shows no relationship, discounting the extreme outlier on both measures. The second plot suggests a moderately strong linear relationship between X and Y. The third plot reveals a rather marked curvilinear relationship between X and Y, indicating that as X increases, Y gets bigger even faster. Despite the great variation in the visual message,

the correlation between X and Y is the same in all three cases.[3]

Emphasis on correlation coefficients, to the exclusion of other techniques, may also lead to the ignoring of relationships that are not additive. An additive relationship, e.g.

$$Y = \alpha + \beta_1 X_1 + \beta_2 X_2 + \in$$

is one in which the effects of X_1 on Y are added to the effects of X_2 on Y. If the relationship between each of the predictor variables and Y is low, then the added effects cannot be high. In fact the total effect will be less than the summed effects because of overlapping explanation due to multicollinearity. In a non-additive relationship, on the other hand, the predictor variables may interact with each other in more complicated ways so that their combined effects may be greater than the sum of their individual effects. For example, linear correlations between the Xs and Y in figure 7.2 are not high. Y, a measure of proneness to coups d'état within states,[4] is correlated with GNP

Figure 7.2a. GNP Per Capita

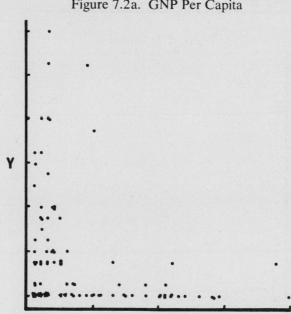

3. Edward R. Tufte, "Improving Data Analysis in Political Science," *World Politics,* 21 (1969): 641-54.

4. For definitions and measurements of the variables and for a fuller description of the model, see Charles L. Taylor, "Turmoil, Economic Development and Organized Political Opposition as Predictors of Irregular Government Change," Proceedings of the Annual Meeting of the American Political Science Association, 1970.

Figure 7.2b. Party Concentration

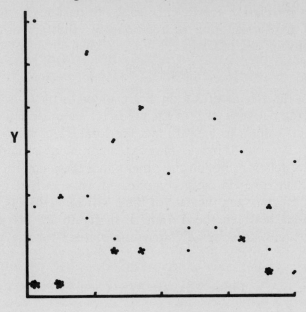

Figure 7.2c. Turmoil

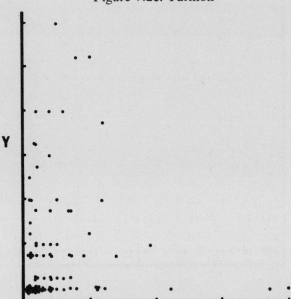

at about .3, with party concentration at about .2, and with turmoil at about
.04. The addition of these three predictors does not explain coup proneness
very well. Their plots, however, reveal triangular-shaped patterns which suggest the possibility of a multiplicative relationship. If the model

$$Y = \alpha X_1^\beta X_2^\gamma X_3^\upsilon \in$$

is fitted to the data, there is reasonably good fit. This equation is mathematically equivalent to an additive relationship among the logarithms of the variables, the constant and the error term and says that coup proneness is likely in countries which are poor *and* tumultuous *and* without organized political opposition, not in those for which only one or two of these conditions is true. (Imagine the Xs as being present or absent. In an additive relationship $1 + 1 + 0 = 2$; in a multiplicative one $1 \times 1 \times 0 = 0$).

About 15 percent of the data circa 1965 in our published collection are missing. In their correlation matrix, the authors of the first edition let the number of cases vary from cell to cell and noted the n as well as the r for each bivariate relationship. But knowing the number involved may not be so interesting as knowing the identity of the units included. Coefficients, regression as well as correlation, may be different depending upon the sample under consideration. A regional or random subsample may produce relationships quite unlike those produced by the whole set. Likewise, a subset produced by missing data can be dissimilar to the whole set in its interrelationships. Unless one looks at the countries for which data are missing and determines whether or not they have common elements that set them apart from the others, one cannot be sure of the results. This is very difficult to do with a large matrix that gives bivariate correlations (although our notes listing countries missing from the tables should be helpful here).

It is not so surprising, then, that John Tukey claims membership in an informal society for the suppression of correlation coefficients, a society whose "guiding principle is that most correlation coefficients should never be calculated."[5] He argues for the fitting of lines through data points; fitting, he says, is the "workhorse of data analysis." It is helpful in summarizing, exposing, and communicating. It provides a functional statement of the relationship among a set of variables and it measures the deviations from that relationship. These residuals are frequently of more interest than the values of the coefficients from the regression equation.[6] Francis Anscombe and John Tukey point out that residuals are important for two reasons: first we learn what they have to tell us of direct interest and second we learn how we might better specify our model. The examination of residuals after a first fitting may lead us to change the form of our model and possibly to add variables to it or transform variables already in it. Or it may lead us to discriminate among individual observations by rejecting outliers (i.e. observations that fall substantially away from the line of the relationship), assigning weights or replacing observed values by modified values.[7] This kind of analysis, of course, requires scatterplots and other

5. John W. Tukey, "Causation, Regression, and Path Analysis," *Statistics and Mathematics in Biology,* ed. Oscar Kempthorne (New York: Hafner, 1964), p. 38.

6. John T. Tukey and M. B. Wilk, "Data Analysis and Statistics: Techniques and Approaches," *The Quantitative Analysis of Social Problems,* ed. Edward R. Tufte (Reading, Mass.: Addison-Wesley, 1970), pp. 370-90.

7. Francis J. Anscombe and John T. Tukey, "The Examination and Analysis of Residuals," *Technometrics,* 5 (1963): 141-60.

displays. Plots of residuals will identify outliers and suggest the need for additional or transformed variables. Time series plots such as those in chapter 3 will demonstrate not only trends but fluctuations as well. Plots such as those in figures 7.1 and 7.2 tell us of relationships that could be made linear if we transform one or more of the variables.[8]

This kind of scrutiny is impossible with either correlation matrices or with factor analyses built upon them. Sensitive model building requires something more than summarization of data.[9] The usual argument for data reduction and summarization, however, is not that they end the process of analysis but that they begin it. Data reduction techniques give the first clues to the structure of the data. There may be some merit to this argument if all of the caveats mentioned earlier are kept in mind. We will therefore briefly report the results of such a summarization of our events data.

Several factor analyses have been done using cross-national events data. By 1967, Rudolph Rummel could list 38 examples of the method's use in conflict studies and international relations.[10] In some types of research it has become a kind of modal method. A great amount of research has been built upon the results of some factor analyses. For example, Rummel found in a study of domestic and foreign conflict data that his nine measures of domestic conflict for the years 1955-57 had three underlying dimensions, which he called turmoil, revolution, and subversion.[11] This study has been cited often and the dimensions have been used as the bases of several other studies.[12] Raymond Tanter replicated the study using the same measures for the years 1958-60. For the domestic conflict variables, he found only two factors, which he labelled turmoil and internal war.[13]

Tanter's results show that the structure of event data at two points in time need not be the same. A cross-sectional analysis can be expected to produce results that duplicate results of a cross-sectional analysis for another point in time if and only if all of the units of analysis have changed variable values at the same rates. If B is twice the size of A at one point in time and grows at

8. Probably one of the most comprehensive introductions to the problem of transformations available is G. E. P. Box and D. R. Cox, "An Analysis of Transformations," *Journal of the Royal Statistical Society,* 26 (1964): 211-43. Someday someone must translate it into a language that we political scientists can understand.

9. For a more complete presentation of this line of thought, see Charles L. Taylor, "The Uses of Statistics in Cross-National Aggregate Data Analysis," *Mathematical Applications in Political Science, VII,* ed. James F. Herndon (Charlottesville: University of Virginia Press, 1972).

10. Rudolph J. Rummel, "Understanding Factor Analysis," *The Journal of Conflict Resolution,* 11 (1967): 444-80, esp. 478-80.

11. Rudolph J. Rummel, "Dimensions of Conflict Behavior Within and Between Nations," *General Systems Yearbook,* 8 (1963): 1-50.

12. For example, see Jonathan Wilkenfeld, "Domestic and Foreign Conflict Behavior of Nations," *Journal of Peace Research,* 5 (1968): 55-69.

13. Raymond Tanter, "Dimensions of Conflict Behavior Within and Between Nations, 1958-1960," *Journal of Conflict Resolution,* 10 (1966): 41-64; and "Dimensions of Conflict Behavior Within Nations, 1955-1960: Turmoil and Internal War," *Peace Research Society: Papers,* 3 (1965), Peace Research Society (International) Chicago Conference, 1964.

twice the rate of A in the period before the second point in time, then B will be more than twice the size of A at the second point in time. Factor analyses on attribute data have tended to yield similar results only because they have included similar variables and because the rates of change for many economic, demographic, and other series are not sufficiently different among countries to have drastic effects over a short period of time.[14] Event data, on the other hand, are not expected to be so stable. Their aggregate levels may fluctuate widely; Hungary has been peaceful for most of the time since 1945, but 1956 was certainly an exception. One of the best predictors of gross national product or total population for a country in year t is that country's score on gross national product or population for year $t-1$, perhaps adjusted by some growth rate. The number of riots in a given country for a given year may not be so simply predicted.

We wished to minimize the effects of this instability over time. The way to do this is to look at within-time or cross-sectional variation.[15] Of course, it is impossible to exclude all longitudinal variation since time is a continuum and a true cross section must be taken at something less than a split second; compromises must be made. Among the smaller of these compromises would be single days or months, but this is impractical since in most countries on most days little of interest is happening; i.e. most cells are zero. Instead we chose the annual period as one long enough to contain a reasonable amount of cross-sectional variation in the number of events and short enough to disallow many time fluctuations.

First we produced regular factor analyses for each of the twenty years separately, These were rotated according to the varimax solution retaining all factors with eigenvalues equal to or greater than one. Now we had twenty separate sets of factors and their loadings, each of which described the event data structure for one year without contamination by between-year variation. We wished, however, a single matrix that would give us some kind of average factor loadings for the whole period. What we needed were factors derived from a matrix that stated the interrelationships among the variables over all of the factors for all of the within-year analyses. To get this, we

14. See Jack Sawyer, "Dimensions of Nations: Size, Wealth and Politics," *American Journal of Sociology,* 73 (1967): 145-72; Bruce M. Russett, *International Regions and the International System: A Study in Political Ecology* (Chicago: Rand McNally, 1967), pp. 14-35; Jun-ichi Kyogoku and Hiroko Inoue, "Multi-Dimensional Scaling of Nations," *Aggregate Data Analysis: Political and Social Indicators in Cross-National Research,* ed. Charles Lewis Taylor (Paris: Mouton, 1968), pp. 165-92; Brian J. L. Berry, "An Inductive Approach to the Regionalization of Economic Development," *Essays on Geography and Economic Development,* ed. Norton Ginsburg (Chicago: University of Chicago Press, 1960), pp. 78-107; and Irma Adelman and Cynthia Taft Morris, *Society, Politics and Economic Development: A Quantitative Approach* (Baltimore: Johns Hopkins Press, 1967).

15. Hayward Alker, using the covariance theorem, puts this problem into the context of inferential fallacies (see Hayward R. Alker, Jr., "A Typology of Ecological Fallacies," *Quantitative Ecological Analysis in the Social Sciences,* ed. Mattei Dogan and Stein Rokkan [Cambridge, Mass.: M.I.T. Press, 1969], pp. 69-86).

hooked together the twenty separate factor matrices to form a giant one of 18 variables (see below) by 112 factors (i.e. the six obtained for 1948 plus the five, for 1949 . . . plus the five, for 1967). This new matrix of within-year factor loadings was multiplied by its transpose to get AA', an 18 x 18 matrix containing the scalar products (and squared lengths in the diagonal) of the eighteen vectors in the assumed 112 dimensional space. This is the usual means for obtaining the covariance matrix (and the correlation matrix if the variables have been normalized). The factors derived from this matrix are reported in tables 7.1 and 7.2. We rotated four, five, and six factors and found four gave the most interpretable results.

Before discussing these interpretations, however, we must be more specific about the original input to the analysis. We included all of the eighteen event series in our collection, the names of which are included in tables 7.1 and 7.2.[16] The list of input series is not the same as Rummel's and Tanter's; it is more like that of Ivo and Rosalind Feierabend's conflict and governmental change study.[17] Our results can be compared only indirectly with all of these studies, however.

All of the series were transformed to the form log (X+1). Logarithms of events are better than numbers of events for giving emphasis to the middle range of values and we did not wish the middle variation to be outweighed by the extreme values. (One is added to the original value simply because there is no logarithm of zero but there are frequently events of zero. Of several solutions to the problem, this one best preserves the original variation). We explicitly reject another reason that has been given for this transformation. There is neither possibility nor need to create normal distributions. Event data are not drawn from some underlying normal distribution; the large number of nil events in the table of chapter 3 show these to be distributions of rare events. If anything, they appear to follow a Poisson distribution.[18] Taking logarithms probably does not create normality and certainly does not create multivariate normality, the characteristic actually assumed in the tests of significance.[19] However, since our purpose is to summarize and to expose what is before us rather than to draw inferences to what is not, this restriction should cause no difficulty.

16. Definitions of the series not included in chapter 3 are to be found in the event data codebooks available from the Inter-University Consortium for Political Research (see appendix 3).

17. Ivo K. Feierabend and Rosalind L. Feierabend, "Aggressive Behaviors Within Polities, 1948-1962: A Cross-National Study," *The Journal of Conflict Resolution*, 10 (1966): 249-71.

18. R. Feron, "Simeon Dénis Poisson," *International Encyclopedia of the Social Sciences*, vol. 12 (1968), pp. 169-72.

19. Carl-Gunnar Janson, "Some Problems of Ecological Factor Analysis," *Quantitative Ecological Analysis in the Social Sciences*, ed. Mattei Dogan and Stein Rokkan (Cambridge, Mass.: M.I.T. Press, 1969), pp. 301-41, esp. p. 332. A standard work on factor analysis is Harry H. Harman, *Modern Factor Analysis* (Chicago: University of Chicago Press, 1960). One that is frequently cited in political science is Rudolph J. Rummel, *Applied Factor Analysis* (Evanston, Ill.: Northwestern University Press, 1970). A short introduction by A. I. Maxwell can be found in the *International Encyclopedia for the Social Sciences*, vol. 5 (1968), pp. 275-81.

Table 7.1 gives the unrotated factor loadings from the analysis of the scalar product matrix along with the communalities and eigenvalues. Table 7.2 identifies the four rotated factors from the same analysis along with the contribution of each to the total communality. No eigenvalue, i.e. the measure of the amount of variation accounted for by a factor, is as high as 1.0, the cut-off often used for factors to be rotated. The communalities, i.e. the proportion of variation of each variable involved in the patterns identified, are all low. The factor loadings, i.e. the measures of a variable's involvement in a factor pattern, are remarkably low as compared with those in ordinary factor analysis (including the original twenty annual analyses of this study). What is important, however, is their relative, not their absolute values.

The factor loadings describe two planes, more or less, with two factors in each. The first might be called the plane of mass activity and the second the plane of the governmental arena. In the first are two factors that concern efforts by persons outside government to have influence on the direction of policy or other political phenomena. The distinction between the two factors in this plane is that of the presence or absence of violence, perhaps, except that riots fits somewhere between the two. An alternative is to label the factor with relatively larger loadings for riots, deaths, assassinations, armed attacks, and elections, the *political violence* dimension, and to name the factor with heavier loadings for riots, protest demonstrations, pro-government demonstrations, political strikes, and renewals of executive power, the *political protest* dimension. These distinctions reflect the definitional discussions of chapter 3. It is not clear why elections and renewals should load highly on these factors. If rotations are allowed more factors, elections becomes a unique factor. These might be left out in future analyses.

The plane of the governmental arena also contains two factors that appear to be gathering areas for vectors that more or less spread out in a fan from adjustment to repression, or from governments able to keep themselves in power by effective control of change through governments of more desperation to governments whose repression has failed and for which instability has set in. The factor with relatively high loadings for executive adjustments, regular executive transfers, executions, sanctions, relaxations of sanctions, and interventions has been labelled the *government controls and adjustment* dimension. We have named the factor with heavier loadings for unsuccessful attempts at regular executive transfer, unsuccessful attempts at irregular executive transfer, and successful irregular executive transfers the *governmental instability* dimension. Again these are more or less to be expected from the definitions in chapter 3.

The results of the factor analysis do not take us much farther than the discussions in chapter 3. Certainly, we must emphasize that these are not the objective dimensions of political stability. Other variables, different rota-

Table 7.1

The Factor Matrix, Communality Estimates, and Eigenvalues for Average Within-Year Scalar Products of the Event Data

Variable	1	2	3	4	Final Communality Estimates
Riots	0.300	−0.097	−0.010	−0.041	0.102
Deaths from political violence	0.301	−0.129	−0.197	0.012	0.145
Assassinations	0.207	−0.133	−0.230	−0.007	0.114
Armed attacks	0.289	−0.075	−0.118	0.015	0.105
Elections	0.255	−0.076	−0.161	−0.176	0.126
Protest demonstrations	0.250	−0.027	0.225	−0.108	0.125
Pro-government demonstrations	0.287	−0.028	0.180	−0.001	0.116
Political strikes	0.236	−0.065	0.166	−0.057	0.092
Renewals of executive tenure	0.169	−0.158	0.109	−0.154	0.089
Unsuccessful attempts at regular executive transfer	0.139	0.197	0.003	−0.228	0.111
Unsuccessful attempts at irregular executive transfer	0.117	0.264	−0.039	−0.182	0.118
Irregular executive transfers	0.164	0.249	−0.053	−0.032	0.093
Executive adjustments	0.160	0.130	−0.014	0.104	0.054
Regular executive transfers	0.231	0.103	0.042	0.139	0.086
Executions for political crimes	0.182	0.132	−0.055	0.050	0.057
Governmental sanctions	0.191	0.160	−0.062	0.145	0.089
Relaxations of governmental restrictions and amnesties	0.301	−0.052	0.077	0.170	0.128
External interventions	0.290	0.038	0.082	0.134	0.110
Eigenvalues	0.988	0.333	0.282	0.260	1.862

Table 7.2

Varimax Rotated Factor Matrix on Average Within-Year Scalar Products
of the Event Data

Variable	Political Protests	Political Violence	Government Controls and Adjustments	Governmental Instability
Riots	0.205	0.224	0.092	-0.023
Deaths from political violence	0.067	0.358	0.114	0.011
Assassinations	-0.002	0.333	0.045	0.016
Armed attacks	0.100	0.273	0.135	-0.012
Elections	0.101	0.314	-0.014	-0.137
Protest demonstrations	0.342	0.012	0.053	-0.077
Pro-government demonstrations	0.303	0.048	0.146	-0.019
Political strikes	0.289	0.054	0.061	-0.021
Renewals of executive tenure	0.263	0.111	-0.085	-0.013
Unsuccessful attempts at regular executive transfer	0.085	0.024	0.016	-0.319
Unsuccessful attempts at irregular executive transfer	0.009	0.006	0.066	-0.337
Irregular executive transfers	-0.009	0.026	0.187	-0.239
Executive adjustments	0.015	0.027	0.222	-0.058
Regular executive transfers	0.095	0.034	0.273	-0.023
Executions for political crimes	0.012	0.075	0.198	-0.105
Governmental sanctions	-0.021	0.058	0.281	-0.065
Relaxations of governmental restrictions and amnesties	0.198	0.112	0.259	0.096
External interventions	0.178	0.068	0.272	0.010
Contribution of factors to total communality	27.8%	27.5%	27.0%	17.7%

tions, more or fewer factors could all have caused the outcome to be different. Every one of the annual analyses was different. *Perhaps, after all, starting out with plots, fittings, and a question gets one just about as far just about as fast.*

Tukey and Wilk write that data have "typically been easier to gather than to analyze. . . . Despite the gains in computation and display—perhaps because of them—this is increasingly true. . . . As in the past, much, perhaps most, of even carefully collected data will not be adequately analyzed."[20] This will possibly be the fate of the handbook data; we hope not. No doubt a lot of mindless work, whether under the guise of barefoot empiricism or of theory building, will go on with these data. We apologize in advance for our responsibility in the results. At the same time, however, we would modestly be willing to take some credit for work well done.

20. Tukey and Wilk, "Data Analysis and Statistics," p. 371.

Appendix 1   The Collection of Political Event Data

Data reported in chapter 3 are part of a dataset whose series were defined, counted, and organized within the World Data Analysis Program. It is incumbent upon us, therefore, to be very specific as to how they came into being. The theory behind and definitions for the 10 series published in this book are given in chapter 3. Definitions for all 18 series are included in the codebook accompanying the dataset available through the Inter-University Consortium for Political Research. Nevertheless, scholars who use the data will also need to know about the training and reliability of coders, the methods by which data from multiple sources were merged into single series, and the contributions of various sources that we used.

The Training and Selection of Coders

Operational definitions for the series achieved final form in cooperative coding among Michael Hudson, Katherine Dolan, and Shirley Schiff. These coders independently applied a set of *a priori* definitions to selected countries for selected years and noted coding difficulties. They met frequently to compare results, check discrepancies, amend definitions, and make coding rules more explicit.

Other coders were added to the project after the definitions were closed to further modification. All but one of these new coders were trained by Katherine Dolan. Insofar as possible, they were assigned to geographical areas to which they had had some previous academic exposure. Each was instructed to become completely familiar with the definitions and to read the relevant history and government sections of the *Worldmark Encyclopedia.* Then each tried sample country-years from the *New York Times Index.* (The use of a single source for the first test allowed direct comparison of a coder's work without adding the complication of varying difficulty among sources for coding.) The new coders kept remark sheets and discussed initial coding problems with the coder training them. Once questions of interpretation had been resolved, the new coders and the training coder tried sample country-years and compared results. The new coders were also tested on sample country-years that other coders had tried earlier, allowing a comparison of several coders in the same sample.

The initial efforts of the new coders almost always were insufficiently accurate. These were not used as a test of coder reliability. Only after the second or third sample run, when misunderstandings had been largely eliminated, were their test results included in the analysis sample. In cases where a coder worked over a long period of time, sample checks were run periodically to assure that he did not develop an implicit understanding of the definitions that differed from the explicit one. One of these checks for

The primary drafts for this appendix were written by Katherine H. Dolan and Edwin C. Dolan.

the one coder who worked from beginning to end is reported as the comparison between coder 0 and coder 1 in tables A.2 and A.3.

Although 13 coders were tested at various stages of the project, only the work of 8 was actually used in this collection. Each of these 8 had a social science background and was familiar with and receptive to the idea of quantitative research. This kind of attitude did seem to have some importance in the success of the coding effort; some intelligent people are simply untrainable as coders. Two other factors proved to be important. Perceptions of events are affected by one's ideological-political position. Most of our coders happened to be of a liberal to radical bent. The one conservative coder was far out of line. (See coder 9 in tables A.2 and A.3.) His work was subsequently recoded. Although ideological dissimilarity was not solely responsible for his larger variances, his high reporting of irregular relative to regular executive transfers, his extremely low reporting of governmental security sanctions relative to that of other coders, and his high reporting of armed attack events can probably be attributed more to his politics than to carelessness or misunderstanding of the definitions. We do not feel conservatives should refrain from using the data; comparability was enhanced for them as well. Secondly, although intelligence was a prerequisite for successful coding, unlimited creativity was a liability, except during the period when the definitions were still open to modification. One had to be able to make distinctions written into the definitions but be disciplined enough to follow what others had specified. Periodic checks helped to ensure that no coder drifted away from the original definitions toward ones he thought to be superior. (This was no small task.)

Intercoder Reliability

The adherence by these coders to the written definitions was estimated by comparing samples of their work. Coders' scores tended to cluster around a mean, yielding a less biased overall account of the events. By looking at the distribution of scores around this mean, variables can be compared on the basis of how well the coders agreed on what was being measured and the coders' reliability can be measured relative to their colleagues.

The selection of country-years for comparison was deliberately not random because such a sample would not have been well suited either for training the coders or for comparing their results efficiently. The eventful country-years, those in which more than one-half of the 18 variables could be scored even once, were a small percentage of the total number of country-years coded. Had they been chosen at random it would have taken longer to expose the coder to the kinds of situations he would encounter for all the variables and overall accuracy would have required rechecking a much larger proportion of his work. At the other extreme, a random sampling procedure would have left open the possibility that some of the country-years that were very eventful and that took an inordinately long time to code would have been selected. To attempt to code such country-years as part of a sample would have discouraged the coder and would have consumed a great deal of time. We needed a group of middle-range country-years, active enough to provide examples of different kinds of events, difficult enough to assess the coder's competence, and short enough to make them feasible to code.

In order to analyze the results of the coder comparison, it was necessary to have a large number of events for each variable on which to compare coders and yet to spend only a relatively small amount of time in the comparative sampling. Thus, it should be kept in mind that the tables do not represent the biases and variances for average years; they are for periods of more than a normal number of events. If anything, the results for average years would have produced less bias and variance than those presented here since agreement on nonexistent events is easy.

Data were collected on sample country-years for pairs and groups of coders. An array X was set up in which each element x_{ikl} denoted the number of events coded by the ith coder for the kth variable and the lth country-year. From these data, as an intermediate step in the calculations, an array of Y of "normalized" scores was derived composed of all possible elements of the form[1]

$$y_{ijkl} = \frac{2x_{ikl}}{x_{ikl} + x_{jkl}}$$

That is, for every pair of x's representing the attempt of two different coders to code the same variable k for the same country-year l a pair of normalized scores was computed with y_{ijkl} representing the ratio of the number of events coded by the ith coder for that country-year to the mean of the number of events coded by the ith and jth coders; y_{jikl} represents the ratio of the number of events coded by j to that mean.

Based on the normalized scores, four kinds of reliability tests can be performed on any subset of the data that is of interest:

(1) the unweighted bias,

$$b_S = \left(\sum_S y_{ijkl}/N\right) - 1$$

where $\sum_S$ signifies the sum taken over all elements in S, and N is the number of elements in S.

(2) the weighted bias,

$$B_S = \left(\sum_S w_{ijkl} y_{ijkl} / \sum_S w_{ijkl}\right) - 1$$

---

1. Observations where both x_{ikl} and x_{jkl} were zero, i.e. where coders agreed that no event occurred, were not included in the sample on the assumption that such agreement is a trivial accomplishment. This agreement most likely is a direct result of no pertinent information in the source.

where

$$w_{ijkl} = \left(x_{ikl} + x_{jkl}\right)/2$$

(3) the unweighted variance,

$$v_S = \sum_S \left(y_{ijkl} - b_S + 1\right)^2/N$$

(4) and the weighted variance,

$$V_S = \sum_S w_{ijkl} \left(y_{ijkl} - B_S + 1\right)^2 / \sum_S w_{ijkl}$$

It is possible, for example, to compare the performance of coders *3* and *5* over all variables by extracting from Y the set $S_{3,5}$ containing all the y_{ijkl} for which i = 3 and j = 5. The unweighted bias b for coder *3* relative to coder *5* is −0.06. This may be interpreted as implying that for a country-year selected at random without regard for the density of events·in that year, coder *3* would be expected to record 6 percent fewer events than coder *5*. The weighted bias for this pairwise combination is 0.025. Since weighting is done by the mean recorded number of events for each country-year, this indicates that the total number of events recorded by coder *3* over a number of country-years would average only 2.5 percent below the total of coder *5*. This weighted bias is the relevant one for considerations of comparability of data on total events occurring in countries coded by different coders. In this case, it is less than the unweighted bias presumably because discrepancies between the two coders tended to be smaller in percentage terms for relatively active country-years.

The same bias tests can be done for two or more coders on individual variables. Figures for coders' weighted biases and variances variable by variable and over all variables are given in tables A.2 and A.3.

Interpretation of the variances is not quite so straightforward as for the biases. The primary interest in the variances is in how much they differ from coder to coder rather than in their exact numerical value. For example, running a test of coder *2* against coder *1* produced a weighted variance (V) of 0.03 over all variables, whereas coder *8* against coder *1* gave a V of 0.10. This would suggest that coder *8* was much more erratic and less consistent in his scoring in relation to coder *1* than was the case for coder *2*. Even though coder *8* has a small relative bias (*0.035*) the data he coded would be somewhat less reliable for comparative analysis because it would contain a higher noise component, the result of less complete internalization of definitions or more careless coding practices. (Coder *1* coded more than one-half of all the country-years and of all the events. For interest in consistency, therefore, it is especially important to know how coders compared with coder *1*.)

A further use of variance scores is for the comparison of variables. A subset S_8 or S_{13} containing all the y_{ijkl} in Y where k = variable 8 and variable 13 respectively can be selected so as to include all the coders' scores. Although the biases computed from such a set would have no meaning, being always equal to one, the variances are of interest. For example, $V_8 = 0.239$ and $V_{13} = 0.438$; this suggests that the definition for variable 8 was either more operational or easier to internalize so that scoring was more accurate for this variable than for variable 13.

Tabular presentation here is limited to a small proportion of the tables generated. Table A.1 compares the 18 variables in terms of the relative consistency of their coding. Reported are the unweighted variance scores calculated from each pair of coders' scores for each variable.

Table A.1

Unweighted Variances for Eighteen Series for All Coders
(Excluding Zero Cells)

		Variance	Sample Size**
5.	Elections	0.081	52
*12.	Irregular executive transfers	0.107	38
* 2.	Deaths from political violence	0.117	152
*16.	Governmental sanctions	0.156	236
* 9.	Renewals of executive tenure	0.170	76
17.	Relaxation of restrictions	0.233	162
8.	Political strikes	0.238	76
* 4.	Armed attacks	0.239	162
*13.	Executive adjustments	0.267	140
* 1.	Riots	0.292	114
*14.	Regular executive transfers	0.314	110
3.	Assassinations	0.389	36
* 6.	Protest demonstrations	0.438	98
15.	Executions for political crimes	0.500	20
10.	Unsuccessful attempts at regular power transfer	0.503	34
11.	Unsuccessful attempts at irregular power transfer	0.656	40
*18.	External interventions	0.681	56
7.	Pro-government demonstrations	0.740	74

*Included in this book.
**Number of events, non-zero agreement.

Data for variables 12, 14, and 18 are included to compare their relative difficulty of operationalization and not as a statement of their final quality. The first two were hand merged (see the section on source merging in this appendix) and many of the difficulties were thereby eliminated. The third was the object of more extensive collection, which is described in chapter 3.

A more detailed picture can be gained by examining the weighted variances and the weighted mean biases of each variable as scored by representative coders. Table A.2 gives the figures for the variances; table A.3, for the biases.

Table A.2

Weighted Variances for Pairs of Coders and Groups that Coded against Each Other

Series**	Coder 0 vs Coder 1	Coder 1 vs Coder 2	Coder 1 vs Coder 3	Coder 1 vs Coder 4	Coder 1 vs Coder 5	Coder 1 vs Coder 6	Coder 1 vs Coder 7	Coder 1 vs Coder 8	Coder 2 vs Coder 3
1	0.101	0.058	0.039	0.062	0.049	0.000	0.056	0.035	0.085
2	0.000	0.011	0.025	0.025	0.011	0.000	0.002	0.082	0.014
3	0.022	0.245	0.000	0.000	0.245	0.000	0.000	0.000	0.000
4	0.125	0.021	0.022	0.049	0.039	0.000	0.011	0.088	0.044
5	0.000	0.000	0.000	0.122	0.000	0.000	0.000	0.000	0.000
6	0.044	0.078	0.190	0.427	0.083	0.000	0.000	0.085	0.364
7	0.292	0.484	0.187	0.122	0.222	0.000	0.000	0.104	0.186
8	0.029	0.051	0.048	0.083	0.034	0.000	0.095	0.010	0.093
9	0.052	0.000	0.122	0.000	0.020	0.000	0.000	0.085	0.000
10	0.143	0.028	0.222	0.000	0.427	0.000	0.000	0.240	0.107
11	0.027	0.250	0.250	0.000	0.000	0.000	0.000	0.000	0.313
12	0.025	0.222	0.245	0.000	0.000	0.000	0.005	0.000	0.010
13	0.050	0.065	0.077	0.108	0.236	0.000	0.000	0.173	0.033
14	0.054	0.074	0.074	0.400	0.000	0.000	0.000	0.071	0.055
15	0.000	0.116	0.000	0.000	0.000	0.000	0.000	0.000	0.000
16	0.013	0.103	0.027	0.193	0.061	0.046	0.002	0.036	0.018
17	0.067	0.086	0.032	0.033	0.043	0.148	0.004	0.360	0.016
18	0.089	0.040	0.160	0.000	0.251	0.000	0.000	0.000	0.160
all	0.013	0.030	0.064	0.156	0.040	0.063	0.021	0.095	0.068

Table A.2—Continued

Series**	Coder 2 vs Coder 5	Coder 3 vs Coder 5	Coder 3 vs Coder 7	Coder 4 vs Coder 8	Coder 5 vs Coder 7	Coder 5 vs Coder 8	Coder 6 vs Coder 8	Coder 7 vs Coder 8	Coder 1 vs all others*
1	0.346	0.027	0.000	0.059	0.037	0.000	0.000	0.000	0.082
2	0.000	0.010	0.000	0.018	0.000	0.001	0.000	0.000	0.032
3	0.000	0.000	0.222	0.000	0.222	0.000	0.000	0.000	0.373
4	0.066	0.018	0.049	0.154	0.000	0.059	0.000	0.000	0.056
5	0.000	0.000	0.000	0.000	0.000	0.083	0.000	0.000	0.031
6	0.278	0.000	0.000	0.182	0.000	0.000	0.000	0.000	0.141
7	0.000	0.000	0.750	0.240	0.000	0.000	0.000	0.000	0.545
8	0.073	0.000	0.000	0.111	0.067	0.000	0.000	0.000	0.111
9	0.027	0.027	0.000	0.250	0.000	0.000	0.000	0.000	0.057
10	0.107	0.000	0.000	0.000	0.000	0.000	0.000	0.000	0.266
11	0.000	0.000	0.000	0.000	0.000	0.000	0.000	0.000	0.204
12	0.000	0.000	0.000	0.000	0.000	0.000	0.000	0.000	0.208
13	0.130	0.109	0.038	0.110	0.071	0.054	0.000	0.000	0.110
14	0.027	0.000	0.071	0.146	0.000	0.667	0.000	0.000	0.099
15	0.000	0.000	0.000	0.000	0.000	0.000	0.000	0.000	0.361
16	0.073	0.049	0.026	0.095	0.080	0.066	0.056	0.000	0.082
17	0.079	0.005	0.084	0.333	0.000	0.265	0.000	0.000	0.076
18	0.172	0.000	0.000	0.432	0.000	0.000	0.000	0.000	0.291
all	0.055	0.028	0.017	0.076	0.081	0.114	0.165	0.174	0.055

Table A.2—Continued

Series**	Coder 2 vs all others*	Coder 3 vs all others*	Coder 4 vs all others*	Coder 5 vs all others*	Coder 6 vs all others*	Coder 7 vs all others*	Coder 8 vs all others*	Coder 9 vs all others*
1	0.091	0.069	0.197	0.120	0.027	0.049	0.061	0.000
2	0.027	0.025	0.029	0.007	0.000	0.002	0.020	0.003
3	0.250	0.222	0.000	0.222	0.000	0.200	0.000	0.000
4	0.043	0.037	0.227	0.063	0.048	0.046	0.160	0.039
5	0.000	0.000	0.099	0.083	0.000	0.000	0.083	0.000
6	0.196	0.252	0.219	0.246	0.000	0.005	0.112	1.000
7	0.378	0.233	0.166	0.413	0.000	1.000	0.292	0.000
8	0.125	0.068	0.267	0.111	0.000	0.094	0.022	0.000
9	0.020	0.067	0.188	0.059	0.000	0.000	0.142	0.000
10	0.110	0.370	0.000	0.309	0.000	0.000	0.222	0.000
11	0.521	0.224	0.000	0.130	0.000	0.000	0.000	0.222
12	0.126	0.120	0.000	0.000	0.000	0.000	0.000	0.000
13	0.068	0.068	0.115	0.160	0.222	0.033	0.113	0.116
14	0.074	0.083	0.259	0.180	0.000	0.039	0.269	0.111
15	0.116	0.000	0.045	0.000	0.000	0.000	0.005	0.000
16	0.087	0.027	0.137	0.080	0.053	0.068	0.104	0.024
17	0.069	0.037	0.242	0.057	0.138	0.041	0.340	0.104
18	0.125	0.166	0.361	0.222	0.000	0.889	0.380	0.000
all	0.045	0.062	0.085	0.047	0.075	0.027	0.088	0.624

*"All others" refers to those against whom a pairwise test was run; except for coder 1, it does not include everyone else.

**For series names, see table A.1.

Table A.3

Weighted Biases for Pairs of Coders and Groups that Coded against Each Other

Series**	Coder 0 vs Coder 1	Coder 1 vs Coder 2	Coder 1 vs Coder 3	Coder 1 vs Coder 4	Coder 1 vs Coder 5	Coder 1 vs Coder 6	Coder 1 vs Coder 7	Coder 1 vs Coder 8	Coder 2 vs Coder 3
1	−0.056	−0.135	0.083	−0.575	0.025	0.333	−0.017	−0.127	0.306
2	0.007	−0.074	−0.289	0.095	−0.009	0.000	−0.021	−0.000	−0.197
3	−0.091	0.571	0.000	0.000	−0.429	0.000	0.000	0.000	0.000
4	0.149	0.084	−0.016	0.708	−0.180	−0.048	−0.011	−0.347	0.039
5	0.000	0.000	0.000	−0.143	0.000	0.000	0.000	0.000	0.000
6	−0.032	−0.136	−0.162	−0.200	0.500	0.000	0.000	−0.169	0.211
7	−0.500	−0.111	−0.692	−0.857	0.333	0.000	−1.000	0.500	−0.448
8	−0.009	−0.176	0.064	−0.500	0.103	0.000	0.556	−0.303	−0.200
9	0.016	0.000	−0.143	0.000	−0.077	0.000	0.000	−0.103	0.000
10	0.125	−0.167	0.333	0.000	0.200	0.000	0.000	0.500	0.800
11	0.143	−0.500	−0.500	0.000	−1.000	0.000	0.000	0.000	−0.143
12	−0.111	−0.333	−0.429	0.000	0.000	0.000	0.000	0.000	−0.111
13	−0.098	−0.103	−0.063	0.030	0.048	−1.000	−0.048	0.111	0.118
14	0.000	0.071	−0.083	0.000	0.000	0.000	0.000	0.077	−0.300
15	0.000	0.133	0.000	−1.000	0.000	−1.000	0.000	1.000	0.000
16	−0.025	0.045	0.102	−0.041	−0.171	0.075	0.179	−0.111	0.151
17	0.106	0.053	−0.049	−0.053	0.000	0.333	0.034	−0.200	−0.000
18	0.333	−0.300	0.200	−1.000	−0.263	0.000	1.000	0.000	0.385
all	−0.013	−0.025	−0.107	−0.119	−0.072	−0.025	0.071	−0.035	0.017

Table A.3—Continued

Series**	Coder 2 vs Coder 5	Coder 3 vs Coder 5	Coder 3 vs Coder 7	Coder 4 vs Coder 8	Coder 5 vs Coder 7	Coder 5 vs Coder 8	Coder 6 vs Coder 8	Coder 7 vs Coder 8	Coder 1 vs all others*
1	0.333	-0.200	-0.286	-0.333	0.017	-0.818	0.000	0.000	-0.104
2	0.021	0.009	0.046	0.116	-0.038	0.077	0.000	0.000	-0.120
3	0.000	0.000	-0.333	0.000	0.333	0.000	0.000	0.000	0.185
4	-0.311	-0.081	0.244	0.085	-1.000	-0.079	-1.000	-1.000	0.009
5	0.000	0.000	0.000	0.000	0.000	-0.500	0.000	0.000	-0.032
6	0.667	-1.000	0.176	0.000	0.000	0.000	0.000	0.000	-0.122
7	-1.000	1.000	0.500	-0.143	-1.000	0.000	1.000	0.000	-0.244
8	-0.429	0.111	0.000	0.000	0.457	0.000	0.000	0.000	-0.050
9	-0.200	-0.200	0.000	-0.333	0.000	-1.000	0.000	0.000	-0.077
10	0.500	1.000	0.000	0.500	0.000	0.000	0.000	0.000	0.120
11	-1.000	0.000	0.000	1.000	0.000	0.000	0.000	0.000	-0.714
12	0.000	0.000	0.000	-1.000	0.000	0.000	0.000	0.000	-0.294
13	0.053	-0.125	0.000	0.133	-0.077	0.429	0.000	0.000	-0.027
14	-0.200	0.333	-0.091	-0.462	0.000	0.000	0.000	0.000	0.011
15	0.000	0.000	0.000	0.000	0.000	0.000	0.000	0.000	-0.143
16	-0.188	-0.065	-0.094	-0.183	0.333	-0.138	-0.333	0.059	-0.017
17	-0.294	-0.077	-0.200	-0.200	0.034	0.143	0.000	-1.000	0.000
18	0.200	-0.400	1.000	0.222	0.000	0.333	0.000	1.000	-0.391
all	-0.102	-0.025	0.046	-0.054	0.041	-0.058	-0.083	-0.157	-0.073

Table A.3—Continued

Series**	Coder 2 vs all others*	Coder 3 vs all others*	Coder 4 vs all others*	Coder 5 vs all others*	Coder 6 vs all others*	Coder 7 vs all others*	Coder 8 vs all others*	Coder 9 vs all others*
1	0.215	-0.190	0.388	-0.087	-0.200	0.030	0.181	0.000
2	-0.042	0.205	0.056	-0.005	0.000	-0.012	-0.111	-0.993
3	-0.500	-0.333	0.000	0.333	0.000	0.000	0.000	1.000
4	-0.080	-0.008	-0.055	0.168	0.000	-0.039	0.062	0.227
5	0.000	0.000	0.111	-0.167	0.000	0.000	0.167	0.000
6	0.203	0.048	-0.108	-0.351	0.000	-0.143	0.140	0.000
7	-0.250	0.500	0.789	-0.636	1.000	0.000	-0.533	0.000
8	-0.091	0.026	0.000	0.097	0.000	-0.480	0.289	0.000
9	-0.077	-0.000	0.250	0.062	0.000	0.000	0.050	-1.000
10	0.354	-0.333	1.000	-0.455	0.000	0.000	-0.567	0.000
11	-0.250	0.176	-1.000	0.845	0.000	0.000	1.000	0.333
12	0.059	0.200	0.000	0.000	0.000	0.000	0.000	1.000
13	0.098	-0.042	0.075	0.026	0.333	0.042	-0.146	0.231
14	-0.170	0.148	-0.333	-0.029	0.000	0.048	0.224	-0.667
15	-0.133	0.000	0.048	0.000	1.000	0.000	-0.006	0.000
16	-0.013	-0.114	-0.114	0.144	-0.101	-0.123	0.125	-0.365
17	-0.059	-0.008	-0.111	0.067	-0.273	-0.000	0.167	-0.357
18	0.283	-0.294	0.622	0.115	0.000	-0.333	-0.273	-1.000
all	-0.015	0.031	0.033	0.045	0.020	-0.062	0.040	-0.198

*All others means all others against whom a coder was compared in the pairwise tests.

**For series names, see table A.1.

Table A.4

Coders and Sources for Countries by Year

*Codings from the Primary Source**

Country	Coder	Years Coded	Coder	Years Coded	Coder	Years Coded	Coder	Years Coded	Coder	Years Coded
Afghanistan	1	(48-65)	7	(66)	8	(67)				
Albania	1	(48-65)	7	(66)	8	(67)				
Algeria	3	(48-56)	1	(57-60)	2	(61-65)	7	(66)	8	(67)
Angola	1	(48-65)	7	(66)	8	(67)				
Argentina	2	(48-65)	7	(66-67)						
Australia	1	(48-65)	7	(66)	8	(67)				
Austria	1	(48-65)	7	(66)	8	(67)				
Barbados	2	(48-65)	7	(66)	8	(67)				
Basuto	1	(48-65)	7	(66)	8	(67)				
Belgium	1	(48-65)	7	(66)	8	(67)				
Bolivia	2	(48-65)	7	(66-67)						
Brazil	2	(48-65)	7	(66)	8	(67)				
Bulgaria	1	(48-65)	7	(66)	8	(67)				
Burma	1	(48-65)	7	(66)	8	(67)				
Burundi	1	(62-65)	7	(66)	8	(67)				
Cambodia	1	(54-65)	7	(66)	8	(67)				
Cameroon	1	(48-65)	7	(66)	8	(67)				
Canada	1	(48-65)	7	(66)	8	(67)				
Central African Republic	1	(48-65)	7	(66)	8	(67)				
Ceylon	1	(48-65)	7	(66)	8	(67)				
Chad	1	(48-65)	7	(66)	8	(67)				
Chile	2	(48-65)	7	(66)	5	(67)				
China	1	(48-65)	7	(66)	8	(67)				
Colombia	2	(48-65)	7	(66)	5	(67)				
Congo-Brazzaville	1	(48-65)	7	(66)	8	(67)				
Congo-Kinshasa	1	(48-65)	7	(66)	8	(67)				
Costa Rica	2	(48-65)	7	(66)	5	(67)				

Table A.4—Continued

Country	Coder	Years Coded	Coder	Years Coded	Coder	Years Coded	Coder	Years Coded	Coder	Years Coded
Cuba	2	(48-65)	7	(66)	5	(67)				
Cyprus	1	(48-65)	7	(66)	8	(67)				
Czechoslovakia	1	(48-65)	7	(66-67)						
Dahomey	1	(48-65)	7	(66)	8	(67)				
Denmark	1	(48-65)	7	(66)	8	(67)				
Dominican Republic	2	(48-65)	7	(66)	5	(67)				
El Salvador	2	(48-65)	7	(66)	5	(67)				
Ethiopia	1	(48-65)	7	(66)	8	(67)				
Finland	1	(48-65)	7	(66)	8	(67)				
France	2	(48-65)	7	(66)	8	(67)				
Gabon	1	(48-65)	7	(66)	8	(67)				
Gambia	1	(48-65)	7	(66)	8	(67)				
East Germany	1	(48-65)	7	(66)	8	(67)				
West Germany	1	(48-65)	7	(66)	8	(67)				
Ghana	1	(48-65)	7	(66)	8	(67)				
Greece	2	(48-65)	7	(66)	8	(67)				
Guatemala	2	(48-65)	7	(66)	5	(67)				
Guinea	1	(48-65)	8	(66-67)						
Guyana	2	(48-65)	8	(66)	5	(67)				
Haiti	2	(48-65)	7	(66)	5	(67)				
Honduras	2	(48-65)	7	(66)	5	(67)				
Hong Kong	1	(48-65)	7	(66)	8	(67)				
Hungary	1	(48-65)	7	(66)	8	(67)				
Ireland	1	(48-65)	7	(66)	8	(67)				
India	1	(48-53)	2	(54-55)	1	(56-62)	2	(63-64)	1	(65)
	7	(66)	5	(67)						
Indonesia	1	(48-65)	8	(66-67)						
Iran	1	(48-65)	7	(66)	8	(67)				
Iraq	3	(48-65)	7	(66)	8	(67)				

Table A.4—Continued

Country	Coder	Years Coded	Coder	Years Coded	Coder	Years Coded	Coder	Years Coded	Coder	Years Coded
Ireland	1	(48-65)	7	(66)	8	(67)				
Israel	1	(48-65)	7	(66)	8	(67)				
Italy	1	(48-65)	7	(66)	8	(67)				
Ivory Coast	1	(48-65)	8	(66-67)	5	(67)				
Jamaica	2	(48-65)	7	(66)	8	(67)				
Japan	1	(48-65)	7	(66)	8	(67)				
Jordan	3	(48-65)	7	(66)	8	(67)				
Kenya	1	(48-65)	8	(66-67)						
North Korea	1	(48-65)	7	(66)	8	(67)				
South Korea	1	(48-65)	7	(66)	8	(67)				
Kuwait	1	(48-65)	7	(66)	8	(67)				
Laos	3	(54-65)	8	(66-67)	8	(67)				
Lebanon	3	(48-65)	7	(66)	8	(67)				
Liberia	1	(48-65)	8	(66-67)						
Libya	3	(48-65)	8	(66-67)	8	(67)				
Luxembourg	2	(48-65)	7	(66)	8	(67)				
Malagasy	1	(48-65)	8	(66-67)						
Malawi	1	(48-65)	8	(66-67)						
Malaysia	1	(48-65)	7	(66)	8	(67)				
Maldives	1	(48-65)	7	(66)	8	(67)				
Mali	1	(48-65)	8	(66-67)	8	(67)				
Malta	1	(48-65)	7	(66)						
Mauritania	1	(48-65)	8	(66-67)						
Mauritius	1	(48-65)	8	(66-67)						
Mexico	2	(48-65)	7	(66)	5	(67)				
Mongolia	1	(48-65)	7	(66)	8	(67)				
Morocco	3	(48-65)	8	(66-67)						
Mozambique	1	(48-65)	8	(66-67)						
Nepal	1	(48-65)	7	(66)	8	(67)				
Netherlands	2	(48-65)	7	(66)	8	(67)				

Table A.4—Continued

Country	Coder	Years Coded	Coder	Years Coded	Coder	Years Coded	Coder	Years Coded
New Zealand	1	(48-65)	7	(66)	8	(67)		
Nicaragua	2	(48-65)	7	(66)	5	(67)		
Niger	1	(48-65)	8	(66-67)				
Nigeria	1	(48-65)	8	(66-67)				
Norway	1	(48-65)	8	(66-67)				
Pakistan	1	(48-65)	7	(66)	8	(67)		
Panama	2	(48-65)	7	(66)	5	(67)		
Papua / New Guinea	1	(48-65)	8	(66-67)				
Paraguay	2	(48-65)	7	(66)	5	(67)		
Peru	2	(48-65)	7	(66)	5	(67)		
Philippines	1	(48-65)	7	(66)	8	(67)		
Poland	1	(48-65)	7	(66)	8	(67)		
Portugal	1	(48-65)	7	(66)	8	(67)		
Puerto Rico	2	(48-65)	7	(66)	5	(67)		
Rhodesia	1	(48-65)	8	(66-67)				
Rumania	1	(48-65)	7	(66)	8	(67)		
Rwanda	1	(62-65)	8	(66-67)				
Saudi Arabia	3	(48-65)	7	(66)	8	(67)		
Senegal	1	(48-65)	8	(66-67)				
Sierra Leone	1	(48-65)	8	(66-67)				
Singapore	1	(48-63)	1	(65)	7	(66)	8	(67)
Somalia	1	(48-65)	8	(66-67)				
South Africa	1	(48-65)	8	(66-67)				
South Arabia	1	(48-65)	7	(66)	8	(67)		
Spain	1	(48-65)	7	(66)	5	(67)		
Sudan	1	(48-65)	8	(66-67)				
Sweden	1	(48-65)	7	(66)	8	(67)		
Switzerland	1	(48-65)	7	(66)	5	(67)		
Syria	3	(48-65)	7	(66)	8	(67)		

Table A.4—*Continued*

Country	Coder	Years Coded	Coder	Years Coded	Coder	Years Coded	Coder	Years Coded	Coder	Years Coded
Taiwan	1	(48-65)	7	(66)	8	(67)				
Tanzania	1	(48-65)	8	(66-67)						
Thailand	1	(48-65)	7	(66)	5	(67)				
Togo	1	(48-65)	8	(66-67)						
Trinidad	2	(48-65)	8	(66-67)						
Tunisia	3	(48-65)	8	(66-67)						
Turkey	1	(48-65)	7	(66)	8	(67)				
Uganda	1	(48-65)	8	(66-67)						
UAR	3	(48-65)	8	(66-67)						
USSR	1	(48-65)	7	(66-67)						
United Kingdom	1	(48-65)	8	(66-67)						
United States	1	(48-65)	8	(66-67)						
Upper Volta	1	(48-65)	8	(66-67)						
Uruguay	2	(48-65)	7	(66)	5	(67)				
Venezuela	2	(48-65)	7	(66)	5	(67)				
North Vietnam	1	(54-65)	7	(66-67)						
South Vietnam	1	(54-65)	7	(66-67)						
Yemen	1	(48-65)	7	(66)	8	(67)				
Yugoslavia	1	(48-65)	7	(66)	8	(67)				
Zambia	1	(48-65)	8	(66-67)						

Primary source: The *New York Times Index* for all countries except the United States; the Associated Press card file in New York for the United States.

Table A.4—Continued

Codings from Secondary Sources**

Country	Source	Coder	Years Coded	Coder	Years Coded	Coder	Years Coded
Afghanistan	AP, AR	6	(48-54)	1	(55-67)		
Albania	AP	6	(48-65)	8	(66-67)		
Algeria	MEJ	5	(48-67)				
Angola	AP, AD	1	(48-61)	4	(61-63)	5	(64-67)
Argentina	AP	5	(48-65)	8	(66-67)		
Australia	AP	1	(48-65)	8	(66-67)		
Austria	AP	1	(48-65)	8	(66-67)		
Barbados	AP	5	(48-65)	8	(66-67)		
Basuto	AP, AD	1	(48-61)	4	(61-63)	5	(64-67)
Bechuanaland	AP, AD	1	(48-61)	4	(61-63)	5	(64-67)
Belgium	AP	1	(48-65)	8	(66-67)		
Bolivia	AP	5	(48-65)	8	(66-67)		
Brazil	AP	5	(48-65)	8	(66-67)		
Bulgaria	AP	6	(48-65)	8	(66-67)		
Burma	AP, AR	6	(48-54)	1	(55-67)		
Burundi	AD	6	(62-63)	5	(64-67)		
Cambodia	AP, AR	6	(54)	1	(55-67)		
Cameroon	AP, AD	1	(48-61)	4	(61-63)	5	(64-67)
Canada	AP	1	(48-65)	8	(66-67)		
Central African Republic	AP, AD	1	(48-61)	4	(61-63)	5	(64-67)
Ceylon	AP, AR	6	(48-54)	1	(55-67)		
Chad	AP, AD	4	(48-63)	5	(64-67)		
Chile	AP	5	(48-65)	8	(66-67)		
China	AP, AR	1	(48-53)	6	(54)	1	(55-67)
Colombia	AP	5	(48-65)	8	(66-67)		
Congo-Brazzaville	AP, AD	4	(48-63)	5	(64-67)		
Congo-Kinshasa	AP, AD	1	(48-61)	4	(61-63)	5	(64-67)

Table A.4–Continued

Country	Source	Coder	Years Coded	Coder	Years Coded	Coder	Years Coded	Coder	Years Coded
Costa Rica	AP	5	(48-65)	8	(66-67)				
Cuba	AP	5	(48-65)	8	(66-67)				
Cyprus	MEJ	1	(48-65)	5	(66-67)				
Czechoslovakia	AP	6	(48-65)	8	(66-67)				
Dahomey	AP, AD	4	(48-63)	5	(64-67)				
Denmark	AP	1	(48-65)	8	(66-67)				
Dominican Republic	AP	5	(48-65)	8	(66-67)				
Ecuador	AP	5	(48-65)	8	(66-67)				
El Salvador	AP	5	(48-65)	8	(66-67)				
Ethiopia	AP, AD	4	(48-63)	5	(64-67)				
Finland	AP	1	(48-65)	8	(66-67)				
France	I'A	1	(48-51)	2	(52-65)	8	(66-67)		
Gabon	AP	1	(48-61)	4	(61-63)	5	(64-67)		
Gambia	AP, AD	4	(48-63)	5	(64-67)				
East Germany	AP	6	(48-65)	8	(66-67)				
West Germany	AP	6	(48-65)	8	(66-67)				
Ghana	AP, AD	4	(48-65)	5	(66-67)				
Greece	AP	1	(48-65)	8	(66-67)				
Guatemala	AP	5	(48-65)	8	(66-67)				
Guinea	AP, AD	1	(48-61)	4	(61-63)	5	(64-65)	8	(66-67)
Guyana	AP	5	(48-49)	1	(50-63)	5	(64-65)	8	(66-67)
Haiti	AP	5	(48-65)	8	(66-67)				
Honduras	AP	5	(48-65)	8	(66-67)				
Hong Kong	AP, AR	6	(48-54)	1	(55-65)	7	(66)	1	(67)
Hungary	AP	6	(48-65)	8	(66-67)				
Iceland	AP	1	(48-65)	8	(66-67)				
India	AP, AR	6	(48-54)	1	(55-65)	7	(66)	5	(67)

Table A.4—Continued

Country	Source	Coder	Years Coded	Coder	Years Coded	Coder	Years Coded	Coder	Years Coded
Indonesia	AP, Ar	6	(48-54)	1	(55-65)	5	(66-67)		
Iran	MEJ	1	(48-65)	5	(66-67)				
Iraq	MEJ	1	(48-65)	8	(66-67)				
Ireland	AP	1	(48-65)	8	(66-67)				
Israel	MEJ	1	(48-65)	5	(66-67)				
Italy	AP	1	(48-65)	8	(66-67)				
Ivory Coast	AP, AD	1	(48-61)	4	(61-63)	5	(64-67)		
Jamaica	AP	1	(48-65)	8	(66-67)				
Japan	AP, AR	6	(48-54)	1	(55-65)	5	(66-67)		
Jordan	MEJ	1	(48-65)	5	(66-67)				
Kenya	AP, AD	4	(48-63)	5	(64-67)				
North Korea	AP, AR	6	(48-54)	1	(55-65)	7	(66)	5	(67)
South Korea	AP, AR	6	(48-54)	1	(55-65)	7	(66)	5	(67)
Kuwait	MEJ	6	(48-65)	5	(66-67)				
Laos	AP, AR	6	(54)	1	(55-65)	5	(66-67)		
Lebanon	MEJ	1	(48-65)	5	(66-67)				
Liberia	AP, AD	4	(48-65)	5	(66-67)				
Libya	MEJ	4	(48-65)	5	(66-67)				
Luxembourg	AP	1	(48-65)	8	(66-67)				
Malagasy	AP, AD	1	(48-61)	5	(61-67)	5	(64-67)		
Malawi	AP, AD	1	(48-61)	4	(61-63)	5	(67)		
Malaysia	AP, AR	1	(48-65)	7	(66)				
Maldives	AP, AR	5	(48-67)						
Mali	AP, AD	1	(48-61)	4	(61-63)	5	(64-67)		
Malta	AP	1	(48-65)	8	(66-67)				
Mauritania	AP, AD	1	(48-61)	4	(61-63)	5	(64-67)		
Mauritius	AP	1	(48-61)	5	(62-67)				
Mexico	AP	5	(48-65)	8	(66-67)			5	(67)
Mongolia	AP, AR	6	(48-54)	1	(55-65)	7	(66)		

Table A.4–*Continued*

Country	Source	Coder	Years Coded	Coder	Years Coded	Coder	Years Coded	Coder	Years Coded
Morocco	MEJ	4	(48-65)	5	(66-67)				
Mozambique	AP, AD	1	(48-61)	4	(61-63)	5	(64-67)		
Nepal	AP, AR	6	(48-54)	1	(55-65)	7	(66)	5	(67)
Netherlands	AP	1	(48-65)	8	(66-67)				
New Zealand	AP	1	(48-65)	8	(66-67)				
Nicaragua	AP	1	(48-65)	8	(66-67)				
Niger	AP, AD	4	(48-63)	5	(64-67)				
Nigeria	AP, AD	4	(48-65)	5	(66-67)				
Norway	AP	1	(48-65)	8	(66-67)				
Pakistan	AP, AR	6	(48-54)	1	(55-65)	7	(66)	5	(67)
Panama	AP	1	(48-65)	8	(66-67)				
Papua/New Guinea	AP	1	(48-67)						
Paraguay	AP	1	(48-65)	8	(66-67)				
Peru	AP	1	(48-65)	8	(66-67)				
Philippines	AP	6	(48-54)	1	(55-67)				
Poland	AP	6	(48-65)	8	(66-67)				
Portugal	AP	1	(48-65)	8	(66-67)				
Puerto Rico	AP	1	(48-65)	8	(66-67)				
Rhodesia	AP, AD	4	(48-63)	5	(64-65)	8	(66-67)		
Rumania	AP	6	(48-65)	8	(66-67)				
Rwanda	AD	4	(62-63)	5	(64-67)				
Saudi Arabia	MEJ	1	(48-65)	5	(66-67)				
Senegal	AP, AD	4	(48-65)	5	(66-67)				
Sierra Leone	AP, AD	1	(48-61)	4	(61-65)	5	(66-67)		
Singapore	AP, AR	6	(48-54)	1	(55-65)	7	(66)	5	(67)
Somalia	AP, AD	1	(48-61)	4	(61-63)	5	(64-65)	8	(66-67)
South Africa	AP, AD	1	(48-61)	4	(61-63)	5	(64-67)		
South Arabia	MEJ	1	(48-65)	5	(66-67)				
Spain	AP	1	(48-65)	8	(66-67)				

Table A.4—Continued

Country	Source	Coder	Years Coded	Coder	Years Coded	Coder	Years Coded
Sudan	AP, AD	1	(48-61)	4	(61-63)	5	(64-67)
Sweden	AP	1	(48-65)	8	(66-67)		
Switzerland	AP	1	(48-65)	8	(66-67)		
Syria	MEJ	1	(48-65)	5	(66-67)		
Taiwan	AP, AR	6	(48-54)	1	(55-65)	5	(66-67)
Tanzania	AP, AD	1	(48-61)	4	(61-63)	5	(64-67)
Thailand	AP, AR	6	(48-54)	1	(55-65)	5	(66-67)
Togo	AP, AD	1	(48-61)	4	(61-63)	5	(64-67)
Trinidad	AP	1	(48-65)	8	(66-67)		
Tunisia	MEJ	4	(48-65)	5	(66-67)		
Turkey	MEJ	1	(48-65)	5	(66-67)		
Uganda	AP, AD	4	(48-63)	5	(64-67)		
UAR	MEJ	1	(48-65)	5	(66-67)		
USSR	AP	6	(48-65)	8	(66-67)		
United Kingdom	AP	1	(48-65)	8	(66-67)		
United States	No second source						
Upper Volta	AP, AD	1	(48-61)	4	(61-63)	5	(64-67)
Uruguay	AP	1	(48-65)	8	(66-67)		
Venezuela	AP	1	(48-65)	8	(66-67)		
North Vietnam	AP, AR	1	(54-65)	5	(66-67)		
South Vietnam	AP, AR	1	(54-65)	7	(66)	5	(67)
Yemen	MEJ	1	(48-65)	5	(66-67)		
Yugoslavia	AP	6	(48-65)	8	(66-67)		
Zambia	AP, AD	4	(48-63)	5	(64-67)		

**Secondary sources:
  AP: Associated Press card file
  AR: Asian Recorder (1955-67)
  MEJ: Middle East Journal

AD: Africa Diary (July, 1961-67)
l'A: l'Année Politique
(The AP was used for African and Asian countries during the years when AR and AD were not published.)

Both tables include figures for coder *0*. Comparing these with the figures for coder *1* shows the effects that coding variables over an extended period of time (three years) had on consistency. The sample from coder *1* was taken during the first six months of coding. The data for coder *0* are from a sample of the same coder taken during the last six months of collection. During the latter period there was a tendency toward a more restricted view of many of the variables but toward a more inclusive interpretation of a few others. The overall change was so small, however, as to suggest that, for this coder at least, no appreciable distortion could be attributed to the time factor. A small sample of coder *9*'s work is also included in these tables for the sake of comparison. As mentioned previously, his results were considered too unlike those of the other coders to be acceptable and his coding was redone. Neither his results against other coders nor the results of coder *0* against coder *1* are included in the summaries in the final row and column of tables A.2 and A.3 and in the calculations made for table A.1. Lists of coders with their countries, years, and sources are given in table A.4.

Source Merging

In order to improve accuracy, data were gathered from two separate sources for each country. Except in the cases of both regular and irregular executive transfers, data from the two sources were merged by computer. The magnitude of the task would have been far too great otherwise. The goal was to provide composite series containing all distinct events reported in at least one source but free from doubly counted events. This is not a simple job because sources, when reporting a given event, may differ about the date of occurrence, the date of the report, and the magnitude or number of events.

For example, consider the coded reports shown in table A.5. (Entries in the table refer to the number of events reported on a given date, e.g. $S(9) - 2$ means that two events of this particular type were reported in the secondary sources on date 9.) The merged series shown would be produced by the following series of merging decisions:

1. It is judged that $P(2)$ and $S(2)$ refer to the same occurrence but that the primary source underreported, i.e. failed to report one of the two events reported by the secondary source.

2. $S(3)$ is close in time to both $P(2)$ and $P(4)$. But since $P(2)$ was already identified with $S(2)$, it is judged that it is $S(3)$ and $P(4)$ that represent the same event, reported a day late in the primary source.

3. $S(9)$ is not close enough to any primary source event to be identified with it. Thus $P(6)$ and $S(9)$ are judged to be distinct events, each of which was reported in only one source.

Table A.5
Hypothetical Example

Date		1	2	3	4	5	6	7	8	9	10
Primary source	(P)		1		1		2				
Secondary source	(S)		2	1						2	
Merged series			2		1		2			2	

A merging algorithm was devised in which such intuitive judgments as these were generalized into formal decision rules unambiguously applicable to all possible situations. This merging algorithm (see figure A.1) produces a merged series with the following characteristics: (1) Two events are judged to be identical if they fall within a given time period of one another; (2) if several events fall within these merge limits, the search sequence defines an order of preference about which should be judged identical; (3) two events from the same source are never merged; and (4) if a secondary source event is judged not to represent double counting, it is included as a net addition to the merged series.

Several possibilities for error exist when this particular merging program is used. The frequency of the various errors discussed below depends to some extent on the search sequence used. After some experimentation, the basic sequence (+1, +2, 0, +3, −1) was adopted. It was chosen because of the differing dates obtained from the primary and secondary sources. The primary source for all countries except the United States was the *New York Times Index*. From this, the coder usually learned only the date on which the story covering the event was published in the *Times*, normally 24 to 48 hours after the actual occurrence. The secondary sources used were the Associated Press Files in New York, which list the dateline of the report in the New York office, usually the actual date of occurrence, and various area-specific sources (e.g. the *Middle East Journal*, the *Asian Recorder*) that give periodical summaries or chronologies also listed by date of actual occurrence. Notice that when an event from a secondary source is added to the merged series under this search sequence, it is shifted to one day later, in order to adjust the merged series to the *New York Times* dating system.

Four of the most significant types of errors made by the program are:

1a. Sequencing errors (total constant). Consider the primary and secondary source data given in table A.6. What really happened was that the event S(1) was not reported at all in the primary source. However, because of the sequential nature of the merging process, S(1) was mistakenly merged with P(3), S(2) with P(4), and S(3), which thus found nothing to merge with because it was blocked from the proper merge with P(4) by the previous merge of S(2) with P(4), was by default added to the merged series at date three.

Figure A.1. Flowchart of Merge Program

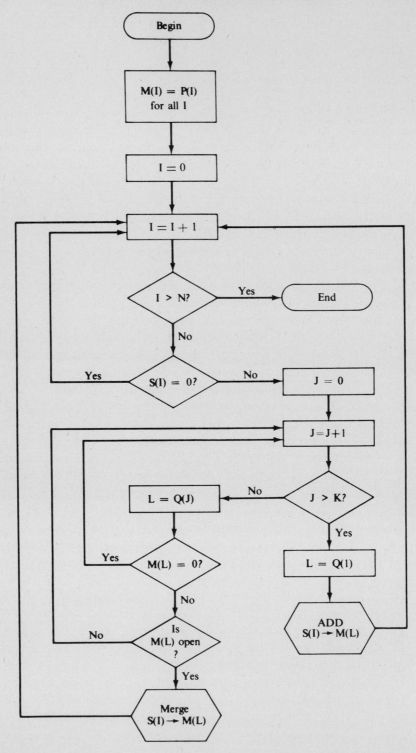

Key to Flowchart of Merging Algorithm (figure A.1).
  Variables:
    M the vector of merged event data
    P the vector of data from primary source
    S the vector of data from secondary source
    Q the search sequence vector, eg. $S = (0, +1, -1)$
    N length of M, P, and S, equal to the total number of days in the time period covered by the data
    K length of Q
    I, J, L indexing variables
  Special Operations:
    Merge: Set the number of events and/or magnitude for the event equal to the greater of the values given in the primary and secondary sources.
    Add: Set the number of events and/or magnitude for the merged series equal to the sum of its previous value, plus the value given by the secondary source.

Table A.6

Example of Sequencing Error: 1a

Date		*1*	*2*	*3*	*4*	*5*	*Total*
Primary source	(P)			1	1		2
Secondary source	(S)	1	1	1			3
Actual sequence			1	1	1		3
Machine merge				1	2		3

Table A.7

Example of Sequencing Error: 1b

Date		*1*	*2*	*3*	*4*	*5*	*Total*
Primary source	(P)			20	1		21
Secondary source	(S)	1	20	1			22
Actual sequence			1	20	1		22
Machine merge				20	21		41

1b. Sequencing errors (totals exaggerated). In contrast to the first type of error, consider the variation of the above situation shown in table A.7. In this case, the total number of events recorded was increased by 19 by the double counting which resulted when S(2), with a multiplicity of 20, was mistakenly merged with P(4).

2. False merges. Sometimes the merged series will differ from the actual sequence of events because two events cannot be distinguished by the merge program on the basis of the coded data. For example, suppose that on a certain day, the *New York Times* reports "Students Riot in Cairo" while the Associated Press reports "Workers Riot in Alexandria." These are clearly distinct events, but will be mistakenly merged by the program.

3. False nonmerges. The reverse of situation 2 can occur. If the Associated Press reports "Ivanov Ousted from Defense Ministry" on

January 5, while the *New York Times* reports "Pravda Story Confirms Ouster of Ivanov" on January 20, the event would be coded with the dates reported in each source and hence would not be merged under the given sequence.

In order to evaluate the overall accuracy of the objective merging procedure and to get a quantitative estimate of the importance of various types of errors, discretionary hand merges were made for a small sample of country-years for the eighteen event variables. The principle of the discretionary merge was to use the judgment of an experienced coder to resolve questionable cases. For example, when doubt existed as to the identity of two events, as in the examples of type 2 and type 3 errors given above, the original news sources were consulted for such additional cues as names and places. The results of the comparison of the hand and machine merges are given in table A.8. The following specific conclusions were drawn from the comparison.

1. Errors of the type 1a were frequent in periods of high event activity, but, since they do not affect yearly or monthly totals, they do not affect most types of research using the data. However, scholars planning projects requiring attention to the time-patterns or spacing of events, when a variation of from +3 to −1 days is critical, should proceed with caution in using the machine-merged event series.

2. Errors of type 1b were not a serious problem in the sample investigated. However, they might potentially be serious in two cases; (a) when a single date accounts for most of a year's total of reported events but the *New York Times* report might not occur with a lag of just 24 hours and (b) when a yearly or monthly total reported in a news source is coded as a single event and assigned to the date reported. The most conspicuous errors of this type are thought to have occurred in the variable, "Deaths from domestic political violence."

3. Errors of types 2 and 3 occurred with a frequency of approximately 3 to 5 times per 100 events. It is most encouraging to note, however, that in the sample checked, the positive and negative effects on yearly totals very nearly cancelled out. Thus the average discrepancy between the hand and machine merges was well below 1 percent.

4. The variables "elections," "irregular executive transfers," and "regular executive transfers" represent special cases. Since these are frequently subject to larger reporting delays, but never occur in dense clusters, the expanded search sequence $(0 + 1, -1 + 2, -2, \ldots +12, -12)$ was used for the machine merge. This gave results comparable in accuracy to those obtained for variables with the short sequence. However, even this small error rate was judged excessive for "regular and irregular executive changes." For these variables, the machine merged data was discarded entirely and replaced with hand merged data for all countries.

Table A.8
Comparison of Hand and Machine Merges

Series*	India 1966		Rhodesia 1966		Guinea 1966		Canada 1967		Pakistan 1966	
	machine	hand	m.	h.	m.	h.	m.	h.	m.	h.
1	108	108	11	11	1	1	0	0	9	9
2	394	395	76	76	0	0	0	0	13	13
3	0	1	0	0	0	0	0	0	0	0
4	74	74	36	35	0	0	4	4	0	0
5	0	0	0	0	0	0	0	0	0	0
6	27	27	10	10	0	0	6	6	16	16
7	0	0	0	0	0	0	1	1	2	2
8	5	5	5	3	0	0	0	0	7	7
9	3	3	0	0	0	0	1	1	0	0
10	0	0	0	0	0	0	0	0	0	0
11	0	0	0	0	0	0	0	0	0	0
12	0	0	0	0	0	0	0	0	0	0
13	6	6	2	2	1	1	3	3	5	4
14	2	2	1	1	0	0	0	0	0	0
15	0	0	0	0	0	0	0	0	0	0
16	76	76	72	81	12	13	3	3	12	12
17	16	16	7	7	2	2	2	2	3	3
18	0	0	8	8	0	0	0	0	0	0

*For names of series, see Table A.1.

Source Comparisons

The *New York Times Index* is probably the best single source to use for coding political event data because it contains more pertinent information about a given country in a more concise and readily accessible form than any other single source. Our evidence for this statement, given below, is corroborated by other scholars who have collected events data. The World Event/Interaction Survey (WEIS), a project for the collection of data on conflictual and cooperative acts of countries, uses the *New York Times Index* as a major source. A comparison of events for this collection reported for January and February 1968 in the *Index* and in *Le Monde* shows no significant difference in the ratios of interaction by the major participants.[2] A similar comparison of the *Index* and the London *Times* for the period July-September 1969, showed that the *New York Times* reported one-third more events than the London *Times* although the latter reported more events for Western Europe and Africa than the former. There was a rank correlation of .83 between the two sources.[3] The Cooperation/Conflict

2. Charles A. McClelland and Gary D. Hoggard, "Conflict Patterns in the Interactions Among Nations," *International Politics and Foreign Policy*, ed. James Rosenau (New York: Free Press, 1969), pp. 711-24, esp. 713.

3. Charles A. McClelland and Robert Young, "The Flow of International Events, July-December, 1969," mimeographed (The University of Southern California, January 1970).

Research Group at Michigan State University compared data on Egypt and
Israel for 1955-58 collected from the *New York Times Index,* the *Middle
East Journal, Deadline Data,* and *Keesing's Contemporary Archives.* The
group found that the *Times* reported more data on these two countries than
did any of the other sources. Since the overlap between the *Times* and the
Middle East Journal was only 9.7 percent, this group concluded that reliance
should not be placed on one source only.[4]

The *New York Times* and the *New York Times Index* are not equivalent,
of course. The latter provides information in a highly condensed manner.
Our coders made sample checks and found that the use of the *Index* rather
than the newspaper probably caused a slight undercount of the events. For
example, a story about riots or demonstrations would often contain the
exact number whereas the shorter account might mention events in "several
cities." These is little loss of information in those series for which multiple
events are not normally reported (e.g. executive transfers). The use of the
newspaper, however, would not have been feasible.

The *New York Times Index* was used as the primary source for all
countries except the United States. The smaller Associated Press card file
seemed more appropriate; even so, the United States is probably over-
reported. For all other countries, we also used secondary sources. For several
reasons, it is impossible for any one source to be expected to report all of
the political events of every country in the world or to report a consistent
proportion of them. It would be unfeasible financially to station a
correspondent in every country. Even were this possible, it would be
impractical to print all of the information that would be generated.
Moreover, there are numerous government restrictions on the establishment
of offices or the entry of correspondents. Finally, a newspaper and its
readers—even readers of the *New York Times*—are not interested equally in
all the happenings of all the countries in the world. We decided, therefore, to
supplement the *Times* accounts with second sources in the hope of
improving areas of weakness and of countering political biases.

A local newspaper from each country as a second source would have been
ideal, but problems of language and time made this choice impractical. The
next best approach was to employ compiled summaries of events taken from
local news sources. It was possible to do this for some regions of the world
although it was not always practical to do so for the entire 20-year period.
For Africa, the *Africa Diary,* a weekly published in New Delhi, was used as a

4. Edward Azar, Stanley Cohen, Thomas Jukam, and James McCormick, "Methodological
Developments in the Quantification of Events Data" (Paper presented at the 1970 Michigan
State University Events Data Conference, April 1970). See also Robert Burrowes, Douglas
Muzzio, and Bert Spector, "Mirror, Mirror on the Wall . . . A Source Comparison Study of
Inter-Nation Event Data" (Paper delivered at the Annual Meeting of the International Studies
Association, San Juan, Puerto Rico, March 1971); and Charles F. Doran, Robert E. Pendley,
and George E. Antunes, "Reliability of Cross-National Measures of Civil Strife and Instability
Events: A Comparison of Indigenous and Secondary Data Sources" (Paper delivered at the
Annual Meeting of the International Studies Association, San Juan, Puerto Rico, March 1971).

second source. To summarize the events of the week for each African country, the *Africa Diary* draws on the London *Times, Le Monde* (Paris), the *New York Times,* various Indian sources, and such African news sources as *Ghanian Times* (Accra), Malawi Information Service, *West African Pilot* (Lagos), Rhodesian Information Department, *Daily Nation* (Nairobi), Liberian Information Department, *Somali News* (Magadiscio), *Standard Tanzania* (Dar es Salaam), *Uganda Argus* (Kampala), Zambian Information Department, *South African Digest* (Pretoria), and the *Sierra Leonian* (Freetown). *Africa Diary* was selected from among several publications containing chronologies because it began at a date (July 1961) earlier than the others. *Africa Research Bulletin* was found to have similar coverage, but it was published only from 1964. (See the discussion of third source comparisons below.) For the period prior to 1961, we decided to use the Associated Press card file in New York.

It was possible to draw on weekly summaries of political events for the countries of Asia by using the *Asian Recorder,* another Indian publication. It also employed Indian and British news sources along with *The Nation* (Rangoon), *Radio Kabul, Dawn* (Karachi), *The Times of Ceylon,* Afghan Embassy, Hsinhua News, *The Manila Times,* Indonesian Information Service, *Times of Vietnam* (Saigon), and *Straits Times* (Singapore). Since this source began only in 1955, it was necessary to rely on the Associated Press card file for the earlier years.

The other area for which a regional source was used was the Middle East. Data were gathered from the quarterly chronologies of the *Middle East Journal.* This source covered the entire 20-year period, but it drew heavily on the *New York Times,* especially in the 1948-58 period when only about 20 percent of the entries came from a source other than that newspaper. These other sources included the *New York Herald Tribune,* London *Times, Palestine Affairs, Akhion Lahzah* (Cairo), the Arab News Agency, *Keesing's Contemporary Archives,* and *Mideast Mirror* (Beirut). A second problem with the *Middle East Journal* was that it did not use the same sources itself throughout the twenty-year period. In 1959 it drew "somewhat more than half" its items from the *New York Times.* However, at that time, in addition to the other sources mentioned above, it began using the Daily Report of the Foreign Broadcast Information Service (Washington, D.C.), *Arab News and Views* (New York), regular and occasional bulletins of Middle East embassies in Washington, *Kashmir Affairs* (Rawalpindi), *Israel Digest* (Jerusalem), *Kabul Times* (Afghanistan), and *Maghreb Digest* (Los Angeles). In 1962 the last two sources were dropped from the list and replaced by *Iran Review* (London) and *Egyptian Economic and Political Review* (Cairo). *Middle Eastern Affairs* was considered as an alternative but was rejected because it was published only from 1950 to 1963.

For Latin America and Europe (except France) the Associated Press card file served as the second source. We used *l'Année Politique* for France.

Radio Free Europe was tried as a source for Eastern Europe but was
abandoned since the very detailed reports required too much effort for the
amount of information it contained. *Keesing's Contemporary Archives* was
tried for Western Europe but proved to be much less complete than the
Associated Press for the countries sampled. (See table A.11.) The *Hispanic
American Report* was initially used as a source for Latin America but it
presented two problems: exact dates of events (needed for merging) were
included only about a fourth of the time and the early years were not as well
reported as in the Associated Press.

The initial hypothesis leading to the use of second sources was that the
New York Times Index covered different countries and regions of the world
with varying degrees of thoroughness. Is this true and does a second source
help to bring more balanced coverage or does it merely accentuate the
differences? If the second source is useful, would a third have been better
still?

The data of tables A.9, A.10, and A.11 help to answer these questions.
Table A.9 gives by region the percentage contribution to total events of the
New York Times Index, the percentage additional contribution by the
secondary sources, and the percentage overlap. (Except for rounding, the
first and second will add to 100 percent; the third is also included within the
first.) Additional information added by the Associated Press card file is quite
consistent from region to region except for Asia. There the contributions by
the Associated Press and the *Asian Recorder* are similar although the overlap
by the latter with the *Index* is much higher than by the former. The very

Table A.9

Percentage Contribution of Sources to Events Reported

	East Europe	West Europe	Latin America	Asia	Africa
NYTI	72	67	72	79	72
Added by AP	28	31	28	20	26
Overlap	22	21	20	12	17

	Middle East	Asia	Africa
NYTI	70	79	55
Added by MEJ	29		
Added by AR		19	
Added by AD			44
Overlap	27	20	21

NYTI: *New York Times Index*
  AP: Associated Press card file
MEJ: *Middle East Journal*
  AR: *Asian Recorder*
  AD: *African Diary*

high contribution by the *New York Times Index* may reflect American military involvement in Asia. Although there is some built-in overlap between *Middle East Journal* and the *New York Times Index* (in that the former uses the latter as one of its primary sources), the net contribution of the journal is of the same order of magnitude as that of the Associated Press. Percentage complementarity in the former case, of course, was higher. The *Africa Diary* (after 1961) contributes a very large percentage of African events; Africa apparently is not one of the more interesting places for either the *New York Times* or for the Associated Press. The *New York Times Index,* therefore, appears to be a consistent guide to events in all regions except Africa. The *Africa Diary,* we think, has done a reasonably good job of amending that fault in the period after 1961.

The regional averages tend to hide reporting differences that coders noticed and that further calculations tend to substantiate. Although the average contribution of the *New York Times Index* is fairly constant between regions, there is a variation among countries within regions. For example, in Latin America the average net contribution of the second source ranges over countries from 6 to 55 percent. The net contributions of second

Table A.10

Net Contributions of Second Sources by Type of Variable

	Violence	Regular Institutional Transfers	Nonviolent Participation	Governmental Repression
Associated Press (Africa)	37	15	22	24
Associated Press (Asia)	16	19	30	20
Associated Press (East Europe)	28	27	46	32
Associated Press (Latin America)	32	24	31	23
Associated Press (West Europe)	32	18	47	38
Asian Recorder	10	31	19	16
African Diary	39	46	51	44
Middle East Journal	24	30	39	31

sources for each variable within each country were calculated but are not published here. Caution must be exercised in the use of these percentages, however, since many of the cells contained small n's.

The coders also felt that some sources paid greater attention to some variables than to others. For example, the Associated Press, they felt, emphasized events of violence and the *Asian Recorder* was weak on these but strong on institutional changes. Table A.10 gives the net contributions of the second sources for groups of variables. The groups are violence (variables

1, 2, 3, 4, 11, 12, 18), regular institutional transfers of power (variables 5, 9, 10, 13, 14), nonviolent participation (variables 6, 7, 8), and governmental repression (variables 15, 16, 17). (See table A.1 for variable numbers and names.)

The table lends some credence to the coders' notions about the *Asian Recorder* but does not substantiate the belief that the Associated Press emphasized violence to the detriment of other series. Indeed for three regions of five, that source made a greater contribution to the series of nonviolent participation than to those of violence.

If, in general, second sources can be said to have a "correcting" rather than aggravating effect, would third and fourth sources continue to improve the data? Would they be worth the additional resources needed? For a sample of seven countries, data from third sources were merged with data from the first and second sources. These are reported in table A.11. We did not feel that the additional information would justify the extra effort. (The newly independent states of Africa may have been the exception.)

Table A.11
Net Contribution of Third Sources
for Sample of Seven Countries

Albania (Radio Free Europe)	9
Rumania (Radio Free Europe)	15
Guinea (Africa Research Bulletin)	21
Rhodesia (Africa Research Bulletin)	8
Iran (Middle Eastern Affairs)	12
Lebanon (Middle Eastern Affairs)	11
Canada (Keesing's Contemporary Archives)	9

Several generalizations about sources seem valid. First, using secondary sources tends to compensate for deficiencies and gaps in the primary source rather than to accentuate them. Second, although there is variation from country to country and from variable to variable, this variation occurs as much within a second source as between them so that the different second sources used do not constitute a barrier to cross-regional comparison. Finally, although using data from third sources would have increased the total number of events by perhaps as much as 15 percent, it would not have substantially altered the overall picture.

A Note on Coding Rules

Data were collected by reports. A report may include one or more events of the same kind reported on the same day. For example, if the source or sources recorded two riots in a country on a particular day, a 2 was entered into the coding sheet. Effects of the riots (deaths, arrests) were entered not here but in their appropriate series. Rules for allowing uniform coding practices were necessary for ambiguous reports of events. If only "several demonstrations" were reported, five events were arbitrarily assigned to the date. Flexibility was allowed the coders so that judgments could be made within the context. Occasionally "widespread rioting" would be assigned a value of 10. If the rioting were reported to continue for three days and no other information were available, the coder would make the minimal assumption that there was one riot a day and enter three events on the date of this report.

Inclusion of more than one event in a report was generally applicable only to riots, armed attacks, demonstrations, political strikes, government security sanctions, and acts of political relaxation. For deaths from domestic violence, assassinations, and executions the number of persons involved was noted. There could be more than one renewal of executive tenure, or of unsuccessful or successful regular or irregular executive transfer, but this rarely happened. In the case of an executive adjustment, if more than one person were involved, only one event was counted.

Size is also important for such series as riots, armed attacks, demonstrations, political strikes, acts of negative sanctions and political relaxations. Whenever the source gave a general idea of size, the numbers were recorded as a power of 10. If 10 to 99 people were involved, magnitude = 1; if 100 to 999, magnitude = 2; and so on. If size were indicated as a part of a report of several events, e.g. "three demonstrations occurred, in one of which 1,000 people participated," two separate reports for this date were recorded, one containing two events of unknown magnitude and another with one event with a magnitude of 3. If size were unknown or if there were fewer than 10 people involved, a magnitude of zero was assigned. Each event is scored on the date it is said to have occurred; the exception to this rule is the occasional event reported in a year different from the date of its occurrence.

Appendix 2   The States and Territories of the World

Names as they appear in tables (upper case) and formal titles (italicized) are given here for the 136 countries included in this book. (Occasionally the two are the same and are given only in upper case.) With the exception of some very small dependent territories, other entities are listed (lower case) with their statuses and their populations. We have noted name changes and defined selected boundaries that might not otherwise be clear.

The list was prepared from standard United Nations Yearbooks and various issues of the United States, Department of State, Bureau of Intelligence and Research, *Status of the World's Nations* (Washington: U.S. Government Printing Office, 1967-70). We are especially appreciative for comments made by Jacques Rapoport of the United Nations Secretariat.

Aden. (*See* Southern Yemen.)

Anglo-Egyptian Sudan. (*See* Sudan.)

AFGHANISTAN. *Kingdom of Afghanistan.*

ALBANIA. *People's Republic of Albania.*

ALGERIA. *Republic of Algeria.*

American Samoa. Territory of United States. Population: 25,000.

Andorra. Co-principality of the President of the French Republic and the Bishop of Urgel, Spain. Population: 11,000.

ANGOLA. Overseas province of Portugal.

Antigua. State in association with the United Kingdom. Population: 57,000.

ARGENTINA. *Argentine Republic.* Data reported do not include those pertaining to Antarctic claims.

AUSTRALIA. *Commonwealth of Australia.*

AUSTRIA. *Federal Republic of Austria.*

Bahama Islands. British colony. Population: 136,000.

Bahrein. Population: 185,000. Became member of the United Nations on 7 October 1971, too late to be included in the study.

Bangladesh. Part of Pakistan at time of data collection.

BARBADOS.

Basutoland. (*See* Lesotho.)

Bechuanaland. (*See* Botswana.)

BELGIUM. *Kingdom of Belgium.*

Bermuda(s). British colony. Population: 48,000.

Bhutan. *Kingdom of Bhutan.* Population: 750,000. Became member of the United Nations on 21 September 1971, too late to be included in the study.

BOLIVIA. *Republic of Bolivia.*

Bonin Islands. Territory of Japan, comprising Parry, Beechey, Bailey,

Volcano, and Marcus islands. Population: 132,000.

BOTSWANA. *Republic of Botswana.* Including Mafeking, the capital before independence, which is located in the Republic of South Africa.

British Borneo. (*See* Brunei, Sabah, and Sarawak.)

British Honduras (Belize). British colony. Population: 106,000.

British Somaliland. (*See* Somalia.)

British Solomon Islands. Protectorate of the United Kingdom, comprising the Solomon Islands group except Bougainville and Buka (*see* New Guinea); also including Ontung, Java, Rennell, and Santa Cruz islands. Population: 137,000.

Brunei. Protectorate of the United Kingdom. Population: 101,000.

BRAZIL. *Federative Republic of Brazil.*

BULGARIA. *People's Republic of Bulgaria.*

'BURMA. *Union of Burma.*

BURUNDI. *Republic of Burundi.* Formerly part of Ruanda-Urundi, a United Nations trust territory under Belgian administration.

CAMBODIA. *Khmer Republic.* (Formerly Kingdom of Cambodia.)

CAMEROON. *Federal Republic of Cameroon.* Comprising former Trust Territory of Cameroons under French administration, which became independent 1 January 1960, and the southern part of the former Trust Territory of the Cameroons under British administration, which became part of independent Cameroon 1 October 1961. On the same date the northern part of the territory under British administration joined Nigeria. (*See* Nigeria.)

CANADA. *Dominion of Canada.* Including Sverdrup group of Arctic islands.

Canal Zone. (*See* Panama.)

Cape Verde Islands. Overseas province of Portugal. Population: 225,000.

CENTRAL AFRICAN REPUBLIC. (Formerly called Ubangi Shari.)

CEYLON. *Dominion of Ceylon.* Recently renamed Sri Lanka.

Channel Islands. Territory of the British Crown, including Jersey, Guernsey, and dependencies of Guernsey. Population: 114,000.

CHAD. *Republic of Chad.*

CHILE. *Republic of Chile.*

CHINA. *The People's Republic of China.* Excluding Taiwan but including Tibet.

China (Taiwan). (*See* Taiwan.)

COLOMBIA. *Republic of Colombia.*

Comoro Islands. Overseas territory of France. Population: 220,000.

CONGO-BRAZZAVILLE. *People's Republic of the Congo.* Formerly known as Middle Congo when under French rule. Brazzaville is the capital.

CONGO-KINSHASA. *Democratic Republic of Congo.* Former Belgian Congo. Kinshasa (formerly Leopoldville) is the capital. Recently renamed Zaire.

Cook Islands. Territory in association with New Zealand. Population: 21,000.

COSTA RICA. *Republic of Costa Rica.*

CUBA. *Republic of Cuba.* Includes Guantanamo and Isle of Pines.

CYPRUS. *Republic of Cyprus.*

CZECHOSLOVAKIA. *Czechoslovak Socialist Republic.*

DAHOMEY. *Republic of Dahomey.*

DENMARK. *Kingdom of Denmark.* Includes the Faeroe Islands and Greenland.

Dominica. State in association with the United Kingdom. Population: 66,000.

DOMINICAN REPUBLIC.

ECUADOR. *Republic of Ecuador.*

Egypt. (*See* United Arab Republic.)

EL SALVADOR. *Republic of El Salvador.*

Equatorial Guinea. *Republic of Equatorial Guinea.* Population: 267,000. Became member of the United Nations on 12 November 1968, too late to be included in the study.

Eritrea. (*See* Ethiopia.)

ETHIOPIA. *Empire of Ethiopia.* Including Eritrea.

Fernando Poo. (*See* Equatorial Guinea.)

Fiji. Became member of United Nations in 1970. Population: 464,000.

FINLAND. *Republic of Finland.*

FRANCE. *French Republic.* Metropolitan (continental) France and Corsica only.

French Equatorial Africa. A former French dependency, whose territories (Chad, Gabon, Middle Congo, and Ubangi Shari) became internally autonomous republics within the French Community in September 1958 and became independent in August 1960.

French Guiana. Overseas department of France. Population: 36,000.

French Polynesia. Overseas territory of France, comprising Austral, Bambier, Marquesas, Rapa, Society, and Tuamotu islands. Population: 88,000.

French Territory of the Afars and Issas. (Formerly French Somaliland.) Overseas territory of France. Population: 81,000.

French West Africa. A former French dependency. Of the territories included within it, French Guinea became independent 1 October 1958; Dahomey, Ivory Coast, Mauritania, Niger, Senegal, French Sudan, and Upper Volta became internally autonomous republics within the Community created by the French referendum 28

September 1958. They became independent during 1960.

GABON. *Republic of Gabon.*

THE GAMBIA.

GERMANY, EAST. *German Democratic Republic.* Including East Berlin.

GERMANY, WEST *Federal Republic of Germany.* Including Saar and West Berlin.

GHANA. *Republic of Ghana.* Comprising former Gold Coast and former Trust Territory of Togoland under British administration.

Gibraltar. British colony. Population: 25,000.

Gilbert and Ellice Islands. Territory of the United Kingdom. Population: 52,000.

GREECE. *Kingdom of Greece.*

Greenland. (*See* Denmark.)

Grenada. State in association with the United Kingdom. Population: 96,000.

Guadeloupe. Overseas department of France. Population: 314,000.

Guam. Territory of the United States. Population: 77,000.

GUATEMALA. *Republic of Guatemala.*

GUINEA. *Republic of Guinea.*

GUYANA. *Republic of Guyana.*

HAITI. *Republic of Haiti.*

Holy See. *State of the Vatican City.* Population: 1,000.

HONDURAS. *Republic of Honduras.*

HONG KONG. British colony. Comprising Hong Kong Island, Kowloon, and the other leased territories on the mainland.

HUNGARY. *Hungarian People's Republic.*

ICELAND. *Republic of Iceland.*

Ifni. Province of Spain. Population: 52,000.

INDIA. *Republic of India.* Including, whenever possible, the parts of Kashmir-Jammu controlled by India.

INDONESIA. *Republic of Indonesia.* Includes West Irian (formerly Netherlands New Guinea).

IRAN. *Empire of Iran.*

IRAQ. *Republic of Iraq.*

IRELAND. *Republic of Ireland.*

Isle of Man. Territory of the British Crown. Population: 50,000.

ISRAEL. *State of Israel.* Excluding the West Bank, the Old City of Jerusalem, the Gaza Strip, Sinai, and the Golan Heights.

ITALY. *Italian Republic.*

Italian Somaliland. (*See* Somalia.)

IVORY COAST. *Republic of Ivory Coast.*

JAMAICA.

JAPAN.

JORDAN. *Hashemite Kingdom of Jordon.* Including the West Bank.

KENYA. *Republic of Kenya.*

Khmer Republic. (*See* Cambodia.)

KOREA, NORTH. *Democratic People's Republic of Korea.*

KOREA, SOUTH. *Republic of Korea.*

KUWAIT. *State of Kuwait.*

LAOS. *Kingdom of Laos.*

LEBANON. *Republic of Lebanon.*

LESOTHO. *Kingdom of Lesotho.* (Formerly British dependency of Basutoland.)

LIBERIA. *Republic of Liberia.*

LIBYA. *Libya Arab Republic.*

Liechtenstein. *Principality of Liechtenstein.* Population: 19,000.

LUXEMBOURG. *Grand Duchy of Luxembourg.*

MADAGASCAR. *Malagasy Republic.*

MALAWI. *Republic of Malawi.* (Formerly Nyasaland.)

Malaya. (*See* Malaysia.)

MALAYSIA. Includes Federation of Malaya, Sabah, and Sarawak. Singapore also was a member for a short time but has been treated separately in this study.

MALDIVE ISLANDS. *Republic of the Maldives.*

MALI. *Republic of Mali.* (Formerly Sudanese Republic.)

MALTA.

Martinique. Overseas department of France. Population: 321,000.

MAURITANIA. *Islamic Republic of Mauritania.*

MAURITIUS.

MEXICO. *United Mexican States.*

Monaco. *Principality of Monaco.* Population: 23,000.

MONGOLIA. *Mongolian People's Republic.*

MOROCCO. *Kingdom of Morocco.* Comprising former French Morocco, former Spanish Morocco, and Tangier.

MOZAMBIQUE. Overseas province of Portugal.

Namibia. (Formerly South West Africa.) Territory held by the Republic of South Africa. Population: 574,000.

Nauru. *Republic of Nauru.* Population: 5,000.

NEPAL. *Kingdom of Nepal.*

NETHERLANDS. *Kingdom of the Netherlands.* Excludes Surinam and Netherlands Antilles.

Netherlands Antilles. Part of the Kingdom of the Netherlands. Population: 208,000.

New Caledonia. Overseas territory of France. Population: 91,000.

NEW GUINEA. United Nations trust territory administered by Australia. Including Northeast New Guinea, the Bismarck Archipelago, Bougainville and Buka of the Solomon Islands group and about 600 smaller islands. Treated with Papua as one unit. (PAPUA/NEW GUINEA).

New Hebrides. Anglo-French condominium. Population: 68,000.

NEW ZEALAND. *Dominion of New Zealand.*

NICARAGUA. *Republic of Nicaragua.*

NIGER. *Republic of Niger.*

NIGERIA. *Federal Republic of Nigeria.* Includes northern part of the former Trust Territory of the Cameroons under British administration.

North Borneo. (*See* Sabah.)

Northern Rhodesia. (*See* Zambia.)

NORWAY. *Kingdom of Norway.*

Nyasaland. (*See* Malawi.)

Oman. Population: 565,000. Became member of the United Nations 21 September 1971, too late to be included in the study.

Pacific Islands. Trust Territory of the Pacific Islands under United States administration, comprising the Carolines, Marianas, and Marshall islands. Also known as Micronesia. Population: 92,000.

PAKISTAN. *Republic of Pakistan.* Data includes those portions of Kashmir-Jammu held by Pakistan, whenever possible.

PANAMA. *Republic of Panama.* Includes Canal Zone.

PAPUA. Territory of Australia. Southeastern part of the island of New Guinea. Treated with New Guinea as one unit (PAPUA/NEW GUINEA).

PARAGUAY. *Republic of Paraguay.*

PERU. *Republic of Peru.*

PHILIPPINES. *Republic of the Philippines.*

POLAND. *Polish People's Republic.*

PORTUGAL. *Republic of Portugal.* Including the Azores and Madeira islands.

Portuguese Guinea. Overseas province of Portugal. Also known as Guinea-Bissau. Population: 527,000.

Portuguese Timor. Overseas province of Portugal. Population: 551,000.

PUERTO RICO. Commonwealth within the United States.

Qatar. Population: 70,000. Became member of the United Nations on 21 September 1971, too late to be included in the study.

Réunion. Overseas department of France. Population: 408,000.

RHODESIA. (Formerly Southern Rhodesia.)

Rhodesia and Nyasaland, Federation of. From 1955-63, included Northern Rhodesia, Southern Rhodesia, and Nyasaland. For Nyasaland, see Malawi; for Northern Rhodesia, see Zambia; for

Southern Rhodesia, see Rhodesia. These countries were treated separately throughout the study.

Rio Muni. (*See* Equatorial Guinea.)

ROMANIA. *Socialist Republic of Romania.*

RWANDA. *Republic of Rwanda.* Formerly part of Ruanda-Urundi, a United Nations trust territory under Belgian administration.

Ryukyu Islands. Administered by the United States. Population: 931,000.

Sabah. (*See* Malaysia.)

San Marino. *Republic of San Marino.* Population: 17,000.

Saõ Tome and Principé. Overseas province of Portugal. Population: 61,000.

Sarawak. (*See* Malaysia.)

SAUDI ARABIA. *Kingdom of Saudi Arabia.*

SENEGAL. *Republic of Senegal.*

Seychelles. British colony. Population: 47,000.

SIERRA LEONE.

Sikkim. *Kingdom of Sikkim.* Under protection of India. Population: 176,000.

SINGAPORE. *Republic of Singapore.* Part of Malaysia, 1963-65, but treated separately throughout the study.

SOMALIA. *Somali Democratic Republic.* Created 1 July 1960 by the union of former British Somaliland with the former United Nations Trust Territory of Somaliland under Italian administration.

SOUTH AFRICA. *Republic of South Africa.* Prior to 31 May 1961, known as the Union of South Africa. Excluding data for Walvis Bay, which is an integral part of South Africa, but is administered as if it were part of South West Africa.

South Arabia. (*See* Southern Yemen.)

Southern Rhodesia. (*See* Rhodesia.)

South West Africa. (*See* Namibia.)

SOUTHERN YEMEN. *Democratic Republic of Yemen.* (Formerly Aden and the Protectorate of South Arabia.)

SOVIET UNION. *Union of Soviet Socialist Republics.*

SPAIN. *(The) Spanish State.* Including the Balearic and Canary islands.

Spanish North Africa. Territory of Spain, including Ceuta, Melilla, Alhucemas, Chafarinas, and Penon de Velez de la Gomera. Population: 158,000.

Spanish Sahara. Territory of Spain. Population: 48,000.

St. Kitts-Nevis and Anguilla. State in association with the United Kingdom. Population: 60,000.

St. Lucia. State in association with the United Kingdom. Population: 103,000.

St. Vincent. State in association with the United Kingdom. Population: 87,000.

SUDAN. *Republic of Sudan.*

Sudanese Republic. (*See* Mali.)

Surinam. Part of the Kingdom of the Netherlands. Population: 335,000.

Swaziland. *Kingdom of Swaziland.* Population: 375,000. Became member of the United Nations on 24 September 1968, too late to be included in the study.

SWEDEN. *Kingdom of Sweden.*

SWITZERLAND. *Swiss Confederation.*

SYRIA. *Syrian Arab Republic.* Part of United Arab Republic 1958-61, but treated separately throughout this study.

TAIWAN. *Republic of China.* Comprising islands of Taiwan and Pescadores.

Tanganyika. (*See* Tanzania.)

TANZANIA. *United Republic of Tanzania.* On 26 April 1964, Tanganyika and Zanzibar merged to form the United Republic of Tanzania.

THAILAND. *Kingdom of Thailand.*

TOGO. *Republic of Togo.* Former Trust Territory of Togoland under French administration.

Tonga. *Kingdom of Tonga.* Population: 73,000.

TRINIDAD AND TOBAGO.

Trucial Oman. Sheikhdoms with special relationship with the United Kingdom. Population: 111,000.

TUNISIA. *Republic of Tunisia.*

TURKEY. *Republic of Turkey.*

UGANDA. *Republic of Uganda.*

UNITED ARAB REPUBLIC. Former Egypt only throughout this study. Including Gaza Strip and Sinai. (*See* Syria.)

Union of South Africa. (*See* South Africa.)

Union of Soviet Socialist Republics. (*See* Soviet Union.)

UNITED KINGDOM. *United Kingdom of Great Britain and Northern Ireland.* Includes England, Wales, Scotland, and Northern Ireland; excludes Channel Islands and Isle of Man.

UNITED STATES. *United States of America.* Data include Alaska and Hawaii throughout this study.

UPPER VOLTA. *Republic of Upper Volta.*

URUGUAY. *Eastern Republic of Uruguay.*

Vatican City. (*See* Holy See.)

VENEZUELA. *Republic of Venezuela.*

VIETNAM, NORTH. *Democratic People's Republic of Vietnam.*

VIETNAM, SOUTH. *Republic of Vietnam.*

Virgin Islands. Territory of the United States. Population: 43,000.

Western Samoa. *The Independent State of Western Samoa.* Population: 127,000.

West Irian. Formerly West New Guinea (Netherlands), included in Indonesia.

YEMEN. *Yemen Arab Republic.*

YUGOSLAVIA. *Socialist Federal Republic of Yugoslavia.*

ZAMBIA. *Republic of Zambia.* (Formerly Northern Rhodesia.)

Zanzibar (and Pemba). (*See* Tanzania.)

Appendix 3   Data and Computer Programs in the World Handbook Archive

Data in this book, along with many other data and with seven computer programs, are archived on magnetic tape in the Inter-University Consortium for Political Research, the University of Michigan, Box 1248, Ann Arbor, Michigan 48106. For a complete description of the holdings, see the codebooks available from the Consortium. A brief catalogue follows.

Daily reports of political events.

Political events, originally collected day by day, are available in this form. A file of 57,268 records gives for each report the identity of the country, the date and type of the event, the number and magnitude of events reported and the source(s).

Event series not given in the book.

Unsuccessful attempts at regular executive transfer
Unsuccessful attempts at irregular executive transfer
Elections
Pro-government demonstrations
Political strikes
Political assassinations
Executions
Acts of relaxation of political restrictions and of political amnesty

Attribute series not given in the book (partial list).

Life expectancy
Working age population (15-64)
Adult population (20+)
Percentage of population living in cities of 20,000 or more
Cinema attendance per capita
Steel consumption
Gross national product in national currencies
Transportation and communications share of gross domestic product
Government consumption as a percentage of gross national product
Schutz coefficients and fairshare points for inequality data
Percentage of economically active male population in wage- and salary-earning occupations
Percentage of total male population in the labor force
Health expenditures
Percentage of legislative seats held by Communists, non-Communist left, center, conservative, and other parties.

Additional information on external interventions.

For each of the external interventions in table 3.6, report is given of intervening country, nature of action, number and type of interveners, group supported, troop intervention, air incursion, naval force employed, casualties, length of stay, and so on.

Data used to create fractionalization, concentration, and Gini indexes.

Included are the names and signs of the several largest ethnic and linguistic divisions, parties (in terms of votes and of legislative seats), export commodities, export-receiving countries and cities. Another file gives the populations and products of sectors of the economy and the areas and numbers of farms by size categories.

Computer programs.

In the archive are programs that ran on the Yale IBM 7040-7094. These have not been converted for use on third generation machines. The programs were used to merge the event data reports from multiple sources, to translate between a six-digit calendar and a four-digit date number (see appendix 1), to create the Gini index, to build most of the tables, and to draw most of the plots of this book.

Index

Tables grouped at ends of chapters are indicated by italicized page numbers.

435